Mohun
Or,
The Last Days Of Lee
And His Paladins

By

John Esten Cooke

Double9
BOOKS

Mohun
Or, The Last Days of Lee And His Paladins
by John Esten Cooke

ISBN: 978-93-59320-68-7

Published by

DOUBLE 9 BOOKS

2/13-B, Ansari Road, Daryaganj
New Delhi – 110002
info@double9books.com
www.double9books.com
Tel. 011-40042856

ABOUT THE AUTHOR

John Esten Cooke (November 3, 1830 – September 27, 1886) was a novelist, writer, and poet from the United States. He was the poet Philip Pendleton Cooke's brother. During the American Civil War, Cooke served as a staff officer in the Confederate States Army cavalry for Maj. Gen. J. E. B. Stuart then, after Stuart's death, for Brig. Gen. William N. Pendleton. Flora, Stuart's wife, was Cooke's first cousin. Cooke was born on November 3, 1830 in Winchester, Virginia, as one of 13 children (five of whom survived childhood) to Bermuda-born planter and lawyer John R. Cooke and Maria Pendleton Cooke. He was born on the family's plantation, "Ambler's Hill," in the Shenandoah Valley near Winchester, Virginia. The family estate to which the Cookes had relocated burned destroyed in 1838. The family relocated to Charles Town, Virginia, and then to Richmond, Virginia, in 1840. Cooke briefly studied and practiced law in Richmond at his father's urging, but dropped out in 1849 when continued financial difficulties stopped him from enrolling at the University of Virginia. In 1851, he founded a law firm with his father, but his writing frequently interfered with his work.

CONTENTS

BOOK I—GETTYSBURG

BOOK II—THE FLOWER OF CAVALIERS

BOOK III—BEHIND THE SCENES

BOOK IV—THE PHANTOMS

BOOK V—THE DEAD GO FAST

BOOK I
GETTYSBURG

I
THE CAVALRY REVIEW

On a beautiful day of June, 1863, the plains of Culpeper, in Virginia, were the scene of an imposing pageant.

Stuart's cavalry was passing in review before Lee, who was about to commence his march toward Gettysburg.

Those of my readers who were fortunate enough to be present, will not forget that scene. They will remember the martial form of Stuart at the head of his *sabreurs;* how the columns of horsemen thundered by the great flag; how the multitude cheered, brightest eyes shone, the merry bands clashed, the gay bugles rang; how the horse artillery roared as it was charged in mimic battle—while Lee, the gray old soldier, with serene carriage, sat his horse and looked on.

Never had the fields of Culpeper witnessed a spectacle more magnificent. The sunshine darted in lightnings from the long line of sabres, lit up beautiful faces, and flashed from scarfs, and waving handkerchiefs, rosy cheeks, and glossy ringlets. All was life, and joy, and splendor. For once war seemed turned to carnival; and flowers wreathed the keen edge of the sword.

Among the illustrious figures gazed at by the crowd, two were the observed of all the observers—those of Lee and Stuart.

Lee sat his powerful horse, with its plain soldierly equipments, beneath the large flag. He was clad in a gray uniform, almost without mark of rank. Cavalry boots reached nearly to his knees; as usual he wore no sword; over his broad brow drooped a plain brown felt hat, without tassel or decoration. Beneath, you saw a pair of frank and benignant, but penetrating eyes, ruddy cheeks, and an iron gray mustache and beard, both cut close. In the poise of the stately head, as in the whole carriage of his person, there was something calm, august and imposing. This man, it was plain, was not only great, but good; — the true type of the race of gentlemen of other times.

Stuart, the chief of cavalry of the army, was altogether different in appearance. Young, ardent, full of life and abandon, he was the true reproduction of Rupert, said to be his ancestor. The dark cavalry feather; the lofty forehead, and dazzling blue eyes; his little "fighting jacket," as he called it, bright with braid and buttons, made a picture. His boots reached to the knee; a yellow silk sash was about his waist; his spurs, of solid gold, were the present of some ladies of Maryland; and with saber at tierce point, extended over his horse's head, he led the charge with his staff, in front of the column, and laughing, as though the notes of the bugle drove him forward.

In every movement of that stalwart figure, as in the glance of the blue eyes, and the laughter curling the huge mustache, could be read youth and joy, and a courage which nothing could bend. He was called a "boy" by some, as Coriolanus was before him. But his Federal adversaries did not laugh at him; they had felt his blows too often. Nor did the soldiers of the army. He had breasted bullets in front of infantry, as well as the sabre in front of cavalry. The civilians might laugh at him — the old soldiers found no fault in him for humming his songs in battle. They knew the man, and felt that he was a good soldier, as well as a great general. He would have made an excellent private, and did not feel "above" being one. Never was human being braver, if he did laugh and sing. Was he not brave? Answer, old sabreurs, whom he led in a hundred charges! old followers of Jackson, with whom he went over the breastworks at Chancellorsville!

Some readers may regard this picture of Stuart as overdrawn; but it is the simple truth of that brave soul. He had his faults; he loved praise, even flattery, and was sometimes irascible — but I have never known a human being more pure, generous and brave.

At sunset the review was over. The long columns of cavalry moved slowly back to their camps. The horse artillery followed; the infantry who had witnessed the ceremony sought their bivouacs in the woods; and the crowd, on foot, on horseback, or in carriages, returned toward the Court-House, whose spires were visible across the fields.

Stuart had approached the flag-staff and, doffing his plumed hat, had saluted Lee, who saluted in return, and complimented the review. After a few moments' conversation, they had then saluted a second time. Lee, followed by his staff, rode toward his quarters; and Stuart set out to return to his own.

We had ridden about half a mile, when Stuart turned his head and called me. I rode to his side.

"I wish you would ride down toward Beverly's Ford, Surry," he said, "and tell Mordaunt to keep a bright lookout to-night. They must have heard our artillery on the other side of the river, and may want to find out what it means."

I saluted, and turned my horse. Stuart cantered on singing.

In a few minutes he was out of sight, and I was riding toward the Rappahannock.

II
HOW I BECAME A MEMBER OF GENERAL STUART'S STAFF

If the reader has done me the honor to peruse the first volume of my memoirs, I indulge the vanity of supposing that he will like to be informed how I became a member of General Stuart's staff.

When oaks crash down they are apt to prostrate the saplings growing around them. Jackson was a very tall oak, and I a very humble sapling. When the great trunk fell, the mere twig disappeared. I had served with Jackson from the beginning of the war; that king of battle dead at Chancellorsville, I had found myself without a commander, and without a home. I was not only called upon in that May of 1863, to mourn the illustrious soldier, who had done me the honor to call me his friend; I had also to look around me for some other general; some other position in the army.

I was revolving this important subject in my mind, when I received a note from General J.E.B. Stuart, Jackson's friend and brother in arms. "Come and see me," said this note. Forty-eight hours afterward I was at Stuart's head-quarters, near Culpeper Court-House.

When I entered his tent, or rather breadth of canvas, stretched beneath a great oak, Stuart rose from the red blanket upon which he was lying, and held out his hand. As he gazed at me in silence I could see his face flush.

"You remind me of Jackson," he said, retaining my hand and gazing fixedly at me.

I bowed my head, making no other reply; for the sight of Stuart brought back to me also many memories; the scouting of the Valley, the hard combats of the Lowland, Cold Harbor, Manassas, Sharpsburg, Fredericksburg, and that last greeting between Jackson and the great commander of the cavalry, on the weird moonlight night at Chancellorsville.

Stuart continued to gaze at me, and I could see his eyes slowly fill with tears.

"It is a national calamity!" he murmured. "Jackson's loss is irreparable!"{1}

{Footnote 1: His words.}

He remained for a moment gazing into my face, then passing his hand over his forehead, he banished by a great effort these depressing memories. His bold features resumed their habitual cheerfulness.

Our dialogue was brief, and came rapidly to the point.

"Have you been assigned to duty yet, my dear Surry?"

"I have not, general."

"Would you like to come with me?"

"More than with any general in the army, since Jackson's death. You know I am sincere in saying that."

"Thanks—then the matter can be very soon arranged, I think. I want another inspector-general, and want *you*."

With these words Stuart seated himself at his desk, wrote a note, which, he dispatched by a courier to army head-quarters; and then throwing aside business, he began laughing and talking.

For once the supply of red tape in Richmond seemed temporarily exhausted. Stuart was Lee's right hand, and when he made a request, the War Office deigned to listen. Four days afterward, I was seated under the canvas of a staff tent, when Stuart hastened up with boyish ardor, holding a paper.

"Here you are, old Surry,"—when he used the prefix "old" to any one's name, he was always excellently well disposed toward them,—"the Richmond people are prompt this time. Here is your assignment—send for Sweeney and his banjo! He shall play 'Jine the Cavalry!' in honor of the occasion, Surry!"

You see now, my dear reader, how it happened that in June, 1863, Stuart beckoned to me, and gave me an order to transmit to General Mordaunt.

III
BLUE AND GRAY PHANTOMS

As I rode toward the Rappahannock to deliver Stuart's order to General Mordaunt, the wide landscape was suddenly lit up by a crimson glare. I looked over my shoulder. The sun was poised upon the western woods, and resembled a huge bloodshot eye. Above it extended a long black cloud, like an eyebrow—and from the cloud issued low thunder.

When a storm is coming, the civilian seeks shelter; but the soldier carrying an order, wraps his cape around him, and rides on. I went on past Brandy and Fleetwood Hill, descended toward the river, entered a great belt of woods—then night and storm descended simultaneously. An artillery duel seemed going on in the clouds; the flickering lightnings amid the branches resembled serpents of fire: the wind rolled through the black wood, tearing off boughs in its passage.

I pushed my horse to full speed to emerge from this scene of crashing limbs and tottering trunks. I had just passed a little stream, when from a by-road on my left came the trample of hoofs. It is good to be on the watch in the cavalry, and I wheeled to the right, listening—when all at once a brilliant flash of lightning showed me, within fifty paces, a column of *blue* cavalry.

"Halt!" rang out from the column, and a pistol-shot followed.

I did not halt. Capture was becoming a hideous affair in June, 1863. I passed across the head of the column at full speed, followed by bullets; struck into a bridle-path on the right, and pushed ahead, hotly pursued.

They had followed me nearly half a mile, firing on me, and ordering me to halt, when suddenly a sonorous "Halt!" resounded fifty yards in front of me; and a moment afterward, a carbine ball passed through my riding cape.

I drove on at full speed, convinced that these in front were friends; and the chest of my horse struck violently against that of another in the darkness.

"Halt, or you are dead!" came in the same commanding voice.

Another flash of lightning showed me a squadron of *gray* cavalry: at their head rode a cavalier, well mounted; it was his horse against which I had struck, and he held a cocked pistol to my breast.

The lightning left nothing in doubt. Gray and blue quickly recognized each other. The blue cavalry had drawn rein, and, at that moment, the leader of the grays shouted—"Charge!" A rush of hoofs, and then a quick clash of sabres followed. The adversaries had hurled together. The wood suddenly became the scene of a violent combat.

It was a rough affair. For ten minutes the result was doubtful. The Federal cavalry were apparently commanded by an officer of excellent nerve, and he fought his men obstinately. For nearly a quarter of an hour the wood was full of sabre-strokes, carbine-shots, and yells, which mingled with the roll of the storm. Then the fight ended.

My friend of the cocked pistol threw himself, sabre in hand, upon the Federal front, and it shook, and gave back, and retreated. The weight of the onset seemed to sweep it, inch by inch, away. The blue squadron finally broke, and scattered in every direction. The grays pressed on with loud cheers, firing as they did so:—five minutes afterward, the storm-lashed wood had swallowed pursuers and pursued.

The whole had disappeared like phantom horsemen in the direction of the Rappahannock.

IV
MOHUN AND HIS PRISONER

Half an hour afterward, the storm had spent its fury, and I was standing by a bivouac fire on the banks of the Rappahannock, conversing with the officer against whom I had driven my horse in the darkness.

Mounted upon a powerful gray, he had led the attack with a sort of fury, and I now looked at him with some curiosity.

He was a man of about thirty, of gaunt face and figure, wearing a hat with a black feather, and the uniform of a colonel of cavalry. The features were regular and might have been called handsome; the eyes, hair, mustache, and imperial—he wore no beard—coal black; the complexion so pale that the effect was startling. More curious than all else, however, was the officer's expression. In the lips and eyes could be read something bitterly cynical, mingled with a profound and apparently ineradicable melancholy. After looking at my new acquaintance for an instant, I said to myself: "This man has either suffered some great grief, or committed some great crime."

His bearing was cold, but courteous.

"I recognized you as soon as I saw you, colonel," he said, in response to my salute. "You probably do not know me, however, as I have just been transferred from the Army of the West. Colonel Mohun, at your service."

I exchanged a pressure of the hand with Colonel Mohun, or, speaking more correctly, I grasped his. It did not return the pressure. I then thanked him for his timely appearance, and he bowed coldly.

"It was lucky that my scout led me in this direction," he said, "that party is whipped back over the river, and will give us no more trouble to-night—the woods are full of their dead and wounded."

As he spoke he took a cigar case from his pocket, and presented it.

"Will you smoke, sir?" he said.

I bowed and selected a cigar. Colonel Mohun imitated me, and was about to commence smoking, when two or three cavalry men were seen approaching through the gloom, apparently escorting some one.

As they drew nearer the figures became plainer in the firelight. The cavalry men had in charge a female prisoner.

She was a woman of petite figure, clad in a handsome gray riding-habit, and mounted upon a superb horse, with rich equipments, apparently belonging to a Federal officer of high rank. From the horse, I glanced at the prisoner's face. It was a strange countenance. She was about twenty-five — her complexion was dead white, except the lips which were as red as carnations; her eyes were large and brilliant, her hair dark and worn plain under a small riding-hat. In one delicately gauntleted hand she held the rein of her horse — with the other, which was ungloved, she raised a lace handkerchief to her lips. On the finger sparkled a diamond.

There was something strange in the expression of this woman. She looked "dangerous" in spite of her calmness.

She sat gazing at some one behind me, with the handkerchief still raised to her lips. Then she took it away, and I could see a smile upon them.

What was the origin of that smile, and at whom was she looking? I turned, and found myself face to face with Colonel Mohun. His appearance almost frightened me. His countenance wore the hue of a corpse, his whole frame shook with quick shudders, and his eyes were distended until the black pupils shone in the centres of two white circles.

Suddenly his teeth clinched audibly; he passed his hand over his forehead streaming with cold sweat; and said in a low voice:

"Then you are not dead, madam?"

"No, sir," the prisoner replied tranquilly.

Mohun gazed at her with a long, fixed look. As he did so his features gradually resumed the cold and cynical expression which I had first observed in them.

"This meeting is singular," he said.

A satirical smile passed over the lips of the prisoner.

"Our last interview was very different, was it not, sir?" she said. "The Nottoway was higher than the Rappahannock is to-night, and you did not expect to meet me again — so soon!"

Mohun continued to gaze at her with the same fixed look.

"No, madam," he said.

"You recall that agreeable evening, do you not, sir?"

Mohun coolly inclined his head.

"And you have not seen me since?"

"Never, madam."

"You are mistaken!"

"Is it possible that I could have forgotten so pleasing a circumstance, madam?"

"Yes!"

"Where and when have I seen you since that time?"

"Everywhere, and at all times! — awake and asleep, day and night!"

Mohun shuddered.

"True," he said, with a bitter smile.

"You remember, then! I am not wrong!" exclaimed the prisoner, gazing intently at him.

Mohun raised his head, and I could see the old cynical expression upon his lips.

"Certainly I remember, madam," he said. "Do you think it possible for any one to forget your charming ladyship? And could any thing be more delightful than this interview between two old friends? But let us reserve these sweet confidences, these gushing emotions! One thing only is wanting, to perfect the happiness of this moment; the presence this evening of *your dear brother*! — but he is doubtless detained elsewhere!"

Mohun's expression was singular as he uttered these words. The prisoner looked at him as he was speaking with an indescribable smile. I can only compare it to that of the swordsman about to deliver a mortal lunge.

"My brother," she said, in accents as soft as a flute; "detained elsewhere, do you say, sir? You are mistaken in supposing so. He commanded the cavalry with which you were fighting to-night!"

At these words, uttered in a strange, mocking voice, I saw Mohun start as if a rattlesnake had bitten his heel. With all his self-possession he could not restrain this exhibition of emotion.

"Impossible! You are deceiving me — "

The prisoner interrupted him with a gay laugh.

"So you do not believe me," she said; "you think, my dear sir, that everybody is dead but yourself! Dismiss that idea from your mind! *I* am not dead, since we have the pleasure of again meeting in the flesh. *He* is not dead! No! it was Colonel Mortimer Darke whom you fought to-night. This is his horse which I borrowed to take a short ride. I have been captured, but *he* is neither dead nor captured, and you will doubtless receive some friendly message from him soon."

Under the mocking accents and the satirical glance, it was easy to read profound hatred. The speaker could not hide that. At that moment she resembled a tigress about to spring.

Mohun had listened with absorbing attention as his companion spoke; but, as on the first occasion, he speedily suppressed his agitation. His face was now as cold and unmoved as though moulded of bronze.

"So be it, madam," he said; "I will respond as I best can to such message as he may send me. For yourself, you know me well, and, I am glad to see, indulge no apprehensions. The past is dead; let it sleep. You think this interview is painful to me. You deceive yourself, madam; I would not exchange it for all the wealth of two hemispheres."

And calling an officer, he said: —

"You will conduct this lady to General Stuart, reporting the circumstances attending her capture."

Mohun made a ceremonious bow to the prisoner as he spoke, saluted me in the same manner, and mounting his horse, rode back at the head of his column.

The prisoner, escorted by the young officer, and still riding her fine horse, had already disappeared in the darkness.

V
STUART

An hour afterward, I had delivered my message to Mordaunt, and was returning by the road over Fleetwood Hill, thinking of the singular dialogue between Mohun and the gray woman.

What had these worthies meant by their mysterious allusions? How had Mohun found himself face to face on this stormy night, with two human beings whom he thought dead?

These questions puzzled me for half an hour; then I gave up the mystery, laughing. An hour afterward I had passed through Culpeper Court-House, crossed the fields, and had reached General Stuart's headquarters.

Stuart's tent, or rather the strip of canvas which he called one, was pitched beneath a great oak on a wooded knoll about a mile south of the little village. Above it drooped the masses of fresh June foliage; around, were grouped the white canvas "flies" of the staff; in a glade close by gleamed the tents d'abri of the couriers. Horses, tethered to the trees, champed their corn in the shadow; in the calm, summer night, the battle-flag drooped and clung to its staff. Before the tent of Stuart, a man on guard, with drawn sabre, paced to and fro with measured steps.

A glance told me that Mohun's singular prisoner had arrived. A courier was holding her fine animal near the general's tent, and as I dismounted, three figures' appeared in the illuminated doorway. These were the figures of Stuart, the "gray woman," and a young aid-de-camp.

"Farewell, madam," said Stuart, bowing and laughing; "I am sorry to have made your acquaintance under circumstances so disagreeable to you; but I trust you will appreciate the situation, and not blame me."

"Blame you? Not in the least, general. You are a very gallant man."

And the gay words were accompanied by a musical laugh.

"You will have an opportunity of seeing the Confederate capital," said Stuart, smiling.

The lady made a humorous grimace.

"And of abusing me upon the way thither; and afterward on the route to Port Monroe and Washington, as you will not be detained, I am sure."

"I shall not abuse you, sir. You are the noblest gentleman I have ever known."{1}

{Footnote 1: The real words of Stuart's prisoner}

And with mutual salutes they parted—the young aid-de-camp accompanying the lady to her horse, and aiding her to mount. They then set forward toward the Court-House. Stuart had ordered the prisoner to be conducted thither, and detained at the village tavern, under guard, until morning, when she would be sent to Richmond.

As they disappeared, I entered the general's tent, and found him laughing. Leaning one hand upon his desk, covered with papers, upon which rested his feather-decorated hat, he carelessly played with the tassel of his yellow sash with the other hand. His blue eyes sparkled, and his mustache curled with humor.

"That is really a beauty, Surry?" he said, "and I have laughed heartily."

He threw himself on his red blanket as he spoke, and began playing with his two setter pups, whose names were "Nip" and "Tuck." He had brought them out of the lines on his saddle.

"Well, you are really a magician," I said. "You charm the evil spirit, and make prisoners laugh."

Stuart laughed in reply.

"That is a curious person that Mohun sent me," he said; "at first she was disdainful enough; but I paid her a few compliments, and now she is in an excellent humor, as you saw."

"Yes."

"But what about the fight?"

I made my report of the events of the evening.

"Well, Mohun is a trump," said Stuart. "A new man, but seems made of the right stuff—real steel. What does Mordaunt say of the attack?"

"Only a scout."

"Right, and this lady is our spoil! She is handsome, is she not? But a more curious face I have never seen. White cheeks and red lips—a sort of devil and angel mixed! Who is she, I wonder, and what was her errand. Something is under it. She gave her name as 'Mrs. Darke,'—and her horse made me break the tenth commandment, Surry! Lady and courser are splendid."

"She is certainly a beauty."

"And what eyes!"

"Dangerous."

Stuart remained silent for some moments, and then I heard him sigh.

"Do you know, my dear Surry," he said, "that if people heard us talk in this way, they would call us libertines—immoral—any thing? There are two things that people will not disbelieve about me—that I am impure, and a drunkard! Do you know what a good man was heard to say of me the other day? 'Stuart would be one of the greatest soldiers in the army, if he did not drink so hard!' {1} And others add: 'if he were not a libertine.' Well, need I defend myself to *you*, from these charges? I promised my mother in my childhood, never to touch ardent spirits, and a drop has never passed my lips, except the wine of the communion.{2} I know I need not tell you that I am equally guiltless of the other imputation. That person does not live who can say that I ever did any thing improper of that description. And yet I am a drunkard—a libertine—I, who never touched drink, and love but one person in this world!"

{Footnote 1: This was actually said of Stuart.}

{Footnote 2: His words}

Stuart's head sank, and he uttered a weary sigh.

"They will not let me alone," he muttered, "and yet I am here fighting for my country. But I defy them to take my good name away from me, Surry!"

And he rose to his feet.

"General Lee knows me! Jackson knew me! I have the regard of the one, and I had the love of the other. What do I care? If my children only will not hear these ignoble charges! *One* can never hear them, Surry—my beloved little Flora! She died while I was fighting near Middleburg in the fall of '62—that nearly broke me down—"

And Stuart paused and covered his eyes with his hand. Between the fingers I saw a tear.

For a moment his breast heaved—something like a sob issued from the brave lip, whereon the heavy mustache trembled.

"I think of her often—I shall never get over her death, Surry!"{1} he murmured. "They think me hard and cold, and bad perhaps—it is nothing. Since she died I care less for men's opinion, and only try to do my duty, till the ball comes that will end me."

{Footnote 1: His words.}

And dashing a tear from his eyes, Stuart walked to the door of his tent, from which he gazed forth upon the stars.

Five minutes passed thus, and I did not speak. Then all at once I heard Stuart call out: "Orderly!"

"Yes, sir," came from the man on post near the tent.

"Tell Sweeney to come and bring his banjo!"

And walking fifty steps, Stuart caressed the glossy neck of his mare "Lady Margaret," who was tethered to a bough, and looked around affectionately at her master.

When he returned he was humming "The dew lay on the blossom," and following him was Sweeney—the same old Sweeney!—ever mild, courteous, almost sad, doffing his cap, saluting with simple grace, and tuning his banjo.

In a moment the tent, the wooded knoll, the whole vicinity was ringing with the uproarious notes of the mirth-inspiring banjo; and Sweeney was chanting, as only that great master *could* chant, the mighty epic of the sabreurs of Stuart:—

"*If you want to have a good time*
Jine the cavalry,
Bully Boys, hey!"

The staff and couriers quickly assembled, the servants were grouped in the starlight, the horses beneath the boughs turned their intelligent heads—and leading in the uproarious chorus might have been heard the sonorous and laughing voice of Stuart.

VI
STUART'S INSTINCT

The festivities were kept up until nearly midnight.

Then Stuart yawned; said with a laugh, "Good morning, gentle-*men*" as was his habit when he wished to work; and the tent was soon deserted.

I retired to rest, but at three in the morning felt a hand upon my shoulder.

"The general is going to move, colonel, and wishes to see you," said the orderly.

I rose, made my brief toilet, and went toward Stuart's tent where a light was shining. He was writing busily at his desk, as fresh and gay as on the preceding evening. His enormous constitution defied fatigue.

All at once I saw that there was another personage in the tent. He was a young man of about twenty, of slight figure, beardless face, and an expression so shy and retiring that he seemed ready to blush if you spoke to him. He wore, nevertheless, the uniform of a captain of artillery; and I remember wondering how this girlish and shrinking personage, with the large, sad eyes, had come to hold a commission.

"Captain Davenant, of my horse artillery, Colonel Surry," said Stuart.

The youth colored, and then with an air of painful embarrassment took a step forward and pressed my hand. The grasp of the slender fingers was like the grip of a steel vice.

"Davenant has been on a scout across the Rappahannock, to keep his hand in," said Stuart, busily writing. "My horse artillery boys do a little of every thing—and Davenant is a wild-cat, Surry, with a touch of the bull dog, in spite of his looks!"

The young officer drew back blushing more than ever at these words. His confusion seemed to deprive him of the power of utterance.

"I'll bet he's blushing now!" said Stuart, laughing and continuing to write with his back turned, as he spoke. "He is blushing or sighing—for the poor Yankees he has killed, doubtless!"

"You are laughing at me, general," said the young man timidly. "Well, my laughter won't hurt you, Davenant. I never joke with people I don't like. But to business. The enemy are going to attack me, Surry. Get ready, I am going to move."

"Ready, general."

"All right!—Hagan!"

"General!"

The voice came like an echo. Then at the door appeared the gigantic, black-bearded Lieutenant Hagan, chief of the general's escort. Have you forgotten him, my dear reader?—his huge figure, his mighty beard, the deep thunder of his tones? I showed you the brave soldier in 1861 and '62. In 1863 his beard was heavier, his voice more like thunder—when the giant walked along he seemed to shake the ground.

"I am going to move in half an hour, Hagan," said Stuart, still writing busily. "Head-quarters will be established on Fleetwood Hill, beyond Brandy; my horse!"

Hagan saluted and vanished without uttering a word. In five minutes the camp was buzzing, and "Lady Margaret" was led up.

"Come on, Surry! Come on, Davenant! I will beat you to the Court-House!"

And Stuart buckled on his sword, drew on his gauntlets, and mounted his horse. I was beside him. Not to be ready when Stuart was—was to be left behind. He waited for nobody. His staff soon learned that.

As Davenant's horse was awaiting him, he was as prompt as Stuart desired. In a minute we were all three riding at full speed toward the village. Stuart was playing with his glove, which he had taken off and dangled to and fro. His brows were knit, and he was reflecting. We did not interrupt him, and in ten minutes we were all clattering over the main street of the hamlet.

Stuart pushed on by the tavern, without pausing, in the direction of Fleetwood, when just as he reached the eastern suburbs of the town a small one-horse wagon, leaving the place, attracted his attention. There was just sufficient light to make out the figures in the wagon. There were two. One was a portly and plainly clad old countryman, with a prominent nose, a double chin, and fat hands decorated with pinchbeck rings. Beside him sat an old woman, as fat as himself, wearing a faded calico gown, a "coal-scuttle" bonnet, and a huge ruffled cap beneath.

Stuart looked keenly at the wagon, called to the driver to halt, and demanded whither he was going, and on what business. The old countryman smiled. The question seemed to strike him as absurd, and his explanation was simple and calculated to remove all suspicion. He stated that his name was Brown—that he lived near the village; had brought in a load of vegetables to sell, on the preceding evening—some friends had persuaded him and "his old woman" to spend the night, and they were now going home.

Stuart peered under the coal-scuttle bonnet.

"And this is your 'old woman' my friend," he said with a laugh.

"Jest so, sir," was the wheezy reply of the fat old countryman, smiling sweetly. "You see she would come along, sir. Womankind is mighty contrary!"

"A profound sentiment!" laughed Stuart, and riding on without further words, he left the countryman free to proceed on his way.

We crossed a little stream, rode on toward Fleetwood, and had nearly reached Brandy when Stuart suddenly reined in his horse.

"Do you know what I think," he said, "that I have done a foolish thing?"

"What, general?"

"To let that old fellow go on. I don't like his looks."

"The old countryman?"

"Yes; I wish I had arrested him—him and his wife."

"Arrested them?"

Stuart nodded.

"I have an instinct about rascals, Surry; and something tells me that I have been guilty of an imprudence."

"Was not his explanation satisfactory?"

"No."

"What could be wrong?"

"Everything."

"And his 'old woman,'" I said, laughing; "think of that highly respectable dame."

"I like her least of all!"

"From instinct?"

"If you choose."

"I think your instinct misleads you this time, general."

"I think not."

"Well, we will see."

And we did see.

In two hours the head-quarters tents were pitched upon Fleetwood Hill beyond Brandy, and Stuart sent his provost marshal to Culpeper Court-House, with orders to conduct the prisoner taken by Mohun on the preceding night, to General Lee, for examination.

An hour afterward the worthy provost returned in hot haste with the astounding information that the fair lady was nowhere to be found. She had disappeared from her chamber, none knew how, before daylight, and as a notoriously suspected individual who had lately been hanging round the tavern had disappeared too, it was probable that they had gone off together. Upon this point, a note left by the lady directed to "General Stuart" would probably give information. This had been found upon her table. And the provost wound up by handing the note to Stuart.

He read it with an air of decided ill-humor. Then throwing it upon his desk, burst into a laugh.

"Well, Surry," he said, "who is right and who is wrong, now? Read that!"

And he pointed to the note, which I opened and read. It was in a delicate female hand, and ran as follows:—

"General Stuart will pardon the attempt his captive is about to make, to effect her escape. He made himself quite charming in their brief interview, but liberty is sweet. Finding a friend unexpectedly in this quarter of the world, I have made every arrangement with him; he is a great master of disguises, and, though the travelling costume which I shall adopt will make me look hideous, I hope it will enable me, before sunrise, to pass a private ford, known to my friend alone, and reach the opposite bank of the Rappahannock.

"Farewell, my dear general. If all the rebels were like yourself, I might change my politics. I have but one other friend in your army — Colonel Mohun, of the cavalry. Present my regards to him, and say that *we will meet again*."

That was all. I raised my eyes from the paper, and looked at the general with stupefaction.

"Then that 'old woman' was the lady?"

"Precisely."

"And we are fooled?"

"Completely. They are by this time on the other side of the Rappahannock."

With these words, Stuart dismissed the whole subject, turned to his desk, and in a moment was busy at his official writing.

VII
THE BALL BEFORE THE BATTLE

On the same evening I was riding with Stuart toward Culpeper Court-House.

"Do you know where we are going, Surry?" he said, with a laugh.

"I can guess, I think."

"Try."

"To the ball given by the young officers to the Charlottesville belles tonight."

"You are wrong, old fellow. I don't dare to go there."

"Don't dare?"

"Well, that is the word," he replied; "I am not afraid of the Yankees, but I am of gossips—above all, of the valorous correspondents of the newspapers."

"I begin to understand now."

"They are dangerous."

"Yes."

Stuart cantered on, playing with his glove as usual. "Think of Messieurs the bomb-proof critics!" he laughed. "They already say I reviewed the cavalry with a wreath of flowers around my horse's neck."

"Is it possible?"

"They say so everywhere; and I will tell you the foundation for the charge. In passing through the Court-House on the morning of the review, a young lady friend of mine ran out from her house and threw a wreath over the neck of my horse. Well, I think it is something to be courteous in this world. I did not throw it off. I thanked her, rode on, and only removed it when I got out of sight. Meeting General Lee, I told him of it, laughing, and he said, with a smile: 'Why did you not wear it?' {1} I might as well have done so, Surry, for you see I have the credit of it. Why try to be temperate, and pure, and soldierly? I am a drunkard, a libertine, and a popinjay! But I care nothing. I intend to do my duty, old fellow, and the next few days will probably show if I can fight."

{Footnote 1: Fact.}

With which words Stuart broke into a song, cantered on more rapidly, and passing without drawing rein through the Court-House, soon reached General Lee's head-quarters on an eminence beyond.

Here he remained for an hour, in private interview with the commander-in-chief. Finally, they came out together. General Lee in his plain uniform, with that sedate dignity of bearing which made the gray old cavalier so superb. I had the honor to receive his salute, and to press his hand, and then I set out with General Stuart for Fleetwood.

In passing through the Court-House we observed the windows of a large building all ablaze with lights, and heard the merry notes of music. Stuart drew rein.

"I think I will drop in for a few minutes, in spite of every thing!" he said. "See the end of all my excellent resolutions, Surry!"

And rapidly dismounting, Stuart entered the ball-room. I followed.

If the review was imposing, the ball was charming. Youths and maidens had assembled promptly at the sound of music, and, if I were a poet or a penny-a-liner, my dear reader, I would compose a fine description of the merry spectacle. But alas! I am neither; and feel unequal to the "ornate" style of writing. I am only a battered old *militaire*, with a number of great events to speak of. Look in the newspapers of that period for an account of the assembly.

Let me say, however, in passing, that there was something sad as well as joyful, gloomy as well as brilliant, in all that echoing laughter, and the movements of these gay figures, on the eve of the bloody battle of Fleetwood. Girls were smiling upon youths who in twelve hours would be dead. Lips were shaping gallant compliments — soon they were going to utter the death-groan. All went merry as a marriage-bell, and they danced to the joyous music. Soon the cannon would begin to roll, and the youths would charge to that stormy music as they danced to this.

I was gazing at the lively assemblage — at the undulating forms moving to and fro, the gay uniforms, the fluttering scarfs, the snowy arms, the rosy cheeks, when my attention was attracted by a figure which made me lose sight of all else.

It was that of a young girl about twenty, tall, stately, and beautiful. Her dark hair was carried back in glossy waves, and ended in profuse curls. Her cheeks resembled blush roses; the eyes were large, brilliant, and full of laughing hauteur; the lips red, and wreathed into a dazzling smile, which was the perfection of satirical mirth.

I grow extravagant; but this young girl was superb. There was something queen like and imposing in her movements and whole appearance. She seemed to look down on the crowd with satirical disdain, and the gay youths who surrounded her were every instant struck by the bright shafts of a wit which spared nothing.

Who was this dangerous beauty, who received the attentions of the young officers with so much careless disdain? I asked that question of a friend and he replied:

"Miss Georgia Conway, a daughter of Judge William Conway."

"Ah," I said, "the statesman? — the successor of Randolph in bitter oratory?"

"Yes, and yonder he is."

I looked in the direction indicated, and saw an elderly gentleman of small stature, with long gray hair, and lips full of benignant smiles. He wore a suit of black, and there was something courtly and attractive in every movement of the slender figure. His low bow and sweet smile were the perfection of old-time courtesy.

I was still looking at this gentleman, whose fame had extended throughout Virginia and the whole South, when a familiar voice near me, attracted my attention. It was that of Captain Davenant, the young officer of the horse artillery, and glancing in the direction of the voice I saw him bending over a young lady who was seated and conversing with him. She was a girl of seventeen, with blue eyes, auburn hair, and a complexion as fair as a lily. As Davenant addressed her in low tones, she gazed up into his face with an expression of confiding affection. In the eyes of the young officer I could read a profound and ardent love.

Turning to my friend I inquired the name of the young lady, in turn.

"Miss Virginia Conway," he replied, "the only sister of Miss Georgia."

He had scarcely uttered the words, when Davenant's interview with the young lady terminated in a very singular manner. Suddenly Judge Conway passed through the crowd, reached the spot where the young people were conversing, and darting a glance of positive fury at the youth — a glance which made his eyes resemble coals of fire — offered his arm to his daughter, and abruptly bore her away.

Davenant's face flushed crimson, and his eyes darted flame. He took a step as though about to follow — but all at once he stopped.

Then from red his face became pale. The old expression of sadness returned to his lips. With head bent down, and a faint color stealing over his cheeks, he went toward the door, and passed though it, and disappeared.

Before I had time to reflect upon this singular incident, I heard the voice of Stuart.

"Come, Surry! to horse! unless you wish to remain!" he said.

"Ready, general!" I replied.

And in five minutes we were galloping toward Fleetwood.

"A gay ball," said Stuart, as we rode along; "but do you remember *my* *instinct*, Surry?"

"Perfectly, general. Has it told you something on the present occasion?"

"Yes."

"What?"

"You have heard of the famous ball at Brussells, broken up by the guns of Waterloo?"

"Certainly."

"Well, I think that this one will prove similar — that cannon are going to thunder before the music stops."

Stuart had scarcely spoken when rapid hoof-strokes were heard in front, and a horseman shot by.

"Have you seen General Stuart?" said a voice in the darkness.

"Here I am — what news, Stringfellow?"

The horseman drew rein so suddenly that his horse was thrown upon his haunches. "You will be attacked at daylight, general."

"Well, — what force?"

"The whole Yankee cavalry, with infantry and artillery supports."

"All right; ride back with me, and tell me every thing, Stringfellow."

In half an hour we were at head-quarters. Stuart dismounted and entered his tent.

"You see I was right, Surry," he said turning toward me, "and there is something in my *instinct* after all!"

VIII
FLEETWOOD

At daylight a long thunder came up from the woods of the Rappahannock. The greatest cavalry combat of the war had begun.

At that sound Stuart leaped to the saddle, and rode rapidly toward the front. Fifteen minutes afterward his head-quarters had vanished. On the green slope of Fleetwood not a tent was visible.

Is the reader familiar with the country along the Upper Rappahannock? If so, he will remember that the river is crossed in Culpeper by numerous fords. The principal — beginning on the left, that is to say, up the river — are Welford's, Beverly's, the Railroad bridge, and Kelly's fords.

Stuart's left, under William H.F. Lee, was opposite Welford's; his centre, under Jones, opposite Beverly's; his right, under Hampton, toward Kelly's; and a force under Robertson was posted in the direction of Stevensburg, to guard the right flank. The whole amounted to about seven or eight thousand cavalry.

The Federal column which now advanced to attack it, is said to have embraced all the cavalry of General Hooker's army; and must have numbered more than twelve thousand sabres.

Stuart rode on rapidly down Fleetwood Hill, and was soon opposite Beverly's Ford where the enemy had crossed in force. General Jones was heavily engaged, and the Napoleons of the horse artillery were roaring steadily. Every moment the round shot crashed, or the shell tore through the woods about three hundred yards in front of the pieces where the dismounted cavalry of the enemy had effected a lodgment. They kept up a hot fire at the cannoneers, and the steady rattle of carbines further up the river told that Lee was also engaged.

In face of the bursting shell, the blue *tirailleurs* could not advance; and Stuart sent an order to Hampton to move in and attack on the right.

The troopers of the Gulf States advanced at the word; their dense column was seen slowly moving, with drawn sabre, across the plain; the moment of decisive struggle seemed rapidly approaching, when suddenly a heavy blow was struck at Stuart's rear.

I had been directed by him to ascertain if "every thing had been sent off from Fleetwood," and to see that no papers had been dropped there in the hurry of departure. Going back at a gallop I soon reached the hill, and rode over the ground recently occupied by the head-quarters. The spot seemed swept. Not a paper was visible. All that I could see was a withered bouquet dropped by some young officer of the staff—a relic, no doubt, of the last night's ball at the village.

I had already turned to ride back to Stuart, when my attention was attracted by a column of cavalry advancing straight on Brandy—that is, upon Stuart's rear. What force was that? Could it be the enemy? It was coming from the direction of Stevensburg; but how could it have passed our force there?

"Look!" I said to an officer of the horse artillery, one battery of which was left in reserve on the hill, "look! what column is that?"

"It must be Wickham's," was his reply.

"I am sure they are Yankees!"

"Impossible!" he exclaimed.

But our doubts were soon terminated. From the rapidly advancing column two guns shot out and unlimbered. Then two white puffs of smoke spouted from their muzzles, and the enemy's shell burst directly in our faces.

The horse artillery returned the fire, and I hastened back with the intelligence to Stuart.

"It is only a squadron, I suppose," he replied with great coolness. "Go back and get all the cavalry you can, and charge the guns and bag them!"{1}

{Footnote: His words}

It is impossible to imagine any thing calmer than the speaker's voice. I knew, however, that the attack was more critical than he supposed; hastened back; came up with two regiments; and they ascended the hill at full gallop, leaping the ravines, and darting toward the crest.

Suddenly it blazed with staggering volleys. The Federal cavalry had rushed straight across the fields toward the hill—ascended its western slope as we ascended the eastern, and met us—coming on, in squadron front, they struck the Confederates advancing in column of fours, and in confusion from the rough ground—they recoiled—were thrown into disorder; and with loud cheers the enemy swarmed all over Fleetwood Hill.

The battle seemed lost. Stuart was cut off, and hemmed in between two powerful bodies of Federal cavalry, supported by infantry and artillery.

All that saved us at that moment, was the "do or die" fighting of the cavalry and horse artillery.

On the crest of Fleetwood took place a bitter and obstinate struggle. It was one of those fights of the giants, which once witnessed is never forgotten. The cannoneers of the horse artillery fought as savagely, hand to hand, as the regular cavalry; and the crest became the scene of a mad wrestle, rather of wild beasts than men.

All at once the form of Davenant appeared amid the smoke. He had come rapidly from the front, and now threw himself into the combat like the bloodhound to which Stuart had compared him. His sad smile had disappeared; his cheeks were flushed; his eyes fiery;—leaping from his horse, he seized the sponge-staff of a gun, from which all the cannoneers had been driven, and ramming home a charge of canister, directed the gun upon a column of the enemy.

Before he could fire, a Federal cavalryman rode at him, and cut furiously at his bare head, with the full weight of his sabre.

Davenant did not try to draw his sword—the attempt would have been useless. In his hand he had a weapon; and with a swing of the rammer he swept the cavalryman from the saddle.{1} He fell headlong, covered with blood; and Davenant aimed and fired the charge of canister—leaped upon his horse—and drawing his sword, plunged into the melee, his head bare, his eyes flaming, his voice rising loud and inspiring, above the combat.

{Footnote 1: Fact.}

It was a stubborn, a superb struggle. Three times the enemy's guns were charged and captured; three times the Confederates were furiously charged in turn, and the pieces recaptured by the enemy.{1} A final charge of the gray cavalry carried all before it. The Federal artillery was seized upon, and their cavalry driven back—but at that moment a heavier force still was seen advancing upon Stuart from the direction of Kelly's ford.

{Footnote 1: Fact.}

It was a splendid spectacle. They came on in solid column, and rapidly formed line of battle on the slope of Fleetwood, with drawn sabres, and flags floating. As they moved they seemed to shake the very ground. I had never before seen so great a force of cavalry drawn up—and the critical moment of the battle had plainly come.

At that instant the great field presented a remarkable appearance. Cavalry were charging in every direction, and it was hard to tell friend from foe. Stuart was fighting, so to say, from the centre outwards. The enemy were in his front, in his rear, and on both his flanks. If they closed in, apparently, he would be crushed as in a vice. The iron hand would strangle him.

That moment tested the nerves. Stuart's "heart of oak" bore the strain. He was aroused, stung, his cheeks burned, his eyes flamed — but the man was sufficient for the work. I looked closely at him. "Do or die" was plain on his face. From that instant I never had any doubts about Stuart.

He rushed two pieces of artillery to a knoll in front of the line of Federal horsemen. A moment afterward two reports were heard, and two shell burst precisely in the middle of the line, making a wide gap in it, and checking the charge which had begun.{1}

{Footnote 1: Fact.}

All at once I saw a column of cavalry coming up from the river, and turning to Stuart, said: —

"General, what cavalry is that?"

"Hampton's!" Stuart exclaimed. "Bring it up like lightning!"{1}

{Footnote 1: His words.}

I set out at full gallop, and soon reached the column. At the head of it rode Young, the *beau sabreur* of Georgia, erect, gallant, with his brave eye and smile.

I pointed out the enemy and gave the order.

"All right!" exclaimed Young, and, turning to his men, he whirled his sabre around his head and shouted,

"Forward!"

The column thundered on, and as it passed I recognized Mohun, his flashing eye and burnished sabre gleaming from the dust-cloud.

In five minutes they were in front of the enemy — the men wheeled and faced the Federal line.

"Charge!" rose from a hundred lips. Spurs were buried in the hot flanks; the mass was hurled at the enemy; and clashing like thunder, sword against sword, swept every thing before it. Not a single shot was fired — the sabre only was used. The enemy were broken to pieces — what I saw was a wild mêlée of whirling swords, flying horses, men cloven to the chin, while others were seen throwing themselves from the saddle, and raising their hands to escape the keen swordsmen slashing at them.{1}

{Footnote 1: Fact.}

The great force of the enemy sweeping down on Stuart's flank was thus routed. The spectacle which followed was ludicrous as well as exciting. The enemy fled in disorder. Never before had I seen the nails in the hind shoes of hundreds of horses—myriads of horses' tails streaming like meteors as they ran!

The force disappeared in the woods, hotly pursued by their foes. The dust followed them in a great cloud—from that cloud arose yells and cheers—cannon thundered; carbines rattled;—but that sound receded more and more rapidly toward the river.

On our left the brave William H.F. Lee had been as successful. He had charged and repulsed the enemy, falling wounded at the head of his men. They had not again advanced upon him. Near the Barbour House he presented an unbroken front to them.

Stuart held with his cavalry, indeed, the whole Fleetwood range. The long thunder of his artillery said to the enemy,

"Come on!"

They did not come. They went back. Their cavalry had crossed the river to ascertain the meaning of the great review. They had discovered nothing, after heavy loss. The ground was strewed with their dead and dying—they retired, shattered and bleeding.

Stuart's loss was also great—even his staff was not spared. One of my brother staff officers was killed, another wounded, a third captured.

But Stuart had won the greatest cavalry fight of the war.

IX
MOHUN FAINTS AT THE RIGHT MOMENT

In a room of the "Barbour House" on Fleetwood Hill, Stuart was writing a dispatch to General Lee.

It was nearly sunset, and the red light was streaming through the windows. On the floor lay a number of wounded men, groaning piteously. Busily attending to their wants were two young girls—the daughters of Judge Conway, whom I had seen on the night of the ball.

The young ladies, I afterward discovered, had been on a visit to the family occupying the Barbour House; had courageously remained during the whole of the battle—and they were now busily attending to the wants of the wounded.

I was gazing at the eldest—the superb beauty with the disdainful eyes, who had held that wit-combat with her circle of admirers—when Stuart finished his dispatches, and turned around.

"Any reports?" he said briefly to a member of his staff.

"None, general—except that Colonel Mohun is reported killed."

"Mohun! It is impossible! He drove the enemy, and was unhurt. I would not swap him for a hundred, nor a thousand of the enemy!"

"Thank you, general!" said a sonorous voice behind us.

And Mohun entered, making the military salute as he did so.

In his bearing I could discern the same cool pride, mingled with satire. There was only one change in him. He was paler than ever, and I could see that his right shoulder was bloody.

As he entered, Miss Georgia Conway, who was bending over a wounded soldier, raised her head and looked at him. Mohun's eye met her own, and he bowed ceremoniously, taking no further notice of her.

At this exhibition of careless indifference I could see Miss Conway's face flush. An expression of freezing hauteur came to the beautiful lips; and the disdainful glance indicated that her *amour propre* was deeply wounded.

She turned her back upon him abruptly — but as Mohun had already turned his, the movement failed in its object. The officer was looking at Stuart, who had grasped his hand. He winced as the general pressed it, and turned paler, but said nothing.

"Then you are not dead, Mohun!" exclaimed Stuart, laughing.

"Not in the least, general, I am happy to inform you," replied Mohun.

"I am truly glad to hear it! What news?"

"Our party is all over. We followed them up until they recrossed the river — and I owed them this little piece of politeness for I recognized an old acquaintance in the commander of the squadron."

"An acquaintance?"

"A certain Colonel Darke — a charming person, general." And Mohun laughed.

"I recognized him yonder when we charged on the hill, and, at first, he followed his men when they broke. As I got close to him, however, in the woods, he recognized me in turn, and we crossed swords. He is brave — no man braver; and he did his utmost to put an end to me. I had somewhat similar views myself in reference to my friend, the colonel, but his men interposed and prevented my carrying them out. They were all around me, slashing away. I was nearly cut out of the saddle — I was carried away from my friend in the mêlée — and the unkindest cut of all was his parting compliment as he retreated through the river."

"What was that, Mohun?"

"A bullet from his pistol, which grazed my shoulder. A mere scratch, but provoking. I saw him grin as he fired."

"An old friend on the Yankee side? Well, that happens," said Stuart —

"Frequently, general," said Mohun; "and this one was *very* dear, indeed — most tenderly attached to me, I assure you. My affection for him is of the same endearing nature: and we only crossed sabres in jest — a mere fencing bout for amusement. We would not hurt each other for worlds!"

And Mohun's mustache curled with laughter. There was something restless and sinister in it.

Suddenly his face grew paler, and his eyes were half closed.

"Well, Mohun," said Stuart, who was not looking at him; "I am going to send you across the river on a reconnaissance to-night."

"All right, general."

And the officer made the military salute. As he did so, he staggered, and Stuart raised his eyes.

"You are wounded!" he exclaimed.

"A trifle," laughed Mohun.

But as he spoke, his frame tottered; his face assumed the hue of a corpse; and he would have fallen, had not Miss Georgia Conway started up unconsciously from the wounded man whom she was attending to, and supported the officer in her arms.

Mohun opened his eyes, and a grim smile came to his pale face.

"A pretty tableau!" I heard him murmur; "it would do to put in a romance. A cup of tea — or a pistol — that would finish — "

As he uttered these singular words, the blood gushed from his wounded shoulder, his eyes closed, and, his head falling on the bosom of the young girl, he fainted.

X
THE SLIM ANIMAL

Fleetwood was the first gun of the great campaign which culminated on the heights of Gettysburg. A week afterward, Lee's columns were in motion toward Pennsylvania.

Was that invasion the dictate of his own judgment? History will answer. What is certain is, that the country, like the army, shouted "Forward!" The people were ablaze with wild enthusiasm; the soldiers flushed with the pride of their great victories of Fredericksburg and Chancellorsville. The authorities at Richmond shared the excitement, and the commissary-general, with unwonted humor, or in sober earnest, indorsed, it is said, upon a requisition for supplies: "If General Lee wishes rations, let him seek them in Pennsylvania."

I doubt if the great commander shared the general agitation. I think he aimed to draw Hooker out of Virginia, leaving the rest to Providence. So he moved toward the Potomac.

The world had called Lee cautious. After this invasion, that charge was not repeated. From first to last audacity seemed the sentiment inspiring him.

With Hooker on the Rappahannock, threatening Richmond, Lee thrust his advance force under Ewell through the Blue Ridge toward Maryland; pushed Longstreet up to Culpeper to support him, and kept only A.P. Hill at Fredericksburg to bar the road to the Confederate capital.

Hooker wished to advance upon it, but President Lincoln forbade him. The dispatch was a queer official document.

"In case you find Lee coming to the north of the Rappahannock," Lincoln wrote, "I would by no means cross to the south of it. I would not take any risk of being entangled upon the river, *like an ox jumped half over a fence, and liable to be torn by dogs, front and rear, without a fair chance to gore one way or kick the other.*"

Ludicrous perhaps, but to the point; the "Rail-Splitter" was not always dignified, but often judicious. Chancellorsville had been defeat—Lee's assault, foreboded thus by Lincoln, would be death.

Hooker fell back, therefore, in the direction of Washington. Lee had foreseen that fact, and had given himself small anxiety. His three corps were already in full motion toward the Potomac; and suddenly the thunder of artillery came on the winds of the mountains.

Ewell, the head of the Southern spear, was driving at Milroy, holding Winchester. The struggle was brief. General Milroy had put the iron heel on the poor valley; had oppressed the unfortunate people beyond the power of words—and suddenly the hand of Fate clutched and shook him to death. Ewell stormed his "Star Fort" near Winchester, with the bayonet; drove him to headlong flight; got in rear of him, capturing nearly all his command; and poor Milroy scarce managed to escape, with a small body-guard, beyond the Potomac.

"In my opinion Milroy's men will fight better *under a soldier!*"

It was his commanding officer, Hooker, who wrote those words a few days afterward. From the hands of his own general came that unkindest cut!

Exit Milroy, thus amid hisses and laughter—the hornet's nest at Winchester was swept away—and Ewell headed straight for Pennsylvania.

Longstreet came up rapidly to fill the gap in the line—Hill followed Longstreet—and then the world beheld the singular spectacle of an army extended in a long skirmish line over a hundred miles, with another army massed not daring to assail it.

Hooker did not see his "opening;" but Lincoln did. One of his dispatches has been quoted—here is another as amusing and as judicious.

"If the head of Lee's army is at Martinsburg," Lincoln wrote Hooker, "and the tail of it on the Plank road, between Fredericksburg and Chancellorsville, *the animal must be very slim somewhere—could you not break him?*"

But Hooker could not. He did not even try. Lee's movements seemed to paralyze him—his chief of staff wrote:—

"We cannot go boggling round, until we know what we are going after."

"Boggling round" exactly described the movements of Hooker. He was still in a grand fog, and knew nothing of his adversary's intent, when a terrific cry arose among the well-to-do farmers of Pennsylvania. The wolf had appeared in the fold. Ewell was rapidly advancing upon Harrisburg.

Behind came the veteran corps of Hill and Longstreet. The gorges of the Blue Ridge were alive with bristling bayonets. Then the waters of the Potomac splashed around the waists of the infantry and the wheels of the artillery carriages. Soon the fields of Maryland and Pennsylvania were alive with "rebels," come, doubtless, to avenge the outrages of Pope and Milroy. Throughout those commonwealths — through Philadelphia, New York, and Boston — rang the cry, "Lee is coming!"

To return to the cavalry. The horsemen of Stuart were going to move in an eccentric orbit. These are my *memoirs*, reader, not a history of the war; I describe only what I saw, and am going to ask you now, to "follow the feather" of Stuart.

Stuart was promptly in the saddle, and when Lee began to move, advanced north of the Rappahannock, drawing a cordon of cavalry across the roads above Middleburg, to guard the approaches to the mountain.

The result was that the infantry defiled through the Blue Ridge without Hooker's knowledge. He knew that something was going on, but there his information terminated. The troopers of Stuart kept watch over fifteen miles of front, and through this wall of sabres the Federal eye could not pierce.

Stuart is regarded by many as only a brave "raider." It was on occasions like this, however, that he performed his greatest services. Everywhere he confronted the enemy in stubborn battle; and the work was hard. It was fighting, fighting, fighting — now, as in 1862, when he covered Lee's retreat after Sharpsburg. Day and night the cavalry had no rest. The crack of carbines, the clash of sabres, and the roar of cannon were incessant. It was a war of giants which Fauquier and Loudoun saw in those days — and not until the rear of Lee's column had nearly reached the Potomac, did General Hooker by a desperate effort succeed in driving Stuart back.

In these pages I must leave that obstinate struggle undescribed. It was full of romantic scenes, and illustrated by daring courage: but all is lost to view in the lurid smoke of Gettysburg.

With one scene in the hurrying drama I shall pass to greater events.

But first, I beg to introduce to the reader a very singular personage, who is destined to play an important part in the history I am writing.

XI

NIGHTHAWK

It was the night of the 20th of June, 1863. Stuart's head-quarters had been established in a house on the roadside above Middleburg.

We had been fighting all day; had returned only at nightfall: and I was exchanging a few words with Stuart, before following the staff to rest, when all at once a third personage, who seemed to have arisen from the floor, stood before us.

His presence was so sudden and unexpected that I started. Then I looked at him, curiously.

He was a man of about forty, thin, wiry, and with a nose resembling the beak of a bird of prey. His eyes, half buried under bushy eyebrows, twinkled like two stars. His mouth was large and smiling; his expression exceedingly benignant. From the face I passed to the costume. The worthy was clad in severe black, with a clerical white cravat: wore a black beaver hat of the "stove-pipe" order; and presented the appearance of a pious and peaceable civilian—almost that of a clergyman, smiling benignantly upon all around him.

Stuart uttered an exclamation of satisfaction.

"Ah! Nighthawk, here you are!" he said.

And turning to me he introduced the new comer as "Mr. Nighthawk, one of my 'private friends,' and true as steel."

Mr. Nighthawk bowed with an air of smiling respect—of benignant sweetness.

"I am glad to know you, colonel, and hope I may have an opportunity of being of service to you some day," he said.

The voice was low, soft, and accorded with the mild expression of the countenance.

"Well, what news, Nighthawk?" asked Stuart; "experience tells me that you have something of importance to communicate?"

"Ah, general!"

"Yes. You pass in the cavalry by the name of the 'man before the battle,' for you always turn up then."

Mr. Nighthawk smiled.

"I try to give you information, general; and perhaps I have some news. But first of my visits to Boston, New York, Philadelphia, and Washington, where I saw many of our friends."

And in his low, quiet voice Mr. Nighthawk, who had taken a seat and smoothed down his white cravat, proceeded to speak of his travels and what he had seen.

The narrative astounded me. He spoke without reserve, for General Stuart had informed him that he might do so before me; and I was startled to find the number of private friends the South had in the North. Mr. Nighthawk was evidently *au fait* at his trade. He had a perfect understanding plainly with persons of the highest political position; and Stuart listened with the greatest interest to the speaker, whose low voice never rose above the half-whisper by which I had been impressed on his first opening his lips.

"So the summing up of all this," said Stuart, "that our friends are not too hopeful?"

"They are not, general."

"They say Lee must win a great victory on the soil of Pennsylvania?"

"Yes, general. Without it there is no hope of peace, they declare."

"Well, I think they are right; and that we shall gain the victory."

Mr. Nighthawk made no reply; and Stuart reflected for some moments without speaking. Then rousing himself: —

"I forgot," he said. "You have not given me your special information, Nighthawk."

The worthy smiled.

"You know I am the 'man before the battle,' general?"

"Yes, go on, Nighthawk."

"I have just left General Hooker's head-quarters."

"Where are they?"

"Beyond Centreville."

"You saw him?"

"I conversed with him."

"Ah!"

"An hour, general, as the Rev. Mr. Ward, from Massachusett, of the 'Grand Union Sanitary Commission'."

And Mr. Nighthawk smiled.

"Of course I urged active movements, and General Hooker became quite animated."

"He agreed with your views then?" said Stuart, laughing.

"Perfectly, general."

"And he intends—"

"There is the important thing. While we were conversing, General Hooker was called for a moment out of his tent, and by accident, my eyes fell upon an order which lay upon his desk."

"An order?"

"For two divisions of cavalry, one of infantry, and a full complement of artillery, to advance and drive you back to the mountain."

"Ah! you saw that order?"

"I did, general; it was just ready to be sent."

"What day did it fix?"

"To-morrow, general."

"Ah, indeed! Two divisions of infantry and one of cavalry?"

Mr. Nighthawk inclined in assent.

"When did you leave Hooker's head-quarters?"

"This afternoon."

"And you came through the lines to-night?"

"Yes, general, in the usual way, by passing through the pickets. I was on foot and nothing was easier."

Stuart knit his brows and reflected. Then he called to the orderly.

"Wake the adjutant-general, and have three couriers ready at once!"

Mr. Nighthawk arose.

"By-the-by, general," he said, "I saw Swartz, whom I have mentioned to you."

"Yes; the best spy, you say, in the Federal army."

"I think he is, general. He is a wonderful man. He recently played a trick upon you."

"Upon *me*?"

"At least he bore off a prisoner from you. It was a lady, captured by Colonel Mohun, one night on the Rappahannock."

"Ah! Is it possible! So Swartz was the old countryman, driving the wagon that morning."

"So he informed me, general."

"You are friends, then?"

"Close friends."

And Mr. Nighthawk smiled.

"We have an agreement—but that would not interest you, general. That was really Swartz, and the old woman was the prisoner."

"Well," said Stuart, "that was a bold stroke, but the lady was handsome enough to make friends. There is something between herself and Colonel Mohun, is there not?"

Mr. Nighthawk glanced quickly at the face of the general. His eyes resembled steel points, but the piercing glance at once sank.

"Something between them, general? What could have made you think that? But here is Major McClellan. I will not detain you, general; I will come back at daylight to receive your orders."

With these words, Mr. Nighthawk distributed a benignant smile, bowed in a friendly manner, and disappeared, it was difficult to say how, from the apartment. I had turned my eyes from him but an instant; when I again looked he was gone.

"And now to work!" exclaimed Stuart. "We are going to fight tomorrow, Surry, since the 'man before the battle' has made his appearance!"

XII
HOW STUART FELL BACK

At daybreak, Stuart was going at full gallop to the front.

A rapid fire of skirmishers, mingled with the dull roar of cannon, indicated that Nighthawk had not been deceived.

All at once the sharp-shooters were seen falling back from the woods.

"Bring me a piece of artillery!" exclaimed Stuart, darting to the front.

But the attack of the enemy swept all before it. Stuart was driven back, and was returning doggedly, when the gun for which he had sent, galloped up, and unlimbered in the road.

It was too late. Suddenly a solid shot screamed above us; the gun was hurled from its carriage, and rolled shattered and useless in the wood; the horses were seen rearing wild with terror, and trying to kick out of the harness.

Suddenly one of them leaped into the air and fell, torn in two by a second round shot.

"Quick work!" said Stuart, grimly.

And turning round to me, he said, pointing to a hill in rear —

"Post three pieces on that hill to rake all the roads."

The order, like the former, came too late, however. The enemy advanced in overpowering force — drove Stuart back beyond his head-quarters, where they captured the military satchel of the present writer — and still rushing forward, like a hurricane, compelled the Confederate cavalry to retire behind Goose Creek. On the high ground there, Stuart posted his artillery; opened a rapid fire; and before this storm of shell the Federal forces paused.

The spectacle at that moment was picturesque and imposing. The enemy's force was evidently large. Long columns of cavalry, heavy masses of infantry and artillery at every opening, right, left, and centre, showed that the task of driving back Stuart was not regarded as very easy. The sunshine darted from bayonet and sabre all along the great line of battle — and from the heavy smoke, tinged with flame, came the Federal shell. With their infantry, cavalry, and artillery, they seemed determined to put an end to us. Stuart galloped to his guns, pouring a steady fire from the lofty hill. Captain Davenant directed it in person, and he was evidently in his right element. All his sadness had disappeared. A cool and resolute smile lit up his features.

"All right, Davenant! Hold your ground!" exclaimed Stuart.

"I will do so, general."

"Can you keep them from crossing?"

"I can try, general."

A whirlwind of shell screamed around the two speakers. For the hundredth time I witnessed that entire indifference to danger which was a trait of Stuart. The fire at this moment was so terrible that I heard an officer say: —

"General Stuart seems trying to get himself and everybody killed."

Nothing more inspiring, however, can be imagined than his appearance at that moment. His horse, wild with terror, reared, darted, and attempted to unseat his rider. Stuart paid no attention to him. He had no eyes or thought for any thing but the enemy. His cheeks were flushed, his eyes flamed — he resembled a veritable king of battle.

From Stuart my glances passed to Davenant. His coolness impressed me deeply. While giving an order, a shell burst right in his face, enveloping horse and rider in a cloud of smoke — but when the smoke drifted away, he was sitting his horse unmoved, and giving the order as quietly as before.

I have not invented this picture, reader, or fancied this character. I had the honor to enjoy the friendship of the brave boy I describe. He was remarkable, in an epoch crowded with remarkable characters.

Stuart held his ground for an hour on the high hills of Goose Creek, but it then became plain that he was going to be driven back. The enemy had felt him, and discovered that the game was in their own hands. Now they rushed on his right, left and centre, at the same moment — cavalry, infantry, and artillery rolling on like a torrent — crossed the stream, charged the hill — in a moment a bitter and savage combat commenced for the possession of the crest.

Stuart rushed toward the guns. As he reached them a cannon ball carried off the head of a cannoneer, and his horse reared with fright, nearly trampling on the headless trunk which spouted blood. Davenant had coolly drawn his sabre, but had given no order to retire.

"Move back the guns!" exclaimed Stuart.

"Is it necessary, general?" asked Davenant.

"Yes, they will be captured in five minutes!"

"It is a pity we can not remain, general. This is an excellent position."

And he gave the order to limber up. The operation was performed amid a hurricane of bullets, striking down the cannoneers.

Suddenly a column of Federal cavalry charged straight at the guns. Davenant met them with his mounted men, armed with sabres, and a stubborn combat followed. It was a hilt to hilt affair, and Davenant was in the midst of it shouting: —

"You are fighting for your guns, boys! You promised to die by your guns!"

The men answered with fierce shouts, and met the enemy with savage resolution. Meanwhile, the guns had rushed at a gallop down the western slope; a regiment came to Davenant's assistance; the fight grew desperate, but was of no avail.

In fifteen minutes we were driven.

Driven! Do you know what that means, reader? Ask old soldiers if it is pleasant. They will growl in reply!

We were forced back, step by step, with the enemy at our very heels. At our backs came on the huge column, yelling and firing, mad with triumph. Stuart the valiant, the obstinate, the unshrinking was driven!

We were forced back to Upperville, and there things looked stormy. On the other roads, Stuart's right and left were rapidly retiring. His centre at Upperville seemed devoted to destruction.

The enemy came on like a whirlwind, with a roaring shout. As far as the eye could see, the great fields were dark with them. Their horse artillery advanced at a gallop, unlimbered, and tore the retreating columns with shot and shell.

I was ten yards from Stuart, just at the edge of the town, when a picked body of Federal horsemen darted straight upon him.

They had evidently recognized him by his major-general's uniform and splendid feather. Bullets hissed around him; blows were struck at him; and for an instant I saw him in the midst of a wild huddle of enemies, defending himself with his revolver only.

In an instant he would have been killed or captured, with his staff and body-guard, when a resounding shout was heard.

I glanced over my shoulder, and saw the cavaliers of Hampton coming on with drawn sabre.

Then a splendid spectacle was presented—that of Wade Hampton in one of his great moments. This stalwart cavalier was leading his men, and in an instant they had struck the enemy with a noise like thunder.

Suddenly a cavalier on a black horse rushed by like the wild huntsman, and I recognized Mohun; who, spurring his animal to headlong speed, drove straight at the leader of the Federal cavalry, almost in contact with us.

Through a rift in the smoke I caught a glimpse of Mohun's opponent. He was a man of low stature, but broad, heavy, and powerful. He came to meet his adversary with the bridle of his horse resting on the animal's neck, while both hands clutched a heavy broad-sword, raised over his right shoulder.

I could only see that the two opponents hurled together like knights tilting; their swords gleamed; they closed in, body to body; then the smoke wrapped them. It was impossible to see more.

XIV
MOSBY COMES TO STUART'S ASSISTANCE

Sore and restive at the reverse which had come to balance his victory of Fleetwood, Stuart bivouacked near Paris, that night, and made every preparation to attack at dawn.

At daylight he was in the saddle, and spurred to the high ground commanding Upperville.

All at once he checked his horse. The enemy had disappeared.

Stuart's blue eye flashed, and half an hour afterward he was advancing at the head of his cavalry. Not a foe was visible. Pressing on through Upperville, and over the trampled fields beyond, he continued to advance upon Middleburg, and near that place came up with the rear of the enemy. They showed little fight, however, and were driven beyond the place. The gray troopers pursued them with shouts and cheers—with which were mingled cries of rejoicing from the people of Middleburg.

An hour afterward the lines were re-established in triumph.

Stuart returned to his former head-quarters amid a drenching rain; and this recalls an incident very honorable to the brave soldier. As night descended, dark and stormy, Stuart gazed gloomily at the torrents of rain falling.

"My poor fellows!" he said, with a sigh, "they will have a hard time to-night."

Then suddenly turning to his servant, he added:—

"Spread my oil-cloth and blankets under that apple tree yonder. I will keep them dry enough when I once get into them."{1}

{Footnote 1: His words.}

"You are not going to sleep out on such a night, general!" exclaimed a staff officer.

"Certainly I am," was his reply, "I don't intend to fare better than my men!"{1}

{Footnote 1: His words.}

And an hour afterward Stuart was asleep under the apple tree, with a torrent pouring on him.

That was the act of a good officer and soldier, was it not, reader?

Before sunrise Stuart was up, and walking uneasily to and fro. As the day wore on, he exhibited more and more impatience. All at once, at the appearance of an officer, approaching rapidly from the front, he uttered an exclamation of pleasure.

"Here is Mosby at last!" he said.

And he went to meet the new-comer. It was the famous chief of partisans whose name by this time had become a terror to the enemy. He wore a plain gray uniform, a brace of revolvers in a swaying belt, rode a spirited gray mare, and I recognized at once the roving glance, and satirical smile which had struck me on that night when he rescued Farley and myself in Fauquier.

Stuart rapidly drew him into a private apartment; remained in consultation with him for half an hour; and then came forth, with a smile of evident satisfaction.

Mosby's intelligence must have pleased him. It at least dispelled his gloom.

An hour afterward his head-quarters had disappeared — every thing was sent toward the mountains. Stuart set out apparently to follow them — but that was only a ruse to blind busybodies.

A quarter of a mile from head-quarters he leaped a fence, and doubled back, going in the direction now of Manassas.

At daylight on the next morning he had forced his way through the Bull Run mountain.

Two hours afterward he had made a sudden attack on the enemy's infantry. It was the rear of Hancock's corps, which was the rear of Hooker's army, then retiring toward the Potomac.

XV
THE SUPPER NEAR BUCKLANDS

Stuart's fight near Haymarket, here alluded to, was a gay affair; but I pass over it, to a scene still gayer and decidedly more pleasant.

The fighting continued throughout the day, and at dusk a heavy rain came on. We were all tired and hungry—the general no less so than his staff—and when an invitation was sent to us by a gentleman near Bucklands, to come and sup with him, we accepted it with fervor, and hastened toward the friendly mansion.

A delightful reception awaited us. The house was full of young ladies, passionately devoted to "rebels," and we were greeted with an enthusiasm which passed all bounds. Delicate hands pressed our own; bright eyes beamed upon us; rosy lips smiled; musical voices said "welcome!"—and soon a savory odor, pervading the mansion, indicated that the wants of the inner man were not forgotten.

An excellent supper was plainly in preparation for the bold Stuart and his military family; and that gay and gallant cavalier, General Fitz Lee having also been invited, the joy of the occasion was complete! The house rang with clashing heels, rattling sabres, and clanking spurs. A more charming sound still, however, was that made by jingling keys and rattling china, and knives and forks. All was joy and uproar: jests, compliments and laughter. Young ladies went and came; the odors grew more inviting. In ten minutes the door of a large apartment opposite the drawing-room was thrown open, and a magnificent, an enthralling spectacle was revealed to every eye. Not to be carried away, however, by enthusiasm, I will simply say that we saw before us a long mahogany table covered with the most appetizing viands—broils, roasts, stews, bread of every variety, and real coffee and tea in real silver! That magical spectacle still dwells in my memory, reader, though the fact may lower me in your good opinion. But alas! we are all "weak creatures."

The most poetical grow hungry. We remember our heroic performances in the great civil war—but ask old soldiers if these recollections are not the most vivid!

An incident connected with the repast made it especially memorable. The servants of the house had deserted to their friends in blue; and as there was thus a deficiency of attendants, the young ladies took their places. Behind every chair stood a maiden—their faces wreathed with smiles. We were shown to our seats, amid joyous laughter. The comedy evidently afforded all engaged in it immense enjoyment—and the cavaliers humoring the angelic maid-servants, gravely advanced toward the table.

Stuart threw his plumed hat upon a chair, and drew near the foot of the table. The light fell full on the ruddy face, the heavy beard and mustache, and brilliant fighting jacket. He looked round with a gay smile. "Was any one absent," asked the kind lady of the house, as she saw the glance. Stuart made a low bow, and said:—

"All are here, madam!"

All at once, however, a voice at the door responded:—

"I think you are mistaken, general!"

And he who had uttered these words advanced into the apartment.

He was a young man, about twenty-three, of medium height, graceful, and with a smile of charming good humor upon the lips. His hair was light and curling; his eyes blue; his lips shaded by a slender mustache. His uniform was brand new, and decorated with the braid of a lieutenant. Yellow gauntlets reached his elbow, he wore a shiny new satchel, and in his hand carried a brown felt hat, caught up with a golden star.

Stuart grasped his hand warmly.

"Here you are, old fellow!" he exclaimed.

And turning to the company, he added:—

"My new aid-de-camp, Lieutenant Herbert, ladies. A fop—but an old soldier. Take that seat by Colonel Surry, Tom."

And every one sat down, and attacked the supper.

I had shaken hands with Tom Herbert, who was far from being a stranger to me, as I had met him frequently in the drawing-rooms of Richmond before the war. He was a fop, but the most charming of fops, when I first knew him. He wore brilliant waistcoats, variegated scarfs, diamond studs, and straw-colored kid gloves. In his hand he used to flourish an ivory-headed whalebone cane, and his boots were of feminine delicacy and dimensions. Such was Tom at that time, but the war had "brought him out." He had rushed into the ranks, shouldered a musket, and fought bravely. So much I knew — and I was soon to hear how he had come to be Stuart's aid.

The supper was charming. The young girls waited on us with mock submission and delighted smiles. Tom and I had fallen to the lot of a little princess with golden ringlets; and Miss Katy Dare — that was her name — acquitted herself marvellously. We supped as though we expected to eat nothing for the next week — and then having finished, we rose, and waited in turn on the fair waiters.

Behind every chair now stood an officer in uniform.

Bright eyes, rosy cheeks, jewelled hands, glossy curls — there was the picture, my dear reader, which we beheld as we "waited" at that magical supper near Buckland. When we wrapped our capes around us, and fell asleep on the floor, the little maidens still laughed in our dreams!{1}

{Footnote 1: A real incident.}

XVI
AN HONEST FOP

Stuart moved again at dawn. The scene of the preceding evening had passed away like a dream. We were in the saddle, and advancing.

Riding beside Lieutenant Tom Herbert, I conversed with that worthy, and found the tedious march beguiled by his gay and insouciant talk.

His "record" was simple. He had volunteered in the infantry, and at the battle of Cold Harbor received a wound in the leg which disqualified him for a foot-soldier thenceforward. His friends succeeded in procuring for him the commission of lieutenant, and he was assigned to duty as drill-master at a camp of instruction near Richmond.

"Here I was really in clover, old fellow," said Tom, laughingly "no more toils, no more hardships, no bullets, or hard tack, or want of soap. A snowy shirt every day—kid gloves if I wanted them—and the sound of cannon at a very remote distance to lull me to repose, my boy. Things had changed, they had indeed! I looked back with scorn on the heavy musket and cartridge-box. I rode a splendidly groomed horse, wore a new uniform shining with gold braid, a new cap covered with ditto, boots which you could see your face in, a magnificent sash, and spurs so long and martial that they made the pavement resound, and announced my approach at the distance of a quarter of a mile! I say the pavement; I was a good deal on the pavement—that of the fashionable Franklin street being my favorite haunt. And as the Scripture says, it is not good for man to be alone, I had young ladies for companions. My life was grand, superb—none of your low military exposure, like that borne by the miserable privates and officers in the field! I slept in town, lived at a hotel, mounted my horse after breakfast, at the Government stables near my lodgings and went gallantly at a gallop, to drill infantry for an hour or two at the camp of instruction. This was a bore, I acknowledge, but life can not be all flowers. It was soon over, however—I galloped gallantly back—dined with all the courses at my hotel, and then lit my cigar and strolled up Franklin. I wore my uniform and spurs on these promenades—wild horses tearing me would not have induced me to doff the spurs! They were so martial! They jingled so! They gave a military and ferocious set-off to my whole appearance, and were immensely admired by the fair sex! Regularly on coming back from my arduous and dangerous duties at camp, I brushed my uniform, put on my red sash, and with one hand resting with dignity on my new sword belt, advanced to engage the enemy — on Franklin street."

Tom Herbert's laugh was contagious; his whole bearing so sunny and *riante* that he was charming.

"Well, how did you awake from your *dolce far niente?*" I said.

"By an effort of the will, old fellow — for I really could not stand that. It was glorious, delightful — that war-making in town; but there was a thorn in it. I was ashamed of myself. 'Tom Herbert you are not a soldier, you are an impostor,' I said; 'you are young, healthy, as good food for powder as anybody else, and yet here you are, safely laid away in a bomb-proof, while your friends are fighting. Wake, rouse yourself, my friend! The only way to regain the path of rectitude is to go back to the army!'"

"I said that, Surry," Tom continued, "and as I could not go back into the infantry on account of my leg, I applied for an assignment to duty in the cavalry. Then the war office had a time of it. I besieged the nabobs of the red tape day and night, and they got so tired of me at last that they told me to find a general who wanted an aid and they would assign me."

"Well, as I was coming out of the den I met General Jeb Stuart going in. I knew him well, and he was tenth cousin to my grandmother, which you know counts for a great deal in Virginia."

"What's the matter, Tom?" he said.

"I want a place in the cavalry, general."

"What claim have you?"

"Shot in the leg — can't walk — am tired of drilling men in bomb-proof."

"Good!" he said. "That's the way to talk. Come in here."

"And he dragged me along. I found that one of his aids had just been captured — he wanted another, and he applied for me. A month afterward his application was approved — short for the war office. That was five days ago. I got into the saddle, — pushed for the Rapidan — got to Middleburg — and arrived in time for supper."

"That's my history, old fellow, except that I have just fallen in love — with the young angel who waited on me at supper, Miss Katy Dare. I opened the campaign in a corner last night — and I intend to win her, Surry, or perish in the attempt!"

XVII
STUART GRAZES CAPTURE

As Tom Herbert uttered these words, a loud shout in front startled us.

Stuart had ridden on ahead of his column, through the immense deserted camps around Wolf Run Shoals, attended only by two or three staff officers.

As I now raised my head quickly, I saw him coming back at headlong speed, directing his horse by means of the halter only, and hotly pursued by a detachment of Federal cavalry, firing on him as they pressed, with loud shouts, upon his very heels.

"Halt!" shouted the enemy. And this order was followed by "bang! bang! bang!"

Stuart did not obey the order.

"Halt! halt!"

And a storm of bullets whistled around our heads. I had drawn my sword, but before I could go to Stuart's assistance, Tom shot ahead of me.

He came just in time. Two of the enemy had caught up with Stuart, and were making furious cuts at him. He parried the blow of one of the Federal cavalry-men—and the other fell from the saddle, throwing up his hands as he did so. Tom Herbert had placed his pistol on his breast, and shot him through the heart.

But by this time the rest had reached us. A sabre flashed above Tom's head; fell, cutting him out of the saddle nearly; and he would have dropped from it, had I not passed my arm around him.

In another instant, all three would have been killed or captured. But the firing had given the alarm. A thunder of hoofs was heard: a squadron of our cavalry dashed over the hill: in three minutes the enemy were flying, to escape the edge of the sabre.

Stuart led the charge, and seemed to enjoy it with the zest of a fox-hunter. He had indeed escaped from a critical danger. He had pushed on with a few of his staff, as I have said, to Fairfax Station, had then stopped and slipped his bridle to allow his horse to eat some "Yankee oats," and while standing beside the animal, had been suddenly charged by the party of Federal cavalry, coming down on a reconnaissance from the direction of the Court-House. So sudden was their appearance that he was nearly "gobbled up." He had leaped on the unbridled horse; seized the halter, and fled at full speed. The enemy had pursued him; he had declined halting — and the reader has seen the sequel.{1}

{Footnote 1: Real.}

Stuart pressed the party hotly toward Sanxter's, but they escaped — nearly capturing on the way, however, a party of officers at a blacksmith's shop. The general came back in high good humor. The chase seemed to have delighted him.

"Bully for old Tom Herbert!" he exclaimed. "You ought to have seen him when they were cutting at him, and spoiling his fine new satchel!"

Tom Herbert did not seem to participate in the general's mirth. He was examining the satchel which a sabre stroke had nearly cut in two.

"What are you looking at?" asked Stuart.

"This hole, general," replied Tom, uttering a piteous sigh.

"Well, it is a trifle."

"It is a serious matter, general."

"You have lost something?"

"Yes."

"What?"

"A joint of my new flute."

And Tom Herbert's expression was so melancholy that Stuart burst into laughter.

"You may have lost your flute, Tom," he said, leaning on his shoulder, "but you have won your spurs at least, in the cavalry!"

XVIII
DROWSYLAND

At daylight, on the next morning, Stuart had crossed the Potomac into Maryland.

He had advanced from Wolf Run Shoals to Fairfax Court House, where the men rifled the sutlers' shops of tobacco, figs, white gloves, straw hats, and every edible and wearable: — then the column pushed on toward Seneca Falls, where the long wavering line of horsemen might have been seen hour after hour crossing the moonlit river, each man, to prevent wetting, holding above his head a shot or shell taken from the caissons. Then the artillery was dragged through: the panting horses trotted on, and the first beams of day saw the long column of Stuart ready to advance on its perilous pathway to the Susquehanna, by the route between the Federal army and Washington.

The word was given, and with the red flags fluttering, Stuart moved toward Rockville, unopposed, save by a picket, which was driven off by the advance guard. Without further incident, he then pushed on, and entered the town in triumph.

A charming reception awaited him. The place was thoroughly Southern; and the passage of the cavalry was greeted with loud cheers. Unbounded was the delight, above all, of a seminary of young girls. Doors and windows were crowded: bright eyes shone; red lips laughed; waving handkerchiefs were seen everywhere; and when Stuart appeared in person, he was received with wild rejoicing.

He bowed low, removing his plumed hat, but suddenly intelligence came which forced him to push on. A long train of "government" wagons had come up from Washington, and on discovering our presence, returned toward the city at a gallop. But the ferocious rebels were after them. Stuart led the charging column — the warlike teamsters were soon halted — the trains became our spoil — and with countless kicking mules driven onward in droves before them, the cavalry, escorting the captured wagons, continued their way toward Pennsylvania.

Moving all that night, Stuart came to Westminster, where Fitz Lee, the gallant, drove the enemy's cavalry from their camp, and the town fell into the hands of Stuart.

Here scowls instead of smiles greeted us. Every face was glum and forbidding, with a few exceptions. So we hastened to depart from that "loyal" town, and were soon on the soil of Pennsylvania.

Approaching Hanover we suddenly waked up the hornets. Chambliss, leading Stuart's advance, pushed ahead and drove in a picket. Then that brave soldier rushed on, and seemed intent on taking the place, when I was sent by Stuart to order him "not to go too far."

I came up with Chambliss as he was charging, but had scarcely given him the order, when he was charged in turn by a heavy force and driven back.

The enemy rushed on, firing volleys, and the road was full of tramping horsemen. To avoid being carried away with them, I diverged into a field, when all at once Stuart appeared, retreating at full gallop before a party who were chasing him.

It was a serious matter then, but I laugh now, remembering that "good run."

Stuart and myself retreated at a gallop, boot to boot; leaped ditches and fences; and got off in safety.

A few moments afterward his artillery opened its thunders. From the lofty hill, that hardy captain of the horse artillery, Breathed, roared obstinately, driving them back. Hampton's guns on the right had opened too—and until night, we held the heights, repulsing every advance of the enemy.

It was truly a fine spectacle, that handsome town of Hanover as I looked at it, on the afternoon of the fair June day. In front extended green fields; then the church spires rose above the roofs of the town; behind, a range of mountains formed a picturesque background. It is true, the adjuncts of the scene were far from peaceful. The green fields were full of blue sharp-shooters; in the suburbs were posted batteries; down the mountain road behind, wound a long compact column of cavalry.

Breathed fought hard that day. From the waving field of rye on the upland his guns thundered on—in the face of that fire, the enemy could not, or would not, advance.

So the night came on, and Stuart's great train moved.

Those wagons were a terrible encumbrance to us on the march. But Stuart determined not to abandon them, and they were dragged on—a line stretched to infinity!

Thenceforth, dear reader, the march was a sort of dream to me. How can I relate my adventures—the numerous spectacles and events of the time? I know not even now if they were events or mere dreams, seeing that, all the long way, I was half asleep in the saddle! It was a veritable Drowsyland that we moved through on horseback! The Dutchmen, the "fraus," the "spreading," the sauer-kraut—the conestogas, the red barns, the guttural voices, the strange faces—were these actual things, or the mere fancies of a somnambulist? Was I an officer of real cavalry making a real march; or a fanciful being, one of a long column of phantoms?

I seem dimly to remember a pretty face, whose owner smiled on me—and a faint memory remains of a supper which she gave me. If I am not mistaken I was left alone in the town of Salem—hostile faces were around me—and I was falling asleep when Hampton's cavalry came up.

I think, then, I rode on with him—having been left to direct him. That we talked about horses, and the superiority of "blood" in animals; that at dawn, Hampton said, "I am perishing for sleep!" and that we lay down, side by side, near a haystack.

All that is a sort of phantasmagoria, and others were no better than myself. Whole columns went to sleep, in the saddle, as they rode along; and General Stuart told me afterward, that he saw a man attempt to climb over a fence, half succeed only, and go to sleep on the top rail!

Some day I promise myself the pleasure of travelling in Pennsylvania. It possesses all the attractions to me of a world seen in a dream!

But after that good sleep, side by side with the great Carolinian, things looked far more real, and pushing on I again caught up with Stuart.

He advanced steadily on Carlisle, and in the afternoon we heard artillery from the south.

I looked at my military map, and calculated the distance. The result was that I said:—

"General, those guns are at a place called Gettysburg on this map."

"Impossible!" was his reply. "They can not be fighting there. You are certainly wrong."

But I was right.

Those guns were the signal of the "First day's fight at Gettysburg."

XIX
CARLISLE BY FIRELIGHT

It can not be said that we accomplished very enormous results at Carlisle. The enemy defended it bravely.

Stuart sent in a flag, demanding a surrender: this proposition was politely declined; and for fear that there might possibly remain some doubts on the subject, the Federal commander of the post, opened with artillery upon the gray cavalry.

That was the signal for a brisk fight, and a magnificent spectacle also.

As soon as the enemy's response to the flag of truce had been received, Stuart advanced his sharp-shooters, replied with his artillery to their own, and dispatched a party to destroy the extensive United States barracks, formerly used as cantonments for recruits to the army.

In ten minutes the buildings were wrapped in flames; and the city of Carlisle was illumined magnificently. The crimson light of the conflagration revealed every house, the long lines of trees, and made the delicate church spires, rising calmly aloft, resemble shafts of rose-tinted marble.

I recall but one scene which was equally picturesque—the "doomed city" of Fredericksburg, on the night of December 11, 1862, when the church spires were illumined by the burning houses, as those of Carlisle were in June, 1863.

So much for this new "Siege of Carlisle." Here my description ends. It was nothing—a mere picture. An hour afterward Stuart ceased firing, the conflagration died down; back into the black night sank the fair town of Carlisle, seen then for the first and the last time by this historian.

The guns were silent, the cavalry retired; and Stuart, accompanied by his staff, galloped back to a great deserted house where he established his temporary head-quarters.

On the bold face there was an expression of decided ill-humor. He had just received a dispatch, by courier, from General Lee.

That dispatch said, "Come, I need you urgently here," and the "here" in question, was Gettysburg, at least twenty miles distant. Now, with worn-out men and horses, twenty miles was a serious matter. Stuart's brows were knit, and he mused gloomily.

Suddenly he turned and addressed me.

"You were right, Surry," he said, "those guns were at Gettysburg. This dispatch, sent this morning, reports the enemy near there."

I bowed; Stuart reflected for some moments without speaking. Then he suddenly said: —

"I wish you would go to General Lee, and say I am coming, Surry. How is your horse?"

"Worn-out, general, but I can get another."

"Good; tell General Lee that I will move at once to Gettysburg, with all my force, and as rapidly as possible!"

"I will lose no time, general."

And saluting, I went out.

From the captured horses I selected the best one I could find, and burying the spurs in his sides, set out through the black night.

XX
THE HOUSE BETWEEN CARLISLE AND GETTYSBURG

You know when you set out, the proverb says, but you know not when you will arrive.

I left Carlisle, breasting the night, on the road to Gettysburg, little thinking that a curious incident was to occur to me upon the way—an incident closely connected with the destinies of some personages who play prominent parts in this history.

I had ridden on for more than an hour, through the darkness, keeping a good look-out for the enemy, whose scouting parties of cavalry were known to be prowling around, when all at once, my horse, who was going at full speed, struck his foot against a sharp point of rock, cropping out from the surface.

The animal stumbled, recovered himself, and went on as rapidly as before. A hundred yards further his speed relaxed; then he began to limp painfully; then in spite of every application of the spur I could not force him out of a slow limping trot.

It was truly unfortunate. I was the bearer of an important message, and was surrounded by enemies. The only chance was to pass through them, under shadow of the darkness; with light they would perceive me, and my capture be certain.

A hundred yards further, and I found I must decide at once upon the course to pursue. My horse seemed about to fall. At every stroke of the spur he groaned piteously, and his limp had become a stagger.

I looked around through the trees, and at the distance of a quarter of a mile I saw the glimmer of a light. To obtain another horse was indispensable under the circumstances; and looking to see that my revolver was loaded and capped, I forced my tottering animal toward the mansion in which the light glimmered.

My design was simply to proceed thither, "impress" a fresh horse at the pistol's muzzle; throw my saddle upon him; leave my own animal, and proceed on my way.

Pushing across the fields, and dismounting to let down the fences which my limping animal could not leap, I soon approached the light. It shone through the window of a house of some size, with ornamental grounds around it, and apparently the abode of a man of means.

At fifty paces from it I dismounted and tethered my horse in the shadow of some trees. A brief reconnaissance under the circumstances was advisable; and approaching the mansion silently, without allowing my sabre to make any clatter, I gained the long portico in front, and went to a window reaching down to the flooring of the verandah.

Through the half-closed venetians I could see into a large apartment, half library, half sitting-room, as the easy chairs, mantel ornaments, desks, and book-cases showed. On the centre-table burned a brilliant lamp — and by its light I witnessed a spectacle which made me draw back in the shadow of the shutter, and rivet my eyes on the interior.

Before me, in the illuminated apartment, I saw the woman whom Mohun had captured on the Rappahannock; and beside her the personage with whom she had escaped that morning in the wagon from Culpeper Court-House. I could not mistake him. The large, prominent nose, the cunning eyes, the double chin, the fat person, and the chubby hands covered with pinchbeck rings, were still fresh in my memory.

The name of this personage had been revealed by Nighthawk. Swartz, the secret agent, blockade-runner, and "best spy in the Federal army" was before me.

A glance at the woman revealed no change in her appearance. Before me was the same lithe and graceful figure, clad as before in a gray dress. I saw the same snow-white cheeks, red lips, and large eyes burning with a latent fire.

The two were busily engaged, and it was not difficult to understand their occupation. The desks, drawers and chests of the apartment were all open; and the female with rapid hands was transferring papers from them to Swartz, who methodically packed them in a leathern valise. These papers were no doubt important, and the aim to remove them to some place of safety beyond the reach of the Confederates.

I gazed for some moments, without moving, upon the spectacle of these two night-birds at their work. The countenance of the lady was animated; her motions rapid; and from time to time she stopped to listen. Swartz, on the contrary, was the incarnation of phlegmatic coolness. His face wore an expression of entire equanimity; and he seemed to indulge no fears whatever of intruders.

All at once, however, I saw his eyes glitter as they fell upon a paper which she handed him to pack away with the rest. It was carefully folded, but one of the folds flew open as he received it, and his eyes were suddenly fixed intently upon the sheet.

Then his head turned quickly, and he looked at his companion. She was bending over a drawer, and did not observe that glance. Thereupon Swartz folded up the paper, quietly put it in his pocket, and went on packing the valise with his former coolness; only a slight color in his face seemed to indicate concealed emotion.

As he pocketed the paper, his companion turned round. It was plain that she had not perceived the manoeuvre.

At the same moment I heard the sound of hoofs in rear of the house, and the clatter of a sabre as a cavalier dismounted. A few indistinct words, apparently addressed to a servant or orderly, followed. Then the door of the apartment opposite the front window was thrown open, and a man entered.

In the new-comer I recognized Mohun's adversary at Upperville— Colonel Darke, of the United States Cavalry.

XXI
FALLEN

Darke entered the apartment abruptly, but his appearance seemed to occasion no surprise. The spy retained his coolness. The lady went on with her work. You would have said that they had expected the officer, and recognized his step.

Their greeting was brief. Darke nodded in apparent approbation of the task in which the man and woman were engaged, and folding his arms in front of the marble mantel, looked on in silence.

I gazed at him with interest, and more carefully than I had been able to do during the fight at Upperville, when the smoke soon concealed him. Let me draw his outline. Of all the human beings whom I encountered in the war, this one's character and career were perhaps the most remarkable. Were I writing a romance, I should be tempted to call him the real hero of this volume.

He was a man approaching middle age; low in stature, but broad, muscular, and powerful. He was clad in the full-dress uniform of a colonel of the United States Cavalry, wore boots reaching to the knee and decorated with large spurs; and his arms were an immense sabre and a brace of revolvers in black leather holsters attached to his belt. His face was swarthy, swollen by excess in drink apparently, and half covered by a shaggy beard and mustache as black as night. The eyes were deep-set, and wary: the poise of the head upon the shoulders, haughty; the expression of the entire countenance cold, phlegmatic, grim.

Such was this man, upon the surface. But there was something more about him which irresistibly attracted attention, and aroused speculation. At the first glance, you set him down as a common-place ruffian, the prey of every brutal passion. At the second glance, you began to doubt whether he was a mere vulgar adventurer—you could see, at least, that this man was not of low birth. There was in his bearing an indefinable something which indicated that he had "seen better days." The surface of the fabric was foul and defiled, but the texture beneath was of velvet, not "hodden gray."

"That brute," I thought, "was once a gentleman, and crime or drink has destroyed him!"

Darke continued to gaze at Swartz and the gray woman as they plied their busy work; and once or twice be pointed to drawers which they had failed to open. These directions were promptly obeyed, and the work went on. The few words which the parties uttered came in an indistinct murmur only through the window at which I was stationed.

Such was the scene within the mansion, upon which I gazed with strong curiosity: suddenly the neigh of a horse was heard in a clump of woods beyond the front gate; and Darke quickly raised his head, and then came out to the portico.

He passed within three feet of me, but did not perceive me, as I was concealed by one of the open venetians. Then he paused and listened. The wind sighed in the foliage, and a distant watch-dog was barking—that was all. No other noise disturbed the silence of the July night.

Darke remained upon the portico for some moments, listening attentively. Then turned and re-entered the house. Through the window, I could see him make his appearance again in the illuminated apartment. In response to the glances of inquiry from his companions he made a gesture only, but that said plainly:—

"Nothing is stirring. You can go on with your work."

In this, however, he was mistaken. Darke had scarcely re-entered the apartment, when I discerned the hoof-strokes of horses beyond the front gate—then the animals were heard leaping the low fence—a moment afterward two figures came on at full gallop, threw themselves from the saddle, and rapidly approached the house.

The rattle of a sabre which one of them wore attracted Darke's attention. He reached the door of the room at a single bound—but at the same instant the new comers rushed by me, and burst in.

As they passed I recognized them. One was Mohun, the other Nighthawk.

XXII
DARKE AND MOHUN

What followed was instantaneous.

The adversaries were face to face, and each drew his pistol and fired at the same moment.

Neither was struck: they drew their swords; and, through the cloud of smoke filling the apartment, I could see Darke and Mohun close in, in a hand to hand encounter.

They were both excellent swordsmen, and the struggle was passionate and terrible. Mohun's movements were those of the tiger springing upon his prey; but Darke met the attack with a coolness and phlegm which indicated unshrinking nerve; his expression seemed, even, to indicate that crossing swords with his adversary gave the swarthy giant extreme pleasure. His face glowed, and a flash darted from beneath the shaggy eyebrows. I could see him smile; but the smile was strange.

From the adversaries my glance passed quickly to the gray woman. She was leaning against the wall, and exhibited no emotion whatever; but the lurid blaze in the great dark eyes, as she looked at Mohun, clearly indicated that a storm was raging in her bosom. Opposite the woman stood Nighthawk—motionless, but grasping a pistol. As to Swartz, that worthy had profited by an open window near, and had glided through it and disappeared.

To return to the combatants. The passionate encounter absorbed all my attention. Mohun and Darke were cutting at each other furiously. They seemed equally matched, and the result was doubtful. One thing only seemed certain—that in a few minutes one of the adversaries would be dead.

Such was the situation of affairs when shots were heard without, the clash of sabres followed, and the door behind Darke was burst open violently by his orderly, who rushed in, exclaiming:—

"Look out, colonel! The enemy are on you!"

As he uttered these words, the man drew a revolver and aimed at Mohun's breast.

Before he could fire, however, an explosion was heard, and I saw the man suddenly drop his weapon, which went off as it escaped from his nerveless grasp. Then he threw up his hands, reeled, took two uncertain steps backward, and fell at full length on the floor. Nighthawk had shot him through the heart.

All this had taken place in far less time than it has taken to write it. I had made violent efforts to break through the window; and finding this impossible, now ran to the door and burst into the apartment.

The singular scene was to have as singular a denouement.

Darke evidently realized the great danger which he ran, for the house was now surrounded, nearly, and his capture was imminent.

From the black eyes shot a glare of defiance, and advancing upon Mohun, he delivered a blow at him which nearly shattered his opponent's sword. Mohun struck in turn, aiming a furious cut at Darke; but as he did so, he stumbled over the dead orderly, and nearly fell. For the moment he was at Darke's mercy.

I rushed forward, sword in hand, to ward off the mortal stroke which I was certain his adversary would deliver, but my intervention was useless.

Darke recoiled from his stumbling adversary, instead of striking at him. I could scarcely believe my own eyes, but the fact was unmistakable.

Then the Federal colonel looked around, and his eye fell upon the woman.

"Kill him!" she said, coldly. "Do not mind me! — only kill him!"

"No!" growled Darke. And seizing the woman in his arms: —

"They shall not take you prisoner!" he said.

And the swarthy Hercules passed through the door in rear at a single bound, bearing off the woman like a feather.

A moment afterward the hoof-strokes of a horse were heard.

Darke had disappeared with the gray woman.

I turned to look at Mohun. He was standing perfectly motionless, and looking after Darke with a strange expression of gloom and astonishment.

"You are unhurt!" I said.

He turned quickly, and held out his hand.

"Slightly wounded — but I am not thinking of that."

"Of what, then?"

"I remember only one thing — that this man might have buried his sword in my heart, and did not."

An hour afterward the skirmish was over; I had explained my presence at the house to Mohun, parted with him, promising to see him soon again; and, mounted upon a fresh animal which Mohun presented to me from among those captured, was once more on my way to Gettysburg.

It was hard to realize that the scenes of the night were actual occurrences. They were more like dreams than realities.

XXIII
GETTYSBURG

I came in sight of Gettysburg at sunrise.

Gettysburg! — name instinct with so many tears, with so much mourning, with those sobs which tear their way from the human heart as the lava makes its way from the womb of the volcano!

There are words in the world's history whose very sound is like a sigh or a groan; places which are branded "accursed" by the moaning lips of mothers, wives, sisters, and orphans. Shadowy figures, gigantic and draped in mourning, seem to hover above these spots: skeleton arms with bony fingers point to the soil beneath, crowded with graves: from the eyes, dim and hollow, glare unutterable things: and the grin of the fleshless lips is the gibbering mirth of the corpse torn from its cerements, and erect, as though the last trump had sounded, and the dead had arisen. No fresh flowers bloom in these dreary spots; no merry birds twitter there; no streamlets lapse sweetly with musical murmurs beneath the waterflags or the drooping boughs of trees. See! the blighted and withered plants are like the deadly nightshade — true flowers of war, blooming, or trying to bloom, on graves! Hear the voices of the few birds — they are sad and discordant! See the trees — they are gnarled, spectral, and torn by cannon-balls. Listen! The stream yonder is not limpid and mirthful like other streams. You would say that it is sighing as it steals away, soiled and ashamed. The images it has mirrored arouse its horror and make it sad. The serene surface has not given back the bright forms of children, laughing and gathering the summer flowers on its banks. As it sneaks like a culprit through the scarred fields of battle, it washes bare the bones of the dead in crumbling uniforms — bringing, stark and staring, to the upper air once more, the blanched skeleton and the grinning skull.

Names of woe, at whose utterance the heart shudders, the blood curdles! Accursed localities where the traveller draws back, turning away in horror! All the world is dotted with them; everywhere they make the sunlight black. Among them, none is gloomier, or instinct with a more nameless horror, than the once insignificant village of Gettysburg.

I reached it on the morning of July 2, 1863.

The immense drama was in full progress. The adversaries had clashed together. Riding across the extensive fields north of the town, I saw the traces of the combat of the preceding day—and among the dying I remember still a poor Federal soldier, who looked at me with his stony and half-glazed eye as I passed; he was an enemy, but he was dying and I pitied him.

A few words will describe the situation of affairs at that moment.

Lee had pressed on northward through the valley of the Cumberland, when news came that General Meade, who had succeeded Hooker, was advancing to deliver battle to the invaders.

At that intelligence Lee arrested his march. Meade menaced his communications, and it was necessary to check him. Hill's corps was, therefore, sent across the South Mountain, toward Gettysburg; Ewell, who had reached York, was ordered back; and Lee made his preparations to fight his adversary as soon as he appeared.

The columns encountered each other in the neighborhood of Gettysburg—a great centre toward which a number of roads converge, like the spokes of a wheel toward the hub.

The head of Hill's column struck the head of Reynolds's—then the thunder began.

The day and scene were lovely. On the waving wheat-fields and the forests in full foliage, the light of a summer sun fell in flashing splendor. A slight rain had fallen; the wind was gently blowing; and the leaves and golden grain were covered with drops which the sunshine changed to diamonds. Over the exquisite landscape drooped a beautiful rainbow.

Soon blood had replaced the raindrops, and the bright bow spanning the sky was hidden by lurid smoke, streaming aloft from burning buildings, set on fire by shell.

I give but a few words to this first struggle, which I did not witness.

The Federal forces rushed forward, exclaiming:—-

"We have come to stay!"

"And a very large portion of them," said one of their officers, General Doubleday, "never left that ground!"

Alas! many thousands in gray, too, "came to stay."

Hill was hard pressed and sent for assistance. Suddenly it appeared from the woods on his left, where Ewell's bayonets were seen, coming back from the Susquehanna.

Rodes, the head of Ewell's corps, formed line and threw himself into the action.

Early came up on the left; Rodes charged and broke through the Federal centre. Gordon, commanding a brigade then, closed in on their right flank, and the battle was decided.

The great blue crescent was shattered, and gave way. The Confederates pressed on, and the Federal army became a rabble. They retreated pellmell through Gettysburg, toward Cemetery Hill, leaving their battle-flags and five thousand prisoners in our hands.

Such was the first day's fight at Gettysburg. Lee's head of column had struck Meade's; each had rapidly been reinforced; the affair became a battle, and the Federal forces were completely defeated.

That was the turning point of the campaign. If this success had only been followed up—if we could only have seized upon and occupied Cemetery Hill!

Then General Meade would have been compelled to retire upon Westminster and Washington. He would doubtless have fought somewhere, but it is a terrible thing to have an army flushed with victory "after" you!

Cemetery Range was not seized that night. When the sun rose the next morning, the golden moment had passed. General Meade was ready.

From right to left, as far as the eye could reach, the heights bristled with blue infantry and artillery. From every point on the ridge waved the enemy's battle flags. From the muzzles of his bronze war-dogs, Meade sent his defiant challenge to his adversary to attack him.

"Come on!" the Federal artillery seemed to mutter fiercely.

And Lee's guns from the ridge opposite thundered grimly in reply,

"We are coming!"

XXIV
THE ARMY

Alas!—

That is the word which rises to the lips of every Southerner, above all to every Virginian, who attempts to describe this terrible battle of Gettysburg.

The cheeks flush, the voice falters, and something like a fiery mist blinds the eyes. What comes back to the memory of the old soldiers who saw that fight is a great picture of heroic assaults, ending in frightful carnage only,— of charges such as the world has rarely seen, made in vain,—of furious onslaughts, the only result of which was to strew those fatal fields with the dead bodies of the flower of the Southern race.

And we were so near succeeding! Twice the enemy staggered; and one more blow—only one more! promised the South a complete victory!

When Longstreet attacked Round Top Hill, driving the enemy back to their inner line, victory seemed within our very grasp—but we could not snatch it. The enemy acknowledge that, and it is one of their own poets who declares that

"The century reeled When Longstreet paused on the slope of the hill."

Pickett stormed Cemetery Heights, and wanted only support. Five thousand men at his back would have given him victory.

There is a name for the battle of Gettysburg which exactly suits it— "The Great Graze!"

You must go to the histories, reader, for a detailed account of this battle. I have not the heart to write it, and aim to give you a few scenes only. In my hasty memoirs I can touch only upon the salient points, and make the general picture.

The ground on which the battle was fought, is familiar to many thousands. A few words will describe it. Cemetery Ridge, where General Meade had taken up his position, is a range of hills running northward toward Gettysburg, within a mile of which place it bends off to the right, terminating in a lofty and rock-bound crest.

This crest was Meade's right. His line stretched away southward then, and ended at Round Top Hill, the southern extremity of the range, about four miles distant. From one end to the other of the extensive range, bayonets glistened, and the muzzles of cannon grinned defiance.

Opposite the Cemetery Range was a lower line of hills, called Seminary Range. Upon this Lee was posted, Ewell holding his left, A. P. Hill his centre, and Longstreet his right.

Between the two armies stretched a valley, waving with grain and dotted with fruit-trees, through which ran the Emmettsburg road, on the western side of a small stream. The golden grain waved gently; the limpid water lapsed away beneath grass and flowers; the birds were singing; the sun was shining — it was the strangest of all scenes for a bloody conflict.

I rode along the line of battle, and curiously scanned the features of the landscape. There is a frightful interest connected with ground which is soon going to become the arena of a great combat. A glance told me that the enemy's position was much the stronger of the two. Would Lee attack it?

From the landscape I turned to look at the army. Never had I seen them so joyous. It would be impossible to convey any idea of the afflatus which buoyed them up. Every man's veins seemed to run with quicksilver, instead of blood. Every cheek was glowing. Every eye flashed with superb joy and defiance. You would have supposed, indeed, that the troops were under the effect of champagne or laughing gas. "I never even imagined such courage," said a Federal officer afterward; "your men seemed to be drunk with victory when they charged us!"

That was scarce an exaggeration. Already on the morning of battle they presented this appearance. Lying down in line of battle, they laughed, jested, sang, and resembled children enjoying a holiday. On the faces of bearded veterans and boy-soldiers alike was a splendid pride. The victories of Fredericksburg, and Chancellorsville had electrified the troops. They thought little of a foe who could be so easily driven; they looked forward to victory as a foregone conclusion — alas! they did not remember that they held the heights at Fredericksburg; and that Meade on Cemetery Hill was an adversary very different from Hooker in the Spottsylvania Wilderness!

Such was the spectacle which I witnessed, when after delivering my message to General Lee, I rode along the Southern line. I think the great commander shared in some measure the sentiment of his troops. His bearing was collected; in his eye you could read no trace of excitement; the lips covered by the gray mustache were firm and composed; and he greeted me with quiet courtesy:—but in the cheeks of the great soldier a ruddy glow seemed to betray anticipated victory.

I confess I shared the general sentiment. That strange intoxication was contagious, and I was drunk like the rest with the thought of triumph. That triumph would open to us the gates of Washington and bring peace. The North scarcely denied that then—though they may deny it to-day. The whole country was completely weary of the war. There seemed to be no hope of compelling the South to return to the Union. A victory over Meade, opening the whole North to Lee, promised a treaty of peace. The day had arrived, apparently when the army of Northern Virginia, musket in hand, was about to dictate the terms of that document.

"Lee has only to slip the leash," I thought, as I gazed at the army, "and these war-dogs will tear down their prey!"

Alas! they tore it, but were torn too! they did all at Gettysburg that any troops could do.

What was impossible, was beyond even their strength.

XXV
THE WRESTLE FOR ROUND TOP HILL

From the morning of the second of July to the evening of the third, the fields south of Gettysburg were one great scene of smoke, dust, uproar, blood; of columns advancing and returning; cannon thundering; men shouting, yelling, cheering, and dying; blue mingled with gray in savage and unrelenting battle.

In that smoke-cloud, with the ears deafened, you saw or heard little distinctly. But above the confused struggle rose two great incidents, which on successive days decided every thing.

The first of them was Longstreet's assault on the enemy's left wing, in front of Round Top Hill.

Lee had displayed excellent soldiership in determining upon this movement, and it will be seen that it came within an inch of success. Standing upon Seminary Range, near his centre, he had reconnoitered General Meade's position through his field-glass, with great attention; and this examination revealed the fact that the Federal line was projected forward in a salient in front of Round Top Hill, a jagged and almost inaccessible peak, near which rested General Meade's extreme left.

If this weak point could be carried, "it appeared" said Lee, "that its possession would give facilities for assailing and carrying the more elevated ground and crest beyond."

As to the importance of that crest—namely Round Top Hill—hear General Meade:—

"If they had succeeded in occupying that, it would have prevented me from holding any of the ground which I subsequently held to the last."

Lee determined to attack the salient, making at the same time a heavy demonstration—or a real assault—upon the Federal right, opposite Ewell.

All his preparations were not made until the afternoon. Then suddenly, Longstreet's artillery opened its thunders.

At that moment the spectacle was grand. The heights, the slopes, the fields, and the rugged crest opposite, were enveloped in smoke and fire from the bursting shell. The sombre roar ascended like the bellowing of a thousand bulls, leaped back from the rocks, and rolled away, in wild echoes through the hills. All the furies seemed let loose, and yet this was only the preface.

At four in the evening the thunder dropped to silence, and along the lines of Hood and McLaws, which formed the charging column, ran a wild cheer, which must have reached the ears of the enemy opposite.

That cheer told both sides that the moment had come. The word was given, and Longstreet hurled his column at the blue line occupying a peach-orchard in his front.

The blow was aimed straight at the salient in the Federal line, and in spite of a brave resistance it was swept away; McLaws advancing rapidly toward the high ground in its rear. At one blow the whole left wing of General Meade's army seemed thrown into irretrievable confusion, and Hood pressing forward on McLaws's right, hastened to seize upon the famous Round Top, from which he would be able to hurl his thunder upon the flank and rear of the Federal line of battle.

The scene, like the conflict which now took place, was wild and singular. The crest of Round Top Hill was a mass of rock, which rose abruptly from the rough and jagged slope. It was unoccupied — for the sudden overthrow of the force in front of it had not been anticipated — and one headlong rush on the part of Hood alone seemed necessary to give him possession of the real key of the whole position.

Hood saw that at a glance, and dashed up the slope at the head of his men. It was scarcely an order of battle which his troops presented at this moment. But one thought burned in every heart. The men swarmed up the hill-side; the woods gave back the rolling thunder of their cheers; already the Southern battle-flags carried by the foremost were fluttering on the crest.

The mass rushed toward the red flags; for an instant the gray figures were seen erect upon the summit — then a sudden crash of musketry resounded — and a mad struggle began with a Federal brigade which had hastened to the spot.

This force, it is said, was hurried up by General Warren, who finding the Federal signal-officers about to retire, ordered them, to remain and continue waving their flags to the last; and then, seizing on the first brigade he could find, rushed them up the slope to the crest.

They arrived just in time. Hood's men were swarming on the crest. A loud cheer arose, but all at once they found themselves face to face with a line of bayonets, while beyond were seen confused and struggling masses, dragging up cannon.

What followed was a savage grapple rather than an ordinary conflict. Only a small part of Hood's force had reached the summit, and this was assailed by a whole brigade. The fight was indescribable. All that the eye could make out for some moments in the dust and smoke, was a confused mass of men clutching each other, dealing blows with the butt-ends of muskets, or fencing with bayonets—men in blue and gray, wrestling, cursing, falling, and dying, in the midst of the crash of small-arms, and the thunder of cannon, which clothed the crest in flame.

When the smoke drifted, it was seen that the Confederates had been repulsed, and driven from the hill. Hood was falling back slowly, like a wounded tiger, who glares at the huntsman and defies him to the last. The slope was strewed with some of his bravest. The Federal cannon roaring on Round Top Hill, seemed to be laughing hoarsely.

McLaws, too, had fallen back after nearly seizing upon the crest in his front. The enemy had quickly re-enforced their left, with brigades, divisions, and corps, and the Confederates had been hotly assailed in their turn. As night descended, the whole Southern line fell back. The pallid moonlight shone on the upturned faces of the innumerable dead.

Longstreet sat on a fence, cutting a stick with his penknife, when an English officer near him exclaimed:—

"I would not have missed this for any thing?"

Longstreet, laughed grimly.

"I would like to have missed it very much!"{1} he said.

{Footnote 1: His words.}

XXVI
THE CHARGE OF THE VIRGINIANS

Lee's great blow at the enemy's left had failed. He had thrown his entire right wing, under Longstreet, against it. The enemy had been driven; victory seemed achieved;—but suddenly the blue lines had rallied, they had returned to the struggle, their huge masses had rolled forward, thrown Longstreet back in turn, and now the pale moon looked down on the battlefield where some of the bravest souls of the South had poured out their blood in vain.

Lee had accomplished nothing, and one of his great corps was panting and bleeding. It was not shattered or even shaken. The iron fibre would stand any thing almost. But the sombre result remained—Longstreet had attacked and had been repulsed.

What course would Lee now pursue? Would he retire?

Retire? The army of Northern Virginia lose heart at a mere rebuff? Lee's veteran army give up the great invasion, after a mere repulse? Troops and commander alike shrunk from the very thought. One more trial of arms—something—an attack somewhere—not *a retreat!*

That was the spirit of the army on the night of the second of July.

A flanking movement to draw the enemy out of their works, or a second attack remained.

Lee determined to attack.

Longstreet and Ewell had accomplished nothing by assailing the right and left of the enemy. Lee resolved now to throw a column against its centre—to split the stubborn obstacle, and pour into the gap with the whole army, when all would be over.

That was hazardous, you will say perhaps to-day, reader. And you have this immense argument to advance, that it failed. Ah! these arguments *after the event!* they are so fatal, and so very easy.

Right or wrong, Lee resolved to make the attack; and on the third of July he carried out his resolution.

If the writer of the South shrinks from describing the bloody repulse of Longstreet, much more gloomy is the task of painting that last charge at Gettysburg. It is one of those scenes which Lee's old soldiers approach with repugnance. That thunder of the guns which comes back to memory seems to issue, hollow and lugubrious, from a thousand tombs.

Let us pass over that tragedy rapidly. It must be touched on in these memoirs — but I leave it soon.

It is the third of July, 1863. Lee's line of battle, stretching along the crest of Seminary Ridge, awaits the signal for a new conflict with a carelessness as great as on the preceding day. The infantry are laughing, jesting, cooking their rations, and smoking their pipes. The ragged cannoneers, with flashing eyes, smiling lips, and faces blackened with powder, are standing in groups, or lying down around the pieces of artillery. Near the centre of the line a gray-headed officer, in plain uniform, and entirely unattended, has dismounted, and is reconnoitring the Federal position through a pair of field-glasses.

It is Lee, and he is looking toward Cemetery Heights, the Mount St. Jean of the new Waterloo — on whose slopes the immense conflict is going to be decided.

Lee gazes for some moments through his glasses at the long range bristling with bayonets. Not a muscle moves; he resembles a statue. Then he lowers the glasses, closes them thoughtfully, and his calm glance passes along the lines of his army. You would say that this glance penetrates the forest; that he sees his old soldiers, gay, unshrinking, unmoved by the reverses of Longstreet, and believing in themselves and in him! The blood of the soldier responds to that thought. The face of the great commander suddenly flushes. He summons a staff officer and utters a few words in calm and measured tones. The order is given. The grand assault is about to begin.

That assault is going to be one of the most desperate in all history. Longstreet's has been fierce — this will be mad and full of headlong fury. At Round Top blood flowed — here the earth is going to be soaked with it. Gettysburg is to witness a charge recalling that of the six hundred horsemen at Balaklava. Each soldier will feel that the fate of the South depends on him, perhaps. If the wedge splits the tough grain, cracking it from end to end, the axe will enter after it — the work will be finished — the red flag of the South will float in triumph over a last and decisive field.

Pickett's division of Virginia troops has been selected for the hazardous venture, and they prepare for the ordeal in the midst of a profound silence. Since the morning scarce a gunshot has been heard. Now and then only, a single cannon, like a signal-gun, sends its growl through the hills.

Those two tigers, the army of Northern Virginia and the army of the Potomac, are crouching, and about to spring.

At one o'clock the moment seems to have arrived. Along the whole front of Hill and Longstreet, the Southern artillery all at once bursts forth. One hundred and forty-five cannon send their threatening thunder across the peaceful valley. From Cemetery Heights eighty pieces reply to them; and for more than an hour these two hundred and twenty-five cannon tear the air with their harsh roar, hurled back in crash after crash from the rocky ramparts. That thunder is the most terrible yet heard in the war. It stirs the coolest veterans. General Hancock, the composed and unexcitable soldier, is going to say of it, "Their artillery fire was most terrific...it was the most terrific cannonade I ever witnessed, and the most prolonged.... It was a most terrific and appalling cannonade, one possibly hardly ever equalled."

For nearly two hours Lee continues this "terrific" fire. The Federal guns reply — shot and shell crossing each other; racing across the blue sky; battering the rocks; or bursting in showers of iron fragments.

Suddenly the Federal fire slackens, and then ceases. Their ammunition has run low,{1} or they are silenced by the Southern fire. Lee's guns also cease firing. The hour has come.

{Footnote: This was the real reason.}

The Virginians, under Pickett, form in double line in the edge of the woods, where Lee's centre is posted. These men are ragged and travel-worn, but their bayonets and gun-barrels shine like silver. From the steel hedge, as the men move, dart lightnings.

From the Cemetery Heights the enemy watch that ominous apparition — the gray line of Virginians drawn up for the charge.

At the word, they move out, shoulder to shoulder, at common time. Descending the slope, they enter on the valley, and move steadily toward the heights.

The advance of the column, with its battle-flags floating proudly, and its ranks closed up and dressed with the precision of troops on parade, is a magnificent spectacle. Old soldiers, hardened in the fires of battle, and not given to emotion, lean forward watching the advance of the Virginians with fiery eyes. You would say, from the fierce clutch of the gaunt hands on the muskets, that they wish to follow; and many wish that.

The column is midway the valley, and beginning to move more rapidly, when suddenly the Federal artillery opens. The ranks are swept by round shot, shell, and canister. Bloody gaps appear, but the line closes up, and continues to advance. The fire of the Federal artillery redoubles. All the demons of the pit seem howling, roaring, yelling, and screaming. The assaulting column is torn by a whirlwind of canister, before which men fall in heaps mangled, streaming with blood, their bosoms torn to pieces, their hands clutching the grass, their teeth biting the earth. The ranks, however, close up as before, and the Virginians continue to advance.

From common time, they have passed to quick time — now they march at the double-quick. That is to say, they run. They have reached the slope; the enemy's breastworks are right before them; and they dash at them with wild cheers.

They are still three hundred yards from the Federal works, when the real conflict commences, to which the cannonade was but child's play. Artillery has thundered, but something more deadly succeeds it — the sudden crash of musketry. From behind a stone wall the Federal infantry rise up and pour a galling fire into the charging column. It has been accompanied to this moment by a body of other troops, but those troops now disappear, like dry leaves swept off by the wind. The Virginians still advance.

Amid a concentrated fire of infantry and artillery, in their front and on both flanks, they pass over the ground between themselves and the enemy; ascend the slope; rush headlong at the breastworks; storm them; strike their bayonets into the enemy, who recoil before them, and a wild cheer rises, making the blood leap in the veins of a hundred thousand men.

The Federal works are carried, and the troops are wild with enthusiasm. With a thunder of cheers they press upon the flying enemy toward the crest.

Alas! as the smoke drifts, they see what is enough to dishearten the bravest. They have stormed the first line of works only! Beyond, is another and a stronger line still. Behind it swarm the heavy reserves of the enemy, ready for the death-struggle. But the column can not pause. It is "do or die." In their faces are thrust the muzzles of muskets spouting flame. Whole ranks go down in the fire. The survivors close up, utter a fierce cheer, and rush straight at the second tier of works.

Then is seen a spectacle which will long be remembered with a throb of the heart by many. The thinned ranks of the Virginians are advancing, unmoved, into the very jaws of death. They go forward — and are annihilated.

At every step death meets them. The furious fire of the enemy, on both flanks and in their front, hurls them back, mangled and dying. The brave Garnett is killed while leading on his men. Kemper is lying on the earth maimed for life. Armistead is mortally wounded at the moment when he leaps upon the breastworks:—he waves his hat on the point of his sword, and staggers, and falls. Of fifteen field officers, fourteen have fallen. Three-fourths of the men are dead, wounded, or prisoners. The Federal infantry has closed in on the flanks and rear of the Virginians—whole corps assault the handful—the little band is enveloped, and cut off from succor—they turn and face the enemy, bayonet to bayonet, and die.

When the smoke drifts away, all is seen to be over. It is a panting, staggering, bleeding remnant only of the brave division that is coming back so slowly yonder. They are swept from the fatal hill—pursued by yells, cheers, cannon-shot, musket-balls, and canister. As they doggedly retire before the howling hurricane, the wounded are seen to stagger and fall. Over the dead and dying sweeps the canister. Amid volleys of musketry and the roar of cannon, all but a handful of Pickett's Virginians pass into eternity.

XXVII
THE GREAT MOMENT OF A GREAT LIFE

I was gazing gloomily at the field covered with detachments limping back amid a great whirlwind of shell, when a mounted officer rode out of the smoke. In his right hand he carried his drawn sword—his left arm was thrown around a wounded boy whom he supported on the pommel of his saddle.

In the cavalier I recognized General Davenant, whom I had seen near the village of Paris, and who was now personally known to me. In the boy I recognized the urchin, Charley, with the braided jacket and jaunty cap.

I spurred toward him.

"Your son—!" I said, and I pointed to the boy.

"He is dying I think, colonel!" was the reply in a hoarse voice. The gray mustache trembled, and the eye of the father rested, moist but fiery, on the boy.

"Such a child!" I said. "Could *he* have gone into the charge?"

"I could not prevent him!" came, in a groan, almost from the old cavalier. "I forbade him, but he got a musket somewhere, and went over the breastworks with the rest. I saw him then for the first time, and heard him laugh and cheer. A moment afterward he was shot—I caught and raised him up, and I have ridden back through the fire, trying to shield him—but he is dying! Look! his wound is mortal, I think—and so young—a mere child—never was any one braver than my poor child—!"

A groan followed the words: and bending down the old cavalier kissed the pale cheek of the boy.

I made no reply; something seemed to choke me.

Suddenly a grave voice uttered some words within a few paces of us, and I turned quickly. It was General Lee—riding calmly amid the smoke, and re-forming the stragglers. Never have I seen a human being more composed.

General Davenant wheeled and saluted.

"We are cut to pieces, general!" he said, with something like a fiery tear in his eye. "We did our best, and we drove them! — but were not supported. My brigade — my brave old brigade is gone! This is my boy — I brought him out — but he is dying too!"

The hoarse tones and fiery tears of the old cavalier made my heart beat. I could see a quick flush rise to the face of General Lee. He looked at the pale face of the boy, over which the disordered curls fell, with a glance of inexpressible sympathy and sweetness. Then stretching out his hand, he pressed the hand of General Davenant, and said in his deep grave voice: —

"This has been a sad day for us, general — a sad day, but we cannot expect always to gain victories. Never mind — all this has been *my* fault. It is *I* who have lost this fight, and you must help me out of it in the best way you can."{1}

{Footnote 1: His words.}

As he uttered these measured words, General Lee saluted and disappeared in the smoke.

General Davenant followed, bearing the wounded boy still upon his saddle.

Ten minutes afterward, I was riding to find General Stuart, who had sent me with a message just before the charge.

I had gloomy news for him. The battle of Gettysburg was lost.

XXVIII
UNSHAKEN

The sun was sinking red and baleful, when I reached Stuart, beyond the left wing of the army.

From the afternoon of the second to this night of the third of July, the cavalry had met that of the enemy in stubborn conflict. The columns had hurled together. General Hampton had been severely wounded in a hand-to-hand encounter with sabres, while leading his men. Stuart had narrowly escaped death or capture in the mêlée; and Fitz Lee had fought hilt to hilt with the Federal horsemen, repulsing them, and coming back laughing, as was his wont.

All these scenes I have passed over, however. The greater drama absorbed me. The gray horsemen were fighting heroically; but what was that encounter of sabres, when the fate of Gettysburg was being decided at Cemetery Hill?

So I pass over all that, and hasten on now to the sequel. Memory finds few scenes to attract it in the days that followed Gettysburg.

But I beg the reader to observe that I should have no scenes of a humiliating character to draw. Never was army less "whipped" than that of Lee after this fight! Do you doubt that statement, reader? Do you think that the Southerners were a disordered rabble, flying before the Federal bayonets? a flock of panic-stricken sheep, hurrying back to the Potomac, with the bay of the Federal war-dogs in their ears?

That idea—entertained by a number of our Northern friends—is entirely fanciful.

Lee's army was not even shaken. It was fagged, hungry, out of ammunition, and it retired,—but not until it had remained for twenty-four hours in line of battle in front of the enemy, perfectly careless of, even inviting, attack.

"I should have liked nothing better than to have been attacked," said Longstreet, "and have no doubt I should have given those who tried, as bad a reception as Pickett received."{1}

{Footnote 1: His words.}

It may be said that this is the boast of the defeated side. But General Meade, when interrogated before the war committee, stated the exact facts.

"My opinion is now," said Meade "that General Lee evacuated that position, not from the fear that he would be dislodged from it by any active operations on my part, but that he was fearful a force would be sent to Harper's Ferry to cut off his communications.... That was what caused him to retire."

"Did you discover," asked one of the committee, "after the battle of Gettysburg, any symptoms of demoralization in Lee's army?"

"No, sir," was General Meade's reply, "I saw nothing of that kind."{1}

{Footnote 1: General Meade's testimony may be found in the Report on the Conduct of the War. Part I., p. 337.}

That statement was just, and General Meade was too much of a gentleman and soldier to withhold it. He knew that his great adversary was still unshaken and dangerous — that the laurels snatched on Round Top and Cemetery Heights might turn to cypress, if the wounded lion were assailed in his own position.

After the repulse of Pickett's column on the third of July, Lee had the choice of two courses — to either attack again or retire. Meade was evidently determined to remain on the defensive. To engage him, Lee must once more charge the Cemetery Heights. But a third failure might be ruinous; the Confederate ammunition was nearly exhausted; the communications with the Potomac were threatened, — and Lee determined to retire.

That is the true history of the matter.

The force which fell back before Meade was an army of veterans, with unshaken nerves. It required only a glance to see that these men were still dangerous. They were ready to fight again, and many raged at the retreat. Like Lee's "old war horse," they were anxious to try another struggle, to have the enemy return the compliment, and come over to charge *them*!

Then commenced that singular retreat.

The trains retired in a long line stretching over many miles, by the Chambersburg road, while the army marched by the shorter route, between the trains and the enemy, ready to turn and tear the blue huntsmen if they attempted to pursue.

So the famous army of Northern Virginia — great in defeat as in victory — took its slow way back toward the soil of Virginia. Never was spectacle stranger than that retreat from Gettysburg. The badly wounded had been sent with the army trains; but many insisted upon keeping their places in the ranks. There was something grim and terrible in these bandaged arms, and faces, and forms of Lee's old soldiers — but you did not think of that as you looked into their pale faces. What struck you in those eyes and lips was the fire, and the smile of an unconquerable courage. Never had I witnessed resolution more splendid and invincible. In the ragged foot soldiers of the old army I could see plainly the evidences of a nerve which no peril could shake. Was it race — or the cause — or confidence, through all, in Lee? I know not, but it was there. These men were utterly careless whether the enemy followed them or not. They were retreating unsubdued. The terrible scenes through which they had passed, the sights of horror, the ghastly wounds, the blood, agony, death of the last few days had passed away from their memories; and they went along with supreme indifference, ready to fight at any moment, and certain that they could whip any enemy who assailed them.

General Meade did not attempt that. He kept Lee at arm's-length, and followed so slowly that the civilians were in enormous wrath, and looked *de haut en bas* on him — on this timid soldier who had not cut Lee to pieces.

Between Meade, however, and the bold civilians, there was this enormous difference. The soldier knew the mettle of the man and the army retiring from Gettysburg. The civilians did not. Meade retained the fruits of his victory over Lee. The civilians would have lost them.

At Williamsport, Lee halted and drew up his army in line of battle. The Potomac, swollen by rains, presented an impassable obstacle.

Meade, following slowly, was met at every step by Stuart's cavalry; but finally faced his adversary.

Every thing presaged a great battle, and Lee's cannon from the hills south of Hagerstown laughed,

"Come on!"

But General Meade did not come. Lee, standing at bay with the army of Northern Virginia, was a formidable adversary, and the Federal commander had little desire to charge the Confederates as they had charged him at Gettysburg — in position.

Day after day the adversaries remained in line of battle facing each other.

Lee neither invited nor declined battle.

At last the Potomac subsided: Lee put his army in motion, and crossing on a pontoon at Falling Waters took up his position on the south bank of the river.

Stuart followed, bringing up the rear with his cavalry column; and the whole army was once more on the soil of Virginia.

They had come back after a great march and a great battle.

The march carried their flags to the south bank of the Susquehanna; the battle resulted in their retreat to the south bank of the Potomac. Thus nothing had been gained, and nothing lost. But alas! the South had counted on a great and decisive victory. When Lee failed to snatch that from the bloody heights of Gettysburg—when, for want of ammunition, and to guard his communications, he returned to the Potomac—then the people began to lose heart, and say that, since the death of Jackson, the cause was lost.

Gettysburg in fact is the turning point of the struggle. From that day dated the decadence of the Southern arms.

At Chancellorsville, the ascending steps of victory culminated—and stopped.

At Gettysburg, the steps began to descend into the valley of defeat, and the shadow of death.

What I shall show the reader in this final series of my memoirs, is Lee and his paladins—officers and privates of the old army of Northern Virginia—fighting on to the end, true in defeat as in victory, in the dark days as in the bright—closing up the thin ranks, and standing by the colors to the last.

That picture may be gloomy—but it will be sublime, too.

BOOK II
THE FLOWER OF CAVALIERS

I
UNDER "STUART'S OAK"

Crossing to the south bank of the Potomac, Stuart established his headquarters at "The Bower," an old mansion on the Opequon.

The family at the ancient hall were Stuart's cherished friends, and our appearance now, with the red flag floating and the bugle sounding a gay salute as we ascended the hill, was hailed with enthusiasm and rejoicing.

All at the "Bower," loved Stuart; they love him to-day; and will love him always.

His tents were pitched on a grassy knoll in the extensive grounds, beneath some ancient oaks resembling those seen in English parks. It was a charming spot. Through the openings in the summer foliage you saw the old walls of the hall. At the foot of the hill, the Opequon stole away, around the base of a fir-clad precipice, its right bank lined with immense white-armed sycamores. Beyond, extended a range of hills: and in the far west, the North Mountain mingled its azure billows with the blue of the summer sky.

Such was the beautiful landscape which greeted our eyes: such the spot to which the winds of war had wafted us. Good old "Bower," and good days there! How well I remember you! After the long, hard march, and the incessant fighting, it was charming to settle down for a brief space in this paradise—to listen idly to the murmur of the Opequon, or the voice of the summer winds amid the foliage of the century oaks!

The great tree on the grassy knoll, under which Stuart erected his own tent, is called "Stuart's Oak" to this day. No axe will ever harm it, I hope; gold could not purchase it; for tender hearts cherish the gnarled trunk and huge boughs, as a souvenir of the great soldier whom it sheltered in that summer of 1863.

So we were anchored for a little space, and enjoyed keenly the repose of this summer nook on the Opequon. Soon the bugle would sound again, and new storms would buffet us; meanwhile, we laughed and sang, snatching the bloom of the peaceful hours, inhaling the odors, listening to the birds, and idly dreaming.

For myself, I had more dreams than the rest of the gray people there! The Bower was not a strange place to me. My brethren of the staff used to laugh, and say that, wherever we went, in Virginia, I found kins-people. I found near and dear ones at the old house on the Opequon; and a hundred spots which recalled my lost youth. Every object carried me back to the days that are dead. The blue hills, the stream, the great oaks, and the hall smiled on me. How familiar the portraits, and wide fireplaces, and deers' antlers. The pictures of hawking scenes, with ladies and gentlemen in the queerest costumes; the engravings of famous race-horses, hanging between guns, bird-bags and fishing-rods in the wide hall—these were not mere dead objects, but old and long-loved acquaintances. I had known them in my childhood; looked with delight upon them in my boyhood; now they seemed to salute me, murmuring—"Welcome! you remember us!"

Thus the hall, the grounds, the pictures, the most trifling object brought back to me, in that summer of 1863, a hundred memories of the years that had flown. Years of childhood and youth, of mirth and joy, such as we felt before war had come to harass us; when I swam in the Opequon, or roamed the hills, looking into bright eyes, where life was so fresh and so young. The "dew was on the blossom" then, the flower in the bud. Now the bloom had passed away, and the dew dried up in the hot war-atmosphere. It was a worn and weary soldier who came back to the scenes of his youth.

Suddenly, as I mused thus, dreaming idly under the great oak which sheltered me, I heard a voice from Stuart's tent, sending its sonorous music on the air. It was the great cavalier singing lustily—

"The dew is on the blossom!"

At all hours of the day you could hear that gay voice. Stuart's headquarters were full of the most mirthful sounds and sights. The knoll was alive with picturesque forms. The horses, tethered to the boughs, champed their bits and pawed impatiently. The bright saddle-blankets shone under the saddles covered with gay decorations. Young officers with clanking sabres and rattling spurs moved to and fro. In front of the head-quarters tent the red battle-flag caught the sunshine in its dazzling folds.

Suddenly, a new charm is added to the picturesque scene. Maiden figures advance over the grassy lawn; bright eyes glimmer; glossy ringlets are lifted by the fingers of the wind; tinkling laughter is heard;—and over all rings the wild sonorous music of the bugle!

The days pass rapidly thus. The nights bring merriment, not sleep. The general goes with his staff to the hospitable mansion, and soon the great drawing-room is full of music and laughter. The song, the dance, the rattling banjo follow. The long hours flit by like a flock of summer birds, and Sweeney, our old friend Sweeney, is the king of the revel.

For Sweeney rattles as before on his banjo; and the "Old Gray Horse" flourishes still in imperishable youth! It is the same old Sweeney, with his mild and deferential courtesy, his obliging smile, his unapproachable skill in "picking on the string." Listen! his voice rings again as in the days of '61 and '62. He is singing still "Oh Johnny Booker, help this nigger!" "Stephen, come back, come back, Stephen!" "Out of the window I did sail!" "Sweet Evelina," and the grand, magnificent epic which advises you to "Jine the Cavalry!"

Hagan listens to him yonder with a twinkle of the eye — Hagan the black-bearded giant, the brave whose voice resembles thunder, the devotee and factotum of Stuart, whom he loves. And Sweeney rattles on. You laugh loud as you listen. The banjo laughs louder than all, and the great apartment is full of uproar, and mirth, and dance.

Then the couples sink back exhausted; a deep silence follows; Sweeney has made you laugh, and is now going to make you sigh. Listen! You can scarcely believe that the singer is the same person who has just been rattling through the "Old Gray Horse." Sweeney is no longer mirthful; his voice sighs instead of laughing. He is singing his tender and exquisite "Faded Flowers." He is telling you in tones as soft as the sigh of the wind in the great oaks, how

"The cold, chilly winds of December,

Stole my flowers, my companions from me!"

Alas! the cold, chilly winds of the coming winter will blow over the grave of the prince of musicians! Sweeney, the pride and charm of the cavalry head-quarters, is going to pass away, and leave his comrades and his banjo forever!

You would say that the future throws its shadow on the present. Sweeney's tones are so sweet and sorrowful, that many eyes grow moist — like Rubini, he "has tears in his voice." The melting strains ascend and sigh through the old hall. When they die away like a wind in the distance, the company remain silent, plunged in sad and dreamy revery.

Suddenly Stuart starts up and exclaims: —

"Stop that, Sweeney! you will make everybody die of the blues. Sing the 'Old Gray Horse' again, or 'Jine the Cavalry!'"

Sweeney smiles and obeys. Then, the gay song ended, he commences a reel. The banjo laughs; his flying fingers race over the strings; youths and maidens whirl from end to end of the great room—on the walls the "old people" in ruffles and short-waisted dresses, look down smiling on their little descendants!

O gay summer nights on the banks of the Opequon! you have flown, but linger still in memory!

In the autumn of 1867, I revisited the old hall where those summer days of 1863 had passed in mirth and enjoyment; and then I wandered away to the grassy knoll where "Stuart's oak" still stands. The sight of the great tree brought back a whole world of memories. Seated on one of its huge roots, beneath the dome of foliage just touched by the finger of autumn, I seemed to see all the past rise up again and move before me, with its gallant figures, its bright scenes, and brighter eyes. Alas! those days were dust, and Stuart sang and laughed no more. The grass was green again, and the birds were singing; but no martial forms moved there, no battle-flag rippled, no voice was heard. Stuart was dead;—his sword rusting under the dry leaves of Hollywood, and his battle-flag was furled forever.

That hour under the old oak, in the autumn of 1867, was one of the saddest that I have ever spent.

The hall was there as before; the clouds floated, the stream murmured, the wind sighed in the great tree, as when Stuart's tent shone under it. But the splendor had vanished, the laughter was hushed—it was a company of ghosts that gathered around me, and their faint voices sounded from another world!

II
BACK TO THE RAPIDAN

But this is a book of incident, worthy reader. We have little time for musing recollections. The halts are brief; the bugle is sounding to horse; events drag us, and we are again in the saddle.

Those gay hours on the Opequon were too agreeable to last. The old hall was a sort of oasis in the desert of war only. We paused for an instant; rested under the green trees; heard the murmur of the waters—then the caravan moved, breasting the arid wastes once more, and the coming simoom.

Stuart's head-quarters disappeared—we bade our kind friends good-bye—and, mounting, set out for the Lowland, whither Lee's column was then marching.

The short lull had been succeeded by new activity. Meade was advancing along the east slope of the Blue Ridge to cut Lee off from Richmond. But the adventure succeeded no better now than in 1862. Meade failed, as McClellan had failed before him.

The army passed the Blue Ridge; drove back the force sent to assail them in flank as they moved; and descended to Culpeper, from which they withdrew behind the Rapidan. Here Lee took up his position, crowned the south bank with his artillery, and, facing General Meade, occupying the north bank, rested.

Such had been the result of the great campaign, in its merely military aspect.

Lee had invaded the North, delivered battle on the territory of the enemy, suffered a repulse, retired, and was again occupying nearly the same ground which he had occupied before the advance. Moving backward and forward on the great chessboard of war, the two adversaries seemed to have gained or lost nothing. The one was not flushed with victory; the other was not prostrated by defeat. Each went into camp, ceased active operations, and prepared for the new conflict which was to take place before the end of the year.

I shall record some incidents of that rapid and shifting campaign, beginning and ending in the month of October; then I pass on to the more important and exciting pages of my memoirs: the mighty struggle between Lee and Grant.

To return for a moment to the cavalry. It held the front along the Rapidan and Robertson rivers, from Madison Court-House on the left, to Chancellorsville on the right. Stuart kept his lynx-eye on all the fords of the two rivers, having his head-quarters in the forks of the streams not far from their junction.

I should like to speak of the charming hours spent at the hospitable mansion near which head-quarters had been established. The sun shone bright, at the house on the grassy hill, but not so bright as the eyes which gave us friendly welcome. Years have passed since that time—all things have changed—but neither time or the new scenes will banish from some hearts the memory of that beautiful face, and the music of that voice! We salute to-day as we saluted in the past—health and happiness attend the fair face and the kindly heart!

I saw much of Mohun in those days, and became in course of time almost his intimate friend. He exhibited still a marked reserve on the subject of his past life: but I thought I could see that the ice was melting. Day by day he grew gayer—gradually his cynicism seemed leaving him. Who was this singular man, and what was his past history? I often asked myself these questions—he persisted in giving me no clue to the secret—but I felt a presentiment that some day I should "pluck out the heart of his mystery."

So much, in passing, for my relations with Mohun. We had begun to be friends, and the chance of war was going to throw us together often. I had caught one or two glimpses of a past full of "strange matters"—in the hours that were coming I was to have every mystery revealed.

Meanwhile Lee was resting, but preparing for another blow. His army was in the highest spirits. The camps buzzed, and laughed, and were full of mirth. Gettysburg was forgotten, or if remembered, it only served to inflame the troops, and inspire them with a passionate desire to "try again." In the blaze of a new victory, the old defeat would disappear.

Such was the condition of things in the army of Northern Virginia in the first days of October, 1863.

III
THE OPENING OF THE HUNT

It soon became obvious that Lee had resolved to strike a blow at his adversary.

How to do so with advantage seemed a hard problem. Between the opponents lay the Rapidan, which would be an ugly obstacle in the path of an army retreating after defeat—and the same considerations which deterred General Meade from attacking Lee, operated to prevent a like movement on the part of his adversary.

Thus an advance of the Southern army on the enemy's front was far too hazardous to be thought of—and the only course left was to assail their flank. This could either be done by crossing lower down, and cutting the enemy off from the Rappahannock, or crossing higher up, and cutting him off from Manassas. Lee determined on the latter—and in a bright morning early in October the great movement began.

Leaving Fitz Lee's cavalry and a small force of infantry in the works on the Rapidan fronting the enemy, General Lee put his columns in motion for the upper fords.

The men hailed the movement with cheers of delight. As they wound along, with glittering bayonets, through the hills and across the river, you could easily see that the old army of Northern Virginia was still in full feather—that Gettysburg had not shaken it—and that Lee could count on it for new campaigns and harder combats than any in the past.

The head of the column was directed toward Madison Court-House, which would enable Lee either to advance directly upon the enemy's flank by the Sperryville road, or continue his flank movement, pass the Rappahannock, and cut off his opponent from Washington.

The advance was an inspiring spectacle. The weather was magnificent, and the crimson foliage of the wood rivalled the tints of the red battle-flags, fluttering above the long glittering hedge of bayonets.

Stuart's cavalry had moved out on the right flank to protect the column from the observation of the enemy. The campaign of October, 1863, had opened.

It was to be one of the briefest, but most adventurous movements of the war. Deciding little, it was yet rich in incident and dramatic scenes. A brilliant comedy, as it were—just tinged with tragedy—was that rapid and shifting *raid* of Lee's whole army, on Meade. Blood, jests, laughter, mourning—these were strangely mingled, in the cavalry movements at least: and to these I proceed.

From the heights, whence you see only the "great events," the movements of armies, and the decisive battles, let us now descend into the lowland, good reader. I will lay before you some incidents, not to be found in the "official reports;" and I promise to carry you on rapidly!

IV
THE GAME A-FOOT

It was a magnificent morning of October,

Stuart leaped to saddle, and, preceded by his red flag rippling gayly in the wind, set out from his head-quarters in the direction of the mountains.

He was entering on his last great cavalry campaign—and it was to be one of his most successful and splendid.

The great soldier, as he advanced that morning, was the beau ideal of a cavalier. His black plume floated proudly; his sabre rattled; his eyes danced with joy; his huge mustache curled with laughter; his voice was gay, sonorous, full of enjoyment of life, health, the grand autumn, and the adventurous and splendid scenes which his imagination painted. On his brow he seemed already to feel the breath of victory.

It was rather an immense war-machine, than a man which I looked at on that morning of October, 1863. Grand physical health, a perfectly fearless soul, the keenest thirst for action, a stubborn dash which nothing could break down—all this could be seen in the face and form of Stuart, as he advanced to take command of his column that day.

On the next morning at daylight he had struck the enemy.

Their outposts of cavalry, supported by infantry, were at Thoroughfare Mountain, a small range above the little village of James City. Here Stuart came suddenly upon them, and drove in their pickets:—a moment afterward he was galloping forward with the gayety of a huntsman after a fox.

A courier came to meet him from the advance guard, riding at full gallop.

"Well!" said Stuart.

"A regiment of infantry, general."

"Where?"

"Yonder in the gap."

And he pointed to a gorge in the little mountain before us.

Stuart wheeled and beckoned to Gordon, the brave North Carolinian, who had made the stubborn charge at Barbee's, in 1862, when Pelham was attacked, front and rear, by the Federal cavalry.

"We have flushed a regiment of infantry, Gordon. Can you break them?"

"I think I can, general."

The handsome face of the soldier glowed — his bright eyes flashed.

"All right. Get ready, then, to attack in front. I will take Young, and strike them at the same moment on the right flank!"

With which words Stuart went at a gallop and joined Young.

That gay and gallant Georgian was at the head of his column; in his sparkling eyes, and the smile which showed the white teeth under the black mustache, I saw the same expression of reckless courage which I had noticed on the day of Fleetwood, when the young Georgian broke the column on the hill.

Stuart explained his design in three words: —

"Are you ready?"

"All ready, general!"

And Young's sabre flashed from the scabbard.

At the same instant the crash of carbines in front, indicated Gordon's charge.

Young darted to the head of his column.

"Charge!" he shouted.

And leading the column, he descended like a thunderbolt on the enemy's flank.

As he did so, Gordon's men rushed with wild cheers into the gorge. Shouts, carbine-shots, musket-shots, yells resounded. In five minutes the Federal infantry, some three hundred in number, were scattered in headlong flight, leaving the ground strewed with new muskets, whose barrels shone like burnished silver.

"Good!" Stuart exclaimed, as long lines of prisoners appeared, going to the rear, "a fair beginning, at least!"

And he rode on rapidly.

V
THE CHASE

The cavalry pressed forward without halting and reached the hills above James City—a magniloquent name, but the "city" was a small affair—a mere village nestling down amid an amphitheatre of hills.

On the opposite range we saw the enemy's cavalry drawn up; and, as we afterward learned, commanded by General Kilpatrick.

They presented a handsome spectacle in the gay autumn sunshine; but we did not attack them. Stuart's orders were to protect the march of Ewell from observation; and this he accomplished by simply holding the Federal cavalry at arm's-length. So a demonstration only was made. Skirmishers advanced, and engaged the enemy. The whole day thus passed in apparent failure to drive the Federals.

A single incident marked the day. Stuart had taken his position, with his staff and couriers, on a hill. Here, with his battle-flag floating, he watched the skirmishers,—and then gradually, the whole party, stretched on the grass, began to doze.

They were to have a rude waking. I was lying, holding my bridle, half asleep, when an earthquake seemed to open beneath me. A crash like thunder accompanied it. I rose quickly, covered with dust. A glance explained the whole. The enemy had directed a gun upon the tempting group over which the flag rose, and the percussion-shell had fallen and burst in our midst.

Strangest of all, no one was hurt.

Stuart laughed, and mounted his horse.

"A good shot!" he said, "look at Surry's hat!" which, on examination, I found covered half an inch deep with earth.

In fact, the shell had burst within three feet of my head—was a "line shot," and with a little more elevation, would have just reached me. Then, exit Surry! in a most unmilitary manner, by the bursting of a percussion-shell.

At nightfall the enemy was still in position, and Stuart had not advanced.

We spent the night at a farm-house, and were in the saddle again at dawn.

The hills opposite were deserted. The enemy had retreated. Stuart pushed on their track down the Sperryville road, passed the village of Griffinsburg, and near Stonehouse Mountain came on, and pushed them rapidly back on Culpeper Court-House.

All at once quick firing was heard on our right.

"What is that?" Stuart asked.

"An infantry regiment, general!" said Weller, one of our couriers, galloping quickly up.

The words acted upon Stuart like the blow of a sword. A wild excitement seemed to seize him.

"Bring up a squadron!" he shouted—for we were riding ahead without support; "bring up the cavalry! I am going to charge! Bring me a squadron!"

And drawing his sword, Stuart rushed at full gallop, alone and unattended, toward the Federal infantry, whose gun-barrels were seen glittering in the woods.

Never had I seen him more excited. He was plainly on fire with the idea of capturing the whole party.

The staff scattered to summon the cavalry, and soon a company came on at full gallop. It was the "Jefferson Company," under that brave officer, Captain George Baylor.

"Charge, and cut them down!" shouted Stuart, his drawn sword flashing as he forced his horse over fallen trees and the debris of the great deserted camp.

A fine spectacle followed. As the Federal infantry double-quicked up a slope, Baylor charged.

As his men darted upon them, they suddenly halted, came to a front-face, and the long line of gun-barrels fell, as though they were parts of some glittering war-machine.

The muzzles spouted flame, and the cavalry received the fire at thirty yards.

It seemed to check them, but it did not. They had come to an impassable ditch. In another moment, the infantry broke, every man for himself, and making a detour, the cavalry pursued, and captured large numbers.

For the second time Stuart had charged infantry and broken them. Pushing on now through the great deserted camps of Stonehouse Mountain, he descended upon Culpeper.

The enemy's cavalry retreated, made a stand on the hills beyond, with their artillery; and seemed to have resolved to retreat no farther.

Suddenly the thunder of artillery came up from the Rapidan. I was sitting my horse near Stuart and Gordon. They were both laughing—indeed, Stuart seemed laughing throughout the campaign.

"That is Fitz Lee!" he said; "he has crossed and driven them."

And turning round,—

"I wish you would go to General Lee, Surry—you will find him toward Griffinsburg—and tell him we are driving the enemy, and Fitz Lee seems to be coming up."

I saluted, and left the two generals laughing as before.

In half an hour I had found General Lee. He was in camp on the Sperryville road, and was talking to Ewell.

It was a singular contrast. Lee, robust, ruddy, erect, with his large frank eye—Ewell, slight, emaciated, pale, with small piercing eyes, and limping on his crutch.

"Thank you, colonel," General Lee said, with his grave but charming courtesy; "tell General Stuart to continue to press them back toward the river."

And turning to Ewell:—

"You had better move on with your command, general," he said, in his measured voice.

Ewell bowed and turned to obey—I returned to Stuart.

He was pushing the Federal cavalry "from pillar to post." Driven back from the hill, where they had planted their artillery, they had retreated on Brandy; Stuart had followed like a fate; Gordon, sent round to the left, struck their right flank with his old sabreurs; Fitz Lee, coming up on the right, thundered down on their left—and in the woods around Brandy took place one of those cavalry combats which, as my friends, the novelists, say, "must be seen to be appreciated!" If the reader will imagine, in the dusk of evening, a grand hurly-burly made up of smoke, dust, blood, yells, clashing swords, banging carbines, thundering cannon, and wild cheers, he will have a faint idea of that "little affair" at Brandy.

A queer circumstance made this fight irresistibly comic.

Fitz Lee had repulsed Buford on the Rapidan; followed him on his retreat, harassing him at every step—when, just as Buford reached Brandy, with Fitz Lee at his heels, Kilpatrick descended on Fitz Lee's rear by the Sperryville road, and Stuart thundered down on *his*!

Thus Fitz Lee was pursuing Buford; Kilpatrick, Fitz Lee; and Stuart, Kilpatrick! It was a grand and comic jumble—except that it came very near being any thing but comic to that joyous cavalier, "General Fitz," as we called him—caught as he was between Generals Buford and Kilpatrick!

General Fitz was the man for a "tight place," however—and "his people," as he called his cavalry, soon cut through to Stuart.

It was a tough and heavy fight.

"Old Jeb cut off more than he could *chaw*, that time!" said a veteran afterward, in describing the fight. And at one time it seemed that the enemy were going to hold their ground.

Fleetwood, beyond, was lined with bayonets, and every knoll was crowned with cannon: when night fell, however, the whole force had retreated and crossed the Rappahannock, leaving the ground strewed with their dead and wounded.

In the dusky woods near Brandy, Stuart sat his horse, looking toward the Rappahannock, and laughing still. He was talking with brave Fitz Lee, whose stout figure, flowing beard, and eyes twinkling with humor, were plain in the starlight. I shall show you that gallant figure more than once in this volume, reader. You had but to look at him to see that he was the bravest of soldiers, and the best of comrades.

So night fell on a victory. Stuart had driven the enemy at every step. He had charged their infantry, cavalry, and artillery, routing all,—and he was once more in sight of Fleetwood Hill, where he had defeated them in the preceding June.

Singular current of war! It used to bear us onward; but be taken with a sudden fancy to flow back to the old spots! See Manassas, Fredericksburg, Cold Harbor, Chancellorsville!

Fleetwood takes its place with them—twice bloody and memorable. In sight of it took place two of Stuart's hardest combats—and both were victories.

VI
THE RUSE

By sunrise Stuart was pushing rapidly up the bank of the Rappahannock toward Warrenton Springs.

Meade had retreated from Culpeper, and was falling back rapidly. Lee was pressing on to cut him off in the vicinity of Auburn.

A hot fight took place at Jeffersonton, a little village beyond Hazel River; and here the enemy fought from house to house, but finally retreated.

Stuart followed, and came up with their rear retreating over the bridge at Warrenton Springs.

On the northern bank the Federal sharp-shooters were posted in double line.

Stuart turned, and saw, not far from him, the Jefferson Company who had charged so gallantly at Stonehouse Mountain. A movement of his hand, and they were charging over the bridge.

Suddenly they recoiled. The head files had stopped, — the horses rearing. The flooring in the centre of the bridge had been torn up — it was impossible to cross.

The men wheeled and came back under a hot fire of sharp-shooters. Stuart's face was fiery.

"To the ford!" he shouted.

And placing himself in front of the men, sword in hand, he led them through the ford, in face of a heavy fire, charged up the opposite slope, and the Federal skirmishers scattered in wild flight.

The Twelfth Virginia Cavalry followed them, and they were cut down or captured.

As the column moved on, Stuart galloped along the line toward the front.

He had just faced death with these men, and at sight of him they raised a cheer.

"Hurrah for old Jeb!" rose in a shout from the column.

Stuart turned: his face glowed: rising in his stirrups, he took off his hat and exclaimed: — -

"Bully for the old Twelfth!"

The words were unclassic, it may be, reader, but they raised a storm.

"I felt like I could die for old Jeb after that," one of the men said to me.

Stuart disappeared, followed by tumultuous cheers, and his column continued to advance upon Warrenton ahead of the army. He had ridden on for a quarter of an hour, when he turned to me, and said: —

"I am getting uneasy about things at Culpeper. I wish you would ride back to Rosser, who is there with two hundred men, and tell him to call on Young, if he is pushed." I turned my horse.

"You know where Young is?"

"On the Sperryville road."

"Exactly — Rosser can count on him. I am going on toward Warrenton."

And the general and myself parted, riding in opposite directions.

I returned toward Hazel River; passed that stream, and the long rows of army wagons; and as the sun was sinking, drew near Culpeper.

As I pressed on, I heard the long thunder of cannon coming up from the direction of Brandy.

What could that sound mean? Had the enemy again advanced and assailed the small force of cavalry there?

Going on now at full speed, I heard the cannon steadily approaching Culpeper Court-House. All at once, as I drew near the village, I heard a tremendous clatter in the streets; a column of cavalry was advancing to the front — soon the crack of carbines was heard beyond the town.

A short ride brought me to the field, and all was explained. Colonel Rosser had been attacked by a whole corps of Federal infantry, and two divisions of cavalry — while his own force was about two hundred men, and a single gun.

He had offered an obstinate resistance, however, fallen back slowly, and when about to be driven into the town, Young had come to his aid.

Then followed one of the gayest comedies of the war. Young was the author of it. You laugh sometimes still, do you not, old comrade, at the trick you played our friends on that October evening?

Young threw himself into the fight with the true cavalry élan. Dismounting his whole brigade, he opened a rapid fire on the advancing enemy; and this obstinate resistance evidently produced a marked effect upon their imaginations. They had been advancing — they now paused.

They had been full of audacity, and now seemed fearful of some trap. It was evident that they suspected the presence of a heavy force of infantry—and night having descended, they halted.

This was the signal for the fifth act of the comedy. Young kindled camp-fires along two miles of front; brought up his brass band and played "The Bonnie Blue Flag," and "Dixie." It was obvious to the enemy that at least a corps of Lee's infantry was there in their front, ready to renew the action at dawn!

The finale was comic—I shared the blankets of the gallant Georgian that night—when we rose the enemy's whole force had disappeared.

Such had been the result of the ruse, and I always regarded the affair as one of the gayest incidents of the war.

When I left the brave Young, he was laughing in triumph.

If your eye meets this page, old comrade, it may give you another laugh—and laughter is something in this dull epoch, is it not?

But whether you laugh or sigh, and wherever you may be, health and happiness attend you!

In the afternoon, I was at Warrenton.

VII
STUART CAUGHT IN THE TRAP

I found the general moving toward Auburn, on a reconnoissance.

Meade had been delayed much by uncertainty as to his adversary's designs—had scarcely advanced beyond the Rappahannock—and the object of Stuart was to discover his position and intentions.

That was the work always assigned to the "Eyes and Ears" of the army Stuart's cavalry; and the stout cavalier, now at the head of his column, was on for the railroad, along which the enemy must retreat.

Another comedy was to follow—which came near being a tragedy.

Stuart steadily advanced, and about sunset had passed Auburn, when, as he was riding at the head of his column, a messenger rode up hastily from Gordon, holding the rear.

"Well!" said Stuart.

"The enemy are in your rear, general!"

"Impossible!"

"General Gordon sent me to say so."

Stuart turned and galloped back. Gordon came to meet him.

"The Yankee army are in our rear, general," said Gordon. "Come, and I will show you."

And riding to an eminence he pointed out across the fields, in the gathering gloom, long lines of infantry and artillery moving toward Manassas.

Stuart gazed at them keenly. As he sat looking toward them, a staff officer from the front came up rapidly.

"Well, captain!"

"The enemy are in front, general."

"Infantry?"

"Yes, with artillery."

Stuart looked at Gordon.

"A real trap," he said coolly, knitting his brows.

"Have they seen you, Gordon?" he asked.

"I think not, general."

"Well, so far all is well. There is nothing to do but to lay low, and take the chances of getting out."

Stuart's voice was never cooler. He looked quietly at the huge column cutting off his retreat.

"A splendid chance to attack them!" he all at once exclaimed.

And tearing a leaf out of his dispatch-book, he wrote a hasty note to General Lee. I afterward knew what it contained. Stuart described his situation, and proposed that Rodes, then near Warrenton, should attack at dawn—when he would open with his artillery, charge with his horsemen, and cut his way out.

"A good man in blue uniform now, Gordon."

Gordon sent off an aid, and the man soon appeared. From top to toe he was of irreproachable blue; and he listened keenly to his instructions.

Five minutes afterward he had dismounted, given his horse to a comrade, and was stealing on foot through the thicket toward the Federal column. A moment afterward he had mingled with their column and disappeared.

Other messengers, also in Federal uniform, were dispatched: the whole force of cavalry was massed, and concealed in the woods: then darkness descended; and the long night of anxiety began.

The situation was not agreeable. Stuart was caught in a veritable trap. On both sides—in his rear and his front—were passing heavy corps of Federal infantry; their numerous artillery; and their long-drawn columns of cavalry. Discovery was destruction; the only hope was that the enemy would not suspect our proximity. If we were once known to be lurking there, good-bye to Stuart and his men!

So the long night commenced. The hours passed on, and still we were not discovered. It seemed miraculous that some noise did not betray Stuart's hiding-place; but an Unseen Eye seemed to watch over him, and an Unseen Hand to guard him.

More than once the neigh of a horse rang out on the air of night; and two or three times the discordant bray of a mule attached to the artillery startled the silence of the woods. But these sounds were unheeded. They evidently attracted no attention from the enemy.

Leaning down in their saddles, the men, half overcome by sleep, but afraid of a rough waking, passed sleepless hours, looking for the dawn.

Stuart was never cooler. On his horse, at the head of his men, he betrayed no emotion. You would not have known, except for his subdued tones when speaking to some one, that he and his command were in a veritable "tight place." Cool and resolute, he was equal to any event. Certain capture or destruction of his whole force was imminent.

Thus the night glided away. We had not been discovered. Over the trees was seen the yellow streak of dawn.

I looked round. The men's faces were haggard from want of sleep. But they evidently felt perfect confidence in Stuart.

He hastened to justify it.

No sooner had light come than he placed his artillery in position. As it grew and broadened, the enemy were seen just on a hill in front of us, busily cooking their breakfasts.

Suddenly a single cannon sent its long thunder, dull and reverberating, through the woods, from the direction of Warrenton.

Stuart rose erect in his saddle, and looked in the direction of the sound, his eyes glowing.

Another followed; then another; then a long, continuous bellow of artillery, making the hills echo.

There was no longer any doubt about the fate of the messengers. Lee had received the dispatches; Rodes had opened on the Federal columns, attacking as that good soldier knew how to attack.

Stuart darted to his guns. On his countenance was a grim smile.

"Attention!" he exclaimed.

The cannoneers ran to their posts, a cheer rose, the next instant the guns spouted flame; shell after shell in rapid succession screamed through the woods—and bursting in the midst of the blue groups, threw them into the wildest disorder.

Stuart did not allow the panic to subside. His sharp-shooters opened at the same instant a determined fire; the great cavalier went at full speed to the head of his column: — then rushing like an avalanche, troopers and artillery, charged the column in front, burst through, trampling it as he went, and at a gallop the gray horsemen, with guns following, broke out; and were again free.

Stuart was out of the trap. From one of the "tightest places" that a commander was ever in he had extricated his whole command.

Once in safety, he turned like a wild boar on his enemies. In ten minutes his artillery had taken a new position—its thunders had opened—its roar told the army, that his feather still floated, his star was still in the ascendant.

Such was that queer affair of Auburn. Few more curious incidents occurred in the war.

A brave officer of the infantry had accompanied us as an amateur.

"I've got enough of the cavalry," he said, laughing; "I am going back to the infantry. It is safer!"

VIII
GENERAL MEADE'S "EYE-TEETH"

Stuart came back laughing from his adventure.

The army hailed his reappearance with joy and cheers.

They had already split the air with shouts in honor of the cavalry, on that evening at Warrenton Springs, when Stuart charged through the ford.

"Hurrah for Stuart!" was now the exclamation everywhere. And let me add that the stout cavalier keenly enjoyed his popularity. He was brave and fond of glory—approbation delighted him. In his ears, praise, sympathy, admiration, sounded sweet.

General Lee continued to press forward, but the golden moment for intercepting Meade had fled.

He had not been cut off in Culpeper; he had not been cut off at Warrenton; he was not going to be cut off at Bristoe, near Manassas. Hill had been sent in that direction to intercept the enemy's retreat, but on the afternoon succeeding the adventure of Stuart, an ugly blow was dealt him on the banks of Deep Run.

He came up with the enemy's rear guard under their brave General Warren; assailed it in front of an embankment furiously, and suffered a heavy repulse.

General Cooke was shot down at the head of his men; the brigade was nearly cut to pieces; and Warren retreated across Deep Run, in grim triumph, carrying off several pieces of Hill's artillery.

It was a grievous blow, and affected the brave Hill deeply. General Lee was no less melancholy; it is said that he was both gloomy and restive. It was reported, I know not upon what authority, that when he and General Hill were riding over the field, and Hill essayed to explain the unfortunate affair, the commander-in-chief shook his head, and said in grave tones:—

"Say no more, general—have these poor dead soldiers buried."

From the hill above Bristoe, General Lee, accompanied by Stuart, looked out in the direction of Manassas. Not a blue coat was to be seen. Meade had made good his retreat. Everywhere he had eluded the blows of his great adversary — and in parting from him, finally, at Bristoe, had left blood in his foot-steps — the blood of some of Lee's best soldiers.

It is said that General Meade made this retreat under protest — and that he was everywhere looking for a position to fight. A Northern correspondent described how, sitting with him by the camp-fire, General Meade had said: —

"It was like pulling out my eye-teeth not to have had a fight!"

Did he say that? Then he was out-generalled.

But he had succeeded in retreating safely. He was behind the works of Centreville: Lee had stopped the pursuit.

There was nothing more, indeed, to be done. Lee must retire, or attack the enemy behind their earth-works. That was not very promising, and he fell back toward his old camps, on the Rapidan.

Nothing prevented the cavalry, however, from "feeling" the enemy in their new position; and Stuart rapidly advanced to Bull Run, across which Fitz Lee drove the Federal horsemen.

A raid toward their rear, by Stuart, followed. He moved toward Groveton; deflected to the left, and crossed the Catharpin in a violent storm; advanced next day toward Frying-Pan; then striking the Second Corps of Meade, and throwing it into confusion, by producing the impression that his force was Lee's whole army, he quietly retired by the way he had come.

His disappearance revealed all. The enemy perceived that the attack was only a "cavalry raid," and were seized with immense indignation. A picked division was sent out in pursuit of the daring raiders — and this force of horsemen, about three thousand in number, hurried across Bull Run to punish Stuart.

They were commanded by the ardent General Kilpatrick: — what followed is known as the "Buckland Races."

IX
WHAT THE AUTHOR HAS OMITTED

Such is a rapid summary of the cavalry operations succeeding the action of Bristoe.

Those readers who cry out for "movement! movement!" are respectfully requested to observe that I have passed over much ground, and many events in a few paragraphs:—and yet I might have dwelt on more than one scene which, possibly, might have interested the worthy reader.

There was the gallant figure of General Fitz Lee, at the head of his horsemen, advancing to charge what he supposed to be the enemy's artillery near Bristoe, and singing as he went, in the gayest voice:—

> *"Rest in peace! rest in peace!*
> *Slumb'ring lady love of mine;*
> *Rest in peace! rest in peace!*
> *Sleep on!"*

There was the charge over the barricade near Yates's Ford, where a strange figure mingled just at dusk with the staff, and when arrested as he was edging away in the dark, coolly announced that he belonged to the "First Maine Cavalry."

There was the march toward Chantilly, amid the drenching storm, when Stuart rode along laughing and shouting his camp songs, with the rain descending in torrents from his heavy brown beard.

There was the splendid advance on the day succeeding, through the rich autumn forest, of all the colors of the rainbow.

Then the fight at Frying-Pan; arousing the hornets' nest there, and the feat performed by Colonel Surry, in carrying off through the fire of the sharp-shooters, on the pommel of his saddle, a beautiful girl who declared that she was "not at all afraid!"

These and many other scenes come back to memory as I sit here at Eagle's Nest. But were I to describe all I witnessed during the war, I should never cease writing. All these must be passed over—my canvas is limited, and I have so many figures to draw, so many pictures to paint, that every square inch is valuable.

That is the vice of "memoirs," reader. The memory is an immense receptacle—it holds every thing, and often trifles take the prominent place, instead of great events. You are interested in those trifles, when they are part of your own experience; but perhaps, they bore your listener and make him yawn—a terrible catastrophe!

So I pass to some real and *bona fide* "events." Sabres are going to clash now, and some figures whom the reader I hope has not forgotten are going to ride for the prize in the famous Buckland Races.

X
I FALL A VICTIM TO TOM'S ILL-LUCK

Stuart had fallen back, and had reached the vicinity of Buckland.

There was a bright light in his blue eyes, a meaning smile on his mustached lip, which in due time I was going to understand.

Kilpatrick was following him. From the rear guard came the crack of skirmishers. It seemed hard to understand, but the fact was perfectly evident, that Stuart was retreating.

I had fallen out of the column, and was riding with Tom Herbert. Have you forgotten that worthy, my dear reader? Has the roar of Gettysburg driven him quite from your memory? I hope not. I have not mentioned him for a long time, so many things have diverted me—but we had ridden together, slept together, fought together, and starved together! Tom had come to be one of my best friends, in fact, and his charming good humor beguiled many a weary march. To hear him laugh was real enjoyment; and when he would suddenly burst forth with,

> *"Oh look at the riggings*
> *On Billy Barlo — o — o — ow!"*

the sternest faces relaxed, the sourest personages could not but laugh.

Brave and honest fop! Where are you to-day, *mon garçon*! I wish I could see you and hear you sing again!

But I am prosing. Riding beside Tom, I was looking down and thinking of a certain young lady, when an exclamation from my companion made me raise my head.

"By George! there's the house, old fellow!"

"The house?"

"Of the famous supper."

"So it is!"

"And my inamorata, Surry! I wonder if she is still there?"

"Inamorata? What is her other name?"

Tom laughed, and began to sing in his gayest voice,

"Oh, Katy! Katy!

Don't marry any other;

You'll break my heart, and kill me dead,

And then be hanged for murder!"

"That is answer enough," I said, laughing.

"Suppose we go and see if they are still alive," Tom said, blushing; "ten minutes will take us to the house."

In fact, I saw across the fields, embowered in foliage, the hospitable mansion in which we had eaten the famous supper, on the route to Pennsylvania.

"It is risky," I said, hesitating.

"But pleasing," retorted Tom, with a laugh.

And I saw, from his flushed face, that he had set his heart on the visit.

That conquered me. I never could refuse Tom Herbert any thing; and we were soon cantering toward the house.

Leaving our horses in a little grove, near the mansion, in order that they might not attract the attention of any of the enemy's vedettes, we hastened up the steps.

As we reached the door, it opened, and Miss Katy Dare, the heroine of Tom's dreams, very nearly precipitated herself into our arms.

"Oh, I am so glad to see you!" she exclaimed, with her auburn ringlets dancing, her eyes sparkling,—and taking care to look at *me* as she uttered the words.

Then a whole bevy of young ladies hastened out to welcome us.

Where had we been? Why were we going back? Could General Stuart intend to leave them in the Yankee lines again? Oh, no! he could not! He could not have the heart to! Was he coming to see them? Oh, the sight of gray uniforms was HEAVENLY!!!

And the young damsels positively overwhelmed me with exclamations and interrogatories. Eyes danced, lips smiled, cheeks glowed—they hung around me, and seemed wild with enthusiasm and delight.

Around *me*, I say—for Tom and Miss Katy had accidentally strolled into a conservatory near at hand. A glass door gave access to it, and they had "gone to examine the flowers," the young ladies said, with rapturous smiles and little nods.

Meanwhile, "the wants of the soldiers" were by no means forgotten. Busy hands brought in china, silver, and snowy napkins. On the table the waiter was soon deposited, containing a splendid, miraculous array of edibles, and these were flanked by decanters containing excellent home-made wine.

This consumed half an hour—but at last the repast was ready, and one of the young ladies hastened toward the conservatory, uttering a discreet little "ahem!" which made her companions laugh.

In an instant Tom made his appearance with a decided color in his cheeks; and Miss Katy—well, Miss Katy's face was the color of a peony, or a carnation.

Shall I reveal to you, gentle reader, what Tom told me long afterward? He had advanced and been repulsed—had attacked and been "scattered." Pardon the slang of the army, and admire the expeditious operations of the gentlemen of the cavalry!

Tom was blushing, but laughing too. He was game, if he *was* unfortunate. He did not even decline the material enjoyment of lunch, and having led in the young Miss Katy, with a charmingly foppish air, took his seat at the table, which promised so much pleasure of another description.

The fates frowned on us. Tom was unlucky that day, and I was drawn into the vortex of bad fortune.

Suddenly a clatter of hoofs came from the grass plat in front of the house; the rattle of sabres from a company of cavalry followed; and the young ladies had just time to thrust us into the conservatory, when the door opened, and an officer in blue uniform, accompanied by a lady, entered the apartment.

XI
I OVERHEAR A SINGULAR CONVERSATION

I recognized the new-comers at a glance. They were Darke, and the gray woman.

There was no mistaking that powerful figure, of low stature, but herculean proportions; that gloomy and phlegmatic face, half-covered with the black beard; and the eye glancing warily, but with a reckless fire in them, from beneath the heavy eye-brows.

The woman wore an elegant gray riding habit — gray seemed a favorite with her. Her cheeks were as white as ever, and her lips as red. Her bearing was perfectly composed, and she advanced, with the long riding skirt thrown over her arm, walking with exquisite grace.

All this I could easily see. The glass door of the conservatory had been left ajar in the hurry of our retreat, and from behind the lemon-trees and flower-bushes, we could see into the apartment without difficulty.

There was evidently little danger of our discovery. The new-comers had plainly entered the house with no design to search it. Darke advanced into the apartment; made the ladies a bow, which more than ever convinced me that he had been familiar with good society; and requested food for the lady. She had tasted none for many hours, and was faint. He would not ask it for himself, inasmuch as he was an enemy.

He bowed again as he spoke, and was silent.

The young ladies had listened coldly. As he finished, they pointed to the waiter, and without speaking, they left the apartment.

Darke was left alone with the woman in gray. She seemed to have regarded ceremony as unnecessary. Going to the table, she had already helped herself, and for some moments devoured, rather than ate, the food before her.

Then she rose, and went and took her seat in a rocking-chair near the fire. Darke remained erect, gazing at her, in silence.

The lady rocked to and fro, pushed back her dark hair with the snowy hand, and looking at her companion, began to laugh.

"You are not hungry?" she said.

"No," was his reply.

"And to think that a romantic young creature like myself *should* be!"

"It was natural. I hoped that you would have given up this fancy of accompanying me. You can not stand the fatigue."

"I can stand it easily," she said. "When we have a cherished object, weariness does not count."

"A cherished object! What is yours?"

"Sit down, and I will tell you. I am tired. You can rejoin the column in ten minutes."

"So be it," said Darke, gloomily.

And he sat down near her.

"You wish to be informed of my object in going with you everywhere," she said. And her voice which had at first been gay and careless, assumed a mocking accent, making the nerves tingle. "I can explain in a very few words my romantic desire. I wish to see *him* fall."

"Humph!" ejaculated Darke, coldly; "you mean—"

"That man—yes. You promised to kill him, when you next met. Did you not promise me that?"

Darke looked at the speaker with grim admiration.

"You are a singular woman," he said; "you never forget a wrong. And yet the wrong, people might say, was committed by *you*—not *him*."

"Do *you* say that?" exclaimed the woman with sudden venom in her voice.

"I say nothing, madam," was the gloomy reply. "I only declare that you hate much more strongly than I do. I hate him—and hate him honestly. But I would not take him at disadvantage. You would strike him, wherever you met him—in the dark—in the back—I think you would dance the war-dance around him, when he was dying!"

And Darke uttered a short jarring laugh.

"You are right," said the woman, coolly. "I wish to see that man die—I expected you to kill him on that night in Pennsylvania. You promised to do it;—redeem your promise!"

"I will try to do so, madam," said Darke, coolly.

"And I wish to be present on the occasion."

Darke laughed as before.

"That doubtless has prevented you from having our good friend Mohun—well—assassinated!"

The woman was silent for a moment. Then she said: —-

"No, I have tried that."

"Ah!—recently?"

"Yes."

"By what means—who was your agent?"

"Swartz."

Darke waited, listening.

"He has three times waylaid *him* behind the rebel lines, and fired on him as he was riding at night through the woods," added the woman.

"Bah!" said Darke; "Swartz told you that?"

"He has done so."

"Hatred blinds you; I do not believe that story. But I design nothing of that description against Colonel Mohun. I will fight him wherever I meet him in battle—kill him, if I can—but no assassination."

A mocking smile came to the woman's lips.

"You seem to dislike the idea of—assassination," she said.

Darke uttered a sound resembling the growl of a wild animal, and a moment after, seizing the decanter, he dashed some of its contents into a glass, and raised it to his lips.

"Cursed stuff!" he suddenly exclaimed, setting the glass down violently. "I want drink—real drink—to-day!"

The woman looked at him curiously, and said quietly: —

"What is the matter?"

Her companion's brows were knit until the shaggy masses united over the gloomy eyes. Beneath burned a lurid fire.

"I have seen *him* again—General Davenant," he said, in a low voice; "it is the second time."

As he uttered these words, Darke seemed the prey of some singular emotion.

"It was at Gettysburg first," he continued. "He was leading the charge, on the third day, against Cemetery Heights. I was there by accident. They were repulsed. When he rode back, he was carrying a bleeding boy in his arms through the smoke. I recognized his tall form and gray hair; and heard his voice in the midst of the cannon, as he cheered on his men."

The speaker's face had flushed. His breast rose and fell.

"That was the first time," he said. "The second was the other day when he was riding among the enemy's guns near Bristoe—I made him out with my glasses."

Darke bent down, and gazed at the floor in silence. The fire in the dark eyes had deepened. His heavy under lip was caught in the large, sharp teeth.

All at once a ringing laugh disturbed the silence. There was a mocking intonation in it which was unmistakable.

"General Davenant!" exclaimed the woman. "Well, who is General Davenant?"

Darke looked at the mocking speaker sidewise.

"Who is General Davenant?" he said. "Is it necessary that I enlighten you, madam? He is my bugbear—my death's head! The sight of him poisons my life, and something gnaws at me, driving me nearly mad! To see that man chills me, like the hand of death!"

The woman looked at him and then began to laugh.

"You do unbend your noble strength, my lord!" she said, "to think so brainsickly of things!" throwing into the word, "brainsickly," exaggerated stage-rant.

"One would say," she continued, "that the brave Colonel Darke had the blues to-day! Take care how you meet Colonel Mohun in this mood! The result might be unfortunate."

Darke made no reply for some moments. He was gazing with knit brows upon the floor. Then he raised his head.

"You return to the subject of your friend," he said, coldly.

"Yes. The subject is agreeable."

"Well, I can give you intelligence of him—unless Swartz has anticipated me."

"What intelligence?"

"Your friend Mohun is in love—again!"

The woman's face flushed suddenly.

"With whom?" she said.

"Ah! there is the curious part of the affair, madam!" returned Darke.

And in a low tone he added:—

"The name of the young lady is—Georgia Conway."

The woman half rose from her chair, with flashing eyes, and said: —

"Who told you that?"

Darke smiled. There was something lugubrious in that chilly mirth.

"An emissary on whom I can rely, brought me the intelligence," he said, "Colonel Mohun was wounded in the battle of Fleetwood, and entering a house where *she* was nursing the wounded, fainted, and was caught in her arms. From that moment the affair began. She nursed him, and he was soon healed. I had myself inflicted the wound with a pistol ball — but the hurt was trifling. He got well in a few days — and was ready to meet me again at Upperville — but in those few days the young lady and himself became enamored of each other. She is proud, they say, and had always laughed at love — he too is a woman-hater — no doubt from some old affair, madam! — but both the young people suddenly changed their views. Colonel Mohun became devoted; the young woman forgot her sarcasm. My emissary saw them riding out more than once near Culpeper Court-House; and since the return of the army, they have been billing and cooing like two doves, quite love sick! That's agreeable, is it not, madam?"

And Darke uttered a singular laugh. As for the woman she had grown so pale, I thought she would faint.

"Do you understand, madam?" continued Darke. "Colonel Mohun is in love *again*; and the name of his friend is — Georgia Conway!"

The woman was silent; but I saw that she was gnawing her nails.

"My budget is not exhausted, madam," continued Darke. "The young lady has a sister; her name is Virginia. She too has a love affair with a young officer of the artillery. His name is William Davenant!"

And the speaker clutched the arm of a chair so violently that the wood cracked in his powerful grasp.

"That is all!" he added. "The Mohuns, Davenants and Conways, are about to intermarry, you see! Their blood is going to mingle, their hands to clasp, in spite of the gulf of fire that divides their people! All is forgotten, or they care nothing. They are yonder, billing, and cooing, and kissing! the tender hearts are throbbing — all the world is bright to them — while I am here, and you, tearing our hearts out in despair!"

Darke stopped, uttering a sound between a curse and a groan. The woman had listened with a bitter smile. As he finished, she rose and approached him. Her eyes burned in the pale face like coals of fire.

"There is a better thing than despair!" she said.

"What?"

"Vengeance!"

And grasping his arm almost violently: —

"That man is yonder!" she said, pointing with the other hand toward Warrenton, "Go and meet him, and kill him, and end all this at once! Remember the banks of the Nottaway! — That sword thrust — that grave! Remember, he hates you with a deadly hatred — has wounded you, laughed at you, — driven you back, when you met him, like a hound under the lash! Remember me! — your oath! Break that oath and I will go and kill him myself!"

As she uttered these words a cannon shot thundered across the woods.

"Listen!" the woman exclaimed.

Darke rose suddenly to his feet.

"You are right!" he said, gloomily. "You keep me to the work. I do not hate him as you do — but he is an enemy, and I will kill him. Why do I yield to you, and obey you thus? What makes me love you, I wonder!"

Suddenly a second gun roared from beyond Buckland.

"We will talk of that afterward," said the woman, with flushed cheeks; "think of one thing only now — that *he* is yonder."

"Good!" said Darke, "and I hope that in an hour one of us will be dead, I care not which — come, madam — but you must not expose yourself!"

"What am I!"

"All I have left!" he said.

And with a gloomy look he rushed from the house, followed by the gray woman.

XII
THE BUCKLAND RACES

In a moment the voice of Darke was heard, ordering "to horse!" a clatter of sabres followed; and the company of cavalry sat out at full gallop toward the firing.

At their head I saw Darke's burly figure. The woman, escorted by an orderly, rode toward the rear.

In a few minutes the company of cavalry had entered a belt of woods and disappeared.

We had hastened into the apartment—Tom and myself, and looked now toward the highway. It was dark with a long column of Federal cavalry which seemed to be in great agitation.

The column, as well as I could make out, numbered at least a division. Neither the head nor the tail of the blue serpent was visible—only the main body, with its drawn sabres glittering like silver scales in the sun.

I hesitated not many seconds. Something was evidently going on, and our present whereabouts dangerous.

With a hasty salute to the young ladies who had hurried in, I made a sign to Tom, and ran to my horse.

My companion did not join me for at least five minutes. Impatience began to master me, when he appeared, laughing, and flourishing a knot of red ribbon, which I had observed in Miss Katy's hair.

With a bound he was in the saddle—I saw him turn and make a gay salute toward the ladies on the steps, and then we set out at full speed across the fields to rejoin Stuart.

He was evidently engaged with the enemy. From the front came quick carbine shots and shouts. From the woods, on the left flank and in rear of the enemy, was heard the rapid thunder of cannon.

Suddenly every thing flashed upon me. I remembered Stuart's significant smile; the absence of Fitz Lee; a trap had evidently been laid, and General Kilpatrick had fallen into it.

I was not deceived. The gallant Fitz Lee had suggested the ruse. He was to move toward Auburn, while Stuart retreated upon Warrenton, pursued by Kilpatrick. Then Fitz Lee was to attack the enemy in flank and rear, from the direction of Auburn—his cannon would be the signal for Stuart to turn. General Kilpatrick, thus assailed in front, flank and rear, *sauve qui pent* would, probably, be the order of the day with him.

Every thing turned out exactly as it had been arranged. Stuart retired steadily on Warrenton. When the Federal rear approached Buckland, Fitz Lee came in on their left flank, and then Stuart turned like a tiger, and bore down on the head of their column.

That gun we had heard was the signal of Fitz Lee's attack. Those carbine shots came from Stuart as his men charged.

We had set out at full speed to rejoin Stuart, as I have said; but he saved Tom and myself the trouble of riding very far. He came to meet us, at full gallop, with drawn sabre, driving the Federal troopers in disorder before him.

The affair that succeeded was one of the most animated of the war.

The enemy were completely dumbfoundered, but a part of Kilpatrick's force made a hard fight. Sabres clashed, carbines cracked, Fitz Lee's artillery roared—the fields and woods around Buckland were full of tumult and conflict.

In ten minutes we had caught up with Stuart. He was leading his column in person. At the head of the front regiment rode Mohun, with drawn sabre, and pressing his magnificent gray to headlong speed. In his eye was the splendid joy of combat; his cheeks glowed; his laughing lips revealed the white teeth under the black mustache. It was difficult to recognize in this gay cavalier, the pale, bitter and melancholy cynic of the previous June.

"Look, Surry!" exclaimed Mohun, "we are driving our friend Kilpatrick! Stuart is down on him like a lion!"

"You are driving a personal friend of yours, besides!" I said. "Yonder he is—Colonel Darke!"

Mohun's smile disappeared suddenly. He looked at Darke, whose burly figure was seen at the head of the charging column; and that glance was troubled and doubtful.

"I am sorry to meet him," he said, in a low tone.

"Why?"

"He would not strike me yonder, in Pennsylvania, when I was in his power."

"But he has sworn to kill you to-day!" I exclaimed. "I have just heard him swear that! Look out, Mohun! here they are!"

In an instant the two columns had clashed together, like thunder. What followed was a fierce and confused struggle — sabres clashing, carbines banging, men shouting, groaning, and falling from their horses, which trampled over the dead and wounded alike.

I was close beside Mohun as he closed in with Darke. The latter had plainly resolved on his enemy's destruction; and in an instant the two men were cutting furiously at each other with their sabres. They were body to body — their faces flamed — it was rather a wrestle on horseback, than a sword fight.

Suddenly Mohun delivered a blow which fell upon his opponent's sword hand, nearly cutting through the fingers. Darke's arm instinctively fell, and he was at his adversary's mercy.

Instead of plunging his sword into Darke's breast, however, as he might have done, Mohun let its point fall, and said: —

"Take your life! Now I am even with you, sir!"

Darke recoiled, and a furious flash darted from his eyes. Then his left hand went to his hilt; he drew a pistol; and spurring close up to Mohun, placed the weapon on his enemy's breast, and fired.

The bullet passed through Mohun's breast, but at the same instant Darke uttered a fierce cry. Mohun had driven his sword's point through the Federal officer's throat — the blood spouted around the blade — a moment afterward the two adversaries had clutched, dragged each other from their rearing horses, and were tearing each other with hands and teeth on the ground, wet with their blood.

One of Mohun's men leaped from horseback and tore them apart.

"A sword! give me a sword," exclaimed Mohun, hoarsely.

And rising to his feet, he clutched at an imaginary weapon,—his lips foamed with blood,—and reeling, he fell at full length on the body of his adversary, who was bathed in blood, and seemed to be dying.

What is here described, all took place in a few minutes. In that time the enemy's column had been broken, and hurled back. Suddenly the wild Southern cheer rang above the woods. Stuart and Fitz Lee had united their forces; in one solid column they pressed the flying enemy, banging and thundering on their rear with carbines and cannon.

Kilpatrick was defeated; his column in hopeless rout.

"Stuart boasts of having driven me from Culpeper;" he is reported to have said just before the fight, "and now I am going to drive *him*."

But Stuart was not driven. On the contrary, he drove Kilpatrick. Some of the enemy's column did not stop, it is said, before they reached the banks of the Potomac.

Such was the dramatic termination of the last great cavalry campaign of Stuart.

The affair came to be known as "The Buckland Races," and Stuart's old sabreurs still laugh as they recall the comedy.

XIII
TWO SCENES IN DECEMBER, 1863

The campaign of October, 1863, was over. Lee was behind the Rapidan.

In December General Meade struck a blow, in turn, at his adversary.

Shall we glance, in passing, at that affair of Mine Run? I saw a spectacle there—and a sad one, too—which I am tempted to describe, though aware it has little to do with my narrative. I have left Colonels Mohun and Darke in a bloody embrace yonder near Buckland. I ought to relate at length how they were not dead, and how they in due time recovered, but for the moment I think of a fine sight, and a weeping face, which I saw in the woods below Verdiersville.

Let us ride thither, reader, it will not take long.

In December, then, General Meade crossed the lower Rapidan, and advanced to assail General Lee in his works above.

A fiasco followed. Meade marched toward Verdiersville; found his adversary behind earth-works, near that place; reconnoitered them, felt them, moved backward and forward before them—and then, one morning, before General Lee was aware of the fact, quietly disappeared, returning to the north bank of the Rapidan.

You see I have no battles to describe on this occasion, reader. We had some hard fighting in the cavalry, but I shall not dwell upon that. It is some handsome fire-necklaces, and a talk with an old woman, which I shall speak of.

The fire-necklaces were manufactured by General Meade's troops, just before their retreat. The men had fallen into line at the word; moved silently toward the Rapidan, and had not taken the trouble, in leaving the rebel woods, to extinguish their bivouac fires, amid the thickets, carpeted with leaves. The result was a splendid spectacle. The fires had gradually burned outward, devouring the carpet of dry leaves. Great circles of flame were seen everywhere in the woods, and these dazzling fire-necklaces grew larger and larger, twined together, became entangled, twisted about, sparkled, crackled, — of all the sights I ever saw I think this was the most curious!

From time to time the flames crawled along and reached the foot of some tall tree, festooned with dry vines. Then the vine would catch; the flame would dart through the festoons; climb the trunk; stream from the summit, — and above the blazing rings, twisting in endless convolutions, would roar a mighty tongue of flame, crimson, baleful, and menacing.

It was a new "torch of war," invented by General Meade.

Such was the picturesque spectacle which rose a moment ago to my memory.

Now for the sad scene which I witnessed, as I rode back with Stuart.

Passing a small house, a poor woman came out, and with eyes full of tears, exclaimed, addressing Stuart: —

"Oh, child! stop a minute! Are they coming back? They have took every thing I had — they are *not* coming back!"[1]

{Footnote 1: Her words.}

Stuart stopped. He was riding at the head of his staff, preceded by his battle-flag. Not a trace of amusement was seen on his features, as he heard himself addressed in that phrase, "Oh, child!"

"Have they treated you so badly?" he said, in his grave, kind voice.

"Oh, yes!" exclaimed the poor woman, weeping bitterly, "they have took every hog, cow, and ear of corn I have, and every thing from my daughter; she is a widow, and lives near us. These are her children, my grandchildren, come to get out of the way."[1]

{Footnote 1: Her words.}

And she pointed to two or three little girls, with frightened faces, and eyes wet with tears.

Stuart seemed deeply affected. Under that stout heart, which never shrunk, was a wealth of sweetness and kindness.

"Well, they are not coming back, my good woman," he said, in a voice of deep feeling. "You need not be afraid — they are gone now."

The poor woman clasped her hands.

"Oh! do you believe that, child!"[1] she said; "do you believe they'll never come back?"

{Footnote 1: Her words.}

"I hope not, at least," Stuart replied, in a low tone.

"She clasped her hands, and for the third time addressing him as 'child,' sobbed:—

"Oh! if they will only never come back!"

That scene affected me deeply. The poor woman's tears brought something into my throat which seemed to choke me. This time the Northern soldiers had been impartial in their marauding. They had not only destroyed the property, and carried off the slaves of the wealthy proprietors, the "bloated aristocrats;" they had taken the bread out of the mouths of the widow and the fatherless—leaving them bare and starving in that bleak December of '63.

War conducted in that manner is barbarous—is it not, reader? The cry of that widow and her children must have gone up to Heaven.

Stuart returned to his bivouac in the pine wood near Verdiersville, where he had slept without tents, by his camp-fire, all these freezing nights. Then the army began to move; soon it resumed its former position; the cavalry was sent to watch the fords of the Rapidan; and Stuart returned to his own head-quarters near Orange Court-House, gayly singing, as he had left them to advance and meet the enemy.

XIV
STUART'S WINTER QUARTERS

COON HOLLOW! —

What gay memories are evoked by that familiar name! How we laughed and sang in that hollow in the hills near Orange, in the cold winter of 1863!

Stuart called his head-quarters "Wigwam Independence," but the officers of his staff gave them the sobriquet of "Coon Hollow;" and I adopt in my memoirs the old familiar designation.

Never were soldiers more comfortable than the inhabitants of Coon Hollow! — and Stuart's tent was the most comfortable of all. He had stretched a large canvas beneath some sheltering trees; and filling up the opening at each end with a picturesque wicker-work of evergreens, ensconced himself there in his sylvan lodge, like some Robin Hood, or ranger of the greenwood in old times. The woodland haunt and open air life seemed, at first, to charm the bold cavalier; nothing seemed wanting to his happiness, lost here in the forest: but soon the freezing airs "demoralized" even the stout cavalryman, and he exchanged his canvas for a regular tent of the largest description, with a plank floor, a camp-couch, and a mighty chimney, wherein sparkled, ere long, a cheerful fire of hickory, driving away the blasts of the cold winter nights, which were sent on their way with song.

Such was Stuart's own domicile. The staff tents were grouped around, with their solid chimneys of rock. The "cavalry head-quarters" was complete — a warm nest in the woods. Couriers came and went; sabres rattled; spurs jingled; the horses whinnied from their stables, woven of pine boughs, near by; and in and out of the general's tent played his two boisterous setters, Nip and Tuck, the companions of his idle hours. We all messed together, under a broad canvas, at one table: music resounded; songs were sung; Sweeney, soon, alas! to be dead, was yet king of the woodland revels; Stuart joined in his songs, to the music of the banjo; and not seldom did the bright faces of fair ladies shine on us, bringing back all the warmth of the summer days — the blue sky, the sunshine, and the smiles!

Such was good old "Coon Hollow." I recall it with delight. The chill airs cut you to the bone when you ventured out on horseback from the sheltered nook; but in Coon Hollow all was warm and bright. In the woods on the crest above, the winds sighed: but in the hollow below, the banjo rattled; laughter resounded; great fires roared; and, as though in open defiance of winter and its tempests, Stuart, carolled in his clear and sonorous voice, his favorite ditty,

"*The dew is on the blossom.*"

So we sang and laughed all those long winter evenings. The winds carried away the sound of jests, and banjo notes. The long hours of winter thus flew by like birds lost, one by one, in the night of the past. Happy days! happy nights! I remember them still. Stuart is dead — more than one of my dear companions have followed him — but their voices sound again, their eyes again flash, their friendly smiles linger in memory.

So the days fled by — and I wonder if our friends across the Rapidan, who were going to crush us, were as gay as the folk about to be crushed? The future looked stormy, but we laughed — and we did right, did we not, friend? That mirth was not unseemly — not unworthy of approval. It is evidence at least of "game," *non fractum esse fortunâ et retinere in rebus asperis, dignitatem* — is it not? Good fortune, wealth, and success, are nothing compared to that. For my part, I would rather have the equal mind in arduous things, than money in my purse, or victory. The army of Northern Virginia had that in the winter of 1863, as they had had it in 1861 and '62, and were going to have it in the dark year and black winter preceding April, 1865.

But I linger too long on those days at "Coon Hollow." The wave of war had wafted us to that quiet nook; for a time, we laughed and sang; but the storm was coming. Soon it struck us; and we left the harbor, driven by the tempest.

So I dismiss Coon Hollow, lost amid the hills of Orange. The spot is desolate to-day, and the bleak wood is silent. But for me, Stuart is singing there now as then — and will sing in my memory forever!

XV
LEE'S "RAGGED REGIMENTS"

It required a stout heart to laugh and sing, *con amore*, in the last days of that winter, and the first days of spring, 1864.

Those very figures, "1864," tell the story, and explain this. Do they not, reader?

Each year of the war has its peculiar physiognomy.

1861—that is mirth, adventure, inexperience, bright faces, wreaths of flowers, "boxes" from home, and "honorable mention" in reports, if you only waved your sword and shouted "Hurrah!" Then you heard the brass bands playing, the drum gayly rolling, the bugles sending their joyous notes across the fields and through the forests—blooming fields, untouched forests!—and that music made the pulses dance. Gayly-clad volunteers marched gallantly through the streets; the crowds cheered; the new flags, shaped by fair hands, fluttered;—not a bullet had torn through them, not a rent was seen in the new uniforms. As the trains swept by with the young heroes on board, bevies of lovely girls cheered, waved handkerchiefs, and threw nosegays. Eyes were sparkling, lips smiling, cheeks glowing in '61. The youths had havelocks to ward off the sun; gaiters to keep out the dust; woollen belts to prevent rheumatism; fanciful shirt bosoms, and pretty needle-cases and tobacco pouches of silk and velvet, decked with beads and gay needle-work, by the dearest fingers in the world!

So they went to the wars—those stout and ruddy youths. Every one anxious to have his head taken off by a cannon ball, all for the honor and glory of it. They marched along cheering, as the white handkerchiefs waved; they proudly kept step to the tap of the drum, or moved briskly beside the cannon, or cantered by on their glossy and spirited horses.

The epoch was agitated, but joy coursed in every vein. And when the first successes came, those small affairs were greeted with "thunders of applause."

General Spoons marched to Bethel; took a look at the gray people; fired a gun or two before retreating—and a thousand Southern journalists shouted "Io, triumphe!—a grand victory!" The brave Del. Kemper fired a shot at the Federal train approaching Vienna, and the journalists cried, "we have driven back the whole Federal army!"

Then some real fighting came, and the applause was again tremendous. When the news of the first Manassas flashed over the wires, the Southern people stood upon their heads, and went wild. The war was ended—the affair was over—the brass bands, and rolling drums, and dazzling uniforms had speedily done the business. The power of the North was broken. She had run upon the breakers. The great hulk was lying stranded, the waves were beating her, and she was about to go to pieces.

Such was 1861—an era of mirth, inexperience, inflated views, brilliant pageants, gay adventures, ruddy cheeks, sparkling eyes and splendid banners, floating proudly in the sunshine of victory!

1862 came, and with it a new phase of the war. Sweat, dust, and blood had replaced the music and wreaths of roses. Faces, were not so ruddy— they began to look war-worn. The rounded cheeks had become gaunt. The bright uniforms were battle-soiled. Smoke had stained them, the bivouac dimmed them, the sun had changed the blue-gray to a sort of scorched yellow. Waving handkerchiefs still greeted the troops—as they greeted them to the end of the war. But few flowers were thrown now—their good angels looked on in silence, and prayed for them.

They were no longer holiday soldiers, but were hardened in battle. They knew the work before them, and advanced to it with the measured tramp of veterans. They fought as well as soldiers have ever fought in this world. Did they not? Answer, Cold Harbor, Malvern Hill, Cedar Mountain, Manassas, Boonsboro', Sharpsburg, and Fredericksburg! And every battle, nearly, was a victory. In the lowlands and the mountains—in Virginia and Maryland—they bore aloft the banner of the South in stalwart hands, and carried it forward with unshrinking hearts, to that baptism of blood awaiting it. That was the great year for the South. The hour was dark—a huge foe fronted us—but wherever that foe was met, he seemed to reel before the mailed hand that buffeted his front. All frippery and decoration had long been stripped from the army. The fingers of war—real war—had torn off the gaudy trappings; and the grim lips had muttered, "What I want is hard muscle, and the brave heart—not tinsel!" The bands were seldom heard—the musicians were tending the wounded. The drums had ceased their jovial rattle, and were chiefly used in the "long roll," which said "Get ready, boys! they are coming!"

So in the midst of smoke and dust,—with yells of triumph, or groans of agony, in place of the gay cheering—passed that year of battles, 1862.

The South was no longer romantic and elated on the subject of the war. The soldiers no longer looked out for adventures, or for the glorious cannonball to carry off their heads, and make their names immortal. At home, the old men were arming, and the women sending words of cheer to their husbands and sons, and praying. In the camps, the old soldiers had forgotten the wreaths of roses. Their havelocks were worn out, and they no longer minded the sun. Gray flannel had replaced the "fancy" shirt bosoms; they carried tobacco in their pockets; and you saw them, seated on some log, busy sewing on buttons, the faces once so round and ruddy, now gaunt and stained with powder.

1863 came, and it was an army of veterans that struck Hooker at Chancellorsville. It was no longer a company of gay gallants marching by, amid music, waving scarfs, and showers of nosegays from fairy hands. It was a stormy wave of gaunt warriors, in ragged clothes and begrimed faces, who clutched their shining muskets, rushed headlong over the breastworks, and, rolling through the blazing and crackling woods, swept the enemy at the point of the bayonet, with the hoarse and menacing cry, "Remember Jackson!" Gettysburg followed—never was grapple more fierce than that, as we have seen; and when the veterans of Lee were hurled back, the soil of the continent seemed to shake. They were repulsed and retreated, but as the lion retreats before the huntsman, glaring back, and admonishing him not to follow too closely, if he would consult his own safety. At Williamsport the wounded lion halted and turned—his pursuer did not assail him—and he crossed the Potomac, and descended to the Rapidan, to strike in turn that dangerous blow in October, when Meade was nearly cut off from Washington.

With that campaign of Bristoe, and the fiasco of Mine Run, the year of 1863 ended.

It left the South bleeding, and what was worse,—discouraged. Affairs were mismanaged. The army had scarcely sufficient meat and bread to live on. The croakers, clad in black coats, and with snowy shirt bosoms, began to mutter under their breath, "It is useless to struggle longer!"—and, recoiling in disgust from the hard fare of "war times," began to hunger for the flesh-pots of Egypt. Manna was tasteless now; the task-master was better than the wilderness and the scant fare. Oh! to sit by the flesh-pots and grow fat, as in the days when they did eat thereof! Why continue the conflict? Why waste valuable lives? Why think of still fighting when flour was a hundred dollars a barrel, coffee twenty dollars a pound, cloth fifty dollars a yard, and good whiskey and brandy not to be purchased at any price? Could patriotism live amid trials like that? Could men cling to a cause which made them the victims of Yankee cavalry? Why have faith any longer in a government that was bankrupt—whose promises to pay originated the scoffing proverb, "as worthless as a Confederate note!" Meat and drink was the religion of the croakers in those days. Money was their real divinity. Without meat and drink, and with worthless money, the Confederacy, in their eyes, was not the side to adhere to. It was unfortunate—down with it! Let it be anathema-maranatha!

The croakers said that—and the brave hearts whom they insulted could not silence them. There were stout souls in black coats—but the croakers distilled their poison, working busily in the darkness. It was the croakers who bought up the supplies, and hoarded them in garrets, and retailed them in driblets, thereby causing the enormous prices which, according to them, foretold the coming downfall. They evaded the conscript officers; grew fat on their extortions; and one day you would miss them from their accustomed haunts—they had flitted across the Potomac, and were drinking their wine in New York, London, or Paris.

Meanwhile, three classes of persons remained faithful to the death:—the old men, the army, and the women.

The gray-beards were taking down their old guns and swords, and forming home-battalions, to fight the enemy to the death when his cavalry came to lay waste the country.

The women were weaving homespun, knitting socks, nursing the wounded, and praying. They had never ceased to pray, nor had they lost the heart of hope. The croakers believed in success, and their patron saint was Mammon. The women believed in the justice of the cause, and in God. In 1861, they had cheered the soldiers, and waved their handkerchiefs, and rained bouquets. In 1862, they had sent brave words of encouragement, and bade their sons, and brothers, and husbands fight to the end. In 1863, they repeated that—sent the laggards back to the ranks—and when they were not sewing, or nursing the sick, were praying. O women of Virginia, and the great South to her farthest limits, there is nothing in all history that surpasses your grand record! You hoped, in the dark days as in the bright;—when bearded men shrunk, you fronted the storm unmoved! Always you hoped, and endured, and prayed for the land. Had the rest done their duty like the women and the army, the red-cross flag would be floating to-day in triumph!

The army—that was unshaken. Gettysburg had not broken its strength, nor affected its stout manhood. Lee's old soldiers believed in him after Gettysburg, in the winter of '63, as they had believed in him after Fredericksburg, in the winter of '62. They had confidence still in their great leader, and in their cause. The wide gaps in their ranks did not dismay them; want of food did not discourage them; hunger, hardships, nakedness, defeat, — they had borne these in the past, they were bearing them still, they were ready to bear them in the future. War did not fright them — though the coming conflict was plainly going to be more bitter than any before. The great array of Grant on the north bank of the Rapidan did not depress them — had they not met and defeated at Fredericksburg and Chancellorsville a force as great, and could not they do it again?

So they lay in their camps on the Rapidan, in that cold winter of 1863 — a little army of ragged and hungry men, with gaunt faces, wasted forms, shoeless feet; with nothing to encourage them but the cause, past victories, and Lee's presence. That was much; what was enough, however, was the blood in their veins; the inspiration of the great race of fighting men from whom they derived their origin. Does any one laugh at that? The winner will — but the truth remains.

That ragged and famished army came of a fighting race. It was starving and dying, but it was going to fight to the last.

When the cannon began to roar in May, 1864, these gaunt veterans were in line, with ragged coats, but burnished bayonets. When Lee, the gray cavalier, rode along their lines, the woods thundered with a cheer which said, "Ready!"

XVI
HAMMER AND RAPIER

I pass to the great collision of armies in the first days of May.

Why say any thing of that dark episode called "Dahlgren's raid?" A full account would be too long—a brief sketch too short. And whatever our Northern friends may think, it is not agreeable to us to dwell on that outrage. Was that *war*? Was it civilized warfare to march in the darkness upon a city full of women and children—to plan the assassination of the Southern President and his cabinet; the destruction of the city by the torch; the release of the Federal prisoners at Belle Isle, to be let loose afterward with fire and sword on Richmond?

Alas! all that was planned. The orders were captured, and exist still. Was that war? I repeat. Answer, friends of the North. Or, did you think us mere wild beasts?

I omit all that, passing on to the real fighting.

General Ulysses S. Grant had been appointed commander-in-chief of the armies of the United States, and had taken command in person of the army of the Potomac, confronting Lee on the Rapidan.

Before the curtain rises, and the cannon begin to roar, let us glance at the relative numbers, and the programme of the Federal leader.

Grant's "available force present for duty, May 1, 1864," was, according to the report of the Federal Secretary of War, 141,166 men.

Lee's force, "present for duty," as his army rolls will show, was 52,626 men. That is to say, rather more than one-third of his adversary's.

Lee afterward received about 10,000 re-enforcements from Beauregard's columns. Grant received about 50,000.

With about 62,000 men Lee repulsed the attacks of Grant with about 200,000 men, from the Rapidan to Petersburg—inflicting a loss on his adversary, by the Federal statement of more than 60,000 men.

These numbers may be denied, but the proof is on record.

The programme of General Grant in the approaching campaign was one of very great simplicity. He intended to "hammer continuously" as he wrote to President Lincoln, and crush his adversary at whatever expense of money and blood. From 1861 to 1864, war had been war, such as the world understands it. Pitched battles had been fought—defeats sustained—or victories gained.

Then the adversaries rested before new pitched battles: more defeats or victories. General Grant had determined to change all that. It had been tried, and had failed. He possessed a gigantic weapon, the army of the United States. In his grasp was a huge sledge-hammer—the army of the Potomac. He was going to clutch that tremendous weapon, whirl it aloft like a new Vulcan, and strike straight at Lee's crest, and try to end him. If one blow did not suffice, he was going to try another. If that failed, in its turn, he would strike another and another. All the year was before him; there were new men to fill the places of those who fell; blood might gush in torrents, but the end was worth the cost. Would it hurl a hundred thousand men into bloody graves? That was unfortunate, but unavoidable. Would the struggle frighten and horrify the world? It was possible. But these things were unimportant. The rebellion must be crushed. The sledge-hammer must strike until Lee's keen rapier was shattered. Hammer and rapier were matched against each other—the combat was *à l'outrance*—the hammer must beat down the rapier, or fall from the grasp of him who wielded it.

Such was the programme of General Grant. It was not war exactly, in the old acceptation of the term. It was not taught by Jomini, or practised by Napoleon. You would have said, indeed, at the first glance, that it rejected the idea of generalship *in toto*. Let us give General Grant his just dues, however. He was not a great commander, but he *was* a man of clear brain. He saw that brute force could alone shatter the army of Northern Virginia;

that to wear it away by attrition, exhaust its blood drop by drop, was the only thing left—and he had the courage to adopt that programme.

To come back to events on the Rapidan in the month of May, 1864.

Lee is ready for the great collision, now seen to be inevitable. His right, under Ewell, occupies the works on the southern bank of the Rapidan, above Chancellorsville. His centre, under A.P. Hill, lies near Orange Court-House. His left, under Longstreet, is in reserve near Gordonsville.

The army of Northern Virginia is thus posted in echelon of corps, extending from Gordonsville, by Orange, toward the fords of the Rapidan.

When the enemy cross on their great advance, Ewell is ready to face east; Hill will close in on his right; and Longstreet in the same manner on Hill's right. Then the army will be in line, ready to strike at Grant's flank as he moves through the Wilderness.

For Lee is going to strike at him. The fifty thousand are going to order the one hundred and forty thousand to halt.

Stuart's cavalry is watching. It extends from Madison Court-House, along Robertson River, on the left of the army; and on the right, from Ewell's camps, past Chancellorsville, to Fredericksburg.

Such was the situation on the first of May. The two tigers were watching each other—and one was about to spring.

XVII
FORT DELAWARE

To descend now from the heights of generalization to the plains of incident and personal observation.

For this volume is not a history of the war in Virginia, but the memoirs of a staff officer belonging to Stuart's cavalry.

May, 1864, had come; we were soon to be in the saddle; the thundering hammer of General Grant was about to commence its performances.

One night — it was the night of the first of May — I was sitting in General Stuart's tent, looking into his blazing log fire, and musing. In this luxury I was not interrupted. It was nearly midnight, and the rest of the staff had retired. Stuart was writing at his desk, by the light of a candle in a captured "camp candlestick," and from time to time, without turning his head, ejaculated some brief words upon any subject which came into his head.

After writing ten minutes, he now said briefly: —

"Surry."

"General," was my as brief response."

"I think Mohun was a friend of yours?"

"Yes, general, we became intimate on the march to Gettysburg."

"Well, I have just received his commission —"

"You mean as —"

"Brigadier-general. You know I long ago applied for it."

"I knew that — pity he has not been exchanged."

"A great pity, — and you miss a pleasure I promised myself I would give you."

"What pleasure, general?"

"To take Mohun his commission with your own hands."

"I am truly sorry I can not. You know he was terribly wounded, and we had to leave him in Warrenton; then the enemy advanced; for a long time we thought him dead. Thus I am sorry I am debarred the pleasure you offer. Some day I hope to accept your offer."

"Accept it now, colonel," said a benignant voice at the door. I turned suddenly, as did the general. At the opening of the tent, a head was seen—the head passed through—was followed by a body,—and Mr. Nighthawk, private and confidential emissary, glided in with the stealthy step of a wild-cat.

He was unchanged. His small eyes were as piercing, his smile as benignant, his costume—black coat, white cravat, and "stove-pipe" hat—as clerical as before.

"Good evening, gentlemen," said Mr. Nighthawk, smiling sweetly; "I bring news of Colonel Mohun."

"And fly in like an owl, or your namesake!" laughed Stuart.

"An owl? I am told that is the bird of wisdom, gentlemen!"

"You hit the nail on the head, when you said 'gentlemen!'"{1} replied Stuart, laughing; "but how about Mohun? Is he exchanged, Nighthawk?"

{Footnote 1: A favorite phrase of Stuart's.}

And Stuart wheeled round and pointed to a chair.

Nighthawk sat down modestly.

"Not exchanged, exactly, general; but safe!" he said.

"He escaped?"

"Exactly, general."

"And you helped him?"

"I believe so."

"Good! You really are a trump, Nighthawk—and you seem to have a peculiar fancy for Mohun."

"He is the best friend I have in the world, general."

"Well, that accounts for it. But how did he escape?"

"I will tell you in a few words, general. I rather pride myself on the manner in which I conducted the little affair. You remember, Colonel Mohun was very badly wounded when you defeated Kilpatrick at Buckland. It was in a fight with Colonel Darke, of the Federal cavalry, who was also wounded and left dying, as was erroneously supposed, at a small house on the roadside, when you fell back. Colonel Mohun was left at Warrenton, his wound being so severe that he could not be brought farther in his ambulance, and here he staid until he was convalescent. His recovery was miraculous, as a bullet had passed through his breast; but he is a gentleman of vigorous constitution, and he rallied at last, but, unfortunately, to find himself a prisoner. General Meade had reoccupied the country, and Colonel Mohun was transferred from hospital to Fort Delaware, as a prisoner of war.

"I have informed you, general," continued Mr. Nighthawk, smiling, and turning the rim of his black hat between his fingers, "that Colonel Mohun was one of my best friends. For that reason, I went to see him at Warrenton, and had arranged a very good plan for his escape, when, unfortunately, he was all at once sent away, thereby disappointing all my schemes. I followed, however, saw that he was taken to Fort Delaware, and proceeded thither at once. You have probably not visited this place, general, or you, colonel. It is a fort, and outside is a pen, or stockade as it is called, covering two or three acres. Inside are cabins for the prisoners, in the shape of a semicircle, and grounds to walk in, except in the space marked off by the 'dead line.' If any prisoner crosses that he is shot by the sentries, whose beat is on a platform running round upon the top of the stockade.

"Well, I went to the place, and found that Colonel Mohun was confined with other officers in the pen, where they had the usual Federal ration of watery soup, bad meat, and musty crackers. For a gentleman, like himself, accustomed before the war to every luxury that unbounded wealth could supply, this was naturally disagreeable, and I determined to omit no exertion to effect his escape.

"Unfortunately, the rules of Fort Delaware are very strict, however. To cross the 'dead line' is death; to attempt to burrow is confinement in irons, and other degrading punishments; and to bribe the sentinels invariably resulted in having the whole affair revealed, after they had received the money. It really seemed as if Colonel Mohun were doomed to the living death of a filthy prison until the end of the war, since exchanges had ceased, and it was only by devising a ruse of very great risk that I accomplished the end in view."

"What was your plan, Nighthawk?" said Stuart, rising and moving to the fireplace, where he stood basking in the warmth. "Original, I lay my life, and—quiet."

"Exactly that, general."

And Nighthawk smiled sweetly.

XVIII
THE UNIFORM

"I have always observed, general," said Mr. Nighthawk, raising his eyes in pious meditation, as it were, "that there is no better rule for a man's conduct in life than to make friends with the mammon of unrighteousness—people in power."

"A profound maxim," laughed Stuart; "friends are useful—that was your principle?"

"Yes, general; and I made one of the quartermaster of the post—a certain major Woodby—who was exceedingly fond of the 'root of all evil.' I made that gentleman's acquaintance, applied for the place of sutler in *the pen*; and this place I acquired by agreeing to pay a heavy bonus in thirty days.

"This was Saturday night. On Monday morning I presented myself before the gate, and demanded admittance as the newly appointed sutler of the pen.

"I was admitted, and taken before the officer of the day, in his quarters.

"'Who are you?' he asked, gruffly.

"'The new sutler, lieutenant.'

"'Where are your papers?'

"I had them ready, and presented them to him. He read them carefully, looked at me superciliously, and said:—

"'That is wholly informal.'

"I looked at him. He had a red nose.

"'I have some excellent French brandy, captain,' I said, promoting him.

"At sight of the portly flask which I drew half from my pocket and exhibited to him, I saw his face relax.

"'You are a keen fellow, and know the world, I perceive,' he said.

"And taking the flask, he poured out nearly a glass full of the brandy, and drank it.

"'Do you intend to keep that article of brandy?' he said.

"'For my friends, captain,' I replied, with a wink which he evidently understood.

"'Let me see your papers again.'

"I unfolded them, and he glanced at them.

"'All right—they are in regular form. There is the key of the sutler's shop, on that nail. Take possession.'

"And my friend the captain emptied a second glass of the brandy, and made me a sign that I could go.

"I bowed profoundly; took the key; and went and opened the sutler's shop; after which I strolled out to look at the prisoners in the area. The sentinel had seen me visit the officer of the day, and go to the sutler's shop.

"Thus he did not interfere with me when I went into the area, as I was obviously a good Union man and an employee of the post.

"Such was the manner in which I secured a private interview with Colonel Mohun: we could talk without the presence of a corporal; and we soon arranged the plan for his escape.

"I had determined to procure a Federal uniform, to be smuggled in to him, and an hour afterward, I left him, promising to see him again as soon as I could visit Wilmington, and return with the intended disguise.

"A strange piece of good fortune aided me, or rather accomplished my purpose at once. I had scarcely returned to the sutler's shop, and spread some blankets to sleep upon, when the officer of the day came in, and I saw at a glance that he was half intoxicated, in consequence of the large amount of brandy which he had swallowed. In a thick and husky voice he cursed the 'stuff' vended at the post, extolled 'the article' I carried, and demanded another pull at the flask. I looked at him—saw that a little more would make him dead-drunk—and all at once resolved on my plan.

"This was," continued Mr. Nighthawk, with modest simplicity, and smiling as he spoke, "to make my friend, the officer of the day, dead-drunk, and then borrow his uniform; and I succeeded. In half an hour he was maudlin. In three-quarters of an hour, drunk. Five minutes afterward he fell out of his chair, and began to snore, where he lay.

"I secured the door tightly, stripped off his uniform, then my own clothing; put on his, and then replaced my own citizen's dress over all, concealed his cap and boots beneath my overcoat, wrapped the prostrate lieutenant in my blankets for fear he would take cold, and going out, locked the door and proceeded to the quarters of the prisoners. Again the sentinel took no notice of me. I found Colonel Mohun in his 'bunk.' Ten minutes afterward he had replaced his gray uniform with that of the Federal lieutenant, and, watching the moment when the back of the sentinel was turned, we walked together toward the gate of the pen.

"That was the moment of real danger. Outside the narrow gate another sentinel was posted, and the man might be personally acquainted with the officer of the day, or have noticed his appearance. Luckily, the guard had been relieved about an hour before—the new sentinel had not seen the officer of the day—and when Colonel Mohun put his head through the little window beside the gate, ordering 'Open!' the gate flew open, the sentinel presented arms as he passed, and I followed modestly—the door banging-to behind us."[1]

{Footnote 1: Fact.}

XIX
THE NOTE

"Thus the colonel was out of the pen," continued Nighthawk, smiling. "The rest was not very dangerous, unless the alarm were given. They might miss the locked-up officer—he might have been seen to go into the sutler's shop—and I admonished Colonel Mohun, in a low tone, to proceed as rapidly as possible in a direction which I pointed out.

"The path indicated led to a spot on the island where I had concealed a small boat among some willows—and, once across on the mainland, I hoped that the danger would be over.

"In spite of my admonitions, Colonel Mohun took his time. He is a cool one! He even turned and walked toward the fort, which he carefully examined—counting the guns, observing the ditches, and the ground around it.

"'That place could be taken, Nighthawk!' he said, with a laugh. And he continued to stroll around the place, receiving at every moment respectful salutes from passing soldiers, which he returned with the utmost coolness, and an air of authority which I never have seen surpassed. I declare to you, general, that it made the sweat burst out on my forehead, and it was fully an hour before we reached the boat. I sprung in and seized the oars, for I saw a dozen soldiers approaching us from the direction of the fort.

"'For heaven's sake, sit down, colonel,' I exclaimed; 'in five minutes we will be lost!'

"He did not reply. He was feeling in the pockets of the lieutenant's coat; and drew out a note-book with a pencil attached. Then, as the men came toward us, he began to write. I looked over his shoulder—a bad habit I acknowledge, general—and I read these words:—-

"'Colonel Mohun, C.S.A., presents his compliments to the commanding officer of Fort Delaware, and recommends the 10-inch Columbiad in place of the 30-lb. Parrotts on the bastion near the southern angle of the work.

"'As Colonel M. is *en route* for Richmond *via* Wilmington, and the train will soon pass, he is compelled to refrain from other suggestions which occur to him.

"'The commandant of the post will pardon the want of ceremony of his departure. This distressing separation is dictated by necessity.'"

Nighthawk smiled as he repeated the words of *Mohun's* note.

"Did you ever hear of a cooler hand, general? But I must end my long story. The colonel wrote this note while the soldiers were coming toward us. When they had come within ten steps, he beckoned to one of them — the man came up, saluting — and the colonel said, 'Take this note to the commandant — go at once.'

"My heart had jumped to my throat, general! The next moment I drew a good long breath of real relief. The Federal soldier touched his cap, took the note, and went back toward the fort. Without further delay, I pushed out and rowed across to the mainland, where we soon arrived.

"Then we left the boat, struck into the fields, and pushed for the nearest station on the railroad. On the way, I could not refrain from upbraiding the colonel with his imprudence. He only laughed, however, and we went on without stopping. An hour afterward we reached the station, and the northern train soon came. We got in, the cars started, and we were *en route* for Baltimore. Suddenly the dull sound of a cannon-shot came from the direction of Fort Delaware. A moment afterward came another, and then a third.

"'A prisoner has escaped from Fort Delaware,' said one of the passengers near us, raising his eyes from a newspaper. Colonel Mohun laughed, and said carelessly, without sinking his voice in the least, 'Ten to one they have found your friend, the lieutenant, Nighthawk!' Such a man, general! It was enough to make your blood run cold! I thought *I* was cool, but I assure you, I never imagined a man could equal *that*.

"We reached Baltimore, made the connection with the train going west to Wheeling, and disembarked at Martinsburg. There the colonel procured a horse — rode to a friend's on the Opequon — changed his blue dress for a citizen's suit, and proceeded to Staunton, thence to Richmond, and yesterday rejoined his regiment, near Chancellorsville."

XX
GENERAL GRANT'S PRIVATE ORDER

Stuart kicked a log, which had fallen on the hearth, back into the fire, and said: —

"Well, Nighthawk, your narrative only proves one thing."

"What, general?"

"That the writer who hereafter relates the true stories of this war, will be set down as a Baron Munchausen."

"No doubt of that, general."

"This escape of Colonel Mohun, for instance, will be discredited."

"No matter, it took place; but I have not told you what brought me over, general."

"Over?"

"Yes, across the Rapidan. I did not go from Martinsburg to Richmond with Colonel Mohun. I thought I would come down and see what was going on in Culpeper. Accordingly I crossed the Blue Ridge at Ashby's Gap, reached Culpeper—and last night crossed the Rapidan opposite Chancellorsville, where I saw Colonel Mohun, before whom I was carried as a spy."

"You bring news, then?" said Stuart, with sudden earnestness and attention.

"Important news, general. The Federal army is about to move."

"To cross?"

"Yes."

"Where—when!—what force!"

"One hundred and forty thousand of all arms. I answer the last question first."

"And—"

"The army will advance in two columns. The right—of Sedgwick's and Warren's corps—will cross at Germanna Ford. The left, consisting of Hancock's corps, at Ely's ford below. They have pontoon and bridge trains — and the movement will commence at midnight on the third — two days from now."

Stuart knit his brows, and buried his hand in his beard. Suddenly he called out to the orderly: —

"Have two horses saddled in five minutes!" And seizing his hat, he said: —

"Get ready to ride to General Lee's head-quarters with me, Nighthawk!"

The clerical looking emissary put on his respectable black hat.

"You are certain of this intelligence?" Stuart said, turning with a piercing glance to him.

"Quite certain, general," said Mr. Nighthawk, serenely.

"You were in the camps?"

"In all, I believe, and at army head-quarters."

"You overheard your intelligence?"

"No, I captured it, general."

"How?"

"A courier was sent in haste — I saw the commander-in-chief speaking to him. I followed — came up with him in a hollow of the woods — and was compelled to blow his brains out, as he would not surrender. I then searched his body, and found what I wanted. There it is general."

And Nighthawk drew forth a paper.

"What is it?" exclaimed Stuart.

"Grant's confidential order to his corps commanders, general, directing the movements of his army."

Stuart seized it, read it hastily, and uttered an exclamation of satisfaction. Ten minutes afterward he was going at full speed, accompanied by Nighthawk, toward General Lee's head-quarters.

XXI
"VIRGINIA EXPECTS EVERY MAN TO DO HIS DUTY!"

Soon after daylight, on the next morning, Stuart was up, and writing busily at his desk.

He was perfectly cool, as always, and his manner when I went in exhibited no sort of flurry. But the couriers going and coming with dispatches indicated clearly that "something was in the wind."

I was seated by the fireplace when Stuart finished a dispatch and came toward me. The next moment he threw himself upon a chair, leaned his head upon my shoulder, and began to caress one of his dogs, who leaped into his lap.

"Well, Surry, old fellow, we are going to get into the saddle. Look out for your head!"

"Excellent advice," I replied. "I recommend you to follow it."

"You think I expose myself, do you?"

"In the most reckless manner."

"For instance—come, an instance!" he laughed.

I saw Stuart was talking to rest himself.

"Well, at Mine Run, when you rode up to that fence lined with sharpshooters—and they fired on us at ten paces, nearly."

"In fact, you might have shot a marble at them—but I am not afraid of any ball *aimed* at me."[1]

{Footnote 1: His words.}

"Then you believe in *chance*, general?"

"There is no chance, Surry," he said, gravely. "God rules over all things, and not a sparrow, we are told, can fall without his permission. How can I, or you, then?"

"You are right, general, and I have always been convinced of your religious faith."

"I believe in God and our Saviour, with all my heart," said Stuart, solemnly. "I may not show it, but I feel deeply."

"On the contrary, you show it—to me at least—even in trifles," I said, moved by his earnestness. "Do you remember the other day, when an officer uttered a sneer at the expense of a friend of his who had turned *preacher*? You replied that the calling of a minister was the noblest in which any human being could engage{1}—and I regretted at that moment, that the people who laugh at you, and charge you with vicious things, could not hear you."

{Footnote 1: His words.}

Stuart shook his head, smiling with a sadness on his lips which I had never seen before.

"They would not believe me, my dear Surry; not one would give me credit for a good sentiment or a pure principle! Am I not a drunkard, because my face is burned red by the sun and the wind? And yet I never touched spirit in all my life! I do not know the taste of it!{1} Am I not given to women? And yet, God knows I am innocent,—that I recoil in disgust from the very thought! Am I not frivolous, trifling,—laughing at all things, reverencing nothing? And yet my laughter is only from high health and animal spirits. I am young and robust; it is natural to me to laugh, as it is to be pleased with bright faces and happy voices, with colors, and music, and approbation. I am not as religious as I ought to be, and wish, with all my heart, I had the deep and devout piety of that good man and great military genius,{2} Stonewall Jackson. I can lay no claim to it, you see, Surry; I am only a rough soldier, at my hard work. I am terribly busy, and my command takes every energy I possess; but I find time to read my Bible and to pray. I pray for pardon and forgiveness, and try to do my duty, and leave the rest to God. If God calls me—and He may call me very soon—I hope I will be ready, and be able to say, 'Thy will be done.' I expect to be killed in this war;{3}—Heaven knows, I would have my right hand chopped off at the wrist to stop it!{4}—but I do not shrink from the ordeal before me, and I am ready to lay down my life for my country."{5}

{Footnote 1: His words.}

{Footnote 2: His words.}

{Footnote 3: His words.}

{Footnote 4: His words.}

{Footnote 5: His words.}

Stuart paused, and leaned his arm upon the rude shelf above the fireplace, passing his hand over his forehead, as was habitual with him.

"A hard campaign is coming, Surry," he said, at length, more cheerfully; "I intend to do my duty in it, and deserve the good opinion of the world, if I do not secure it. I have perilled my life many times, and shall not shrink from it in future. I am a Virginian, and I intend to live or die for Old Virginia! The tug is coming; the enemy are about to come over and 'try again!' But we will meet them, and fight them like men, Surry! Our army is small, but with strong hands and brave hearts much can be done. We must be up and doing, and do our duty to the handle.{1} For myself, I am going to fight whatever is before me, — to win victory, with God's blessing, or die trying! Once more, Surry, remember that we are fighting for our old mother, and that Virginia expects every man to do his duty!"

{Footnote 1: His words.}

His face glowed as he spoke; in his dazzling blue eyes burned the fire of an unconquerable resolution, a courage that nothing seemed able to crush.

Years have passed since then, a thousand scenes have swept before me; but still I see the stalwart cavalier, with his proud forehead raised, and hear his sonorous voice exclaim: —

"Virginia expects every man to do his duty!"{1}

{Footnote 1: His words.}

XXII
WHAT OCCURRED AT WARRENTON

This conversation took place at an early hour of the morning. Two hours afterward, I was in the saddle and riding toward Chancellorsville, with the double object of inspecting the pickets and taking Mohun his commission.

I have described in my former *Memoirs* that melancholy country of the Wilderness; its unending thickets; its roads, narrow and deserted, which seem to wind on forever; the desolate fields, here and there covered with stunted bushes; the owls flapping their dusky wings; the whip-poor-will, crying in the jungle; and the moccasin gliding stealthily amid the ooze, covered with its green scum.

Strange and sombre country! lugubrious shades where death lurked! Already two great armies had clutched there in May, 1863. Now, in May, '64, the tangled thicket was again to thunder; men were going to grapple here in a mad wrestle even more desperate than the former!

Two roads stretch from Orange Court-House to Chancellorsville — the old turnpike, and the plank road — running through Verdiersville.

I took the latter, followed the interminable wooden pathway through the thicket, and toward evening came to the point where the Ely's Ford road comes in near Chancellorsville. Here, surrounded by the rotting weapons, bones and skulls of the great battle already fought, I found Mohun ready for the battle that was coming.

He commanded the regiment on picket opposite Ely's Ford; and was pointed out to me at three hundred yards from an old torn down house which still remains there, I fancy.

Mohun had dismounted, and, leaning against the trunk of a tree, was smoking a cigar. He was much thinner and paler than when I had last seen him; but his eye was brilliant and piercing, his carriage erect and proud. In his fine new uniform, replacing that left at Fort Delaware, and his brown hat, decorated with a black feather, he was the model of a cavalier, ready at a moment's warning to meet the enemy.

We exchanged a close grasp of the hand. Something in this man had attracted me, and from acquaintances we had become friends, though Mohun had never given me his confidence.

I informed him of Nighthawk's visit and narrative, congratulated him on his escape, and then presented him with his appointment to the grade of brigadier-general.

"Hurrah for Stuart! He is a man to count on!" exclaimed Mohun, "and here inclosed is the order for me to take command of four regiments!"

"I congratulate you, Mohun."

"I hope to do good work with them, my dear Surry — and I think they are just in time."

With which words Mohun put the paper in his pocket.

"You know the latest intelligence?" he said.

"Yes; but do not let us talk of it. Tell me something about yourself — but first listen to a little narrative from me."

And I described the visit which I had made with Tom Herbert to the house near Buckland; the scene between Darke and his companion; and, to keep back nothing, repeated the substance of their conversation.

Mohun knit his brows; then burst into a laugh.

"Well!" he said, "so those two amiable characters are still bent on making mince-meat of me, are they? Did you ever hear any thing like it? They are perfect tigers, thirsting for blood!"

"Nothing more nor less," I said; "the whole thing is like a romance."

"Is it not?"

"A perfect labyrinth."

"The very word!"

"And I have not a trace of a key."

Mohun looked at me for some moments in silence. He was evidently hesitating; and letting his eyes fall, played with the hilt of his sword.

Then he suddenly looked up.

"I have a confidence to make you, Surry," he said, "and would like to make it this very day. But I cannot. You have no doubt divined that Colonel Darke is my bitter enemy — that his companion is no less, even more, bitter — and some day I will tell you what all that means. My life has been a strange one. As was said of Randolph of Roanoke's, 'the fictions of romance cannot surpass it.' These two persons alluded to it — I understand more than you possibly can — but I do *not* understand the allusions made to

General Davenant. I am *not* the suitor of his daughter—or of any one. I am not in love—I do not intend to be—to be frank with you, friend, I have little confidence in women—and you no doubt comprehend that this strange one whom you have thrice met, on the Rappahannock, in Pennsylvania, and near Buckland, is the cause."

"She seems to be a perfect viper."

"Is she not? You would say so, more than ever, if I told you what took place at Warrenton."

And again Mohun's brows were knit together. Then his bitter expression changed to laughter.

"What took place at Warrenton!" I said, looking at him intently.

"Exactly, my dear friend—it was a real comedy. Only a poignard played a prominent part in the affair, and you know poignards belong exclusively to tragedy."

Mohun uttered these words with his old reckless satire. A sort of grim and biting humor was plain in his accents.

"A poniard—a tragedy—tell me about it, Mohun," I said.

He hesitated a moment. "Well, I will do so," he said, at length. "It will amuse you, my guest, while dinner is getting ready."

"I am listening."

"Well, to go back. You remember my fight with Colonel Darke near Buckland?"

"Certainly; and I was sure that you had killed each other."

"You were mistaken. He is not dead, and you see I am not. He was wounded in the throat, but my sabre missed the artery, and he was taken to a house near at hand, and thence to hospital, where he recovered. My own wound was a bullet through the chest; and this gave me so much agony that I could not be carried in my ambulance farther than Warrenton, where I was left with some friends who took good care of me. Meanwhile, General Meade had again advanced and occupied the place—I was discovered, and removed as soon as possible to the Federal hospital, where they could have me under guard. Faith! they are smart people—our friends the Yankees! They are convinced that 'every little helps,' and they had no idea of allowing that tremendous Southern paladin, Colonel Mohun, to escape! So I was sent to hospital. The removal caused a return of fever—I was within an inch of the grave—and this brings me to the circumstance that I wish to relate for your amusement.

"For some days after my removal to the Federal hospital, I was delirious, but am now convinced that much which I then took for the wanderings of a fevered brain, was real.

"I used to lie awake a great deal, and one gloomy night I saw, or dreamed I saw, as I then supposed, *that woman* enter my ward, in company with the surgeon. She bent over me, glared upon me with those dark eyes, which you no doubt remember, and then drawing back said to the surgeon:—

"'Will he live?'

"'Impossible to say, madam,' was the reply. 'The ball passed through his breast, and although these wounds are almost always mortal, men do now and then recover from them.'

"'Will this one?'

"'I cannot tell you, madam, his constitution seems powerful.'

"I saw her turn as he spoke, and fix those glaring eyes on me again. They were enough to burn a hole in you, Surry, and made me feel for some weapon. But there was none—and the scene here terminated—both retired. The next night, however, it was renewed. This time the surgeon felt my pulse, touched my forehead, placed his ear to my breast to listen to the action of the heart, and rising up said, in reply to madam's earnest glance of inquiry:—

"'Yes, I am sure he will live. You can give yourself no further anxiety about your cousin, madam.'

"*Her cousin!* That was not bad, you see. She had gained access, as I ascertained from some words of their conversation, by representing herself as my cousin. I was a member of her family who had 'gone astray' and embraced the cause of the rebellion, but was still dear to her! Womanly heart! clinging affection! not even the sin of the prodigal cousin could sever the tender chord of her love! I had wandered from the right path—fed on husks with the Confederate swine; but I was wounded—had come back; should the fatted calf remain unbutchered, and the loving welcome be withheld?

"'*You can give yourself no further uneasiness about your cousin, madam!*'

"Such was the assurance of the surgeon, and he turned away to other patients, of whom there were, however, very few in the hospital, and none near me. As he turned his back, madam looked at me. Her face was really diabolical, and I thought at the moment that she was a nightmare—that I *dreamed her!* Closing my eyes to shut out the vision, I kept them thus shut for some moments. When I reopened them she was gone.

"Well, the surgeon's predictions did not seem likely to be verified. My fever returned. Throughout the succeeding day I turned and tossed on my couch; as night came, I had some hideous dreams. A storm was raging without, and the rain falling in torrents. The building trembled, the windows rattled—it was a night of nights for some devil's work; and I remember laughing in my fever, and muttering, 'Now is the time for delirium, bad dreams, and ugly shapes, to flock around me!'

"I fell into a doze at last, and had, as I thought, a decidedly bad dream—for I felt certain that I was dreaming, and that what I witnessed was the sport of my fancy. What I saw, or seemed to see, was this: the door opened slowly—a head was thrust in, and remained motionless for an instant; then the head moved, a body followed; madam, the lady of the dark eyes, glided stealthily toward my cot. It was enough to make one shudder, Surry, to have seen the stealthy movement of that phantom. I gazed at it through my half-closed eyelids—saw the midnight eyes burning in the white face half covered by a shawl thrown over the head—and, under that covering, the right hand of the phantom grasped something which I could not make out.

"In three quick steps *it* was beside me. I say *it*, for the figure resembled that of a ghost, or some horrible *thing*. From the eyes two flames seemed to dart, the lips opened, and I heard, in a low mutter:—

"'Ah! he is going to recover, then!'

"As the words left the phantom's lips, it reached my cot at a bound; something gleamed aloft, and I started back only in time to avoid the sharp point of a poniard, which grazed my head and nearly buried itself in the pillow on which I lay.

"Well, I started up and endeavored to seize my assailant; but she suddenly broke away from me, still clutching her weapon. Her clothing was torn from her person—she recoiled toward the door—and I leaped from my couch to rush after and arrest her. I had not the strength to do so, however. I had scarcely taken three steps when I began to stagger.

"'Murderess!' I exclaimed, extending my arms to arrest her flight.

"It was useless. A few feet further I reeled—my head seemed turning round—and again shouting 'Murderess!' I fell at full length on the floor, at the moment when the woman disappeared.

"That was curious, was it not? It would have been a tragical dream—it was more tragical in being no dream at all, but a reality. What had taken place was simple, and easy to understand. That woman had come thither, on this stormy night, to murder me; and she had very nearly succeeded. Had she found me asleep, I should never have waked. Fortunately, I was awake. Some noise frightened her, and she disappeared. A moment afterward one of the nurses came, and finally the surgeon.

"When I told him what had taken place, he laughed.

"'Well, colonel, go back to bed,' he said, 'such dreams retard your recovery more than every thing else.'

"I obeyed, without taking the trouble to contradict him. My breast was bleeding again, and I did not get over the excitement for some days. The phantom did not return. I slowly recovered, and was taken in due time to Fort Delaware — the rest you know.

"I forgot to tell you one thing. The surgeon almost persuaded me that I had been the victim of nightmare. Unfortunately, however, for the theory of the worthy, I found a deep hole in my pillow, where the poniard had entered.

"So you see it was madam, and not her ghost, who had done me the honor of a visit, Surry."

XXIII
THE GRAVE OF ACHMED

An hour afterward I had dined with Mohun at his head-quarters, in the woods; mounted our horses; and were making our way toward the Rapidan to inspect the pickets.

This consumed two hours. We found nothing stirring. As sunset approached, we retraced our steps toward Chancellorsville. I had accepted Mohun's invitation to spend the night with him.

As I rode on, the country seemed strangely familiar. All at once I recognized here a tree, there a stump—we were passing over the road which I had followed first in April, 1861, and again in August, 1862, when I came so unexpectedly upon Fenwick, and heard his singular revelation.

We had been speaking of Mordaunt, to whose brigade Mohun's regiment belonged, and the young officer had grown enthusiastic, extolling Mordaunt as 'one of the greatest soldiers of the army, under whom it was an honor to serve.'

"Well," I said, "there is a spot near here which he knows well, and where a strange scene passed on a night of May, 1863."

"Ah! you know the country, then?" said Mohun.

"Perfectly well."

"What are you looking at?"

"That hill yonder, shut in by a thicket. There is a house there."

And I spurred on, followed by Mohun. In five minutes we reached the brush-fence; our horses easily cleared it, and we rode up the hill toward the desolate-looking mansion.

I surveyed it intently. It was unchanged, save that the porch seemed rotting away, and the window-shutters about to fall—that on the window to the right hung by a single hinge. It was the one through which I had looked in August, 1862. There was the same door through which I had burst in upon Fenwick and his companion.

I dismounted, threw my bridle over a stunted shrub, and approached the house. Suddenly I stopped.

At ten paces from me, in a little group of cedars, a man was kneeling on a grave, covered with tangled grass. At the rattle of my sabre he rose, turned round — it was Mordaunt.

In a moment we had exchanged a pressure of the hand; and then turning to the grave: —

"That is the last resting-place of poor Achmed," he said; adding, in his deep, grave voice: —

"You know how he loved me, Surry."

"And how you loved *him*, Mordaunt. I can understand your presence at his grave, my dear friend."

Mordaunt sighed, then saluted Mohun, who approached.

"This spot," he said, "is well known to Colonel Surry and myself, Mohun."

Then turning to me, he added: —

"I found a melancholy spectacle awaiting me here."

"Other than Achmed's grave?"

"Yes; come, and I will show you."

And he led the way into the house. As I entered the squalid and miserable mansion, the sight which greeted me made me recoil.

On a wretched bed lay the corpse of a woman; and at a glance, I recognized the woman Parkins, who had played so tragic a part in the history of Mordaunt. The face was hideously attenuated; the eyes were open and staring; the lower jaw had fallen. In the rigid and bony hand was a dry and musty crust of bread.

"She must have starved to death here," said Mordaunt, gazing at the corpse. And, approaching it, he took the crust from the fingers. As he did so, the teeth seemed grinning at him.

"Poor creature!" he said; "this crust was probably all that remained to her of the price of her many crimes! I pardon her, and will have her buried!"

As Mordaunt turned away, I saw him look at the floor.

"There is Achmed's blood," he said, pointing to a stain on the plank; "and the other is the blood of Fenwick, who was buried near his victim."

"I remember," I murmured. And letting my chin fall upon my breast, I returned in thought to the strange scene which the spot recalled so vividly.

"There is but one other actor in that drama of whom I know nothing, Mordaunt!"

"You mean—"

"Violet Grafton."

Mordaunt raised his head quickly. His eyes glowed with a serene sweetness.

"She is my wife," he said; "the joy and sunlight of my life! I no longer read *Les Misérables*, and sneer at my species—I no longer scowl, Surry, and try to rush against the bullet that is to end me. God has rescued a lost life in sending me one of his angels; and it was she who made me promise to come hither and pray on the grave of our dear Achmed!"

Mordaunt turned toward the door as he spoke, and inviting me to ride with him, left the mansion. As I had agreed to stay with Mohun, I was obliged to decline.

Five minutes afterward he had mounted, and with a salute, the tall form disappeared in the forest.

We set out in turn, and were soon at Mohun's bivouac.

XXIV
A NIGHT BIRD

I shared Mohun's blankets, and was waked by the sun shining in my face.

My companion had disappeared, but I had scarcely risen when he was seen approaching at full gallop.

Throwing himself from his horse, he grasped my hand, his face beaming.

"All right, Surry!" he exclaimed; "I have seen Mordaunt; my command is all arranged; I have four superb regiments; and they are already in the saddle."

"I congratulate you, my dear general! Make good use of them—and I think you are going to have the opportunity at once."

"You are right—the enemy's cavalry are drawn up on the north bank of the river."

"Any firing in front?"

"They are feeling at all the fords."

"Are you going there?"

"At once."

"I will go with you."

And I mounted my horse which stood saddled near by.

Swallowing some mouthfuls of bread and beef as we rode on, we soon reached Mohun's command. It consisted of four regiments, drawn up in column, ready to move—and at sight of the young *sabreur*, the men raised a shout.

Mohun saluted with drawn sabre, and galloped to the front.

A moment afterward the bugle sounded, and the column advanced toward the Rapidan, within a mile of which it halted—Mohun and myself riding forward to reconnoitre at Germanna Ford, directly in our front.

The pickets were engaged, firing at each other across the river. On the northern bank were seen long columns of Federal cavalry, drawn up as though about to cross.

I rode with Mohun to the summit of the lofty hill near the ford, and here, seated on his horse beneath a tree, we found Mordaunt. It was hard to realize that, on the evening before, I had seen this stern and martial figure, kneeling in prayer upon a grave—had heard the brief deep voice grow musical when he spoke of his wife. But habit is every thing. On the field, Mordaunt was the soldier, and nothing but the soldier.

"You see," he said, "the game is about to open," pointing to the Federal cavalry. "You remember this spot, and that hill yonder, I think."

"Yes," I replied, "and your charge there when we captured their artillery in August, '62."

As he spoke, a dull firing, which we had heard for some moments from the direction of Ely's Ford, grew more rapid. Five minutes afterward, an officer was seen approaching from the side of the firing, at full speed. When he was within a hundred yards, I recognized Harry Mordaunt. He was unchanged; his eyes still sparkled, his plume floated, his lips were smiling.

He greeted me warmly, and then turned to General Mordaunt, and reported the enemy attempting to cross at Ely's.

"I will go, then; will you ride with me, Surry? Keep a good look out here, Mohun."

I accepted Mordaunt's invitation, and in a moment we were galloping, accompanied by Harry, toward Ely's.

"Glad to see you again, colonel!" exclaimed the young man, in his gay voice, "you remind me of old times, and a young lady was speaking of you lately."

"A certain Miss Fitzhugh, I will wager!"

"There's no such person, colonel."

"Ah! you are married!"

"Last spring; but I might as well be single! That's the worst of this foolishness,—I wish they would stop it! I don't mind hard tack, or fighting, or sleeping in the rain; what I do mind is never being able to go home! I wish old Grant would go home and see *his* wife, and let me go and see *mine*! We could then come back, and blaze away at each other with some satisfaction!"

Harry was chattering all the way, and I encouraged him to talk; his gay voice was delightful. We talked of a thousand things, but they interested me more than they would interest the reader, and I pass on to matters more important.

Pushing rapidly toward Ely's, we soon arrived, and found the enemy making a heavy demonstration there. It lasted throughout the day, and I remained to witness the result. At sunset, however, the firing stopped, and, declining Mordaunt's invitation to share the blankets of his bivouac, I set out on my way back to Orange.

Night came almost before I was aware of it, and found me following the Brock road to get on the Orange plank road.

Do you know the Brock road, reader? and have you ever ridden over it on a lowering night? If so, you have experienced a peculiar sensation. It is impossible to imagine any thing more lugubrious than these strange thickets. In their depths the owl hoots, and the whippoorwill cries; the stunted trees, with their gnarled branches, are like fiends reaching out spectral arms to seize the wayfarer by the hair. Desolation reigns there, and you unconsciously place your hand on your pistol as you ride along, to be ready for some mysterious and unseen enemy.

At least, I did so on that night. I had now penetrated some distance, and had come near the lonely house where so many singular events had occurred.

I turned my head and glanced over my shoulder, when, to my surprise, I saw a light glimmering through the window. What was its origin? The house was certainly uninhabited, even by the dead—for Mordaunt had informed me that a detail had, that morning, buried the corpse.

There was but one means of solving the mystery, and I leaped the fence, riding straight toward the house; soon reaching it, I dismounted and threw open the door.

What should greet my eyes, but the respectable figure of Mr. Nighthawk, seated before a cheerful blaze, and calmly smoking his pipe!

XXV
THE APPOINTMENT

As I entered, Mr. Nighthawk rose politely, without exhibiting the least mark of astonishment.

"Good evening, colonel," he said, smiling, "I am glad to see you."

"And I, never more surprised to see any one than you, here, Nighthawk!"

"Why so, colonel?"

I could not help laughing at his air of mild inquiry.

"Did I not leave you at our head-quarters?"

"That was two days ago, colonel."

"And this is your residence, perhaps?"

"I have no residence, colonel; but am here, temporarily, on a little matter of business."

"Ah! a matter of business!"

"I think it might be called so, colonel."

"Which it would be indiscreet to reveal to me, however. That is a pity, for I am terribly curious, my dear Nighthawk!"

Nighthawk looked at me benignly, with a philanthropic smile.

"I have not the least objection to informing you, colonel. You are a gentleman of discretion, and have another claim on my respect."

"What is that?"

"You are a friend of Colonel Mohun's."

"A very warm one."

"Then you can command me; and I will tell you at once that I am awaiting the advance of General Grant."

"Ah! Now I begin to understand."

"I was sure you would at the first word I uttered, colonel. General Grant will cross the Rapidan to-night—by to-morrow evening his whole force will probably be over—and I expect to procure some important information before I return to General Stuart. To you I am Mr. Nighthawk, an humble friend of the cause, employed in secret business,—to General Grant I shall be an honest farmer, of Union opinions, who has suffered from the depredations of his troops, and goes to head-quarters for redress. You see they have already stripped me of every thing," continued Mr. Nighthawk, waving his arm and smiling; "not a cow, a hog, a mule, or a mouthful of food has been left me. They have destroyed the very furniture of my modest dwelling, and I am cast, a mere pauper, on the cold charities of the world!"

Mr. Nighthawk had ceased smiling, and looked grave; while it was I who burst into laughter. His eyes were raised toward heaven, with an expression of meek resignation; he spread out both hands with the eloquence of Mr. Pecksniff; and presented the appearance of a virtuous citizen accepting meekly the most trying misfortunes.

When I had ceased laughing, I said:—

"I congratulate you on your histrionic abilities, Nighthawk. They deserve to be crowned with success. But how did you discover this house?"

"I was acquainted with its former owner, Mrs. Parkins. She was a sister of a friend of mine, whom I think you have seen, colonel."

"What friend?"

"His name is Swartz, colonel."

"Not the Federal spy?"

"The same, colonel."

"Whom we saw last in the house between Carlisle and Gettysburg?"

"I saw him the other day," returned Mr. Nighthawk, smiling sweetly.

"Is it possible!"

"Near Culpeper Court-House, colonel. And, to let you into a little secret, I expect to see him to-night."

I looked at the speaker with bewilderment.

"That man will be here!"

"If he keeps his appointment, colonel."

"You have an appointment?"

"Yes, colonel."

"In this house?"

"To-night."

"With what object, in heaven's name!"

Nighthawk hesitated for some moments before replying.

"The fact is, colonel," he said, "that I inadvertently mentioned my appointment with Swartz without reflecting how singular it must appear to you, unless I gave you some explanation. But I am quite at my ease with you—you are a friend of Colonel Mohun's—and I will explain, as much of my business as propriety will permit. To be brief, I am anxious to procure a certain document in Swartz's possession."

"A certain document?" I said, looking intently at the speaker.

"Exactly, colonel."

"Which Swartz has?"

"Precisely, colonel."

"And which he stole from the papers of Colonel Darke on the night of Mohun's combat with Darke, in the house near Carlisle?"

Mr. Nighthawk looked keenly at me, in turn.

"Ah! you know that!" he said, quickly.

"I saw him steal it, through the window, while the woman's back was turned."

"I am deeply indebted to you, colonel," said Mr. Nighthawk, gravely, "for informing me of this fact, which, I assure you, is important. Swartz swore to me that he had the paper, and had procured it in that manner, but I doubted seriously whether he was not deceiving me. He is a *very* consummate rascal, knows the value of that document, and my appointment with him to-night is with an eye to its purchase from him."

"Do you think he will come?"

"I think so. He would sell his soul for gold."

"And that woman? he seems to be her friend."

"He would sell *her* for *silver!*"

After uttering which *bon mot*, Mr. Nighthawk smiled.

This man puzzled me beyond expression. His stealthy movements were strange enough—it was singular to meet him in this lonely house—but more singular still was the business which had brought him. What was that paper? Why did Nighthawk wish to secure it? I gave up the inquiry in despair.

"Well," I said, "I will not remain longer; I might scare off your friend, and to eaves-drop is out of the question, even if you were willing that I should be present."

"In fact, colonel, I shall probably discuss some very private matters with my friend Swartz, so that — "

"You prefer I should go."

Mr. Nighthawk smiled; he was too polite to say "yes."

"You are not afraid to meet your friend in this lonely place?" I said, rising.

"Not at all, colonel."

"You are armed?"

Mr. Nighthawk opened his coat, and showed me a brace of revolvers.

"I have these; but they are unnecessary, colonel."

"Unnecessary?"

"I have an understanding with Swartz, and he with me."

"What is that?"

"That we shall not employ the carnal weapon; only destroy each other by superior generalship."

"You speak in enigmas, Nighthawk!"

"And yet, my meaning is very simple. If I can have Swartz arrested and hung, or he me, it is all fair. But we have agreed not to fight."

"So, if you caught him to-night, you could have him hung as a spy?"

"Yes, colonel; but nothing would induce me to betray him."

"Ah!"

"I have given him my parol, that he shall have safe conduct!"

I laughed, bade Nighthawk good-bye, and left him smiling as I had found him. In ten minutes I was again on the Brock road, riding on through the darkness, between the impenetrable thickets.

XXVI
STUART SINGS

My reflections were by no means gay. The scenes at the lonely house had not been cheerful and mirth-inspiring.

That grinning corpse, with the crust of bread in the bony fingers; that stain of blood on the floor; the grave of Achmed; lastly, the appointment of the mysterious Nighthawk with the Federal spy; all were fantastic and lugubrious.

Who was Nighthawk, and what was his connection with Mohun? Who was Mohun, and what had been his previous history? Who was this youth of unbounded wealth, as Nighthawk had intimated, in whose life personages supposed to be dead, but still alive, had figured?

"Decidedly, Mohun and Nighthawk are two enigmas!" I muttered, "and I give the affair up."

With which words I spurred on, and soon debouched on the Orange plank road, leading toward Mine Run.

As I entered it, I heard hoof-strokes on the resounding boards, and a company of horsemen cantered toward me through the darkness. As they came, I heard a gay voice singing the lines: —

"I wake up in the morning,

I wake up in the morning,

I wake up in the morning,

Before the break o' day!"

There was no mistaking that gay sound. It was Stuart, riding at the head of his staff and couriers.

In a moment he had come up, and promptly halted me.

"Ah! that's you, Surry!" he exclaimed with a laugh, "wandering about here in the Wilderness! What news?"

I reported the state of things in front, and Stuart exclaimed: —

"All right; we are ready for them! Coon Hollow is evacuated—head-quarters are in the saddle! Hear that whippoorwill! It is a good omen. Whip 'em well! Whip 'em well!—and we'll do it too!"{1} Stuart laughed, and began to sing—

"*Never mind the weather*

But get over double trouble!

We are bound for the Happy land of Lincoln!"

{Footnote 1: His words.}

As the martial voice rang through the shadowy thickets, I thought, "How fortunate it is that the grave people are not here to witness this singular 'want of dignity' in the great commander of Lee's cavalry!"

Those "grave people" would certainly have rolled their eyes, and groaned, "Oh! how undignified!" Was not the occasion solemn? Was it not sinful to laugh and sing? No, messieurs! It was right; and much better than rolling the eyes, and staying at home and groaning! Stuart was going to fight hard—meanwhile he sang gayly. Heaven had given him animal spirits, and he laughed in the face of danger. He laughed and sang on this night when he was going to clash against Grant, as he had laughed and sung when he had clashed against Hooker—when his proud plume floated in front of Jackson's veterans, and he led them over the breastworks at Chancellorsville, singing, "Old Joe Hooker, will you come out of the Wilderness!"

Stuart cantered on: we turned into the Brock road, and I found myself retracing my steps toward the Rapidan.

As I passed near the lonely house, I cast a glance toward the glimmering light. Had Nighthawk's friend arrived?

We soon reached Ely's Ford, and I conducted Stuart to Mordaunt's bivouac, which I had left at dusk. He had just wrapped his cloak around him, and laid down under a tree, ready to mount at a moment's warning.

"What news, Mordaunt?" said Stuart, grasping his hand.

"Some fighting this evening, but it ceased about nightfall, general."

Stuart looked toward the river, and listened attentively.

"I hear nothing stirring."

And passing his hand through his beard he muttered half to himself:—

"I wonder if Grant can have made any change in his programme?"

"The order at least was explicit—that brought by Nighthawk," I said.

Stuart turned toward me suddenly.

"I wonder where he could be found? If I knew, I would send him over the river to-night, to bring me a reliable report of every thing."

I drew the general aside.

"I can tell you where to find Nighthawk."

"Where."

"Shall I bring him?"

"Like lightning, Surry! I wish to dispatch him at once!"

Without reply I wheeled my horse, and went back rapidly toward the house in the Wilderness. I soon reached the spot, rode to the window, and called to Nighthawk, who came out promptly at my call.

"Your friend has not arrived?" I said.

"He will not come till midnight, colonel."

"When, I am afraid, he will not see you, Nighthawk—you are wanted."

And I explained my errand. Nighthawk sighed—it was easy to see that he was much disappointed.

"Well, colonel," he said, in a resigned tone, "I must give up my private business—duty calls. I will be ready in a moment."

And disappearing, he put out the light—issued forth in rear of the house—mounted a horse concealed in the bushes—and rejoined me in front.

"Swartz will not know what to think," he said, as we rode rapidly toward the river; "he knows I am the soul of punctuality, and this failure to keep my appointment will much distress him."

"Distress him, Nighthawk?"

"He will think some harm has happened to me."

And Mr. Nighthawk smiled so sadly, that I could not refrain from laughter.

We soon reached the spot where Stuart awaited us. At sight of Nighthawk he uttered an exclamation of satisfaction, and explained in brief words his wishes.

"That will be easy, general," said Nighthawk.

"Can you procure a Federal uniform?"

"I always travel with one, general."

And Mr. Nighthawk unstrapped the bundle behind his saddle, drawing forth a blue coat and trousers, which in five minutes had replaced his black clothes. Before us stood one of the "blue birds." Nighthawk was an unmistakable "Yankee."

Stuart gave him a few additional instructions, and having listened with the air of a man who is engraving the words he hears upon his memory, Nighthawk disappeared in the darkness, toward the private crossing, where he intended to pass the river.

Half an hour afterward, Stuart was riding toward Germanna Ford. As we approached, Mohun met us, and reported all quiet.

Stuart then turned back in the direction of Chancellorsville, where Nighthawk was to report to him, before daylight, if possible.

XXVII
MOHUN RIDES

I lingered behind a moment to exchange a few words with Mohun. Something told me that he was intimately connected with the business which had occasioned the appointment between Nighthawk and Swartz—and at the first words which I uttered, I saw that I was not mistaken.

Mohun raised his head quickly, listened with the closest attention, and when I had informed him of every thing, said abruptly:—

"Well, I'll keep Nighthawk's appointment for him!"

"You!" I said.

"Yes, my dear Surry—this is a matter of more importance than you think. The business will not take long—the enemy will not be moving before daylight—and you said, I think, that the appointment was for midnight?"

"Yes."

Mohun drew out his watch; scratched a match which he drew from a small metal case.

"Just eleven," he said; "there is time to arrive before midnight, if we ride well—will you show me the way?"

I saw that he was bent on his scheme, and said no more. In a few moments we were in the saddle, and riding at full speed toward the house where the meeting was to take place.

Mohun rode like the wild huntsman, and mile after mile disappeared behind us—flitting away beneath the rapid hoofs of our horses. During the whole ride he scarcely opened his lips. He seemed to be reflecting deeply, and to scarcely realize my presence.

At last we turned into the Brock road, and were soon near the lonely house.

"We have arrived," I said, leaping the brushwood fence. And we galloped up the knoll toward the house, which was as dark and silent as the grave.

Dismounting and concealing our horses in the bushes, we opened the door. Mohun again had recourse to his match-case, and lit the candle left by Nighthawk on an old pine table, and glanced at his watch.

"Midnight exactly!" he said; "we have made a good ride of it, Surry."

"Yes; and now that I have piloted you safely, Mohun, I will discreetly retire."

"Why not remain, if you think it will amuse you, my dear friend?"

"But you are going to discuss your private affairs, are you not?"

"They are not private from you, since I have promised to relate my whole life to you."

"Then I remain; but do you think our friend will keep his appointment?"

"There he is," said Mohun, as hoof-strokes were heard without. "He is punctual."

XXVIII
THE SPY

A moment afterward we heard the new-comer dismount. Then his steps were heard on the small porch. All at once his figure appeared in the doorway.

It was Swartz. The fat person, the small eyes, the immense double chin, and the chubby fingers covered with pinchbeck rings, were unmistakable.

He was clad in citizens' clothes, and covered with dust as from a long ride.

Mohun rose.

"Come in, my dear Mr. Swartz," he said coolly; "you see we await you."

The spy recoiled. It was plain that he was astonished beyond measure at seeing us. He threw a glance behind him in the direction of his horse, and seemed about to fly.

Mohun quietly drew his revolver, and cocked it.

"Fear nothing, my dear sir," he said, "and, above all, do not attempt to escape."

Swartz hesitated, and cast an uneasy glance upon the weapon.

"Does the sight of this little instrument annoy you?" said Mohun, laughing. "It shall not be guilty of that impoliteness, Mr. Swartz."

And he uncocked the weapon, and replaced it in its holster.

"Now," he continued, "sit down, and let us talk."

Swartz obeyed. Before Mohun's penetrating glance, his own sank. He took his seat in a broken-backed chair; drew forth a huge red bandanna handkerchief; wiped his forehead; and said quietly:—

"I expected to meet a friend here to-night, gentlemen, instead of—"

"Enemies?" interrupted Mohun. "We are such, it is true, my dear sir, but you are quite safe. Your friend Nighthawk is called away; he is even ignorant of our presence here."

"But meeting him would have been different, gentlemen. I had his safe conduct!"

"You shall have it from me."

"May I ask from whom?" said Swartz.

"From General Mohun, of the Confederate army."

Swartz smiled this time; then making a grotesque bow, he replied: —

"I knew you very well, general — that is why I am so much at my ease. I am pleased to hear that you are promoted. When I last saw you, you were only a colonel, but I was certain that you would soon be promoted or killed."

There was a queer accent of politeness in the voice of the speaker. He did not seem to have uttered these words in order to flatter his listener, but to express his real sentiment. He was evidently a character.

"Good!" said Mohun, with his habitual accent of satire. "These little compliments are charming. But I am in haste to-night — let us come to business, my dear sir. I came hither to ask you some questions, and to these I expect plain replies."

Swartz looked at the speaker intently, but without suspicion. His glance, on the contrary, had in it something strangely open and unreserved.

"I will reply to all your questions, general," he said, "and reply truthfully. I have long expected this interview, and will even say that I wished it. You look on me as a Yankee spy, and will have but little confidence in what I say. Nevertheless, I am going to tell you the whole truth about every thing. Ask your questions, general, I will answer them."

Mohun was leaning one elbow on the broken table. His glance, calm and yet fiery, seemed bent on penetrating to the most secret recess of the spy's heart.

"Well," he said, "now that we begin to understand each other, let us come to the point at once. Where were you on the morning of the thirteenth of December, 1856?"

Swartz replied without hesitation: —

"On the bank of Nottoway River, in Dinwiddie, Virginia, and bound for Petersburg."

"The object of your journey?"

"To sell dried fruits and winter vegetables."

"Then you travelled in a cart, or a wagon?"

"In a cart, general."

"You reached Petersburg without meeting with any incident on the way?"

"I met with two very curious ones, general. I see you know something about the affair, and are anxious to know every thing. I will tell you the whole truth; but it will be best to let me do it in my own way."

"Do so, then," said Mohun, fixing his eyes more intently upon the spy.

Swartz was silent again for more than a minute, gazing on the floor. Then he raised his head, passed his red handkerchief over his brow, and said:—

"To begin at the beginning, general. At the time you speak of, December, 1856, I was a small landholder in Dinwiddie, and made my living by carting vegetables and garden-truck to Petersburg. Well, one morning in winter—you remind me that it was the thirteenth of December,—I set out, as usual, in my cart drawn by an old mule, with a good load on board, to go by way of Monk's Neck. I had not gone two miles, however, when passing through a lonely piece of woods on the bank of the river, I heard a strange cry in the brush. It was the most startling you can think of, and made my heart stop beating. I jumped down from my cart, left it standing in the narrow road, and went to the spot. It was a strange sight I saw. On the bank of the river, I saw a woman lying drenched with water, and half-dead. She was richly dressed, and of very great beauty—but I never saw any human face so pale, or clothes more torn and draggled."

The spy paused. Mohun shaded his eyes from the light, with his hands, and said coolly:—

"Go on."

"Well, general—that was enough to astonish anybody—and what is more astonishing still, I have never to this day discovered the meaning of the woman's being there—for it was plain that she was a lady. She was half-dead with cold, and had cried out in what seemed to be a sort of delirium. When I raised her up, and wrung the wet out of her clothes, she looked at me so strangely that I was frightened. I asked her how she had come there, but she made no reply. Where should I take her? She made no reply to that either. She seemed dumb—out of her wits—and, to make a long story short, I half led and half carried her to the cart in which I put her, making a sort of bed for her of some old bags.

"I set out on my way again, without having the least notion what I should do with her—for she seemed a lady—and only with a sort of idea that her friends might probably pay me for my trouble, some day.

"Well, I went on for a mile or two farther, when a new adventure happened to me. That was stranger still—it was like a story-book; and you will hardly believe me—but as I was going through a piece of woods, following a by-road by which I cut off a mile or more, I heard groans near the road, and once more stopped my cart. Then I listened. I was scared, and began to believe in witchcraft. The groans came from the woods on my left, and there was no doubt about the sound—so, having listened for some time, I mustered courage to go in the direction of the sound. Can you think what I found, general?"

"What?" said Mohun, in the same cool voice; "tell me."

"A man lying in a grave;—a real grave, general—broad and deep—a man with a hole through his breast, and streaming with blood."

"Is it possible?"

And Mohun uttered a laugh.

"Just as I tell you, general—it is the simple, naked truth. When I got to the place, he was struggling to get out of the grave, and his breast was bleeding terribly. I never saw a human being look paler. 'Help!' he cried out, in a suffocated voice like, when he saw me—and as he spoke, he made such a strong effort to rise, that his wound gushed with blood, and he fainted."

"He fainted, did he? And what did you do?" said Mohun.

"I took him up in my arms, general, as I had taken the woman, carried him to my cart, when I bound up his breast in the best way I could, and laid him by the side of the half-drowned lady."

"To get a reward from *his* friends, too, no doubt?"

"Well, general, we must live, you know. And did I not deserve something for being so scared—and for the use of my mule?"

"Certainly you did. Is not the laborer worthy of his hire? But go on, sir—your tale is interesting."

"Tale, general? It is the truth—on the word of Swartz!"

"I no longer doubt now, if I did before," said Mohun; "but tell me the end of your adventure."

"I can do that in a few words, general. I whipped up my old mule, and went on through the woods, thinking what I had best do with the man and the woman I had saved, I could take them to Petersburg, and tell my story to the mayor or some good citizen, who would see that they were taken care of. But as soon as I said 'mayor' to myself, I thought 'he is the chief of police.' *Police!* — that is one of the ugliest words in the language, general! Some people shiver, and their flesh crawls, when you cut a cork, or scratch on a window pane — well, it is strange, but I have always felt in that way when I heard, or thought of, the word, *police!* And here I was going to have dealings with the said *police!* I was going to say 'I found these people on the Nottoway — one half-drowned, and the other in a newly dug grave!' No, I thank you! We never know what our characters will stand, and I was by no means certain that mine would stand that! Then the reward — I wished to have my lady and gentleman under my eye. So, after thinking over the matter for some miles, I determined to leave them with a crony of mine near Monk's Neck, named Alibi, who would take care of them and say nothing. Well, I did so, and went on to Petersburg, where I sold my truck. When I got back they were in bed, and on my next visit they were at the point of death. About that time I was taken sick, and was laid up for more than three months. When I went to see my birds at Monk's Neck, they had flown!"

"Without leaving you their adieux?"

"No, they were at least polite. They left me a roll of bank notes — more than I thought they had about them."

"You had searched them, of course, when they were lying in your cart," said Mohun.

Swartz smiled.

"I acknowledge it, general — I forgot to mention the fact. I had found only a small amount in the gentleman's pocket-book — nothing on the lady — and I never could understand where he or she had concealed about their persons such a considerable amount of money — though I suppose, in a secret pocket."

Mohun nodded.

"That is often done — well, that was the last of them?"

Swartz smiled, and glanced at Mohun.

"What is the use of any concealment, my dear Mr. Swartz?" said the latter. "You may as well tell the whole story, as you have gone this far."

"You are right, general, and I will finish. The war broke out, and I sold my truck patch, and invested in a better business—that is, running the blockade across the Potomac, and smuggling in goods for the Richmond market. On one of these trips, I met, plump, in the streets of Washington, no less a person than the lady whom I had rescued. She was richly dressed, and far more beautiful, but there was no mistaking her. I spoke to her; she recognized me, took me to her house, and here I found *the gentleman*, dressed in a fine new uniform. He was changed too—his wound had long healed, he was stout and strong, but I knew him, too, at a glance. Well, I spent the evening, and when I left the house had accepted an offer made me to combine a new business with that of blockade runner."

"That of spy, you mean?" said Mohun.

Swartz smiled.

"You speak plainly, general. We call ourselves 'secret agents'—but either word expresses the idea!"

XXIX
THE PAPER

Mohun raised his head, and looked Swartz full in the face. His glance had grown, if possible, more penetrating than before, and a grim smile responded to the unctuous expression of the spy.

"Well, my dear Mr. Swartz," he said coolly, "that is a curious history. Others might doubt its accuracy, but I give you my word that I do not! I did well to let you proceed in your own way, instead of questioning you—but I have not yet done; and this time shall return to the method of interrogation."

"At your orders, general," said Swartz, whose quick glance showed that he was on his guard, and foresaw what was coming.

Mohun leaned toward the spy.

"Let us proceed to 'call names,'" he said. "The man you rescued from the grave was Colonel Darke?"

"Exactly, general."

"Is that his real name, or a false one?"

Swartz hesitated; then replied:—

"A false one."

"His real name?"

"Mortimer."

"And the lady is—?"

"His wife, general."

"Good," said Mohun, "you are well informed, I see, my dear Mr. Swartz; and it is a pleasure to converse with a gentleman who knows so much, and knows it so accurately."

"You flatter my pride, general!"

"I do you justice—but to the point. Your story was cut off in the middle. After the interview in Washington, you continued to see Colonel Darke and his wife?"

"I saw them frequently, general."

"In the army—and at their home, both?"

"Yes, general."

"Where did they live?"

"Near Carlisle, Pennsylvania."

"Where you were on a visit, just before the battle of Gettysburg?"

"Yes, general."

"Very good!"

And rising quickly, Mohun confronted the spy, who drew back unconsciously.

"Where is the paper that you stole from the woman that night?" he said.

Swartz was unable to sustain the fiery glance directed toward him by Mohun.

"Then Nighthawk has told you all!" he exclaimed.

"Colonel Surry saw you hide the paper."

Swartz looked suddenly toward me—his smiles had all vanished.

"The paper! give me the paper!" exclaimed Mohun; "you shall have gold for it!"

"I have left it in Culpeper, general."

"Liar!—give me the paper!"

Swartz started to his feet.

Mohun caught at his throat—the spy recoiled—when suddenly a quick firing was heard coming rapidly from the direction of Germanna Ford.

"The enemy have crossed, Mohun!" I cried.

Mohun started, and turned his head in the direction of the sound.

"They are advancing!" I said, "but look out!—the spy!—"

Mohun wheeled, drawing his pistol.

Swartz had profited by the moment, when our attention was attracted by the firing, to pass through the door, gain his horse at a bound, and throw himself into the saddle, with an agility that was incredible in one so fat.

At the same moment Mohun's pistol-shot responded, but the bullet whistled harmlessly over the spy's head. In an instant he had disappeared in the woods.

Mohun rushed to his horse, I followed, and we were soon riding at full speed in the direction of the firing.

As we advanced, however, it receded. We pushed on, and reached the bank of the Rapidan just as Mohun's men had driven a party of the enemy over.

It was only a small body, who, crossing at a private ford and surprising the sleepy picket, had raided into the thicket, to retire promptly when they were assailed.

The affair was nothing. Unfortunately, however, it had enabled the Federal spy to elude us.

Swartz had disappeared like a bird of the night; and all pursuit of him in such a wilderness was impossible.

An hour afterward, I had rejoined Stuart.

XXX
GRANT STRIKES HIS FIRST BLOW

Such were the singular scenes which I witnessed, amid the shadows of the Spottsylvania Wilderness, in the first days of May, 1864.

The narrative has brought the reader now to an hour past midnight on the third of May.

An hour before—that is to say, at midnight precisely—the Federal forces began to move: at six in the morning, they had massed on the north bank of the Rapidan; and as the sun rose above the Wilderness, the blue columns began to cross the river.

General Grant, at the head of his army of 140,000 men, had set forth on his great advance toward Richmond—that advance so often tried, so often defeated, but which now seemed, from the very nature of things, to be destined to succeed.

Any other hypothesis seemed absurd. What could 50,000 do against nearly thrice their number? What could arrest the immense machine rolling forward to crush the Confederacy? A glance at Grant's splendid array was enough to make the stoutest heart sink. On this 4th day of May, 1864, he was crossing the Rapidan with what resembled a countless host. Heavy masses of blue infantry, with glittering bayonets—huge parks of rifled artillery, with their swarming cannoneers—long columns of horsemen, armed with sabre and repeating carbines, made the earth shake, and the woods echo with their heavy and continuous tramp, mingled with the roll of wheels.

In front of them, a little army of gaunt and ragged men, looked on and waited, without resisting their advance. What did that waiting mean? Did they intend to dispute the passage of that multitude toward Richmond? It seemed incredible, but that was exactly the intention of Lee.

It is now known that General Grant and his officers felicitated themselves greatly on the safe passage of the Rapidan, and were convinced that Lee would hasten to retreat toward the South Anna.

Instead of retreating, Lee advanced and delivered battle.

The first collision took place on the 5th of May, when the Federal army was rapidly massing in the Wilderness.

Ewell had promptly advanced, and about noon was forming line of battle across the old turnpike, when he was vigorously attacked by Warren, and his advance driven back. But the real obstacle was behind. Ewell's rear closed up—he advanced in his turn; assailed Warren with fury; swept him back into the thicket; seized two pieces of his artillery, with about 1,000 prisoners; and for the time completely paralyzed the Federal force in his front.

Such was the first blow struck. It had failed, and General Grant turned his attention to A.P. Hill, who had hastened up, and formed line of battle across the Orange plank road, on Ewell's right.

Hancock directed the assault here, and we have General Lee's testimony to the fact, that the Federal attempts to drive back Hill were "repeated and desperate." All failed. Hill stubbornly held his ground. At night the enemy retired, and gave up all further attempts on that day to make any headway.

Grant had expected to find a mere rear-guard, while Lee's main body was retreating upon Richmond.

He found two full corps in his front; and there was no doubt that a third—that of Longstreet—was approaching.

Lee was evidently going to fight—his aim was, plainly, to shut up Grant in the Wilderness, and drive him back beyond the Rapidan, or destroy him.

XXXI
THE REPORT

It was twilight and the fighting was over.

The two tigers had drawn back, and, crouching down, panted heavily, — resting and gathering new strength for the fiercer conflict of the next day.

From the thickets rose the stifled hum of the two hosts. Only a few shots were heard, now and then, from the skirmishers, and these resembled the last drops of a storm which had spent its fury.

I had been sent by General Stuart with an order to General Hampton, who commanded the cavalry on Hill's right.

Hampton was sitting his horse in a field extending, at this point, between us and the enemy; and, if it were necessary, I would draw his outline. It is not necessary, however; every one is familiar with the figure of this great and faithful soldier, in his old gray coat, plain arms and equipments, on his large and powerful war-horse, — man and horse ready for battle. In the war I saw many great figures, — Hampton's was one of the noblest.

Having delivered my message to General Hampton, who received it with his air of grave, yet cordial courtesy, I turned to shake hands with Captain Church — a thorough-bred young officer, as brave as steel, and one of my best friends — when an exclamation from the staff attracted my attention, and looking round, I saw the cause.

At the opposite extremity of the extensive field, a solitary horseman was seen darting out of the woods occupied by the Federal infantry, and this man was obviously a deserter, making his way into our lines.

At a sign from General Hampton, Captain Church went to meet him, and as my horse was fresh, I accompanied my friend in his ride.

The deserter came on at full speed to meet us, and for a moment, his horse skimmed the dusky expanse like a black-winged bird.{1} Then, all at once, his speed moderated; he approached at a jog-trot, and through the gathering gloom I recognised, above the blue uniform, the sweetly smiling countenance of Nighthawk!

{Footnote 1: This scene is real.}

"Good evening, colonel," said Nighthawk; "I am glad to see you again, and hope you are well."

"So you have turned deserter, Nighthawk?" I said, laughing heartily.

"Precisely, colonel. I could not get off before. Will you inform me where I can find General Stuart?"

"I will take you to him."

And riding back with Captain Church and Nighthawk, I soon found myself again in presence of General Hampton.

A word from me explained the real character of the pseudo-deserter. General Hampton asked a number of questions, Nighthawk replied to them, and then the latter begged me to conduct him to General Stuart. I did so without delay, and we soon reached Stuart's bivouac, where he was talking with his staff by a camp-fire.

At sight of the blue figure he scarcely turned; then suddenly he recognized Nighthawk, and burst into laughter.

"Well, my blue night-bird!" he exclaimed, "here you are at last! What news? Is Grant going to cross the river?"

Nighthawk hung his head, and sighed audibly.

"I could not help it, general."

"Why didn't you come before?"

"It was impossible, general."

Stuart shook his head.

"Strike that word out of your dictionary, my friend."[1]

{Footnote 1: His words.}

"That is good advice, general; but this time they nonplussed me. They blocked every road, and I had to join their army."

"Well, I hope you got the $600 bounty," said Stuart, laughing.

"That was another impossibility, general; but I enjoyed the very best society yonder."

"What society, Nighthawk?"

"That of Grant, Meade, and Sedgwick."

"Ah! my old friend, General Sedgwick! But where are Grant's headquarters, Nighthawk? Tell me every thing!"

"At Old Wilderness Tavern, general."

"And you saw him there?"

"In the midst of his generals,—I was temporarily one of his couriers."

"I understand. Well, their intended movements?"

Nighthawk shook his head.

"I could have foretold you those of to-day, general."

"How?"

"I heard General Meade dictating his order, through the window of his head-quarters, and can repeat it *verbatim*, if you desire."

"By all means, Nighthawk,—it will reveal his programme. But is it possible that you can do so?"

"I can, general; I engraved every word on my memory."

And, fixing his eyes intently upon vacancy, Nighthawk commenced in a low, monotonous voice:—

"The following movements are ordered for the 5th May, 1864. General Sheridan, commanding cavalry corps, will move with Gregg's and Torbert's divisions against the enemy's cavalry, in the direction of Hamilton's Crossing. General Wilson, with the Third cavalry division, will move at 5 A.M., to Craig's meeting-house, on the Catharpin road. He will keep out parties on the Orange Court-House pike, and plank road, the Catharpin road, Pamunkey road, and in the direction of Troyman's store and Andrew's store, or Good Hope church. 2. Major-General Hancock, commanding Second Corps, will move at 5 A.M., to Shady Grove church, and extend his right toward the Fifth Corps at Parker's store. 3. Major-General Warren, commanding Fifth Corps, will move at 5 A.M., to Parker's store, on the Orange Court-House plank road, and extend his right toward the Sixth Corps at Old Wilderness Tavern. 4. Major-General Sedgwick, commanding Sixth Corps, will move to the Old Wilderness Tavern, on the Orange Court-House pike, as soon as the road is clear."

The monotonous voice stopped. I had listened with astonishment, and found it difficult to credit this remarkable feat of memory, though it took place before my eyes, or rather, in my ears.

"It is really wonderful," said Stuart, gravely.

"You see," said Nighthawk, returning to his original voice, so to speak, "you see, general, this would have been of some importance yesterday."

"It is very important now," said Stuart; "it indicates Grant's programme—his wish to get out of the Wilderness. He is at Old Wilderness Tavern?"

"He was this morning, general, with Meade and Sedgwick."

"You were there?"

"I was, general."

"What did you gather, Nighthawk?"

"Little or nothing, general. True, I heard one or two amusing things as I loitered among the couriers near."

"What?"

"General Grant came out talking with Meade, Sedgwick, and Warren. General Meade said, '*They have left a division to fool us here, while they concentrate, and prepare a position toward the North Anna, – and what I want is to prevent these fellows from getting back to Mine Run.*'"[1]

{Footnote 1: His words.}

Stuart laughed.

"Well, 'these fellows' don't appear to be going back. What did Grant say?"

"He smoked, general."

"And did not open his lips?"

"Only once, when General Meade said something about 'manoeuvring.'"

"What did he say?"

"I can give you his words. He took his cigar from his lips – puffed out the smoke – and replied, '*Oh! I never manoeuvre!*'"[1]

{Footnote 1: His words.}

"So much the better," said Stuart: "the general that does not manoeuvre sacrifices his men: and I predict that General Grant will soon alter his programme."

Stuart had ordered his horse to be saddled, and now mounted to go to General Lee's head-quarters.

"By the bye," he said, "did you hear Warren or Sedgwick say any thing, Nighthawk?"

Nighthawk smiled.

"I heard Sedgwick utter a few words, general."

"What?"

"He said to Warren, '*I hear Hood is to take Stuart's place. I am glad of it, for Stuart is the best cavalry officer ever foaled in North America!*'"[1]

{Footnote 1: His words.}

XXXII
THE UNSEEN DEATH

The morning of the 6th of May was ushered in with thunder.

The battle of the preceding day had been a sort of "feeler"—now the real struggle came.

By a curious coincidence, Grant and Lee both began the attack and at the same hour. At five o'clock in the morning the blue and gray ranks rushed together, and opened fire on each other. Or rather, they fired when they heard each others' steps and shouts. You saw little in that jungle.

I have already spoken more than once of this sombre country—a land of undergrowth, thicket, ooze; where sight failed, and attacks had to be made by the needle, the officers advancing in front of the line with drawn— compasses!

The assaults here were worse than night fighting; the combats strange beyond example. Regiments, brigades, and divisions stumbled on each other before they knew it; and each opened fire, guided alone by the crackling of steps in the bushes. There was something weird and lugubrious in such a struggle. It was not a conflict of men, matched against each other in civilized warfare. Two wild animals were prowling, and hunting each other in the jungle. When they heard each others' steps, they sprang and grappled. One fell, the other fell upon him. Then the conqueror rose up and went in pursuit of other game—the dead was lost from all eyes.

In this mournful and desolate country of the Spottsylvania Wilderness, did the bloody campaign of 1864 begin. Here, where the very landscape seemed dolorous; here, in blind wrestle, as at midnight, did 200,000 men, in blue and gray, clutch each other—bloodiest and weirdest of encounters.

War had had nothing like it. Destruction of life had become a science, and was done by the compass.

The Genius of Blood, apparently tired of the old common-place mode of killing, had invented the "Unseen Death," in the depths of the jungle.

On the morning of May 6th, Lee and Grant had grappled, and the battle became general along the entire line of the two armies. In these rapid memoirs I need only outline this bitter struggle—the histories will describe it.

Lee was aiming to get around the enemy's left, and huddle him up in the thicket—but in this he failed.

Just as Longstreet, who had arrived and taken part in the action, was advancing to turn the Federal flank on the Brock road, he was wounded by one of his own men; and the movement was arrested in mid career.

But Lee adhered to his plan. He determined to lead his column in person, and would have done so, but for the remonstrances of his men.

"To the rear!" shouted the troops, as he rode in front of them; "to the rear!"

And he was obliged to obey.

He was not needed.

The gray lines surged forward: the thicket was full of smoke and quick flashes of flame: then the woods took fire, and the scene of carnage had a new and ghastly feature added to it. Dense clouds of smoke rose, blinding and choking the combatants: the flames crackled, soared aloft, and were blown in the men's faces; and still, in the midst of this frightful array of horrors, the carnival of destruction went on without ceasing.

At nightfall, General Lee had driven the enemy from their front line of works—but nothing was gained.

What *could* be gained in that wretched country, where there was nothing but thicket, thicket!

General Grant saw his danger, and, no doubt, divined the object of his adversary,—to arrest and cripple him in this tangle-wood, where numbers did not count, and artillery could not be used.

There was but one thing to do—to get out of the jungle.

So, on the day after this weird encounter, in which he had lost nearly 20,000 men, and Lee about 8,000, Grant moved toward Spottsylvania.

The thickets of the Wilderness were again silent, and the blue and gray objects in the undergrowth did not move.

The war-dogs had gone to tear each other elsewhere.

XXXIII
BREATHED AND HIS GUN

In the din and smoke of that desperate grapple of the infantry, I have lost sight of the incessant cavalry combats which marked each day with blood.

And now there is no time to return to them. A great and sombre event drags the pen. With one scene I shall dismiss those heroic fights—but that scene will be superb.

Does the reader remember the brave Breathed, commanding a battalion of the Stuart horse artillery? I first spoke of him on the night preceding Chancellorsville, when he came to see Stuart, at that time he was already famous for his "do-or die" fighting. A Marylander by birth, he had "come over to help us:" had been the right-hand man of Pelham; the favorite of Stuart; the admiration of the whole army for a courage which the word "reckless" best describes;—and now, in this May, 1864, his familiar name of "Old Jim Breathed," bestowed by Stuart, who held him in high favor, had become the synonym of stubborn nerve and *élan*, unsurpassed by that of Murat. To fight his guns to the muzzles, or go in with the sabre, best suited Breathed. A veritable bull-dog in combat, he shrank at nothing, and led everywhere. I saw brave men in the war—none braver than Breathed. When he failed in any thing, it was because reckless courage could not accomplish it.

He was young, of vigorous frame, with dark hair and eyes, and tanned by sun and wind. His voice was low, and deep; his manners simple and unassuming; his ready laugh and off-hand bearing indicated the born soldier; eyes mild, friendly, and full of honesty. It was only when Breathed was fighting his guns, or leading a charge, that they resembled red-hot coals, and seemed to flame. To come to my incident. I wish, reader, to show you Breathed; to let you see the whole individual in a single exploit. It is good to record things not recorded in "history." They are, after all, the real glory of the South of which nothing can deprive her. I please myself, too, for Breathed was my friend. I loved and admired him—and only a month or two before, he had made the whole army admire—and laugh with—him too.

See how memory leads me off! I am going to give ten words, first, to that incident which made us laugh.

In the last days of winter, a force of Federal cavalry came to make an attack on Charlottesville—crossing the Rapidan high up toward the mountains, and aiming to surprise the place. Unfortunately for him, General Custer, who commanded the expedition, was to find the Stuart horse artillery in winter quarters near. So sudden and unexpected was Custer's advance, that the artillery camps were entirely surprised. At one moment, the men were lying down in their tents, dozing, smoking, laughing—the horses turned out to graze, the guns covered, a profound peace reigning—at the next, they were running to arms, shouting, and in confusion, with the blue cavalry charging straight on their tents, sabre in hand.

Breathed had been lounging like the rest, laughing and talking with the men. Peril made him suddenly king, and, sabre in hand, he rushed to the guns, calling to his men to follow.

With his own hands he wheeled a gun round, drove home a charge, and trained the piece to bear upon the Federal cavalry, trampling in among the tents within fifty yards of him.

"Man the guns!" he shouted, in his voice of thunder. "Stand to your guns, boys! You promised me you would never let these guns be taken!"[1]

{Footnote 1: His words.}

A roar of voices answered him. The bull-dogs thrilled at the voice of the master. Suddenly the pieces spouted flame; shell and canister tore through the Federal ranks. Breathed was everywhere, cheering on the cannoneers. Discharge succeeded discharge; the ground shook: then the enemy gave back, wavering and losing heart.

Breathed seized the moment. Many of the horses had been caught and hastily saddled. Breathed leaped upon one of them, and shouted:—

"Mount!"

The men threw themselves into the saddle—some armed with sabres, others with clubs, others with pieces of fence-rail, caught up from the fires.

"Charge!" thundered Breathed.

At the head of his men, he lead a headlong charge upon the Federal cavalry, which broke and fled in the wildest disorder, pursued by the ragged cannoneers, Breathed in front, with yells, cheers, and cries of defiance.

They were pursued past Barboursville to the Rapidan, without pause. That night Stuart went after them: their officers held a council of war, it is said, to decide whether they should not bury their artillery near Stannardsville, to prevent is capture. On the day after this, they had escaped.

In passing Barboursville, on their return from Charlottesville, one of the Federal troopers stopped to get a drink of water at the house of a citizen.

"What's the matter?" asked the citizen.

"Well, we are retreating."

"Who is after you?"

"Nobody but old Jim Breathed and his men, armed with fence-rails."{1}

{Footnote 1: His words.}

Such was one of a dozen incidents in Breathed's life. Let me come to that which took place near Spottsylvania Court-House.

Grant had moved, as we have seen, by his left flank toward that place. General Fitzhugh Lee opposed him on the way, and at every step harassed the head of the Federal column with his dismounted sharp-shooters and horse artillery. Near Spottsylvania Court-House, it was the stand made by Fitz Lee's cavalry that saved the position, changing the aspect of the whole campaign.

Sent by Stuart with a message to the brave "General Fitz," I reached him near Spottsylvania Court-House, at the moment when he had just ordered his cavalry to fall back slowly before the advancing enemy, and take a new position in rear.

Two guns which had been firing on the enemy were still in battery on a hill; upon these a heavy Federal skirmish line was steadily moving: and beside the guns, Breathed and Fitzhugh Lee sat their horses, looking coolly at the advancing line.

"Give them a round of canister, Breathed!" exclaimed General Fitz Lee.

Breathed obeyed, but the skirmish line continued bravely to advance. All at once, there appeared in the woods behind them, a regular line of battle advancing, with flags fluttering.

To remain longer on the hill was to lose the guns. The bullets were whizzing around us, and there was but one course left—to fall back.

"Take the guns off, Breathed!" exclaimed the general; "there is no time to lose! Join the command in the new position, farther down the road!"

Breathed looked decidedly unwilling.

"A few more rounds, general!"

And turning to the men, he shouted:—

"Give them canister!"

At the word, the guns spouted flame, and the canister tore through the line of skirmishers, and the Federal line of battle behind; but it did not check them. They came on more rapidly, and the air was full of balls.

"Look out for the guns, Breathed! Take them off!" exclaimed the general.

Breathed turned toward one of the pieces, and ordered: —

"Limber to the rear!"

The order was quickly obeyed.

"Forward!"

The piece went off at a thundering gallop, pursued by bullets.

"Only a few more rounds, general!" pleaded Breathed; "I won't lose the guns!"

"All right!"

As he spoke, the enemy rushed upon the single gun.

Breathed replied by hurling canister in their faces. He sat his horse, unflinching. Never had I seen a more superb soldier.

The enemy were nearly at the muzzle of the piece.

"Surrender!" they were heard shouting; "surrender the gun!" Breathed's response was a roar, which hurled back the front rank.

Then, his form towering amid the smoke, his eyes flashing, his drawn sabre whirled above his head, Breathed shouted, —

"Limber up!"

The cannoneers seized the trail; the horses wheeled at a gallop; the piece was limbered up; and the men rushed down the hill to mount their horses, left there.

Then around the gun seemed to open a volcano of flame. The Federal infantry were right on it. A storm of bullets cut the air. The drivers leaped from the horses drawing the piece, thinking its capture inevitable, and ran down the hill.

In an instant they had disappeared. The piece seemed in the hands of the enemy — indeed, they were almost touching it — a gun of the Stuart horse artillery for the first time was to be captured!

That thought seemed to turn Breathed into a giant. As the drivers disappeared, his own horse was shot under him, staggered, sunk, and rolled upon his rider. Breathed dragged himself from beneath the bleeding animal, rose to his feet, and rushing to the lead horses of the gun, leaped upon one of them, and struck them violently with his sabre to force them on.

As he did so, the horse upon which he was mounted fell, pierced by a bullet through the body.

Breathed fell upon his feet, and, with the edge of his sabre, cut the two leaders out of the traces. He then leaped upon one of the middle horses — the gun being drawn by six — and started off.

He had not gone three paces, when the animal which he now rode fell dead in turn. Breathed rolled upon the ground, but rising to his feet, severed the dead animal and his companion from the piece, as he had done the leaders.

He then leaped upon one of the wheel-horses — these alone being now left — struck them furiously with his sabre — started at a thundering gallop down the hill — and pursued by a hail-storm of bullets, from which, as General Lee says in his report, "he miraculously escaped unharmed," carried off the gun in safety, and rejoined the cavalry, greeted by a rolling thunder of cheers.

Such was the manner in which Breathed fought his artillery, and the narrative is the barest and most simple statement of fact.

Breathed came out of the war a lieutenant-colonel only. Napoleon would have made him a marshal.

XXXIV
MY LAST RIDE WITH STUART

More than one stirring incident marked those days of desperate fighting, when, barricading all the roads, and charging recklessly, Stuart opposed, at every step, Grant's advance toward the Po.

But I can not describe those incidents. They must be left to others. The pen which has paused to record that exploit of Breathed, is drawn onward as by the hand of Fate toward one of those scenes which stand out, lugubrious and bloody, from the pages of history.

From the moment when Grant crossed the Rapidan, Stuart had met the horsemen of Sheridan everywhere in bitter conflict; and the days and nights had been strewed all over with battles.

Now, on the ninth of May, when the two great adversaries faced each other on the Po, a more arduous service still was demanded of the great sabreur. Sheridan had been dispatched to sever General Lee's communications, and, if possible, capture Richmond. The city was known to be well nigh stripped of troops, and a determined assault might result in its fall. Sheridan accordingly cut loose a heavy column, took command of it in person, and descended like a thunderbolt toward the devoted city.

No sooner, however, had he begun to move, than Stuart followed on his track. He had no difficulty in doing so. A great dust-cloud told the story. That cloud hung above the long column of Federal cavalry, accompanied it wherever it moved, and indicated clearly to Stuart the course which his adversary was pursuing.

If he could only interpose, with however small a force, between Sheridan and Richmond, time would be given for preparation to resist the attack, and the capital might be saved. If he failed to interpose, Sheridan would accomplish his object — Richmond would fall.

It was a forlorn hope, after all, that he could arrest the Federal commander. General Sheridan took with him a force estimated at 9,000. Stuart's was, in all, about 3,000; Gordon, who was not in the battle at Yellow Tavern, included. That action was fought by Fitz Lee's division of 2,400 men all told. But the men and officers were brave beyond words; the incentive to daring resistance was enormous; they would do all that could be done.

Such was the situation of affairs on the 9th of May, 1864.

Stuart set out at full gallop on his iron gray, from Spottsylvania Court-House, about three o'clock in the day, and reached Chilesburg, toward Hanover Junction, just as night fell.

Here we found General Fitz Lee engaged in a hot skirmish with the enemy's rear-guard; and that night Stuart planned an attack upon their camp, but abandoned the idea.

His spirits at this time were excellent, but it was easy to see that he realized the immense importance of checking the enemy.

An officer said in his presence: —

"We won't be able to stop Sheridan."

Stuart turned at those words; his cheeks flushed; his eyes flamed, and he said: —

"No, sir! I'd rather die than let him go on!"[1]

{Footnote 1: His words}

On the next morning, he moved in the direction of Hanover Junction; riding boot to boot with his friend General Fitz Lee. I had never seen him more joyous. Some events engrave themselves forever on the memory. That ride of May 10th, 1864, was one of them.

Have human beings a presentiment, ever, at the near approach of death? Does the shadow of the unseen hand ever reveal itself to the eye? I know not, but I know that no such presentiment came to Stuart; no shadow of the coming event darkened the path of the great cavalier. On the contrary, his spirits were buoyant beyond example, almost; and, riding on with

General Fitz Lee, he sang in his gallant voice his favorite ditties "Come out of the Wilderness!" and "Jine the Cavalry!"

As he rode on thus, he was the beau ideal of a cavalier. His seat in the saddle was firm; his blue eyes dazzling; his heavy mustache curled with laughter at the least provocation. Something in this man seemed to spring forward to meet danger. Peril aroused and strung him. All his energies were stimulated by it. In that ride through the May forest, to attack Sheridan, and arrest him or die, Stuart's bearing and expression were superbly joyous and inspiring. His black plume floated in the spring breeze, like some knight-errant's; and he went to battle humming a song, resolved to conquer or fall.

Riding beside him, I found my eyes incessantly attracted to his proud face; and now I see the great cavalier as then, clearly with the eyes of memory. What a career had been his! what a life of battles!

As we went on through the spring woods, amid the joyous songs of birds, all the long, hard combats of this man passed before me like an immense panorama. The ceaseless scouting and fighting in the Shenandoah Valley; the charge and route of the red-legged "Zouaves" at Manassas; the falling back to the Peninsula, and the fighting all through Charles City; the famous ride around McClellan; the advance and combats on the Rapidan and Rappahannock, after Cedar Mountain; the night attack on Catlett's, when he captured Pope's coat and papers; the march on Jackson's flank, and the capture of Manassas; the advance into Maryland; the fights at Frederick, Crampton's, and Boonsboro', with the hard rear-guard work, as Lee retired to Sharpsburg; his splendid handling of artillery on the left wing of the army there; the retreat, covered by his cavalry; the second ride around McClellan, and safe escape from his clutches; the bitter conflicts at Upperville and Barbee's, as Lee fell back; the hard fighting thereafter, on the banks of the Rappahannock; the "crowding 'em with artillery," on the night of Fredericksburg; the winter march to Dumfries; the desperate battle at Kelly's Ford; the falling back before Hooker; the battle of Chancellorsville, when he succeeded Jackson; the stubborn wrestle of Fleetwood; the war of giants below Upperville; the advance across Maryland into Pennsylvania, when the long march was strewed all over with battles, at Westminister, Hanover, Carlisle, Gettysburg, where he met and repulsed the best cavalry of the Federal army; the retreat from Gettysburg, with the tough affair near Boonsboro'; guarding the rear of the army as it again crossed the Potomac; then the campaign of October, ending with Kilpatrick's route at Buckland; the assault on Meade's head of column, when he came over to Mine Run; the bold attack on his rear there; and the hard, incessant fighting since Grant had come over to the Wilderness;—I remembered all these splendid scenes and illustrious services as I rode on beside Stuart, through the fields and forests of Hanover, and thought, "This is one of those great figures which live forever in history, and men's memories!"

To-day, I know that I was not mistaken, or laboring under the influence of undue affection and admiration. That figure has passed from earth, but still lives!

Stuart is long dead, and the grass covers him; but there is scarce a foot of the soil of Virginia that does not speak of him. He is gone, but his old mother is proud of him—is she not?

Answer, mountains where he fought—lowlands, where he fell—river, murmuring a dirge, as you foam through the rocks yonder, past his grave!

XXXV
"SOON WITH ANGELS I'LL BE MARCHING"

Let me rapidly pass over the events of the tenth of May.

Gordon's little brigade had been ordered to follow on the rear of the enemy, while Fitz Lee moved round by Taylorsville to get in front of them.

Stuart rode and met Gordon, gave the brave North Carolinian, so soon to fall, his last orders; and then hastened back to Fitz Lee, who had continued to press the enemy.

They had struck the Central railroad, but the gray cavaliers were close on them. Colonel Robert Randolph, that brave soul, doomed like Gordon, charged them furiously here, took nearly a hundred prisoners, and drove them across the road.

At this moment Stuart returned, and pushed forward toward Taylorsville, from which point he intended to hasten on and get in their front.

About four in the afternoon we reached Fork church, and the command halted to rest.

Stuart stretched himself at full length, surrounded by his staff, in a field of clover; and placing his hat over his face to protect his eyes from the light, snatched a short sleep, of which he was very greatly in need.

The column again moved, and that night camped near Taylorsville, awaiting the work of the morrow.

At daylight on the 11th, Stuart moved toward Ashland. Here he came up with the enemy; attacked them furiously, and drove them before him, and out of the village, killing, wounding, and capturing a considerable number.

Then he put his column again in motion, advanced rapidly by the Telegraph road toward Yellow Tavern, a point near Richmond, where he intended to intercept the enemy — the moment of decisive struggle, to which all the fighting along the roads of Hanover had only been the prelude, was at hand.

Stuart was riding at the head of his column, looking straight forward, and with no thought, apparently, save that of arriving in time.

He was no longer gay. Was it the coming event; was it the loss of sleep; the great interest at stake; the terrible struggle before him? I know not; but he looked anxious, feverish, almost melancholy.

"My men and horses are tired, jaded, and hungry, but all right," he had written to General Bragg, from Ashland.

And these words will serve in large measure to describe the condition of the great commander himself.

I was riding beside him, when he turned to me and said, in a low tone:—

"Do you remember a conversation which we had at Orange, Surry, that night in my tent?"

"Yes, general."

"And what I said?"

"Every word is engraved, I think, upon my memory."

"Good. Do not let one thing ever escape you. Remember, that I said what I say again to-day, that 'Virginia expects every man to do his duty!'"

"I will never forget that, general."

He smiled, and rode on. For half a mile he was silent. Then I heard escape from his lips, in a low, musing voice, a refrain which I had never heard him sing before—

"Soon with angels I'll be marching!"{1}

{Footnote 1: Real}

I know not why, but that low sound made me shiver.

XXXVI
YELLOW TAVERN, MAY 11, 1864

Yellow Tavern! At the mention of that name, a sort of tremor agitates me even to-day, when nearly four years have passed.

In my eyes, the locality is cursed. A gloomy cloud seems ever hanging over it. No birds sing in the trees. The very sunshine of the summer days is sad there.

But I pass to my brief description of the place, and the event which made it one of the black names in Southern history.

Yellow Tavern is an old dismantled hostelry, on the Brook road, about six miles from Richmond. Nothing more dreary than this desolate wayside inn can be imagined. Its doors stand open, its windows are gone, the rotting floor crumbles beneath the heel, and the winds moan through the paneless sashes, like invisible spirits hovering near and muttering some lugubrious secret. "This is the scene of some deed of darkness!" you are tempted to mutter, as you place your feet upon the threshold. When you leave the spot behind you, a weight seems lifted from your breast — you breathe freer.

Such was the Yellow Tavern when I went there in the spring of 1864. Is it different to-day? Do human beings laugh there? I know not; but I know that nothing could make it cheerful in my eyes. It was, and is, and ever will be, a thing accursed!

For the military reader, however, a few words in reference to the topographical features of the locality are necessary.

Yellow Tavern is at the forks of the Telegraph and Mountain roads, six miles from Richmond. The Telegraph road runs north and south — over this road Stuart marched. The Mountain road comes into it from the northwest. By this road Sheridan was coming.

Open the left hand, with the palm upward; the index finger pointing north. The thumb is the Mountain road; the index-finger the Telegraph road; where the thumb joins the hand is the Yellow Tavern in open fields; and Richmond is at the wrist.

Toward the head of the thumb is a wood. Here Wickham, commanding Stuart's right, was placed, his line facing the Mountain road so as to strike the approaching enemy in flank.

From Wickham's left, or near it, Stuart's left wing, under Lomax, extended along the Telegraph road to the Tavern—the two lines thus forming an obtuse angle.

On a hill, near Lomax's right, was Breathed with his guns.

The object of this disposition of Stuart's force will be seen at a glance. Lomax, commanding the left, was across the enemy's front; Wickham, commanding the right, was on their flank; and the artillery was so posted as to sweep at once the front of both Stuart's wings.

The enemy's advance would bring them to the first joint of the thumb. There they would receive Lomax's fire in front; Wickham's in flank; and Breathed's transversely. The cross fire on that point, over which the enemy must pass, would be deadly. Take a pencil, reader, and draw the diagram, and lines of fire. That will show Stuart's excellent design.

Stuart had reached Yellow Tavern, and made his dispositions before the arrival of Sheridan, who was, nevertheless, rapidly advancing by the Mountain road. Major McClellan, adjutant-general, had been sent to General Bragg, with a suggestion that the latter should attack from the direction of the city, at the moment when the cavalry assailed the Federal flank. All was ready.

It was the morning of May 11th, 1864.

Never was scene more beautiful and inspiring. The men were jaded, like their horses; but no heart shrank from the coming encounter. Stretching in a thin line from the tavern into the woods on the right of the Mountain road, the men sat their horses, with drawn sabres gleaming in the sun; and the red battle-flags waved proudly in the fresh May breeze, as though saluting Stuart, who rode in front of them.

Such was the scene at Yellow Tavern. The moment had come. At about eight, a stifled hum, mixed with the tramp of hoofs, was heard. Then a courier came at a gallop, from the right, to Stuart. The enemy were in sight, and advancing rapidly.

Stuart was sitting his horse near Yellow Tavern when that intelligence reached him. He rose in his saddle, took his field-glasses from their leathern case, and looked through them in the direction of the woods across the Mountain road.

Suddenly, quick firing came on the wind—then, loud shouts. Stuart lowered his glasses, shut them up, replaced them in their case, and drew his sabre.

Never had I seen him present an appearance more superb. His head was carried proudly erect, his black plume floated, his blue eyes flashed—he was the *beau ideal* of a soldier, and as one of his bravest officers{1} afterward said to me, looked as if he had resolved on "victory or death." I had seen him often aroused and strung for action. On this morning he seemed on fire, and resembled a veritable king of battle.

{Footnote 1: Breathed.}

Suddenly, the skirmish line of the enemy appeared in front of the woods, and a quick fire was opened on Stuart's sharp-shooters under Colonel Pate, in the angle of the two roads; Stuart hastened to take the real initiative. He posted two guns on a rising ground in the angle, and opened a heavy fire; and galled by this fire, the enemy suddenly made a determined charge upon the guns.

Stuart rose in his stirrups and gazed coolly at the heavy line advancing upon him, and forcing Pate's handful back.

"Take back the guns!" he said.

They were limbered up, and went off rapidly.

At the same moment Colonel Pate appeared, his men obstinately contesting every foot of ground as they fell back toward the Telegraph road, where a deep cut promised them advantage.

Colonel Pate was a tall, fair-haired officer, with a ready smile, and a cordial bearing. He and Stuart had bitterly quarrelled, and the general had court-martialed the colonel. It is scarcely too much to say that they had been deadly enemies.

For the first time now, since their collision, they met. But on this day their enmity seemed dead. The two men about to die grasped each other's hands.

"They are pressing you back, colonel!" exclaimed Stuart.

"Yes, general, I have but three skeleton squadrons! and you see their force."

"You are right. You have done all that any man could. Can you hold this cut?"

"I will try, general."

Their glances crossed. Never was Stuart's face kinder.

"If you say you will, you will do it! Hold this position to the last, colonel."

"I'll hold it until I die, general."{1}

{Footnote 1: His words.}

With a pressure of the hand they parted.

Fifteen minutes afterward, Pate was dead. Attacked at once in front and on both flanks in the road, his little force had been cut to pieces. He fell with three of his captains, and his handful were scattered.

Stuart witnessed all, and his eye grew fiery.

"Pate has died the death of a hero!"{1} he exclaimed.

{Footnote 1: His words.}

"Order Wickham to dismount his brigade, and attack on the right!" he added to Lieutenant Garnett, aid-de-camp. Twenty minutes afterward, Wickham's men were seen advancing, and driving the enemy before them. This relieved the left, and Wickham continued to push on until he struck up against a heavy line behind rail breastworks in the woods.

He then fell back, and each side remained motionless, awaiting the movement of the other.

Such was the preface to the real battle of Yellow Tavern, — the species of demonstration which preluded the furious grapple.

Stuart's melancholy had all vanished. He was in splendid spirits. He hastened back his artillery to the point from which it had been driven, and soon its defiant roar was heard rising above the woods.

At the same moment a courier galloped up.

"What news?"

"A dispatch from Gordon, general."

Stuart took it and read it with high good humor.

"Gordon has had a handsome little affair this morning," he said; "he has whipped them."

And looking toward the northwest—

"I wish Gordon was here,"{1} he said.

{Footnote 1: His words.}

The guns continued to roar, and the enemy had not again advanced. It was nearly four o'clock. Night approached.

But the great blow was coming.

Stuart was sitting his horse near the guns, with Breathed beside him. Suddenly the edge of the woods on the Mountain road swarmed with blue horsemen. As they appeared, the long lines of sabres darted from the scabbards; then they rushed like a hurricane toward the guns.

The attack was so sudden and overpowering, that nothing could stand before it. For a short time the men fought desperately, crossing sabres and using their pistols. But the enemy's numbers were too great. The left was driven back. With triumphant cheers, the Federal troopers pressed upon them to drive them completely from the field.

Suddenly, as the men fell back, Stuart appeared, with drawn sabre, among them, calling upon them to rally. His voice rose above the fire, and a wild cheer greeted him.

The men rallied, the enemy were met again, sabre to sabre, and the field became a scene of the most desperate conflict.

Stuart led every charge. I shall never forget the appearance which he presented at that moment; with one hand he controlled his restive horse, with the other he grasped his sabre; in his cheeks burned the hot blood of the soldier.

"Breathed!" he exclaimed.

"General!"

"Take command of all the mounted men in the road, and hold it against whatever may come! If this road is lost, we are gone!"{1}

{Footnote 1: His words.}

Breathed darted to the head of the men and shouted:—

"Follow me!"

His sword flashed lightning, and digging the spur into his horse, he darted ahead of the column, disappearing in the middle of a swarm of enemies.

A superb sight followed. Breathed was seen in the midst of the Federal cavalry defending himself, with pistol and sabre, against the blows which were aimed at him on every side.

He cut one officer out of the saddle; killed a lieutenant with a pistol ball; was shot slightly in the side, and a sabre stroke laid open his head. But five minutes afterward he was seen to clear a path with his sabre, and reappear, streaming with blood.{1}

{Footnote: This incident, like all here related as attending this battle, is rigidly true.}

The momentary repulse effected nothing. The enemy re-formed their line, and again charged the guns, which were pouring a heavy fire upon them. As they rushed forward, the hoofs of their horses shook the ground. A deafening cheer arose from the blue line.

Stuart was looking at them, and spurred out in front of the guns. His eyes flashed, and, taking off his brown felt hat, he waved it and cheered.

Then he wheeled to take command of a column of Lomax's men, coming to meet the charge.

They were too late. In a moment the enemy were trampling among the guns. All but one were captured, and that piece was saved only by the terror of the drivers. They lashed their horses into a gallop, and rushed toward the Chickahominy, followed by the cannoneers who were cursing them, and shouting:—

"For God's sake, boys, let's go back! They've got Breathed! Let's go back to him!"{1}

{Footnote 1: Their words.}

That terror of the drivers, which the cannoneers cursed so bitterly, ended all. The gun, whirling on at wild speed, suddenly struck against the head of the column advancing to meet the enemy. A war-engine hurled against it could not have more effectually broken it. Before it could re-form the enemy had struck it, forced it back; and then the whole Federal force of cavalry was hurled upon Stuart.

His right, where Fitz Lee commanded in person, was giving back. His left was broken and driven. The day was evidently lost; and Stuart, with a sort of desperation, rushed into the midst of the enemy, calling upon his men to rally, and firing his pistol in the faces of the Federal cavalrymen.

Suddenly, one of them darted past him toward the rear, and as he did so, placed his pistol nearly on Stuart's body, and fired.

As the man disappeared in the smoke, Stuart's hand went quickly to his side, he reeled in the saddle, and would have fallen had not Captain Dorsay, of the First Virginia Cavalry, caught him in his arms.

The bullet had passed through his side into the stomach, and wounded him mortally. In its passage, it just grazed a small Bible in his pocket. The Bible was the gift of his mother—but the Almighty had decreed that it should not turn the fatal bullet.

Stuart's immense vitality sustained him for a moment. Pale, and tottering in the saddle, he still surveyed the field, and called on the men to rally.

"Go back," he exclaimed, "and do your duty, as I have done mine! And our country will be safe!"[1]

{Footnote 1: His words.}

A moment afterward he called out again to the men passing him:—

"Go back! go back! I'd rather die than be whipped!"[1]

{Footnote 1: His words.}

The old lightning flashed from his eyes as he spoke. Then a mist passed over them; his head sank upon his breast; and, still supported in the saddle, he was led through the woods toward the Chickahominy.

Suddenly, Fitzhugh Lee, who had been stubbornly fighting on the right, galloped up, and accosted Stuart. His face was flushed, his eyes moist.

"You are wounded!" he exclaimed.

"Badly," Stuart replied, "but look out, Fitz! Yonder they come!"

A glance showed all. In the midst of a wild uproar of clashing sabres, quick shots, and resounding cries, the Federal cavalry were rushing forward to overwhelm the disordered lines.

Stuart's eye flashed for the last time. Turning to General Fitzhugh Lee, he exclaimed in a full, sonorous voice: —

"Go ahead, Fitz, old fellow! I know you will do what is right!"[1]

{Footnote 1: His words.}

This was the last order he ever gave upon the field. As he spoke, his head sank, his eyes closed, and he was borne toward the rear.

There was scarcely time to save him from capture. His wound seemed to have been the signal for his lines to break. They had now given way everywhere—the enemy were pressing them with loud shouts. Fighting with stubborn desperation, they fell back toward the Chickahominy, which they crossed, hotly pressed by the victorious enemy.

Stuart had been placed in an ambulance and borne across the stream, where Dr. Randolph and Dr. Fontaine made a brief examination of his wound. It was plainly mortal—but he was hastily driven, by way of Mechanicsville, into Richmond.

His hard fighting had saved the city. When Sheridan attacked, he was repulsed.

But the capital was dearly purchased. Twenty-four hours afterward Stuart was dead.

The end of the great cavalier had been as serene as his life was stormy. His death was that of the Christian warrior, who bows to the will of God, and accepts whatever His loving hand decrees for him.

He asked repeatedly that his favorite hymns should be sung for him; and when President Davis visited him, and asked: —

"General, how do you feel?"

"Easy, but willing to die," he said, "if God and my country think I have fulfilled my destiny, and done my duty."[1]

{Footnote 1: His words.}

As night came, he requested his physician to inform him if he thought he would live till morning. The physician replied that his death was rapidly approaching, when he faintly bowed his head, and murmured: —

"I am resigned, if it be God's will. I should like to see my wife, but God's will be done."[1]

{Footnote 1: His words.}

When the proposed attack upon Sheridan, near Mechanicsville, was spoken of in his presence, he said: —

"God grant that it may be successful. I wish I could be there." *

Turning his face toward the pillow, he added, with tears in his eyes, "but I must prepare for another world."{1}

{Footnote 1: His words.}

Feeling now that his end was near, he made his last dispositions.

"You will find in my hat," he said to a member of his staff, "a little Confederate flag, which a lady of Columbia, South Carolina, sent me, requesting that I would wear it on my horse in battle, and return it to her. Send it to her."{1}

{Footnote 1: His words.}

He gave then the name of the lady, and added: —

"My spurs — those always worn in battle — I promised to give to Mrs. Lily Lee, at Shepherdstown. My sabre I leave to my son."

His horses and equipments were then given to his staff — his papers directed to be sent to his wife.

A prayer was then offered by the minister at his bedside: his lips moved as he repeated the words. As the prayer ended he murmured: —

"I am going fast now — I am resigned. God's will be done!"{1}

{Footnote 1: His words.}

As the words escaped from his lips, he expired.

BOOK III
BEHIND THE SCENES

I
WHAT I DID NOT SEE

I was not at Stuart's bedside when he died. While aiding the rest to hold him in the saddle, I had been shot through the shoulder; and twenty-four hours afterward I lay, at the house of a friend in Richmond, turning and tossing with fever.

In my delirium I heard a mournful tolling of bells. It was many days, however, before I knew that they were tolling for Stuart.

When, at last, after more than a month's confinement to my bed, I rose, and began to totter about, — pale, faint, and weak, but convalescent — my great loss, for the first time, struck me in all its force.

Where should I turn now — and whither should I go? Jackson dead at Chancellorsville — Stuart at Yellow Tavern — thenceforth I seemed to have lost my support, to grope and totter in darkness, without a guide! These two kings of battle had gone down in the storm, and, like the Knight of Arthur, I looked around me, with vacant and inquiring eyes, asking whither I was now to direct my steps, and what work I should work in the coming years. Jackson! Stuart! — who could replace them? They had loved and trusted me — their head-quarters had been my home. Now, when they disappeared, I had no friends, no home; and an inexpressible sense of loss descended upon me, as a dark cloud descends and obscures a landscape, smiling and full of sunshine.

Another woe had come to me. My father was dead. The war had snapped the chords of that stout heart as it snapped the chords of thousands, and the illustrious head of the house had descended into the tomb. From this double blow I scarcely had strength to rise. For weeks I remained in a sort of dumb stupor; and was only aroused from it by the necessity of looking after my family affairs.

As soon as I had strength to mount my horse, I rode to Eagle's Nest. A good aunt had come and installed herself as the friend and protector of my little Annie; and with the arms of my young sister around me, I wept for my father.

I remained at Eagle's Nest more than two months. The long ride had made the wound in my shoulder reopen, and I was again stretched upon a bed of illness, from which, at one time, I thought I should not rise. More than once I made a narrow escape from scouting parties of Federal cavalry in the neighborhood; and on one occasion, an officer entered my chamber, but left me unmolested, under the impression that I was too ill to live.

It was late in the month of August before I rose from my bed again, and set out on my return.

In those three months and a half—counting from the time I left Spottsylvania with Stuart—great events had happened in Virginia. Grant's hammer and Lee's rapier had been clashing day and night. Hill and valley, mountain and lowland—Virginia and Maryland—had thundered.

General Grant had hastened forward from the Wilderness, only to find Lee confronting him behind breastworks at Spottsylvania Court-House. The Confederate commander had taken up a defensive position on the line of the Po; and for more than two weeks Grant threw his masses against the works of his adversary, in desperate attempts to break through.

On the 12th of May, at daylight, he nearly succeeded. "The Horse Shoe" salient was charged in the dusk of morning; the Southerners were surprised, and bayoneted in the trenches; the works carried; the artillery captured; and a large number of prisoners fell into the hands of the enemy.

The blow was heavy, but General Grant derived little advantage from it. Lee rallied his troops; formed a new line; and repulsed every assault made on it, throughout the entire day. When night fell, Grant had not advanced further; Lee's position was stronger than before, and plainly impregnable.

For many days, Grant was occupied in reconnoitring and feeling his adversary. At the end of a week, the hope of breaking Lee's line was seen to be desperate.

Then commenced the second great "movement by the left flank" toward Richmond.

Grant disappeared one morning, and hastened toward Hanover Junction. When he arrived, Lee was there in his front, ready to receive him. And the new position was stronger, if any thing, than that of Spottsylvania. Grant felt it; abandoned the attempt to carry it, at once; and again moved, on his swift and stealthy way, by the left flank toward Richmond. Crossing the

Pamunkey at Hanovertown, he made straight for the capital; but reaching the Tottapotomoi, he found Lee again awaiting him.

Then the days and nights thundered, as they had been thundering since the day when Grant crossed the Rapidan. Lee could not be driven, and the Federal movement by the left flank began again.

Grant made for Cold Harbor, and massed his army to burst through the Chickahominy, and seize Richmond. The huge engine began to move at daylight, on the third of June. Half an hour afterward, 13,000 of General Grant's forces were dead or wounded. He was repulsed and driven back. His whole loss, from the moment of crossing the Rapidan, had been about 60,000 men.

That ended all hopes of forcing the lines of the Chickahominy. The Federal commander gave up the attempt in despair, and resumed his Wandering-Jew march. Moving still by the left flank, he hastened to cross James River and advance on Petersburg. But Lee was again too rapid for him. In the works south of the Appomattox the gray infantry, under the brave General Wise, confronted the enemy. They repulsed every assault, and Grant sat down to lay siege to Richmond from the distance of thirty miles.

Such had been the great campaign of the summer of 1864 in Virginia. Lee had everywhere stood at bay, and repulsed every attack: he had also struck in return a great aggressive blow, in Maryland.

At Cold Harbor, early in June, news had arrived that a Federal column, under Hunter, was advancing on Lynchburg. A force was sent to intercept Hunter, under the command of Early. That hard fighter crossed the mountains; attacked his adversary; drove him beyond the Alleghanies; and then, returning on his steps, hurried down the Shenandoah Valley toward the Potomac, driving every thing before him. Once at the Potomac, he hastened to cross into Maryland. Once in Maryland, Early advanced, without loss of time, upon Washington. At Monocacy he met and defeated General Wallace; pressed after him toward Washington; and reaching the outer works, advanced his lines to the assault. But he had but a handful, after the long and prostrating march. His numbers were wholly inadequate to storm the defences of the capital. Grant had sent forward, in haste, two army corps to defend the city, and Early was compelled to retreat across the Potomac to the Shenandoah Valley, with the sole satisfaction of reflecting that he had given the enemy a great "scare," and had flaunted the red-cross flag in front of the ramparts of Washington.

I have not space to describe the cavalry movements of the summer. Hampton had succeeded Stuart in command of all the cavalry, and the country soon heard the ring of his heavy blows.

In June, Sheridan was sent to capture Gordonsville and Charlottesville; but Hampton checked and defeated him in a fierce action near Trevillian's, and in another at Charlottesville; pursued him to the White House; hurried him on to James River; and Sheridan crossed that stream on pontoons, glad, no doubt, to get back to the blue infantry. Hampton crossed also; penetrated to Dinwiddie; defeated the enemy at Sappony church, capturing their men and artillery—everywhere they had been routed, with a total loss of more than 2,000 prisoners.

Such were the events which had taken place during my tedious illness. They came to me only in vague rumors, or by means of chance newspapers sent by my neighbors. At last, however, I rose from my sick couch, and embracing my aunt and sister, who were to remain together at Eagle's Nest, set out on my return.

Stuart's staff were all scattered, and seeking new positions. I was one of them, and I again asked myself more gloomily than at first, "Where shall I go?" The gentlemen of the red tape at Richmond would doubtless inform me, however; and riding on steadily, with a keen look out for scouting parties, I at last reached the city.

On the next day I filed my application in the war office, to be assigned to duty.

A week afterward I had not heard from it.

Messieurs, the red tapists, were evidently not in the least bit of a hurry—and hat in hand I awaited their good pleasure.

II

THE "DOOMED CITY"

Richmond presented a singular spectacle in that summer of 1864.

It was styled "the doomed city," by our friends over the border, and in truth there was something gloomy and tragic in its appearance — in the very atmosphere surrounding it.

On every countenance you could read anxiety, poverty, the wasting effect of the terrible suffering and suspense of the epoch. All things combined to deepen the colors of the sombre picture. Hope long deferred had sickened the stoutest hearts. Men were nervous, anxious, burnt up by the hot fever of war. Provisions of every description were sold at enormous prices. Fathers of families could scarcely procure the plainest food for their wives and children. The streets were dotted with poor widows, bereaved sisters, weeping mothers, and pale daughters, whose black dresses told the story of their loss to all eyes. Hunger clutched at the stomach; agony tore the heart. Soldiers, pale and tottering from their wounds, staggered by. Cannon rattled through the streets. Couriers dashed backward and forward from the telegraph office to the war office. The poor starved — the rich scarcely fared any better. Black hair had become white. Stalwart frames were bent and shrunken. Spies and secret emissaries lurked, and looked at you sidewise. Forestallers crowded the markets. Bread was doled out by the ounce. Confederate money by the bushel. Gold was hoarded and buried. Cowards shrunk and began to whisper — "the flesh pots! the flesh pots! they were better!" Society was uprooted from its foundations. Strange characters were thrown up. The scum had come to the top, and bore itself bravely in the sunshine. The whole social fabric seemed warped and wrenched from its base; and in the midst of this chaos of starving women, feverish men, spies, extortioners, blockade-runners, — over the "doomed city," day and night, rolled the thunder of the cannon, telling that Grant and Lee were still holding their high debate at Petersburg.

Such was Richmond at the end of summer in 1864. Society was approaching one of those epochs, when all things appear unreal, monstrous, gliding toward some great catastrophe. All rascaldom was rampant. The night-birds had come forth. Vice stalked, and flaunted its feathers in the light of day. Chaos seemed coming, and with it all the powers of darkness.

That spectacle was singular to a soldier, bred in camps, and habituated, now, for some years, to the breezy airs of "the field." I looked on with astonishment. The whole drama seemed unreal—the characters mere players. Who was A, and B, and what did C do for a living? You knew not, but they bowed, and smiled, and were charming. They grasped your hand, offered you cigars, invited you to supper—they wanted nothing. And they found no difficulty in procuring guests. I was no better than the rest, reader—there is an honest confession—and, looking back now, I can see that I knew, and dined or supped with some queer characters in those days.

Shall I give you a brief sketch of one of these worthies and his surroundings? It will afford some idea of the strange contrasts then presented in the "doomed" and starving city.

III
I DINE WITH MR. BLOCQUE

He was a prominent personage at that time—my friend (in a parliamentary sense at least) Mr. Blocque.

He was a charming little fellow, acquainted with everybody—an "employee of government," but employed to do heaven knows what; and while others were starving, Mr. Blocque was as plump as a partridge. He wore the snowiest shirt bosoms, glittering with diamond studs; the finest broadcloth coats; the most brilliant patent leather shoes; and his fat little hands sparkled with costly rings. He was constantly smiling in a manner that was delightful to behold; hopped about and chirped like a sparrow or tomtit; and was the soul of good humor and enjoyment. There was no resisting his charms; he conquered you in five minutes. When he linked his arm in yours, and chirped, "My dear friend, come and dine with me—at five o'clock precisely—I shall certainly expect you!" it was impossible to refuse the small gentleman's invitation. Perhaps you asked yourself, "Who is my dear friend, Mr. Blocque—how does he live so well, and wear broadcloth and fine linen?" But the next moment you smiled, shrugged your shoulders, elevated your eye-brows, and—went to dine with him.

I was like all the world, and at five o'clock one evening was shown into Mr. Blocque's elegant residence on Shockoe Hill, by a servant in white gloves, who bowed low, as he ushered me in. Mr. Blocque hastened to receive me, with his most charming smile; I was introduced to the guests, who had all arrived; and ten minutes afterward the folding doors opened, revealing a superb banquet—for the word "dinner" would be too common-place. The table was one mass of silver. Waxlights, in candelabra, were already lit; and a host of servants waited, silent and respectful, behind every chair.

The guests were nearly a dozen in number, and more than one prominent "government official" honored Mr. Blocque's repast. I had been introduced among the rest to Mr. Torpedo, member of Congress, and bitter foe of President Davis; Mr. Croker, who had made an enormous fortune by buying up, and hoarding in garrets and cellars, flour, bacon, coffee, sugar, and other necessaries; and Colonel Desperade, a tall and warlike officer in a splendid uniform, who had never been in the army, but intended to report for duty, it was supposed, as soon as he was made brigadier-general.

The dinner was excellent. The table literally groaned with every delicacy. Everywhere you saw canvass-back ducks, grouse, salmon, paté de foie gras, oysters; the champagne, was really superb; the Madeira and sherry beyond praise; and the cigars excellent Havanas, which at that time were rarely seen, and cost fabulous prices. Think, old army comrades, starving on a quarter of a pound of rancid bacon during that summer of '64—think of that magical bill of fare, that array of wonders!

Who was the magician who had evoked all this by a wave of his wand? How could smiling Mr. Blocque roll in luxury thus, when everybody else was starving? How could my host wear broadcloth, and drink champagne and smoke Havanas, when ragged clothing, musty bacon, and new apple-abomination, were the order of the day with all others?

These questions puzzled me extremely; but there was the magician before us, smiling in the most friendly manner, and pressing his rich wines on his guests, as they sat around the polished mahogany smoking their cigars. Elegantly clad servants hovered noiselessly behind the convives— the wine circulated—the fragrant smoke rose—the conversation became general—and all was animation.

"No, sir!" says Mr. Torpedo, puffing fiercely at his cigar, "the President never will assign Johnston to command again, sir! You call Mr. Davis 'pig-headed,' Mr. Croker—you are wrong, sir! You do injustice to the pigs, sir! Pigs are not insane, sir!"

And Mr. Torpedo sucks at his cigar, as though he were a vampire, extracting the blood of his victim.

Mr. Croker sips his wine; he is large and portly; ruddy and pompous; his watch seals jingle; and he rounds his periods with the air of a millionaire, who is accustomed to be listened to with deference.

"You are right, my dear, sir," says Mr. Croker, clearing his throat. "The government has assuredly been administered, from its very inception, in a manner which the most enthusiastic adherents of the Executive will scarcely venture to characterize as either judicious or constitutional. In the year which has just elapsed, things have been managed in a manner which must excite universal reprobation. Even the alleged performances of the army are problematical, and—"

"I beg your pardon, sir," says Colonel Desperade, twirling his mustache in a warlike manner; "do I understand you to call in question the nerve of our brave soldiers, or the generalship of our great commander?"

"I do, sir," says Mr. Croker, staring haughtily at the speaker. "I am not of those enthusiasts who consider General Lee a great soldier. He has succeeded in defensive campaigns, but is deficient in genius—and I will add, sir, as you seem to be surprised at my remarks, sir, that in my opinion the Southern Confederacy will be overwhelmed, sir, and the South compelled to return to the Union, sir!"

"Upon what do you ground that extraordinary assumption, may I ask, sir?"

"On common sense and experience, sir," returns Mr. Croker, severely; "look at the currency—debased until the dollar is merely a piece of paper. Look at prices—coffee, twenty dollars a pound, and sugar the same. Look at the army starving—the people losing heart—and strong, able-bodied men," adds Mr. Croker, looking at Colonel Desperade, "lurking about the cities, and keeping out of the way of bullets."

The mustached warrior looks ferocious—his eyes dart flame.

"And who causes the high prices, sir? Who makes the money a rag? I answer—the forestallers and engrossers—do you know any, sir?"

"I do not, sir!"

"That is singular!" And Colonel Desperade twirls his mustache satirically—looking at the pompous Mr. Croker in a manner which makes that worthy turn scarlet.

I was laughing to myself quietly, and listening for the expected outbreak, when Mr. Blocque interposed with his winning voice.

"What are you discussing, gentlemen?" he said, with his charming smile. "But first tell me your opinion of this Madeira and those cigars. My agent writes me word that he used every exertion to procure the best. Still, I am not entirely pleased with either the wine or brand of cigars, and hope you will excuse them. Were you speaking of our great President, Mr. Torpedo? And you, Mr. Croker—I think you were referring to the present state of affairs. They appear to me more hopeful than at any previous time, and his Excellency, President Davis, is guiding the helm of state with extraordinary courage and good judgment. I know some of you differ with me in these views, my friends. But let us not be censorious—let us look on the bright side. The troubles of the country are great, and we of the South are suffering every privation—but we must bear up, gentlemen; we must keep brave hearts, and endure all things. Let us live on dry bread if it comes to that, and bravely fight to the last! Let us cheerfully endure hardships, and oppose the enemy at all points. Our present troubles and privations will soon come to an end—we shall again be surrounded by the comforts and luxuries of life—and generations now unborn will bless our names, and pity our sufferings in these days that try men's souls!"

Mr. Blocque ceased, and smoothing down his snowy shirt bosom, pushed the wine. At the same moment, an alabaster clock on the marble mantelpiece struck seven.

"So late?" said Colonel Desperade. "I have an appointment at the war office!"

Mr. Blocque drew out a magnificent gold watch.

"The clock is fast," he said, "keep your seats, gentlemen,—unless you fancy going to the theatre. My private box is at your disposal, and carriages will be ready in a few minutes."

As the charming little gentleman spoke, he led the way back to the drawing-room—the folding doors flanked by silent and respectful servants as the guests passed in.

In five minutes, coffee and liqueurs were served; both were superb, the white sugar sparkled like crystal in the silver dish, and the cream in the solid jug was yellow and as thick as a syrup.

"Shall it be the theatre, gentlemen?" said Mr. Blocque, with winning smiles. "We can amuse ourselves with cards for an hour, as the curtain does not rise before eight."

And he pointed to a silver basket on the centre table of carved walnut, surmounted by a slab of variegated marble. I looked, and saw the crowning wonder. The silver basket contained piles of gold coin and greenbacks! Not a trace of a Confederate note was visible in the mass!

Packs of fresh cards were brought quickly by a servant, on a silver waiter; the guests helped themselves to the coin and bank notes; in ten minutes they were playing furiously.

As I do not play, I rose and took my leave. Mr. Blocque accompanied me to the door, smiling sweetly to the last.

"Come again very soon, my dear colonel," he said, squeezing my hand, "my poor house, and all in it, is at your service at all times!"

I thanked my host, shook hands, and went out into the darkness, — determined never to return.

I had had an excellent dinner, and, physically, had never felt better. Morally, I must say, I felt contaminated, for, unfortunately, I had begun to think of Lee's hungry soldiers, lying in rags, in the Petersburg trenches.

"Eight o'clock! All is well!" came from the sentinel, as I passed by the capitol.

IV
JOHN M. DANIEL

On the day after this scene, a trifling matter of business led me to call on John M. Daniel, editor of the *Examiner*.

The career of this singular personage had been as remarkable as his character. He was not a stranger to me. I had known him in 1849 or '50, when I accompanied my father on a visit to Richmond, and I still recall the striking appearance of the individual at that time. He had come, a poor boy of gentle birth, from the bleak hills of Stafford, to the city of Richmond, to seek his fortune, and, finding nothing better to do, had accepted the position of librarian to the Richmond library, waiting for something to "turn up," and ready to grasp it. About the same time, that experienced journalist, the late B.M. De Witt, had founded the *Examiner*. He, no doubt, saw the eminent talents of the youth from Stafford, and the result had been an invitation to assist in the editorial department of the journal.

Going to the Richmond library, to procure for my father some volume for reference, I had made the acquaintance of the youthful journalist. At the first glance, I felt that I was in the presence of an original character. His labors on the *Examiner* had just commenced. He was seated, half-reclining, in an arm-chair, surrounded by "exchanges," from which he clipped paragraphs, throwing the papers, as soon as he had done so, in a pile upon the floor. His black eyes, long black hair, brushed behind the ears, and thin, sallow cheeks, were not agreeable; but they made up a striking physiognomy. The black eyes glittered with a sullen fire; the thin lips were wreathed with a sardonic smile; and I was informed that the youth lived the life of a *solitaire*, voluntarily absenting himself from society, to give his days and nights to exhausting study.

He read every thing, it was said—history, poetry, political economy, and theology. Swift was said to be his literary divinity, and Rabelais was at his elbow always. Poor, uneducated, ignorant of nearly every thing, he was educating himself for the future — sharpening, by attrition with the strongest minds in all literatures, ancient and modern, that trenchant weapon which afterward flashed its superb lightnings in the heated atmosphere of the great epoch in which he figured.

Bitter, misanthropic, solitary; burning the midnight lamp, instead of moving among his fellows in the sunshine, he yet possessed hardy virtues and a high pride of gentleman. He hated the world at large, it was said, but loved his few friends with an ardor which shrank at nothing. One of them owed a sum of money — and Daniel went on foot, twenty-two miles, to Petersburg, paid it, and returned in the same manner. Afterward he went in person to Charlottesville, to purchase a house for the use of another friend of limited means. For his friends he was thus willing to sacrifice his convenience and his means, without thought of return. All who were not his friends, he is said to have hated or despised. An acquaintance was in his room one day, and showed him a valuable pen-knife. Daniel admired it, and the gentleman said "You may have it, if you like it." Daniel turned upon him, scowled at him, his lip curled, and he replied, "What do you expect me to do for you?"

His other virtues were self-denial, and a proud independence. At the library, he lived on bread and tea — often making the tea himself. Too poor to possess a chamber, he slept on a lounge in the public room. He would owe no man any thing, asked no favors, and fawned on nobody. He would fight his own fight, make his own way; with the intellect heaven had sent him, carve out his own future, unassisted. The sallow youth, groaning under dyspepsia, with scarce a friend, and nothing but his brain, promised himself that he would one day rise from his low estate, and wield the thunderbolts of power, as one born to grasp and hurl them.

He was not mistaken, and did not overestimate his powers. When I saw him in 1849 or '50, he was obscurest of the obscure. Two or three years afterward he had made the *Examiner* one of the great powers of the political world, and was living in a palace at Turin, minister to Sardinia. He had achieved this success in life by the sheer force of his character; by the vigor and recklessness of his pen, and the intensity of his invective. Commencing his editorial career, apparently, with the theory that, in order to rise into notice, he must spare nothing and no one, he had entered the arena of partisan politics like a full armed gladiator; and soon the whole country resounded with the blows which he struck. Bitter personality is a feeble phrase to describe the animus of the writer in those days. There was something incredibly exasperating in his comments on political opponents. He flayed and roasted them alive. It was like thrusting a blazing torch into the raw flesh of his victims. Nor was it simple "abuse." The satirist was too intelligent to rely upon that. It was his scorching wit which made opponents shrink. His scalpel divided the arteries, and touched the vitals of the living subject. Personal peculiarities were satirized with unfailing acumen. The readers of the *Examiner*, in those days, will still recall the tremendous flaying which he administered to his adversaries. It may almost be said, that when the remorseless editor had finished with these gentlemen, there was "nothing of them left"—what lay before him was a bleeding and mortally wounded victim. And what was worse, all the world was laughing. Those who looked with utter disapproval upon his ferocious course, were still unable to resist the influence of his mordant humor. They denounced the *Examiner* without stint, but they subscribed to it, and read it every morning. "Have you seen the *Examiner* to-day?" asked the friend whom you met on the street. "John M. Daniel is down on Blank!" said A to B, rubbing his hands and laughing. Blank may have been the personal acquaintance and friend of Mr. A, but there was no resisting the cartoon of him, traced by the pen of the satirist! The portrait might be a caricature, but it was a terrible likeness! The long nose was very long; the round shoulders, very round; the cast in the eye, a frightful squint; but the individual was unmistakable. The bitter humor of the artist had caught and embodied every weakness. Thenceforth, the unfortunate adversary went on his way before all eyes, the mark of suppressed ridicule and laughing whispers. Whether you approved or disapproved, you read those tremendous satires. Not to see the *Examiner* in those days was to miss a part of the history of the times. The whole political world felt the presence of a *power* in journalism. Into all the recesses of the body politic, those shafts of ridicule or denunciation penetrated. That venomous invective pierced the hardest panoply. For the first time in American journalism, the world saw the full force of ridicule; and tasted a bitterness of invective unknown since the days of Swift.

Out of these personal attacks grew numerous duels. The butts of the editor's ridicule sent him defiances, and he was engaged in several affairs, which, however, resulted in nothing, or nearly nothing, as I believe he was wounded only once. They did not induce him to change his course. He seemed to have marked out his career in cold blood, and was plainly resolved to adhere to his programme—to write himself into power. In this he fully succeeded. By dint of slashing and flaying, he attracted the attention of all. Then his vigorous and masculine intellect riveted the spell. Hated, feared, admired, publicly stigmatized as one who "ruled Virginia with a rod of iron," he had reached his aim; and soon the material results of success came. The director of that great political engine, the Richmond *Examiner*, found no difficulty in securing the position which he desired; and he received the appointment of minister to Sardinia, which he accepted, selling his newspaper, but reserving the right to resume editorial control of it on his return.

His ambition was thus gratified—for the moment at least. The unknown youth, living once on bread and tea, and too poor to possess a bed, was now a foreign minister; had an Italian count for his *chef de cuisine*; and drew a salary which enabled him to return, some years afterward, to the United States with savings amounting to $30,000.

It was a contrast to his past. The sallow youth was *M. le ministre*! The garret in Richmond had been turned into a marble palace in Turin. He had a nobleman for a cook, instead of making his own tea. And the *Examiner* had done all that for him!

When war became imminent, he returned to Virginia, and resumed control of the *Examiner*. With the exception of brief military service with General Floyd, and on the staff of A.P. Hill, in the battles around Richmond, when he was slightly wounded in the right arm, he remained in editorial harness until his death.

As soon as he grasped the helm of the *Examiner* again, that great battleship trembled and obeyed him. It had been powerful before, it was now a mighty engine, dragging every thing in its wake. Commencing by supporting the Government, it soon became bitterly inimical to President Davis and the whole administration. The invective in which it indulged was not so violent as in the past, but it was even more powerful and dangerous. Every department was lashed, in those brief, terse sentences which all will remember—sentences summing up volumes in a paragraph, condensing oceans of gall into a drop of ink. Under these mortal stabs, delivered coolly and deliberately, the authors of public abuses shrank, recoiled, and sought safety in silence. They writhed, but knew the power of their adversary too well to reply to him. When once or twice they did so, his rejoinder was more mortal than his first attack. The whole country read the *Examiner*, from the chief officers of the administration to the humblest soldier in the trenches. It shaped the opinions of thousands, and this great influence was not due to trick or chance. It was not because it denounced the Executive in terms of the bitterest invective; because it descended like a wild boar on the abuses or inefficiency of the departments; but because this journal, more, perhaps, than any other in the South, spoke the public sentiment, uttered its views with fearless candor, and conveyed those views in words so terse, pointed, and trenchant—in such forcible and excellent English—that the thought of the writer was driven home, and remained fixed in the dullest apprehension.

The *Examiner*, in one word, had become the controlling power, almost, of the epoch. Its views had become those even of men who bitterly stigmatized its course. You might disapprove of its editorials often, and regret their appearance—as I did—but it was impossible not to be carried onward by the hardy logic of the writer: impossible not to admire the Swift-like pith and vigor of this man, who seemed to have re-discovered the lost well of undefiled English.

When I went to see John M. Daniel, thus, in this summer of 1864, it was not a mere journalist whom I visited, but a historic character. For it was given to him, invisible behind the scenes, to shape, in no small degree, the destiny of the country, by moulding the views and opinions of the actors who contended on the public arena.

Was that influence for good or for evil? Let others answer. To-day this man is dead, and the cause for which he fought with his pen has failed. I reproduce his figure and some scenes of that great cause—make your own comments, reader.

V
THE EDITOR IN HIS SANCTUM

Knocking at the door of the journalist's house on Broad Street, nearly opposite the "African church," I was admitted by a negro servant, sent up my name, and was invited by Mr. Daniel to ascend to his sanctum on the second story.

I went up, and found him leaning back in a high chair of black horsehair, in an apartment commanding a view southward of James River and Chesterfield. On a table beside him were books and papers—the furniture of the room was plain and simple.

He greeted me with great cordiality, bowing very courteously, and offering me a cigar. I had not seen him since his return from Europe, and looked at him with some curiosity. He was as sallow as before—his eyes as black and sparkling; but his long, black hair, as straight as an Indian's, and worn behind his ears, when I first knew him, was close-cut now; and his upper lip was covered by a black mustache. His dress was simple and exceedingly neat. It was impossible not to see that the famous journalist was a gentleman.

As I had visited him purely upon a matter of business, I dispatched it, and then rose to take my departure. But he urged me with persistent cordiality, not to desert him. He saw few persons, he said; I must stay and dine with him. I had business? Then I could attend to it, and would do him the favor to return.

Looking at my watch, I found that it was nearly two o'clock—he had informed me that he dined at four—and, not to detain the reader with these details, recurring to a very retentive memory, I found myself, two hours afterward, seated at table with the editor of the *Examiner*.

The table was of ancient, and brilliantly-polished mahogany. The dinner consisted of only two or three dishes, but these were of the best quality, excellently cooked, and served upon china of the most costly description. Coffee followed—then a great luxury—and, not only the sugar-dish, cream-jug and other pieces of the service were of silver; the waiter upon which they rested was of the same material—heavy, antique, and richly carved.

We lingered at table throughout the entire afternoon, my host having resisted every attempt which I made to depart, by taking my hat from my hand, and thrusting upon me another excellent Havana cigar. Cordiality so extreme, in one who bore the reputation of a man-hater, was at least something *piquant*—and as my host had appealed to my weak side, by greatly praising a slight literary performance of mine ("he would be proud," he assured me, "to have it thought that *he* had written it)," I yielded, surrendered my hat, lit the cigar offered me, and we went on talking.

I still recall that conversation, the last but one which I ever had with this singular man. Unfortunately, it does not concern the narrative I now write, and I would not like to record his denunciations and invective directed at the Government. He handled it without mercy, and his comments upon the character of President Davis were exceedingly bitter. One of these was laughable for the grim humor of the idea. Opening a volume of Voltaire—whose complete works he had just purchased—he showed me a passage in one of the infidel dramas of the great Frenchman, where King David, on his death-bed, after invoking maledictions upon his opponents, declares that "having forgiven all his enemies *en bon Juif*, he is ready to die."

A grim smile came to the face of the journalist, as he showed me the passage.

"That suits Mr. Davis exactly," he said. "He forgives his enemies *en bon Juif!* I believe I will make an editorial, and quote the passage on him—but he wouldn't understand it!"

That was bitter—was it not, reader? I raised my pen to draw a line through the incident, but it can do no harm now.

The solitary journalist-politician spoke freely of himself and his intentions for the future. With a few passages from our talk on this point, I will terminate my account of the interview.

"You see I am here chained to the pen," he said, "and, luckily, I have that which defies the conscript officers, if the Government takes a fancy to order editors into the ranks."

Smiling slightly as he spoke, he showed me his right hand, the fingers of which he could scarcely bend.

"I was wounded at Cold Harbor, in June, 1862," he added; "not much wounded either; but sufficient to prevent me from handling a sword or musket. It is a trifle. I should like to be able to show an honorable scar{1} in this cause, and I am sorry I left the army. By this time I might have, been a brigadier—perhaps a major-general."{2}

{Footnote 1: His words.}

{Footnote 2: His words.}

"Possibly," I replied; "but the position of an editor is a powerful one."

"Do you think so?"

"Don't you?"

"Yes, colonel; but what good is the *Examiner* doing? What can all the papers in the Confederacy effect? Besides, I like to command men. I love power."{1}

{Footnote 1: His words.}

I laughed.

"I would recommend the philosophic view of things," I said. "Why not take the good the gods provide? As a soldier, you would be in fetters— whatever your rank—to say nothing of the bullet that might cut short your career. And yet this life of the brain is wearing too,—"

"But my health is all the better for it," he said. "A friend was here to see me the other day, and I startled him by the observation 'I shall live to eat the goose that eats the grass over your grave.'{1} When he inquired my meaning, I replied, 'For two reasons—I come of a long-lived race, and have an infallible sign of longevity; I never dream, and my sleep is always sound and refreshing.'"{2}

{Footnote 1: His words.}

{Footnote 2: His words.}

"Do you believe in that dictum?" I said.

"Thoroughly," he replied, laughing. "I shall live long, in spite of the enmities which would destroy me in an instant, if the secret foes I have could only accomplish their end without danger to themselves."

"You do not really believe, surely, that you have such foes?"

"Not believe it? I know it. *You* have them, colonel, too. How long do you think you would live, if your enemies had their way with you? Perhaps you think you have no enemies who hate you enough to kill you. You are greatly mistaken—every man has his enemies. I have them by the thousand, and I have no doubt you, too, have them, though they are probably not so numerous as mine."{1}

{Footnote 1: His words.}

"But their enmity comes to nothing."

"Because to indulge it, would bring them into trouble," he replied. "Neither your enemies or mine would run the risk of murdering us in open day; but suppose they could kill us by simply *wishing it?* I should drop down dead before your eyes—and you would fall a corpse in Main Street before you reached your home!"{1}

{Footnote 1: His words.}

"A gloomy view enough, but I dare not deny it."

"It would be useless, colonel. That is the way men are made. For myself, I distrust all of them—or nearly all."

He uttered the words with intense bitterness, and for a moment remained silent.

"This is gloomy talk," he said, "and will not amuse you. Let us change the topic. When I am not discussing public affairs—the doings of this wretched administration, and the old man of the sea astride upon the country's back—I ought to try and amuse myself."

"You find the *Examiner* a heavy weight upon you?"

"It is a mill-stone around my neck."{1}

{Footnote 1: His words.}

"Why not throw it off, if you find it onerous?"

"Because I look to this journal as a father does to an only son—as my pet, my pride, and the support and honor of myself and my name in the future."

"You are proud of it."

"It has made me, and it will do more for me hereafter than it has ever done yet."

He paused, and then went on, with a glow in his swarthy face:

"Every man has his cherished object in this world, colonel. Mine is the success and glory of the *Examiner*. I intend to make of it what the London *Times* is in England, and the world—a great power, which shall lay down the law, control cabinets, mould parties, and direct events. It has given me much trouble to establish it, but *ça ira* now! From the *Examiner* I expect to realize the great dream of my life."

"The dream of your life? What is that?—if I may ask without intrusion."

"Oh! I make no secret of it, and as a gentleman speaking to a gentleman, can say what I could not in the society of *roturiers* or common people. My family is an old and honorable one in Virginia—this, by way of explanation only, I beg you to note. We are thus, people of old descent, but my branch of the family is ruined. My object is to reinstate it; and you will perhaps compare me to the scheming young politician in Bulwer's 'My Novel,' who seeks to restore the family fortunes, and brighten up the lonely old house—in Yorkshire, is it? You remember?"

"Yes," I said.

"Well, I always sympathized with that character. He is morally bad, you say: granted; but he is resolute and brave—and his object is noble."

"I agree with you, the object *is* noble."

"I am glad you think so, colonel. I see I speak to one who has the old Virginia feeling. You respect family."

"Who does not? There are those who profess to care naught for it, but it is because they are new-comers."

"Yes," was the journalist's reply, "mushrooms—and very dirty ones!"

I laughed at the speaker's grimace.

"For my own part," I said, "I do not pretend to be indifferent whether or not my father was a gentleman. I bow as politely to the new-comer as if it were the Conqueror he came over with; but still I am glad my father was a gentleman. I hope no one will quarrel with that."

"You are mistaken. They will hate you for it."

"You are right—but I interrupted you."

"I am glad the interruption came, colonel, for it gave you an opportunity of showing me that my views and your own are in exact accord on this subject. I will proceed, therefore, without ceremony, to tell you what I design doing some day."

I listened with attention. It is always interesting to look into the recesses of a remarkable man's character. This human being was notable in an epoch filled with notabilities; and chance was about to give me an insight into his secret thoughts.

He twirled a paper-cutter in his fingers, reflected a moment, and said:—

"I am still young—not very young either, for I will soon be forty—but I know no young man who has better prospects than myself, and few who have done so well. I suppose I am worth now nearly $100,000 in good money. I have more gold coin than I know what to do with. The *Examiner* is very valuable property, and is destined to be much more so. I expect to live long, and if I do, I shall be rich. When I am rich, I shall buy the old family estate in Stafford County, and shall add to it all the land for miles around. I shall build a house to my fancy, and, with all my possessions walled in, I shall teach these people what they never knew — how to live like a gentleman."{1}

{Footnote 1: This paragraph is in Mr. J.M. Daniel's words.}

The glow had deepened on the sallow face. It was easy to see that the speaker had unfolded to me the dream of his life.

"Your scheme is one," I said, "which takes my fancy greatly. But why do you intend to wall in your property?"

"To keep out those wolves called men."

"Ah! I forgot. You do not like those bipeds without feathers."

"I like some of them, colonel; but the majority are worse than my dogs, Fanny and Frank, yonder. Sometimes I think they are human — they bite each other so!"

I laughed. There was something *piquant* in the grim humor of this singular personage.

"What is your ideal man?" I said, "for, doubtless, you have such an ideal?"

"Yes. I like a man of bronze, who does not snivel or weep. I like Wigfall for his physique and his magnificent courage. It is the genuine thing. There is no *put on* there. He has native pluck — the actual article — and it is no strain on him to exhibit it. The grit is in him, and you can't shake him."{1}

{Footnote 1: This paragraph is in Mr. J.M. Daniel's words.}

"You would admit your men of bronze, then, into the walled-up domain in Stafford?"

"I don't know," he said grimly. "With my violin, a good cook, English books and papers — I hate your Yankee trash — and occasional travel, I think I could get through life without very great ennui. I do not expect to be governor of Virginia for ten years yet!"

And smiling, the journalist said: —

"Let us change the subject. What are people talking about? I never ask what is the news.{1} Is any thing said of evacuating Virginia? That is a pernicious idea!{2} Whom have you seen lately?"

{Footnote 1: His words.}

{Footnote 2: His words.}

"A queer set," I said.

And I gave him an account of my dinner at Mr. Blocque's.

"What a little wretch!" he said. "I think I will run a pin through that bug, and impale him. He would make a fine dish served up *à la Victor Hugo*. You have read *Les Misérables* yonder? It is a trashy affair."

And taking up the elegantly bound volume, which must have cost him a considerable sum, he quietly pitched it out of the window.

As he did so, the printer's devil appeared at the door, holding proof in his hand.

"You see I am never safe from intrusion, colonel. This *Examiner* newspaper keeps me at the oar."

I rose and put on my hat.

"Come and see me again soon, if it suits your convenience," he said. "I am going to write an editorial, and I think I will serve up your host, Blocque."

"Do not use his name."

"Be tranquil. He will be the type only."

And, escorting me to the door, Mr. Daniel bestowed a courteous bow upon me, which I returned. Then the door closed.

VI
AN EDITORIAL IN THE EXAMINER

On the following morning I opened the *Examiner,* and the first article which I saw was the following one, on

THE BLOCKADE-RUNNER.

"We owe to the kindness of SHEM'S Express Company, which has charge

of the line between the front door of the State Department and the

back door of the Tuileries kitchen, the advance sheets of a new

novel by VICTUS HAUTGOUT, which bears the striking title, Les

Fortunés, and which consists of five parts — ABRAHAM, ISAAC, JACOB,

JUDAH, and BENJAMIN. Of course, the discerning reader will not

suppose for a moment that there is any connection between Les

Fortunés and Les Misérables; between the chaste style of

HAUTGOUT and the extravaganzas of HUGO; whose works, in former

days, were not considered fit reading for an Anglo-Saxon public,

whose latest and most corrupt fiction owes its success (let us

hope) rather to the dearth of new literature than to the vitiated

taste of the Southern people. How great the difference between the

two authors is, can best be appreciated by comparing the

description of the gamin in Marius, with the following extracts

from HAUTGOUT'S portraiture of the BLOCKADE-RUNNER: —

"Yankeedom has a bird, and the crocodile has a bird. The crocodile's bird is called the Trochilus. Yankeedom's bird is called the blockade-runner. Yankeedom is the crocodile. The blockade-runner is the Trochilus.

"Couple these two ideas — Yankeedom and the crocodile. They are worth the coupling. The crocodile is asleep. He does not sleep on both ears; he sleeps with one eye open; his jaws are also open. Rows of teeth appear, sharped, fanged, pointed, murderous, carnivorous, omnivorous. Some of the teeth are wanting: say a dozen. Who knocked those teeth out? A demon. What demon? Or perhaps an angel. What angel? The angel is secession: the demon is rebellion. ORMUZD and AHRIMAN: BALDUR and LOKI:
the DEVIL and ST. DUNSTAN. So we go.

"The Trochilus picks the crocodile's teeth. Does the crocodile object? Not he. He likes to have his teeth picked. It is good for his health. It promotes his digestion. It is, on the whole, a sanitary measure. 'Feed yourself,' he says, 'my good Trochilus, on the broken meats which lie between my grinders. Feed your little ones at home. I shan't snap you up unless I get very hungry. There are Confederates enough. Why should I eat you?'

"This little creature — this Trochilus obsidionalis — this blockade-running tomtit — is full of joy. He has rich food to eat every day. He goes to the show every evening, when he is not on duty. He has a fine shirt on his back; patent-leather boots on his feet; the pick and choice of a dozen houses. He is of any age — chiefly of the conscript age; ranges singly or in couples; haunts auction houses; dodges enrolling officers; eats canvass-backs; smells of greenbacks; swears allegiance to both

sides; keeps faith with neither; is hand and glove with ABE'S

detectives as well as with WINDER'S Plugs; smuggles in an ounce of

quinine for the Confederate Government, and smuggles out a pound of

gold for the Lincolnites; fishes in troubled waters; runs with the hare and hunts with the hounds; sings Yankee Doodle through one nostril, and My Maryland through the other; is on good terms with

everybody — especially with himself — and, withal, is as great a rascal as goes unhung.

"He has sports of his own; roguish tricks of his own, of which a hearty hatred of humdrum, honest people is the basis. He has his own occupations, such as running for hacks, which he hires at fabulous prices; crossing the Potomac in all kinds of weather; rubbing off Yankee trade-marks and putting English labels in their stead. He has a currency of his own, slips of green paper, which have an unvarying and well regulated circulation throughout this gipsy band.

"He is never satisfied with his pantaloons unless they have a watch-fob, and never satisfied with his watch-fob unless it contains a gold watch. Sometimes he has two watch-fobs; sometimes

a score.

"This rosy child of Richmond lives, develops, gets into and out of scrapes — a merry witness of our social unrealities. He looks on ready to laugh; ready also for something else, for pocketing whatever he can lay his hands on. Whoever you are, you that call yourselves Honor, Justice, Patriotism, Independence, Freedom, Candour, Honesty, Right, beware of the grinning blockade-runner. He is growing. He will continue to grow.

"Of what clay is he made? Part Baltimore street-dirt, part James River mud, best part and worst part sacred soil of Palestine. What will become of him in the hands of the potter, chance? Heaven grant that he may be ground into his original powder before he is stuck up on our mantel-pieces as a costly vase, in which the choice flowers of our civilization can but wither and die."

Admire that grim humor, reader—the firm stroke with which this Aristophanes of 1864 drew my friend, Mr. Blocque. See how he reproduced every trait, delineated the worthy in his exact colors, and, at the foot of the picture, wrote, as it were, "Here is going to be the founder of 'one of the old families,'—one of the ornaments of the future, who will come out of the war rich, and be a costly vase, not a vessel of dishonor, as at present."

Grim satirist! You saw far, and I think we want you to-day!

VII
UNDER THE CROSSED SWORDS

I had dined with Mr. Blocque; two days afterward I went to sup with Judge Conway.

Does the reader remember his appearance at Culpeper Court-House, on the night of the ball after the review in June, 1863? On that evening he had excited my astonishment by abruptly terminating the interview between his daughter and Captain Davenant; and I little supposed that I would ever penetrate the motive of that action, or become intimate with the performer.

Yet the chance of war had decreed that both events should occur. All will be, in due time, explained to the reader's satisfaction; at present we will simply make the acquaintance of one of the most distinguished statesmen of the epoch.

My friendly relations with the judge came about in a very simple manner. He was an intimate associate of the gentleman at whose house I was staying; had taken great interest in my recovery after Yellow Tavern; and therefore had done me the honor to bestow his friendship upon me.

On the day to which we have now come, Judge Conway had made a speech of surpassing eloquence, in Congress, on the condition of the country, and I had listened, thrilling at the brave voice which rang out its sonorous, "All's well!" amid the storm. I was now going to call on the statesman to express my admiration of his eloquent appeal, and converse upon the exciting topics of the hour.

I found him in a mansion not far from the splendid residence of Mr. Blocque. Here he occupied "apartments," or rather a single room,—and, in 1864, my dear reader, that was a very common mode of living.

Like others, Judge Conway was too poor to occupy a whole house,— even too poor to board. He had a single apartment, containing a few chairs and a bed; was waited on by a maid; and, I think, prepared his own meals, which were plain to poverty.

He met me at the door of his bare and poor-looking apartment, extending his hand with the gracious and stately courtesy of the ancient régime. His figure was small, slight, and bent by age; his face, thin and pale; his hair nearly white, and falling in long curls upon his shoulders; under the gray brows sparkled keen, penetrating, but benignant eyes.

As I pressed the hand of my host, and looked around the poor apartment, I could not refrain from a sentiment of profound bitterness. Two days before I had dined at the table of a peddling blockade-runner, who ate canvass-backs, drank champagne, wore "fine linen," and, dodging the conscript officers, revelled in luxury and plenty. And now here before me was a gentleman of ancient lineage, whose ancestors had been famous, who had himself played a great part in the history of the commonwealth, — and this gentleman was poor, lived in lodgings, had scarce a penny; he had been wealthy, and was still the owner of great possessions; but the bare land was all that was left him for support. He had been surrounded with luxury, but had sacrificed all to the cause. He had had two gallant sons, but they had fallen at the first Manassas — their crossed swords were above his poor bare mantel-piece.

From the splendid table of the sneaking blockade-runner, I had come to the poverty-stricken apartment of this great statesman and high-bred gentleman. "Oh, Juvenal!" I muttered, "it is your satires, not the bucolics of Virgil, that suit this epoch!"

The old statesman pointed, with all the grace of a nobleman, to a bare rocking-chair, and received my congratulations upon his speech with modest simplicity.

"I am glad that my views are honored by your good opinion, colonel," he said, "and that you approve of the tone of them. I am naturally given to invective—a habit derived from my friend, the late Mr. Randolph; but the country wants encouragement."

"And yet not to satirize is so hard, my dear sir!"

"Very hard."

"Think of the army depleted—the soldiers starving—the finances in ruin, and entire destruction threatening us!"

The old statesman was silent. A moment afterward he raised his head, and with his thin finger pointed to the crossed swords above his mantelpiece.

"I try to bear and forbear since I lost my poor boys," he said. "They died for their country—I ought to live for it, and do what I can in my sphere—to suppress my bitterness, and try to utter words of good cheer. But we are discussing gloomy topics. Let us come to more cheerful matters. I am in very good spirits to-day. My daughters have come to make me a visit," and the old face glowed with smiles; its expression was quite charming.

"I see you do not appreciate that great treat, my dear colonel," he added, smiling. "You are yet unmarried, though I rejoice to hear you are soon to be united to a daughter of my old friend, Colonel Beverly, of "The Oaks." Some day I hope you will know the great charm of paternity. This morning I was lonely—this evening I am no longer so. Georgia and Virginia have come up from my house, "Five Forks," escorted by my faithful old Juba, and they burst in upon me like the sunshine!"

The words had scarcely been uttered when a tap came at the door; a voice said, "May we come in, papa?" and a moment afterward the door opened, and admitted Miss Georgia Conway and her sister Virginia.

Miss Georgia was the same tall and superb beauty, with the dark hair and eyes; Miss Virginia the same winning little blonde, with the blue eyes, and the smiles which made her lips resemble rose-buds. The young ladies were clad in poor, faded-looking calicoes, and the slippers on the small feet, peeping from their skirts, were full of holes. Such was the appearance presented in that summer of 1864, my dear reader, by two of the most elegant and "aristocratic" young ladies of Virginia!

But you did not look at the calicoes, and soon forgot the holes in the shoes. My bow was such as I should have bestowed on two princesses, and the young ladies received it with a grace and courtesy which were charming.

In ten minutes we were all talking like old friends, and the young ladies were making tea.

This was soon ready; some bread, without butter, was placed upon the little table; and the meal was the most cheerful and happy imaginable. "Oh, my dear Mr. Blocque!" I could not help saying to myself, "keep your champagne, and canvass-backs, and every luxury, and welcome! I like dry bread and tea, with this company, better!"

I have not room to repeat the charming words, mingled with laughter, of the young women, on that evening. Their presence was truly like sunshine, and you could see the reflection of it upon the old statesman's countenance.

Only once that countenance was overshadowed. I had uttered the name of Willie Davenant, by accident; and then all at once remembering the scene at Culpeper Court-House, had looked quietly at Judge Conway and Miss Virginia. A deep frown was on his face—that of the young girl was crimson with blushes, and two tears came to her eyes, as she caught her father's glance of displeasure.

I hastened to change the topic—to banish the dangerous subject; and in a few moments everybody was smiling once more. Miss Georgia, in her stately and amusing way, was relating their experiences from a scouting party of the enemy, at "Five Forks."

"I heard something of this from old Juba," said the Judge; "you do not mention your deliverer, however."

"Our deliverer, papa?"

"General Mohun."

Miss Georgia unmistakably blushed in her turn.

"Oh, I forgot!" she said, carelessly, "General Mohun *did* drive them off. Did I not mention it? — I should have done so before finishing, papa."

As she spoke, the young lady happened to catch my eye. I was laughing quietly. Thereupon her head rose in a stately way — a decided pout succeeded — finally, she burst into laughter.

The puzzled expression of the old Judge completed the comedy of the occasion — we all laughed in a perfectly absurd and foolish way — and the rest of the evening passed in the most cheerful manner imaginable.

When I bade my friends good evening, I knew something I had not known before: — namely, that Mohun the woman-hater, had renewed his "friendly relations" with Miss Georgia Conway, at her home in Dinwiddie.

Exchanging a pressure of the hand with my host and his charming daughters, I bade them good evening, and returned homeward. As I went along, I thought of the happy circle I had left; and again I could not refrain from drawing the comparison between Judge Conway and Mr. Blocque.

At the fine house of the blockade-runner — champagne, rich viands, wax-lights, gold and silver, and profuse luxury.

At the poor lodgings of the great statesman, — a cup of tea and cold bread; stately courtesy from my host, charming smiles from his beautiful daughters, clad in calico, with worn-out shoes — and above the simple happy group, the crossed swords of the brave youths who had fallen at Manassas!

VIII
MR. X———-

It was past ten in the evening when I left Judge Conway. But I felt no disposition to retire; and determined to pay a visit to a singular character of my acquaintance.

The name of this gentleman was Mr. X— —-.

Looking back now to the days spent in Richmond, in that curious summer of '64, I recall, among the representative personages whom I encountered, no individual more remarkable than the Honorable Mr. X— —--. You are acquainted with him, my dear reader, either personally or by reputation, for he was a prominent official of the Confederate Government, and, before the war, had been famous in the councils of "the nation."

He resided at this time in a small house, on a street near the capitol. You gained access to his apartment after night—if you knew the way—by a winding path, through shrubbery, to the back door of the mansion. When you entered, you found yourself in presence of a tall, powerful, gray-haired and very courteous personage, who sat in a huge arm-chair, near a table littered with papers, and smoked, meditatively, a cigar, the flavor of which indicated its excellent quality.

I enjoyed the intimacy of Mr. X— —-- in spite of the difference of our ages and positions. He had been the friend of my father, and, in my turn, did me the honor to bestow his friendship upon me. On this evening I was seized with the fancy to visit him—and passing through the grounds of the capitol, where the bronze Washington and his great companions looked silently out into the moonlight, reached the small house, followed the path through the shrubbery, and opening the door in the rear, found myself suddenly enveloped in a cloud of cigar smoke, through which loomed the portly figure of Mr. X— —-.

He was seated, as usual, in his large arm-chair, by the table, covered with papers; and a small bell near his hand seemed placed there for the convenience of summoning an attendant, without the trouble of rising. Near the bell lay a package of foreign-looking documents. Near the documents lay a pile of telegraphic dispatches. In the appearance and surroundings of this man you read "Power."

Mr. X— —- received me with easy cordiality.

"Glad to see you, my dear colonel," he said, rising and shaking my hand; then sinking back in his chair, "take a cigar, and tell me the news." I sat down,—having declined the proffered cigar.

"The news!" I said, laughing; "I ought to ask that of you."

"Ah! you think I am well-informed?"

I pointed to the dispatches. Mr. X— —- shrugged his shoulders.

"Papers from England and France—they are not going to recognize us.

"And those telegrams—nothing. We get little that is worth attention, except a line now and then, signed 'R.E. Lee.'"

"Well, there is that signature," I said, pointing to an open paper.

"It is a private letter to me—but do you wish to see a line which I have just received? It is interesting, I assure you."

And he handed me a paper.

It was a telegram announcing the fall of Atlanta!

"Good heavens!" I said, "is it possible? Then there is nothing to stop Sherman."

"Nothing whatever," said Mr. X— —-, coolly.

"What will be the consequence?"

"The Confederacy will be cut in two. Sherman will be at Savannah before Grant reaches the Southside road—or as soon, at least."

"You think Grant will reach that?"

"Yes, by April; and then—you know what!"

"But Lee will protect it."

Mr. X— —- shrugged his shoulders.

"Shall I tell you a secret?"

I listened.

"Lee's force is less than 50,000—next spring it will not number 40,000. Grant's will be at least four times that."

"Why can not our army be re-enforced?"

Mr. X— —- helped himself to a fresh cigar.

"The people are tired, and the conscript officers are playing a farce," he said. "The commissary department gives the army a quarter of a pound of rancid meat. That even often fails, for the quartermaster's department does not supply it. The result is—no conscripts, and a thousand desertions. The soldiers are starving; their wives and children are writing them letters that drive them mad—the end is not far off; and when Grant reaches the Southside road we are gone."

Mr. X— —- smoked his cigar with extreme calmness as he spoke.

"But one thing remains," I said.

"What is that?"

"Lee will retreat from Virginia."

Mr. X— —- shook his head.

"He will not."

"Why not?"

"He will be prevented from doing so."

"Under any circumstances?"

"Until too late, at least."

"And the result?"

"Surrender—though he said to me the other day, when he came to see me here, 'For myself, I intend to die sword in hand.'"

I could not refrain from a sentiment of profound gloom, as I listened to these sombre predictions. It seemed incredible that they could be well founded, but I had more than once had an opportunity to remark the extraordinary prescience of the remarkable man with whom I conversed.

"You draw a black picture of the future," I said. "And the South seems moving to and fro, on the crust of a volcano."

"No metaphor could be more just."

"And what will be the result of the war?"

"That is easy to reply to. Political slavery, negro suffrage, and the bayonet, until the new leaven works."

"The new leaven?"

"The conviction that democratic government is a failure."

"And then—?"

"An emperor, or dictator—call him what you will. The main fact is, that he will rule the country by the bayonet—North and South impartially."

Mr. X— —- lit a fresh cigar.

"Things are going on straight to that," he said. "The future is perfectly plain to me, for I read it in the light of history. These events are going to follow step by step. Lee is brave—no man is braver; a great leader. I think him one of the first captains of the world. But in spite of his courage and skill—in spite of the heroism of his army—in spite of the high character and pure motives of the president—we are going to fail. Then the rest will follow—negro suffrage and the bayonet. Then the third era will begin—the disgust of the white man at the equality of the negro; his distrust of a government which makes such a farce possible; consequent revulsion against democracy; a tendency toward monarchy; a king, emperor or dictator, who will restore order out of the chaos of misrule and madness. England is rushing toward a democracy, America is hastening to become an empire. For my own part I think I prefer the imperial to the popular idea—Imperator to Demos. It is a matter of taste, however."

And Mr. X——- turned his head, calling out, calmly,

"Come in!"

The door opened and a stranger glided into the apartment. He was clad in a blue Federal uniform, half-concealed by a brown linen overall. His face was almost covered by a red beard; his lips by a mustache of the same color; and his eyes disappeared behind huge green goggles.

"Come in," repeated Mr. X——-, who seemed to recognize the intruder; "what news?"

The personage glanced quickly at me.

"Speak before him," said Mr. X——-, "he is a friend."

"I am very well acquainted with Colonel Surry," said the other, smiling, "and have the honor to number him, I hope, among my own friends."

With which words, the new-comer quietly removed his red beard, took off his green spectacles, and I saw before me no less a personage than Mr. Nighthawk!

IX

"SEND ME A COPY.
IN CANADA!"

Nothing was more surprising in this singular man than these sudden appearances at places and times when you least expected him.

I had parted with him in Spottsylvania, on the night when he "deserted" from the enemy, and rode into our lines; and he was then the secret agent of General Stuart. Now, he reappeared in the city of Richmond, with an excellent understanding, it was evident, between himself and Mr. X— —-!

Our greeting was cordial, and indeed I never had classed Nighthawk among professional spies. General Stuart assured me one day, that he invariably refused all reward; and his profound, almost romantic devotion to Mohun, had deeply impressed me. Love of country and watchful care of the young cavalier, whose past life was as mysterious as his own, seemed the controlling sentiments of Nighthawk; and he always presented himself to me rather in the light of a political conspirator, than as a "spy."

His first words now indicated that he was a secret agent of the Government. He seemed to have been everywhere, and gained access to everybody; and once more, as in June, 1863, when he appeared at Stuart's head-quarters, near Middleburg, he astonished me by the accuracy and extent of his information. Political and military secrets of the highest importance, and calling for urgent action on the part of the Government, were detailed by Nighthawk, in his calm and benignant voice; he gave us an account of a long interview which he had had at City Point, with General Grant; and wound up as usual by announcing an impending battle—a movement of the enemy, which duly took place as he announced.

Mr. X— —- listened with close attention, asking few questions.

When Nighthawk had made his report, the statesman looked at his watch, said, *sotto voce*, "Midnight—too late," and added aloud:—

"Come back at ten to-morrow morning, my friend; your information is highly interesting and important."

Nighthawk rose, and I did likewise, declining the courteous request of Mr. X— —- to prolong my visit. He held the door open with great politeness and said, smiling:—

"I need not say, my dear colonel, that the views I have expressed this evening are confidential—for the present, at least."

"Assuredly," I replied, with a bow and a smile.

"Hereafter you are at liberty to repeat them, if you wish, only I beg you will ascribe them to Mr. X— —-, an unknown quantity. If you write a book, and put me in it, send me a copy—in Canada!"

A moment afterward I was wending my way through the shrubbery, thinking of the curious personage I had left.

At the gate Nighthawk awaited me, and I scarcely recognized him. He had resumed his red beard, and green glasses.

"I am glad to see you again, colonel," he said benignantly; "I heard that you were in the city and called at your lodgings, but found you absent."

"You wished to see me particularly, then, Nighthawk."

"Yes, and to-night, colonel."

"Ah!"

"I know you are a friend of General Mohun's."

"A very sincere friend."

"Well, I think we will be able to do him a very great service by attending to a little matter in which he is interested, colonel. Are you disengaged, and willing to accompany me?"

X
THE WAY THE MONEY WENT

I looked intently at Nighthawk. He was evidently very much in earnest.

"I am entirely disengaged, and perfectly willing to accompany you," I said; "but where?"

Nighthawk smiled.

"You know I am a mysterious person, colonel, both by character and profession. I fear the habit is growing on me, in spite of every exertion I make. I predict I will end by burning my coat, for fear it will tell some of my secrets."

"Well," I said with a smile, "keep your secret then, and lead the way. I am ready to go far to oblige Mohun in any thing."

"I thank you, colonel, from my heart. You have only to follow me."

And Nighthawk set out at a rapid pace, through the grounds of the capitol, toward the lower part of the city.

There was something as singular about the walk of my companion, as about his appearance. He went at a great pace, but his progress was entirely noiseless. You would have said that he was skimming along upon invisible wings.

In an incredibly short time we had reached a street below the capitol, and my companion, who had walked straight on without turning his head to the right or the left, all at once paused before a tall and dingy-looking house, which would have appeared completely uninhabited, except for a bright red light which shone through a circular opening in the door.

At this door Nighthawk gave a single tap. The glass covering the circular space glided back, and a face reconnoitred. My companion uttered two words; and the door opened, giving access to a stairs, which we ascended, the janitor having already disappeared.

At the head of the stairs was a door which Nighthawk opened, and we found ourselves in an apartment where a dozen persons were playing faro.

Upon these Nighthawk threw a rapid glance—some one whom he appeared to be seeking, was evidently not among the players.

Another moment he returned through the door, I following, and we ascended a second flight of stairs, at the top of which was a second door. Here another janitor barred the way, but my companion again uttered some low words,—the door opened; a magnificently lit apartment, with a buffet of liquors, and every edible, presented itself before us; and in the midst of a dozen personages, who were playing furiously, I recognized—Mr. Blocque, Mr. Croker, Mr. Torpedo, and Colonel Desperade.

For some moments I stood watching the spectacle, and it very considerably enlarged my experience. Before me I saw prominent politicians, officers of high rank, employees of government holding responsible positions, all gambling with an ardor that amounted to fury. One gentleman in uniform—apparently of the quartermaster's department—held in his hand a huge package of Confederate notes, of the denominations, of $100 and $500, and this worthy staked, twice, the pretty little amount of $10,000 upon a card, and each time lost.

The play so absorbed the soldiers, lawgivers, and law-administrators, that our presence was unperceived. My friend, Mr. Blocque, did not turn his head; Mr. Croker, Mr. Torpedo, and Colonel Desperade, were red in the face and oblivious.

After that evening I knew where some of the public money went.

As I was looking at the strange scene of reckless excitement, one of the players, a portly individual with black mustache, rich dark curls, gold spectacles, and wearing a fine suit of broadcloth—rose and looked toward us. Nighthawk was already gazing at him; and suddenly I saw their glances cross like steel rapiers. They had evidently recognized each other; and going up to the gentleman of the spectacles, Nighthawk said a few words in a low voice, which I did not distinguish.

"With pleasure, my dear friend," said the portly gentleman, "but you are sure you are not provided with a detective of General Winder's?"

"Can you believe such a thing?" returned Nighthawk, reproachfully.

"I thought it possible you might have one waiting below; but if you give me your word, Nighthawk—"

And without further objection the worthy followed Nighthawk and myself down the stairs.

As we approached the outer door, the invisible janitor opened it; we issued forth into the street; and the portly gentleman, fixing a keen look upon me in the clear moonlight, said: —

"I believe we have had the pleasure of meeting before, colonel."

"I am ashamed to say I do not remember where, sir," I said.

"My memory is better, colonel; we met last May, in a house in the Wilderness, near Chancellorsville."

"Is it possible that you are—"

"Swartz, very much at your service. It is wonderful what a difference is made by a wig and spectacles!"

As he spoke, he gracefully removed his black wig and the gold spectacles. In the man with gray hair, small eyes, and double chin, I recognized the spy of the Wilderness.

XI
THE PASS

Replacing his wig and spectacles, Mr. Swartz smiled in a good-humored manner, and said: —

"May I ask to what I am indebted for this visit?"

Nighthawk replied even more blandly: —

"I wish to have a conversation with you, my dear Swartz, before arresting you."

"Ah! you intend to arrest me!"

"Unless you make it unnecessary."

"How?"

"By producing the paper which we spoke of in the Wilderness," said Nighthawk, briefly.

Swartz shook his head.

"That is not in my power, my friend. I did not bring it with me."

"Will you think me very impolite if I say I do not believe you, my dear Swartz?"

Swartz smiled.

"Well, that would be speaking without ceremony, my friend — but I assure you I am unable to do as you desire."

"Aha! you repeat that curious statement, my dear Swartz! Well, oblige me by accompanying me to the provost-marshal's."

"You arrest me?"

"Precisely."

"As a spy?"

"Why not?"

"It is impossible, Nighthawk!"

"You resist?"

"I might do so."

And, opening his coat, Mr. Swartz exhibited a bowie-knife and revolver.

"I show you these little toys," said he, laughing good-humoredly, "to let you see, my friend, that I might oppose your project—and you know I am not backward in using them on occasion. But I make a difference. You are not a common police-officer or detective, Nighthawk—you are a friend and comrade, and I am going to prove that I appreciate your feelings, and respect your wishes."

Nighthawk fixed his eyes on the speaker and listened.

"You are a friend of General Mohun's," said Mr. Swartz, with bland good humor; "you wish to secure a certain document in which he is interested; you fancy I have that document here in the city of Richmond; and your object, very naturally, is to force me to surrender it. Well, I do not object to doing so—for a consideration. I fully intend to produce it, when my terms are accepted. I would have stated them to you in the Wilderness, but you were unable to meet me—or to General Mohun, but his violence defeated every thing. You meet me now, and without discussion, demand the paper. I reply, that I have not brought it with me, but three days from this time will meet you at a spot agreed on, with the document, for which you will return me—my consideration."

Nighthawk shook his head.

"Unfortunately, my dear Swartz, experience tells me that the present is always the best time for business—that 'a bird in the hand is worth two in the bush.'"

Mr. Swartz smiled sweetly.

"And I am the bird in your hand?"

"Something like it."

"I am a spy?"

"Don't use hard names, my friend."

"By no means, my dear Nighthawk, and if I have hurt your feelings, I deeply regret it. But I am speaking to the point. You regard me as a Federal spy, lurking in Richmond—you penetrate my disguise, and are going to arrest me, and search my lodgings for that paper."

"The necessity is painful," said Nighthawk.

"It is useless, my friend."

"I will try it."

Swartz smiled, and drew a paper from his pocket, which he unfolded.

"You are then determined to arrest your old comrade, Nighthawk."

"Yes, my dear Swartz."

"As a spy?"

"Exactly."

"In spite of this?"

And Mr. Swartz held out the paper.

"Do me the favor to read this, colonel, and then oblige me by returning it."

I took the paper, and easily read it by moonlight. It contained the following words: —

"The bearer is employed on secret service, by the Confederate Government, and will not be molested."

The paper was signed by a personage of high position in the government, and was stamped with the seal of the department over which he presided. There could be no doubt of the genuineness of the paper. The worthy Mr. Swartz loomed up before me in the novel and unexpected light of a *Confederate* emissary!

I read the paper aloud to Nighthawk, and pointed to the official signature and seal.

Nighthawk uttered a groan, and his chin sank upon his breast.

That spectacle seemed to excite the sympathy of his friend.

"There, my dear Nighthawk," said Mr. Swartz, in a feeling tone, "don't take the blow too much to heart. I have beaten you, this game, and your hands are tied at present. But I swear that I will meet you, and produce that paper."

"When?" murmured Nighthawk.

"In three days from this time."

"Where?"

"At the house of our friend Alibi, near Monk's Neck, in Dinwiddie."

"On your word?"

"On the word of Swartz!"

"That is enough, my dear Swartz; I will be at Alibi's, when we will come to terms. And now, pardon this visit, which has put you to so much inconvenience. I was merely jesting, my dear friend, when I spoke of arresting you. Arrest you! Nothing could induce me to think of so unfriendly a proceeding. And now, good night, my dear friend. I will return with you, colonel."

With which words Nighthawk saluted his "friend," and we returned toward the upper part of the city.

Such were the scenes of a night in the summer of 1864.

XII
THE GRAVE OF STUART

On the next morning a piece of good fortune befell me. In spite of continued visits to the war-office, and an amount of importunity which must have been exceedingly annoying to the gentlemen of the red tape, I found myself, at the end of August, apparently no nearer to an "assignment to duty" than at first.

It really seemed that the Confederate States had no need of my services; that the privilege of performing military duty in behalf of the Government was one jealously guarded, and not to be lightly bestowed upon any one. I was in despair, and was revolving the project of resigning my empty commission, and enlisting in the cavalry as a private soldier, when the *deus ex machinâ* to extricate me from all my troubles, appeared in the person of Colonel P— —-, of army head-quarters.

This accomplished soldier and gentleman met me as I was coming out of the war-office, on the morning after the visit to Mr. X— —-, looking I suppose, like some descendant of the Knight of the Sorrowful Countenance, and stopped to inquire the cause of my dejection. I informed him of the whole affair, and he laughed heartily. "You have set about your affairs, my dear colonel, in a manner entirely wrong," he said. "You should have gone to some general, discovered that your grandmother and his own were third cousins; expressed your admiration of his valor; denounced the brother-general with whom he was quarreling; written puffs to the papers about him; and then, one morning said, 'By the by, general, you are entitled to another staff officer.' The result would have been a glowing letter to the war department, requesting your assignment—you would have attained your object—you would have been torn from the horrors of Richmond, and once more enjoyed the great privilege of being shot at!"

I echoed the colonel's laugh.

"Alas!" I said, "I have no genius for all that. I never yet could 'crook the hinges of the knee that thrift might follow fawning,' and I suppose I shall be compelled to resign, and enter the ranks. Why not? Better men are there, carrying musket or carbine, or pulling the lanyard."

"Still you gained your rank by your services—and I am going to make you an offer which will enable you to retain it. Come and be my assistant inspector-general—an officer is required to inspect the cavalry and horse artillery, which is so distant, often, that I have no time to visit them."

"A thousand thanks, colonel! You could not offer me a more pleasant duty."

"You will have to ride a great deal, but will have a great deal of freedom. If you consent to my proposition, I will have the matter arranged at once, and will request you to make a tour of inspection to General Early's army, near Winchester."

He looked at me, laughing.

"'The Oaks' is—a charming place," he added, "and you are certain to be very tired when you reach the vicinity of Markham's! If you find it convenient to stop there—say, for a day or more—present my regards to Colonel Beverly, and any of the family you find present!"

With which words he laughed again, shook me by the hand, and then his tall form disappeared in the doorway of the war office.

On the next day I found my assignment awaiting me. I was appointed assistant inspector-general of the cavalry and horse artillery of the army of Northern Virginia. Tremendous title!

That evening I went by railway to Petersburg, to visit Colonel P——-, and receive his instructions. Returning the same night, the next day set out on horseback for the Valley of the Shenandoah, by way of Orange, Gaines's Cross Roads, and Ashby's Gap.

Of this journey it is unnecessary for me to speak in the present volume. Some curious adventures occurred to me, in the valley, near Millwood, and I made the acquaintance of St. Leger Landon, of "Bizarre," one of the bravest and truest gentlemen I have ever known. The adventures alluded to, and some events in the strange history of my friend, Captain Landon, are embraced in a separate memoir, to which I have given the fanciful title, *Hilt to Hilt, or Days and Nights on the Banks of the Shenandoah.*

I remained in the valley from the first to the eighteenth of September, when I set out on my return to Petersburg, little thinking that, on the very next day, General Early would be attacked on the Opequon, driven from Winchester, and forced to retreat up the valley, in spite of fighting which was never surpassed.

I had received some rough handling in a cavalry combat near the Old Chapel, beyond Millwood, and my ride back was tedious. But at last I reached Richmond, and made preparations to set out at once for the army. On the evening before my departure, I went to visit the grave of Stuart at Hollywood, on the beautiful hill above the falls, west of the city.

As I approached the lonely spot, where the great cavalier was lying beside his little Flora, of whom he had often spoken to me with tears, a thousand memories knocked at the door of my heart. With head bent down, and chin resting on my breast, I drew near the grassy mound over which waved the autumn foliage, tinted with yellow and crimson—and in these few moments, all the splendid career of Stuart passed before me, as on that day when I rode with him toward the fatal field of Yellow Tavern.

I remembered all his hard combats, his glorious encounters, his victories over such odds as vindicated his claim to a descent from the dashing Rupert, and ranked him with the most famous leaders of cavalry in all history. I recalled the courage, the joy, the gay laughter of the great soldier—the blue eyes that flashed so—the sonorous voice singing the merry songs. I remembered all the occasions when he had led his men in the charge—how he had wept for Jackson, bowed his head above the cold face of Pelham—how he had met the torrent unmoved, shrunk from nothing in his path, fallen to save the Virginia capital, and died murmuring "God's will be done!"—I remembered all that, and with something in my throat that seemed choking me, drew near the quiet mound, beneath which rested such a career, and so much glory.

The birds were twittering and singing, the foliage waving gently—I raised my head—when suddenly I became aware that a solitary mourner was bending over the grave.

He was an officer in gray uniform. He held a flower in his hand, which he dropped upon the grave, uttering a low sob as he did so.

At the same moment he turned round, and I 'l'' Mosby.{1}

{Footnote 1: Real.}

XIII
THE CEDARS

Twenty-four hours after, I had passed over the same number of miles, and found myself at the staff head-quarters, on the left bank of the Appomattox, above Petersburg.

I had soon pitched my tent, with the assistance of a servant; had erected a hedge of cedar boughs to protect it from the cutting blasts of the coming winter; and, a few days afterwards, was surrounded with many objects of comfort. My tent had been floored; at one end rose an excellent chimney; strips of planks, skillfully balanced on two logs, supplied a spring bed; I had secured a split bottom chair, and my saddle and bridle were disposed upon a rough rack, near a black valise containing my small stock of apparel, and the pine table and desk holding official papers.

Having christened this castle "The Cedars," I settled down for a long winter,—and it was not a great while before I congratulated myself on the good fortune which had provided me with that warm nest. More than once, however, I experienced something like a sentiment of shame, when, in the dark and freezing nights, with the hail rattling on my tent, I sat by my warm fire, and heard the crack of the sharp-shooters, along the lines beyond Petersburg. What right had I to be there, by that blazing fire, in my warm tent, when my brethren—many of them my betters— were yonder, fighting along the frozen hills? What had I done to deserve that comfort, and exemption from all pain? I was idling, or reading by my blazing fire,—*they* were keeping back the enemy, and, perhaps, falling and dying in the darkness. I was musing in my chair, gazing into the blaze, and going back in memory to the fond scenes of home, so clearly, that I laughed the heart's laugh, and was happy. And they? They, too, were thinking of home, perhaps,—of their wives and children, to sink down the next moment shivering with cold, or stagger and fall, with spouting blood, as the bullet pierced them. Why should *I* be thus favored by a good Providence? I often asked myself that question, and I could not answer it. I could only murmur, "I did not sneak here to get out of the way of the bullets, — those, yonder, are my betters, — God guard and keep the brave soldiers of this army!"

And now, worthy reader, having given you some idea of the manner in which the more fortunate ones wintered near Petersburg, in 1864, I am going to drop the subject of army head-quarters, and my surroundings there. Jackson and Stuart are dead, and have become figures of history. I have drawn them as well as I could, — I dare not attempt to do the same with the great commander-in-chief. He is alive. May he live long! — and, saluting him, I pass on.

So if I speak of General Lee, it will be of the individual in his official character. What he utters, he will have uttered in the hearing of many.

With these words of preface, I resume the thread of my history.

XIV
THE SITUATION

October, 1864, had come.

The "situation" may be described in a few words.

Grant had drawn his lines from a point in Charles City, on the left bank of James River, across that stream and across the Appomattox, around Petersburg to the Squirrel Level road, where he threatened the Southside railroad, Lee's line of communication with the south and west. Fort Harrison had just been taken. Grant was gradually hemming in his opponent along the immense line extending across the two rivers, past the scene of the famous "Crater" explosion, to the vicinity of the Rowanty, a distance of nearly forty miles. One incessant crash and thunder went up, day and night. Grant was "hammering continuously," carrying out his programme; and, the military view apart, never was spectacle more picturesque than that presented in these combats.

The long lines of works were wreathed with the smoke of battle. The glare of cannon lit the smoke-cloud; mortar shells rose, described their fiery curves, and descended in the trenches, and these were saluted as they rose and fell by the crack of musketry, the roar of artillery, the echoing cheers of the blue and gray people, who never seemed weary of fighting, yelling, and paying their compliments to each other. At night the spectacle was superb; the mortars were like flocks of fire-birds, swooping down upon their prey. The horizon glared at each cannon-shot; shell burst in vivid lightnings, shining for a moment, then extinguished. And yonder object, like a bloodshot eye, shining grimly through the darkness, — what is that? It is a lamp, my dear reader, with a transparent shade; and on this shade is written, for the information of the graybacks: —

"While yet the lamp holds out to burn,

The vilest rebel may return."

Lee's lines faced Grant's, following the blue cordon across the rivers, around Petersburg, toward the Southside railroad.

Beyond the right of the Confederate infantry stretched the cavalry, which consisted of the divisions of Wade Hampton and W.H.F. Lee, — the former commanding. Fitz Lee, with his division, was in the Valley.

Such, reader was the situation, when I joined the army. The great fifth act of the tragic drama was approaching.

XV
MOHUN AGAIN

Three days after my arrival, I mounted my horse, crossed the Appomattox, followed the Boydton road, struck southward at the Quaker road, and soon found myself in the heart of the shadowy pine woods of that singular country, Dinwiddie.

My official duty was to inspect and report the condition of the cavalry and horse artillery of the army at the beginning and middle of each month. And now, first assuring the reader that I performed my duty in all weather, and amid every difficulty, I will drop the official phase of my history, and proceed to matters rather more entertaining.

On the day after my departure from Petersburg, I had made my inspections, and was returning.

I had been received by my old friends of the cavalry with every mark of cordial regard. General Hampton, General Lee, and the various officers and men whom I had known as a staff-officer of General Stuart, seemed to welcome the sight of a face which, perhaps, reminded them of their dead leader; and I had pressed all these warm hands, and received these friendly greetings not without emotion—for I, too, was carried back to the past.

I saw Mordaunt and Davenant, but not Mohun—he was absent, visiting his picket line. Mordaunt was the same stately soldier—his grave and friendly voice greeted me warmly as in old days; and Willie Davenant, now a major, commanding a battalion of horse artillery, shook hands with me, as shy and blushing as before—and even more sad.

"How had his suit prospered? Were things more encouraging?"

I asked him these questions with a laugh, apologizing for my intrusion.

He assured me sadly that it was not in the least an intrusion; but that he had not seen the person to whom I alluded, for many months.

And executing a blush which would have become a girl, this young tiger of the horse artillery—for such he always proved himself, in a fight—

hastened to change the subject. Soon afterward I took my departure, turned my horse's head toward Petersburg, and set out at a round trot between the walls of pine.

It was dusk when I reached the debouchment of the "military road," and, tired and hungry, I was contemplating ruefully the long ride still before me, when rapid hoof-strokes behind me attracted my attention, and, turning my head, I recognized the bold figure of Mohun.

He was mounted on a fine animal, and came at full speed.

In a moment he had caught up, recognized, and we exchanged a warm grasp of the hand.

"I am delighted to see you, Surry. I thought you had deserted us, old fellow. The sight of you is a treat!"

"And the sight of you, my dear Mohun. You look beaming."

Indeed, Mohun had never presented a better appearance, with his dark eyes; his tanned and glowing cheeks; his raven mustached lips, which, parting with a smile, showed white and regular teeth. He was the picture of a gallant soldier; all his old melancholy and cynical bitterness gone, as mist is swept away by the morning sunshine.

"You are positively dazzling, Mohun. Where are you going, and what has happened to you? Ah!—I begin to understand!"

And pointing northward, I said:—

"Five Forks is not far from here, is it?"

Mohun colored, but, the next moment, burst into laughter.

"You are right, old friend! It is impossible to hide any thing from you."

"And a friend of yours is there—whom you are going to see?"

"Yes, my dear Surry," was his reply, in a voice of sudden earnestness, "you are not mistaken, and you see I am like all the rest of the world. When we first met on the Rapidan, I was a woman-hater. I despised them all, for I had had reason. That was my state of mind, when a very beautiful and noble girl, whom you have seen, crossed my path. Events threw us together—first, the wound I received at Fleetwood—she caught me as I was falling on that day—and several times afterward I saw and conversed with her, finding her proud, satirical, indifferent to admiration, but as honest and true as steel. Still, our relations did not proceed beyond friendship, and when I told you one day in the Wilderness that I was not her suitor, I spoke the truth. I am not exactly able to say as much to-day!—But to finish my account of myself: I came here to Dinwiddie on the right of the army, and a week or two after my arrival the enemy made a cavalry raid toward the Southside railroad. I followed, and came up with them as they were plundering a house not far from Five Forks. Well, I charged and drove them into the woods—when, who should make her appearance at the door but Miss Conway, whom I had last seen in Culpeper! As you know, her father resides here—he is now at Richmond—and, after following the enemy back to their own lines, hurrying them up with sabre and carbine, I came back to inquire the extent of their depredations at Five Forks.

"Such is the simple explanation of the present 'situation,' my dear friend. Miss Virginia cordially invited me to come whenever I could do so, and although Miss Georgia was less pressing—in fact, said nothing on the subject—I was not cast down thereby! I returned, have been often since, and—that's all."

Mohun laughed the heart's laugh. You have heard that, have you not, reader? "Now tell me about yourself," he added, "and on the way to Five Forks! I see you are tired and hungry. Come! they have the easiest chairs yonder, and are the soul of hospitality!"

The offer was tempting. Why not accept it? My hesitation lasted exactly three seconds.

At the end of that time, I was riding beside Mohun in the direction of Five Forks, which we reached just as I terminated my account of myself since Mohun and I had parted in the Wilderness.

XVI
"FIVE FORKS"

"Five Forks" was an old mansion not far from the place of the same name, now become historical. It was a building of large size; the grounds were extensive, and had been elegant; the house had evidently been the home of a long line of gentlemen, whose portraits, flanked by those of their fair helpmates, adorned the walls of the great drawing-room, between the lofty windows. In the hall stood a tall bookcase, filled with law books, and volumes of miscellany. From the woodwork hung pictures of racehorses, and old engravings. Such was the establishment which the Federal cavalry had visited, leaving, as always, their traces, in broken furniture, smashed crockery, and trampled grounds.

I shall not pause to describe my brief visit to this hospitable house. The young ladies had returned from Richmond some time before, escorted by the gray-haired Juba, that faithful old African retainer; and, as a result of the evenings which I had spent with them and their father, I had the honor to be received in the character of an old friend.

Ten minutes after my arrival I saw that Mohun was passionately in love with Miss Georgia; and I thought I perceived as clearly that she returned his affection. Their eyes — those tell-tales — were incessantly meeting; and Mohun followed every movement of the queenly girl with those long, fixed glances, which leave nothing in doubt.

The younger sister, Miss Virginia, received me with charming sweetness, but a secret melancholy weighed down the dusky eye-lashes. The blue eyes were sad; the very smiles on the rosy lips were sad. All was plain here, too, at a single glance. The pure girl had given her heart to the brave Willie Davenant, and some mysterious hostility of her father toward the young officer, forced them apart.

What was the origin of that hostility? Why had Judge Conway so abruptly torn his daughter away from Davenant at the ball in Culpeper —

and why had that shadow passed over the old statesman's brow when I uttered the name of the young man in Richmond?

I asked myself these questions vainly—and decided in my mind that I should probably never know.

I was mistaken. I was going to know before midnight.

After an excellent supper, over which Miss Georgia presided with stately dignity—for she, too, had changed, in as marked a degree as Mohun,—I rose, declared I must return to Petersburg, and bade the young ladies, who cordially pressed me to remain, good-night.

Mohun declared that he would remain an hour longer—and having promised a visit soon, at his camp on the Rowanty, I mounted my horse, and set out, through the darkness, for Petersburg.

XVII
GENERAL DAVENANT

Following the White Oak road, I passed Hatcher's Run at Burgess's mill, and went on over the Boydton road, reflecting upon the scene I had just left.

All at once my horse placed his foot upon a sharp root in the road, stumbled, nearly fell, and when I touched him with the spur I found that he limped painfully.

Dismounting, I examined his foot. The sharp point had entered it, and it was bleeding profusely. The accident was unfortunate—and, attempting to ride on, I found the hurt worse than I had expected. My gray staggered on as if the limb were broken.

I dismounted once more, led him slowly by the bridle, and continued my way on foot. A quarter of a mile farther, the animal was in such agony that I looked around for some light, by which to examine the hurt more fully.

On the right, a glimmer was seen through the trees. I made straight toward it, through the woods, and soon found myself near a group of tents, one of which was lit up.

"Whose head-quarters are these?" I asked of a man on post, near.

"Mine, my dear colonel," said a voice in the darkness near. "My candle yonder is hospitable and enables me to recognize you."

With which words the figure advanced into the light, and I recognized the tall and stately form of General Davenant.

He gave me his hand cordially, and I explained my dilemma. "You are unfortunate, but fortunate, too," said Davenant, "as I have a man among my couriers who knows all about horses. I will send yours to him; meanwhile come into my tent."

And intrusting my horse to the orderly with some brief directions, the general led the way into his head-quarters tent.

A cheerful fire burned in the rude log-built chimney. On one side were a plain desk and two camp-stools; on the other a rough couch of pine logs, filled with straw, and spread with blankets. Upon the blankets a boy of about fourteen was sound asleep, the light auburn curls tossed in disorder over the rosy young face. At a glance I recognized the youth who had entered the ranks at Gettysburg, taken part in Pickett's charge, and been borne out through the smoke, wounded and bleeding, in the arms of his father. The young Charley had evidently recovered, and was as ruddy as before. His little braided jacket was as jaunty, his face as smiling, as on that evening near Paris.

An hour afterward, General Davenant and myself were conversing like old friends. We were by no means strangers, as I had repeatedly been thrown with him in the army, and my intimacy with Will doubtless commended me to the brave soldier's regard. An accident now seemed about to make us still better acquainted. The orderly had reported that it would be impossible to proceed farther with my horse that night, and I had accepted the invitation of General Davenant to remain with him until morning.

"My brigade is holding the right of the army, colonel," he had said; "we have just moved to this position, and have not had time to become very comfortable. But I can offer you a tolerable supper and a camp-bed after it, with a warm welcome, I assure you."

I declined the supper, but accepted the bed; and seated opposite the grizzled old cavalier, in his gray uniform, had begun to converse.

Something about the stately general of infantry, drew me irresistibly toward him. His bearing was lofty, and not without a species of hauteur; but under all was an exquisite high-breeding and courtesy, which made his society quite charming.

At some words of mine, however, in reference to my visit on this day to his son, a decided expression of gloom had obscured the smiles of the old soldier.

"Yes, colonel," he said, with something like a sigh, "Willie has lost his good spirits, and has been much depressed for more than a year. You are his friend—you share his confidence—you doubtless know the origin of this depression."

"I do, general; a very common cause of trouble to young men — a young lady."

"A young lady," repeated General Davenant, in the same gloomy tone. "He has committed the imprudence of falling in love, as the phrase is, with — Miss Conway."

He paused before the words "Miss Conway," and uttered them with evident repugnance. They issued from his lips, indeed, with a species of jerk; and he seemed glad to get rid of them, if I may so express myself.

"I can talk of this affair with you, colonel," he added, gloomily, "for Will has told me of your regard for him."

I bowed, and said: —

"You are not wrong in supposing that I am one of your son's best friends, general. I was long in the cavalry with him — there is no more heroic soldier in the army — and it has given me sincere sorrow to see him laboring under such melancholy."

General Davenant, with his hand covering his brow, listened in silence.

"I have not inquired the origin of this depression," I added — "that would have been indiscreet — though I know Will would tell me. I guessed it, however, and I have visited the young lady at her house to-night. I will certainly use my utmost exertions to remove all obstacles."

General Davenant suddenly rose erect. His eye was flashing.

"I beg you will not, colonel!" he exclaimed. "The barrier between himself and — Miss Conway — can never be removed."

I looked at the speaker's flushed face with positive wonder, and replied: —

"You astonish me, general! Are there any such obstacles in life?"

"There are!"

I made no reply.

"There are, colonel," repeated the now fiery old soldier. "Judge Conway has been guilty of a gross wrong to me. No son of mine shall ever form an alliance with his family!"

I looked up with deep astonishment.

"This is a very great surprise to me, my dear general," I said; "I thought, from many things, that it was Judge Conway who opposed this alliance; and from the belief that *you* had done *him* some great wrong."

General Davenant had taken his seat again, after his outburst. Once more his forehead was covered with his hand. For some moments he preserved a silence so profound, that nothing disturbed the night but the long breathing of the sleeping boy, and the measured tramp of the sentinel.

Then, all at once, the general raised his head. His expression was no longer fiery — it was unutterably sad.

"I have been reflecting, colonel," he said gravely, "and, in these few minutes, have come to a somewhat singular determination."

"What is that, general?"

"To tell you why *my* son can never marry the daughter of Judge Conway!"

XVIII
TWO MEN AND A WOMAN

General Davenant leaned his elbow on the desk, rested his forehead in his hand, and said in a deep, measured voice: —

"My story need not be a long one, colonel. Those who relate gay adventures and joyous experiences, indulge in endless details — memory is charming to them at such moments — they go back to the past, with a smile on the lips, recalling every little detail, every color of the bright picture.

"My own narrative will be brief, because it is a gloomy one. It is far from pleasant to return to the scenes I propose to describe. I only do so to erase a stigma which seems to attach to my family and myself; to show you that, in spite of Judge Conway, I deserve your good opinion. Assuredly I do not propose any pleasure to myself in relating these events. Alas! one of the bitterest things to a proud man — and I am proud — is to even seem to defend his good name from imputed dishonor!"

Knitting his brows as he spoke, the old soldier looked gloomily into the blaze before us. In a moment, he went on: —

"I was born in the county of Dinwiddie, colonel, where my family had lived from the time of the first settlement of Virginia. My father was a large landholder, and his most intimate friend was Mr. Conway, the father of the present judge. The family friendship was inherited by the young people of the two families — and my two most intimate friends were George and William Conway. One is dead, the other is Judge William Conway, member of Congress. We had played together as children, been companions at school. When our fathers died, and we in turn became the representatives of the two families, our friendship became even more close. I was half my time at 'Five Forks' — they paid long visits to me at 'The Pines' — we hunted together, went to entertainments together, drank wine together, and were inseparable.

"George was especially my favorite. He was the soul of amiability; everybody loved him; and I entertained for him the most tender friendship. His brother William was equally estimable, but did not attract you as strongly. Although a person of the highest sense of honor, and universally respected for talents of the first order, he was irascible, bitter, and, when once aroused, allowed nothing to restrain him. At such moments his best friends avoided him, for he was dangerous. He brooked no opposition. His anger was like a consuming fire; and a friendship which he had formed with that gentleman of splendid powers, but venomous antipathies, John Randolph of Roanoke, served still more to encourage him in the indulgence of the natural acerbity of his disposition. More than once, I have seen him almost foam at the mouth as he denounced some political adversary from the stump, and when one of these fits of passion seized him, he became as ungovernable as a wild animal. You can scarcely realize that, now. Sorrow has chastened him; trouble has softened him; I have nothing to say against the Judge William Conway of to-day. He is a self-sacrificing patriot, a gentleman of irreproachable courtesy, and sweetness of character; but, as a young man, he was a firebrand, and I think the fire is still unquenched beneath the gray hairs of the man of seventy.

"Such were George and William Conway, when I knew them as young men—the one mild, amiable, the soul of kindness and good-nature; the other proud, honorable, but subject to fits of stormy passion, which made all avoid him when the paroxysm was upon him.

"From this hasty description, you will understand why George was a greater favorite with me than his brother. Our friendship was, indeed, as close and tender as possible, and we passed our majority and approached the age of twenty-five, without ever having had a moment's interruption of our intimacy.

"Then, all at once, there appeared upon the stage, that cause of so much happiness, woe, joy, grief, to mankind—a woman. To make a long story short, George Conway and myself were so unfortunate as to become attached to the same young lady, and very soon this sentiment amounted, both on his part and on my own, to a wild and consuming passion. The young lady—it is unnecessary to mention her name—was a person of rare beauty, and mistress of all the wiles which bring young men to the feet of women. She used these unsparingly, too, for nothing delighted her so much as to attract admiration and inspire love. Perceiving the effect which her grace and loveliness had produced upon myself and George, she made every exertion to increase our infatuation—encouraged first one, then the other; and, in the end, succeeded in breaking those close ties of friendship which had bound us from the time when we had played together as children.

"That is a sad confession, colonel, but it is the truth. The bright eyes and smiles of a girl had terminated a life-long friendship. The mere love of admiration in the heart of a young girl had interrupted the affection of years—making George and myself cold and *distrait* toward each other. Soon things became still worse. From friends we had become mere acquaintances—from acquaintances we became strangers, and finally foes. Busy-bodies whispered, tale-bearers blew the flames. If the young lady smiled on me at a party where George was present, the good people around us looked at *him* with satirical meaning. If she smiled on George, their eyes were turned toward me, and they giggled and whispered.

"That is all tedious—is it not? An old story, which every country neighborhood knows. You laugh, perhaps, at hearing it told of A and B,—but you do not laugh when you are one of the actors. Well, not to lengthen my history unduly, an open rivalry and enmity at last arose between myself and poor George. We had been spurred on to hate each other, and narrowly escaped having an 'affair' together—appealing to the pistol as the arbiter.

"It never came to that, however. I saw, ere long, that the young lady had made up her mind. George was in every way a more attractive and lovable person than myself; and after drawing me on, encouraging me, and inducing me to offer her my hand, she turned her back on me, and married George!

"Such was the result of the campaign. George had won,—and I am obliged to say that I hated him cordially. I should never have done so, from the simple fact of his success. I am not so ignoble as that, my dear colonel. Bitter as was my disappointment, I could have bowed to the fiat—pardoned the young lady—and offered my hand to dear George; but there were our 'friends,' the busy-bodies and talebearers. They were unresting in their exertions—took the whole affair under their personal supervision, and invented a hundred fables to sting and arouse me. You would have said that they were bloody minded—the busy-bodies—and bent on trouble; that their aim was to profoundly enrage me, and cause bloodshed. George had laughed at me, they said; never had had a moment's doubt of the young lady's sentiments; had often jested about me, and expressed his pity for my 'silly presumption;' had even amused himself and the young lady, by mimicking my peculiarities, and raising a laugh at my expense.

"These reports were persistently and regularly repeated for my information: I was baited, and worried, and driven nearly mad by them — finally a duel nearly resulted; but that last step was not taken. I simply made my bow to the happy pair, left them without a word, and returned home, determined to drop the whole matter — but none the less enraged and embittered.

"From that moment George and myself rarely met, and never as friends. I had been brought to hate him — he knew the fact — and although he was innocent of all wrong to me, as I know to-day, made no effort to win my regard again. He was as proud as myself — he said nothing — and our paths here separated forever.

"Such is the necessary introduction, colonel," said General Davenant, "to the events which I propose to relate."

XIX
THE MURDER

"More than twenty years had passed," continued General Davenant, "when that old hatred which had been aroused in me, toward George Conway, produced bitter fruits.

"I was to be taught by a terrible experience that hatred is a deadly sin; that God punishes it more severely than all other sins, for it is the poison which turns the whole heart to bitterness. I had indulged it—made no effort to banish it—nourished it like a snake in the recesses of my breast, and now God decreed, as a punishment, that the snake should turn and sting me.

"To go back for a moment, however. George had married—a year afterward I had imitated him. My wife was an angel upon earth—she is an angel in heaven now—and in comparison with the deep affection which I felt for her, the ephemeral fancy for the young lady whom my rival had married, appeared the veriest trifle. William Conway had also married, and he and George, with their wives, were living at Five Forks. William was judge of the circuit—George managed the estate—and their affection for each other, at this period of their mature manhood, was said to exceed that of their youth.

"'Was said to,' I say, colonel; for I never saw either of them. All intercourse between "The Pines" and "Five Forks" had ceased twenty years before; and George and William Conway were as much strangers to me, as if we lived in opposite quarters of the globe; for time had not changed—or rather restored—the *entente cordial* of the past. On the contrary, the feud had become chronic—the gulf separating us had grown deeper. When I met either of the brothers, we exchanged no greetings—passed without looking at each other—and the 'family feud' between the Davenants and the Conways was not even alluded to; it had become an old story, and lost its interest.

"Such was the condition of things—such the attitude which I occupied toward the two brothers—when the event, which I am about to relate, took place. The event in question was tragic and terrible. It came without warning, to shock the entire surrounding country. One night, on his return from the county seat, whither he was said to have gone upon some matter of business, George Conway was murdered, and his body concealed in some bushes by the roadside.

"The body was not discovered until the morning succeeding the murder. His riderless horse was then seen standing at the door of the stable at Five Forks, and in great terror. Judge Conway set out rapidly to look for his brother, who was supposed to have met with some accident. Two or three neighbors, whom he chanced to meet, joined in the search; the body was discovered; and, on examination, revealed a deep gash in the region of the heart, apparently inflicted by a dagger or a knife.

"The blow had evidently been mortal—no other hurt was visible. George Conway seemed to have been waylaid by some unknown person, and murdered on his return from the court-house.

"It was impossible to divine the perpetrator of the crime, or form any idea of his motive. Upon the person of the murdered man a large sum of money, which he had received that day, was discovered. He had not been waylaid, thus, by one designing to rob him; and his peaceful and amiable character excluded the hypothesis that he had aroused such enmity as could have led to the bloody deed. The whole affair was a profound mystery—no clue could be discovered to the perpetrator, or the motive of the crime—and the body was borne to "Five Forks," where it was laid in state to await burial on the next day.

"Judge Conway, it was said, had nearly lost his reason at this sudden and terrible blow. He had loved his brother with extraordinary affection; and the event struck him like a thunderbolt. His stupor of grief was succeeded by rage. He fell into one of his paroxysms. With flushed face, bloodshot eyes, and mouth foaming with a species of fury, he mounted his horse, went at full speed to the court-house, made inquiries of everybody who had seen his brother, asked with whom he had last been seen, and left no stone unturned to ferret out the author of the crime.

"Meanwhile, the whole county was discussing, with awe-struck eyes, the extraordinary event. Who could have perpetrated the act? Who could have waylaid and murdered a man so universally popular? Who was safe, if such a state of things could exist in a peaceful community,—if a good citizen could not ride to see a neighbor, or to the county seat, without danger of being murdered?

"Grief, indignation, horror, were the universal sentiments. Some one must be discovered upon whom to lay the crime. And that some one was the individual before you, colonel!"

XX
THE KNIFE

"Let me continue, I beg," continued General Davenant, gloomily. "Your look of astonishment is quite natural; you feel the indignation of a gentleman at my words; but allow me to go on with my narrative.

"Poor George Conway was buried on the day after the discovery of his body, and an immense concourse accompanied him to his grave. The funeral procession was a mile long, for the notoriety attached to the event had drawn people from far and near; and when the body reached the grave-yard, the crowd nearly filled the small enclosure.

"I was present in my carriage with my wife, and my son Charles yonder, then a child in arms. You will understand, colonel, that I had not the heart to be absent. I had long ceased to feel a sentiment of any great regard for the Conways; but at the intelligence of George's sudden death, all my old friendship had revived—the old kindly feeling came back; pity banished all enmity. I thought of his former love for me, and I determined to do all that remained in my power to show my sympathy—attend his funeral among those who mourned him.

"Well, the body was borne to the grave, the service read, and the remains of the unfortunate gentleman deposited in their last resting-place. Then the clods rattled on the coffin, the service ended, and George Conway had passed away from all eyes.

"I looked at his poor wife and brother with tears in my eyes. All my enmity was gone—my memory went back to the old scenes; at that instant I could have reached out my arms, and drawn the bereaved brother to my heart, mingling my tears with his own.

"All at once, however, I looked at Judge Conway with astonishment. I had expected to see him overwhelmed with grief—but as he now raised his head, and turned in the direction of the spot where I was standing, I saw that his features were convulsed with wrath. His cheeks were crimson, his teeth clenched, his eyes injected with blood. Suddenly these bloodshot eyes met my own—the cheeks a moment before so red, grew pale—and exclaiming, 'It is you who murdered my brother!' he threw himself upon me with the fury of a wild animal, and his fingers were nearly buried in my throat.

"The assault was so sudden and terrible that I staggered back, and nearly fell over the grave.

"Then regaining my self-possession, I caught Judge Conway by the throat in turn, hurled him from me, and stood confronting him, pale, panting, my throat bleeding—and resolved if he attacked me again to put him to death with the first weapon upon which I could lay my hand.

"He was, meanwhile, struggling in the hands of his friends, who, by main force, held him back.

"'Let me go!' he shouted, foaming at the mouth with rage—'that man murdered my brother! I will take the law into my own hands! he shall not leave this spot alive! He dares to come here in the presence of the dead body of George Conway—and he is his murderer!'

"These words were rather howled than uttered. The speaker seemed to have lost his reason, from pure excess of rage. If his friends had not restrained him by main force, he would have thrown himself upon me a second time, when one of us would have lost his life, colonel, for I was now as violently enraged as himself.

"That *I* should be thus publicly branded with the basest crime! that the representative of the old and honorable house of the Davenants, should be thus grossly insulted, his person assailed, his good name torn from him—that he should be denounced thus in the presence of all as a felon and murderer!

"'You are insane, sir!' I at length said, struggling to regain my coolness. 'Your grief has affected your brain! I can pardon much in you today, sir, but beware how you again attempt to degrade me!'

"'Hear him!' was the hoarse and furious reply of Judge Conway; and reaching out his thin fingers, a habit he had caught from Mr. Randolph—he pointed at me where I stood.

"'Hear him! He affects innocence! He is outraged! He is indignant! And yet he waylaid my brother, whom he has hated for twenty years—he waylaid him like an assassin, and murdered him! There is the proof!'

"And drawing from his pocket a knife, covered with clotted blood, he threw it upon the grave before all eyes.

"Good God! It was my own!"

XXI
THE CHAIN OF EVIDENCE

"At the sight of that terrible object" continued General Davenant, "I staggered back, and nearly fell. I could not believe my eyes—never thought of denying the ownership of the fearful witness,—I could only gaze at it, with a wild horror creeping over me, and then all these terrible emotions were too much for me.

"I took two steps toward the grave, reached out with a shudder to grasp the knife whose clots of blood seemed to burn themselves into my brain—then vertigo seized me, and letting my head fall, I fainted.

"When I regained my senses, I was in my carriage, supported by the arms of my wife, and rolling up the avenue to my own house.

"Opposite me, in the carriage, little Charley, who, dimly realized apparently that some trouble had come to me, was crying bitterly, and a rough personage was endeavoring to quiet his sobbing.

"The personage in question was a constable. When I fainted at the grave, my friends had caught me in their arms—protested with burning indignation that the charge against me was a base calumny—and the magistrate who was summoned by Judge Conway to arrest me, had declined to do more than direct a constable to escort me home, and see that I did not attempt to escape.

"That was kind. I was a murderer, and my proper place a jail. Why should *I* be more favored than some poor common man charged with that crime? Had such a person been confronted with such a charge, supported by such damning evidence as the bloody knife, would any ceremony have been observed? 'To jail!' all would have cried, 'No bail for the murderer!' And why should the rich Mr. Davenant be treated with more consideration?

"On the day after my arrest—I spare you all the harrowing scenes, my poor wife's agony, and every thing, colonel—on the day after, I got into my carriage, and went and demanded to be confined in jail. It was the first time a Davenant had ever been *in jail*—but I went thither without hesitation, if not without a shudder. No sooner had I taken this step than the whole country seemed to have left their homes to visit me in my prison. On the evening of the scene at the grave, twenty persons had called at the 'Pines,' to express their sympathy and indignation at the charge against me. Now, when the iron door of the law had closed upon me, and I was a real prisoner, the visitors came in throngs without number. One and all, they treated the charge as the mere result of Judge Conway's fury—some laughed at, others denounced it as an attempt to entrap and destroy me—all were certain that an investigation would at once demonstrate my innocence, and restore me to liberty and honor.

"Alas! I could only thank my friends, and reply that I hoped that such would be the result. But when they had left me alone, I fell into fits of the deepest dejection.

"What proofs could I give that I was innocent? There was a terrible array of circumstances, on the contrary, to support the hypothesis of my guilt—much more than I have mentioned, colonel. I had visited the courthouse on the same day with poor George Conway, and for the first time in twenty years had exchanged words with him. And the words were unfriendly. We had both been in the clerk's office of the county, when that gentleman asked me some common-place question—in what year such a person had died, and his will had been recorded, I think. I replied, mentioning a year. The clerk shook his head, declaring that it must have been later, and appealed to poor George Conway, who agreed with him, adding, 'Mr. Davenant is certainly in the wrong.' I was much annoyed that day—made some curt reply—poor George made a similar rejoinder, and some harsh, almost insulting words, passed between us. The affair went no further, however. I left the clerk's office, and having attended to the business which brought me, left the court-house about dusk. As I mounted my horse, I saw poor George Conway riding out of the place. I followed slowly, not wishing to come up with him, turning into a by-road which led toward my own house—and knew nothing of the murder until it was bruited abroad on the next day.

"That is much like the special pleading of a criminal—is it not, colonel? If I had really murdered the poor man, would not this be my method of explaining every thing? You see, I do not deny what several witnesses could prove; the fact that I quarreled with Conway, came to high words, uttered insults, exhibited anger, followed him from the court-house at dusk—I acknowledge all that, but add, that I struck into a by-road and went home! That sounds suspicious, I assure you, even to myself, to-day. Imagine the effect it promised to have then, when I was a man charged with murder—who would naturally try to frame such a statement as would clear him—and when a large portion of the community were excited and indignant at the murder.

"Such had been the truly unfortunate scene in the clerk's office,—the fatality which made me follow the man going to his death, and my known enmity of long standing, supported the hypothesis of my guilt. There was another, and even more fatal circumstance still,—the discovery of the knife with which George Conway had been slain. That knife was my own; it was one of peculiar shape, with a handle of tortoise-shell, and I had often used it in presence of my friends and others. A dozen persons could make oath to it as my property; but it was not needed; the scene at the grave made that useless. I evidently did not deny the ownership of the weapon which had been used in the commission of the murder. At the very sight of it, on the contrary, in the hands of the brother of my victim, I had turned pale and fainted!

"This was the condition of things when the special term of the court, held expressly to try me, commenced at Dinwiddie."

XXII
THE TRIAL

"A great crowd assembled on the day of the trial. Judge Conway had vacated the bench, as personally interested, and the judge from a neighboring circuit had taken his place.

"Below the seat of the judge sat the jury. Outside the railing, the spectators were crowded so closely that it was with difficulty the sheriff made a passage for my entrance.

"To one resolution I had adhered in spite of the remonstrances of all my friends,—to employ no counsel. In this determination nothing could shake me. A disdainful pride sustained me, mingled with bitter obstinacy. If I, the representative of one of the oldest and most honorable families in the county of Dinwiddie was to be branded as a murderer,—if my past life, my family and personal character, did not refute the charge,—if I was to be dragged to death on suspicion, gibbeted as a murderer, because some felon had stolen my pocket-knife, and committed a crime with it,—then I would go to my death unmoved. I would disdain to frame explanations; let the law murder *me* if it would; no glib counsel should save my life by technicalities; I would be vindicated by God and my past life, or would die.

"Such was my state of mind, and such the origin of my refusal to employ counsel. When the court now assigned me counsel, I rose and forbade them to appear for me. In the midst of a stormy scene, and with the prosecuting attorney sitting dumb in his chair, resolved to take no part in the trial, the witnesses appeared upon the stand, and, rather by sufferance than the judge's consent, the jury proceeded to interrogate them.

"The circumstances which I have detailed to you were all proved in the clearest manner; the altercation in the clerk's office on the day of the murder; my long enmity against him, dating back more than twenty years; the fact that I had followed him out of the village just at dusk on the fatal night; and the discovery of my knife in the tall grass by the roadside near the body.

"I had summoned no witnesses, but some appeared of their own accord, and gave important testimony. Many neighbors testified that my enmity toward George Conway had almost entirely disappeared in the lapse of years, and that I had spoken of him, upon more than one occasion, with great kindness. The clerk of the county described the scene in his office, stating that the affair had appeared to him a mere interchange of curt words, without exhibition of the least malice on my part. The most important witness, however, was a poor man, living in the neighborhood, who made oath that he had been riding toward the court-house on the evening of the murder; had passed Mr. Conway, and, riding on farther, came in sight of me, and he had, before reaching me, seen me turn into the by-road which led toward my own residence. I could not have committed the murder, he added, for Mr. Conway had time to pass the spot where his body was found before I could have ridden back to the highroad and caught up with him.

"Unfortunately, the witness who gave this testimony bore a very indifferent character, and I could see that more than one of the jurors suspected that he was perjuring himself.

"Another ugly-looking circumstance also intervened to neutralize the favorable impression thus made. From the irregular mode of proceeding, the fatal knife had not been exhibited in court. Suddenly, a juror called for it, and it could nowhere be found! The sheriff swore that he had left it in the clerk's office, where he supposed it to be entirely safe. Upon searching for it, however, in the drawer where he had deposited it, the weapon was missing.

"When that fact was stated, I saw a curious expression pass over the faces of more than one of the jury. They evidently suspected foul play.

"'Was the door of the office locked?' asked one of them.

"'Yes, sir,' was the reply.

"'Were the windows secured?'

"'By shutters with bolts.'

"'Are all the bolts on the windows of this building firm?'

"'I think so, sir.'

"'There is one, that is not!' said the juror.

"And he pointed to a long iron bolt on one of the windows, which bore evident traces of having been rent from its socket.

"The sheriff looked in amazement in the direction indicated.

"'You are right, sir!' he said; 'some one has entered the court-house by breaking open the shutter, and stolen that knife from the clerk's office, which is never locked.'

"A meaning silence followed the words. It was not difficult to understand it. The jury looked at each other, and in their glances I could read this—'Mr. Davenant is on trial for his life. He or his friends suborn testimony to prove an alibi on the night of the murder, and not content with that, they hire a burglar to enter the court-house and steal the knife which proves his connection with the deed—that it may not appear in evidence against him.'

"The evidence closed. I had not uttered a word. I had sworn in my heart that I would not stir a finger in the matter—but now, stung beyond endurance, I rose and addressed the jury in impassioned words. 'Their verdict,' I told them, 'was of little importance if I was to lose the respect of my fellow-citizens. I had made no effort to shape their decision, but now on the brink, it might be of a felon's grave, I would utter my dying words. I would confine myself to protesting before God, and on my honor, that I had long since forgiven George Conway the wrongs done me—that the scene on the day of his murder was the result of momentary irritability, caused by business annoyances, and not malice—that I had forgotten it in an hour—returned directly to my own house—and only heard of the murder on the day after its commission. As to the knife—I had been suspected if not charged with having had the weapon stolen. Well! my answer to that was to declare that, to the best of my knowledge and belief, *the murder was committed with my own knife!* More than that. A witness had sworn that he saw me turn into the road to my own residence, at such a distance behind George Conway that I could not have rejoined him before he had passed the fatal spot. The witness was mistaken. There was time. *By riding across the angle through the thicket, I could easily have rejoined him!*

"'And now, gentlemen,' I said, 'I have done. I have left you no ground to charge me with suborning testimony—with having the evidence of my crime stolen—with plotting in darkness, to hide my crime and blind your eyes in determining my guilt or innocence. That knife was mine, I repeat. It was possible for me to rejoin Mr. Conway, and do him to death by a blow with it. Now, retire, gentlemen! Bring in your verdict! Thank God! no taint of real dishonor will rest upon a Davenant, and I can appear before my Maker as I stand here to-day—innocent!'

"Ten minutes afterward the jury had retired, with every mark of agitation upon their faces. The great concourse of spectators seemed moved almost beyond control.

"Suddenly the crowd opened, I saw my wife hastening through the space thus made—a living wall on each side—and in an instant she had thrown herself into my arms, with a low cry which brought tears to the roughest faces of the auditory. I placed my arm around her, remonstrated with her for this ill-advised proceeding, and was trying to soothe her, when she hastily gave me a letter. A strange man had brought it an hour before, she said—it was marked 'In haste—this will save Mr. Davenant's life.' She had mounted her riding horse, and brought it at full speed in person, without waiting to question the stranger, who had at once disappeared.

"I opened the letter—glanced at its contents—at the same instant the jury made their appearance—and the clerk said:—

"'Gentlemen of the jury, have you agreed upon a verdict?'

"'We have, sir,' said the foreman.

"'What is it?'

"'Not guilty!'

"The court-house rang with applause. The crowd rushed toward me to shake me by the hand and congratulate me. Suddenly, in the midst of the tumult, I heard the furious words:—

"'Murderer! you have escaped, but I brand you before God and man as the murderer of my brother!'

"It was Judge Conway, who, mounted upon a bench, with glaring eyes, foaming lips, teeth clenched, in a wild fury, shook his arm at me, and denounced me as a convict before God, if not before man."

XXIII
WHAT THE LETTER CONTAINED

General Davenant was silent for a moment. The deep voice, so long resounding in my ears, made the silence oppressive.

"Now you know, my dear colonel," he suddenly added, "why my son can not form an alliance with a daughter of Judge Conway."

I bowed my head. The whole mystery was patent before me.

"The family opposition is mutual," said General Davenant, with a proud smile; "he objects because he believes that I murdered his brother—and I object because he believes it! He insulted me, outraged me—at the grave, in the court-house, in public, as in private; and I could not think of beseeching his honor to give his consent to the marriage of his daughter with the son of an 'escaped murderer.'"

The old soldier uttered these words with gloomy bitterness; but in a moment he had regained his coolness.

"That was the end of the affair," he said. "I went home, accompanied by a *cortége* of friends who seemed never weary of congratulating me; and on the next day, I wrote a mortal defiance to Judge Conway, which I placed in the hands of a friend to convey to him. An hour afterward, I had mounted my horse, ridden rapidly, caught up with this friend on his way to Five Forks, and had taken from him the challenge, which I tore to pieces. You will probably comprehend the motive which compelled me to do this. It was not repugnance to the modern form of single combat, I am sorry to say. Old as I was, I had still the ancient hallucination on that subject. I did not then know that duels were mere comedies—child's play; that one infantry skirmish results in the shedding of more blood than all the affairs of a generation. The motive that induced me to withdraw my challenge, was one which you will probably understand. The pale face of the dead George Conway had risen up before me—I knew his brother's deep love for him—that he regarded me as the dead man's murderer; and I no longer writhed under that public insult in the court-house, or, at least controlled myself. 'Let him go on his way, poor, stricken heart!' I said with deep pity; 'I forgive him, and will not avenge that affront to me!'

"Such is my history, colonel. It is sad, you see. I have related it to explain what has come to your knowledge—the bitter hostility which Judge Conway indulges toward me, and his frowns at the very name of Davenant. These events occurred more than ten years ago. During all that time, he has been laboring under the belief that I am really guilty of his brother's blood. See where my 'high pride' has conducted me," said General Davenant, with a smile of inexpressible melancholy and bitterness. "I was proud and disdainful on the day of my trial—I would not use the common weapons of defence—I risked my life by refusing counsel, and acknowledging the ownership of that knife. Pride, hauteur, a sort of disdain at refuting a charge of base dishonor—that was my sentiment then, and I remain as haughty to-day! I am a Davenant—I was found 'not guilty'—why go and tell Judge Conway the contents of that letter received in the court-house?"

"The contents of the letter, general?"

"Yes, colonel."

"What did it contain?—I beg you to tell me!"

"The confession of the murderer of George Conway!"

XXIV
"BLOOD"

General Davenant had scarcely uttered the words which I have just recorded, when rapid firing was heard in the woods, a quarter of a mile from his head-quarters; and a moment afterward a courier came at a gallop, bearing a dispatch.

"My horse!" came in the brief tone of command.

And General Davenant tore open the dispatch, which he read attentively.

"The enemy are advancing to attack me," he said; "this note was written ten minutes since. The attack has commenced. Will you go and see it, colonel?"

"Willingly."

General Davenant ordered another horse, as my own was useless; we mounted and rode at full speed through the woods; in five minutes we were at the scene of action.

A heavy assault was in progress. The enemy had massed a large force in front of the hastily erected earth-works, and were endeavoring, by a determined charge, to carry them.

General Davenant was everywhere amid the fight, the guiding and directing head, and beside him I saw distinctly in the starlight, the brave figure of little Charley, who had started from his couch, buckled on a huge sword, and was now galloping to and fro, cheering on the men as gallantly as his father. It was an inspiring sight to see that child in his little braided jacket, with his jaunty cap balanced gallantly on his auburn curls — to see his rosy cheeks, his smiling lips, and his small hand flourishing that tremendous sabre, as he galloped gaily amid the fire.

"And yet," I said, "there are those who will not believe in *blood* — or race!"

Fill the space which that dash occupies, my dear reader, with an abrupt "duck" of the head, as a bullet went through my hat!

The charge was repulsed in twenty minutes; but the firing continued throughout the night. When it ceased, toward daybreak, and I rode back with General Davenant and Charley, who was as gay as a lark, and entertained me with reminiscences of Gettysburg, I was completely broken down with fatigue. Throwing myself upon a bed, in General Davenant's tent, I fell asleep.

When I opened my eyes the sun was high in the heavens. I looked around for the general, he was invisible.

I rose, and at the door of the tent met Charley, with bright eyes, and cheeks like roses.

"The general has gone to corps head-quarters, colonel, and told me to present you his compliments, and beg that you will remain to breakfast."

After which formal and somewhat pompous sentence the youthful Charley drew near, slapped me in a friendly way upon the back, and exclaimed, with dancing eyes: —

"I say, colonel! wasn't that a jolly old he-fight we had last night?"

My reply was a laugh, and a glance of admiration at the gay boy.

I declined the invitation of General Davenant, as I had to return. My horse was brought, and I found his foot much easier. In half an hour I was on the road to Petersburg.

XXV
THE BLUE SERPENT

Once back at the "Cedars," I reflected deeply upon the history which I had heard from the lips of General Davenant.

I shall refrain, however, from recording these reflections. If the reader will cast his eyes back over the pages of these memoirs, he will perceive that I have confined myself generally to the simple narration of events — seldom pausing to offer my own comments upon the scenes passing before me. Were I to do so, what an enormous volume I should write, and how the reader would be bored! Now, to bore a reader, is, in my eyes, one of the greatest crimes of which an author can be guilty. It is the unpardonable sin, indeed, in a writer. For which reason, and acting upon the theory that a drama ought to explain itself and be its own commentator, I spare the worthy reader of these pages all those reflections which I indulged in, after hearing General Davenant's singular narrative.

"Pride! pride!" I muttered, rising at the end of an hour. "I think I can understand that — exceptional as is this instance; but I wish I had heard who was the 'real murderer' of George Conway!"

Having thus dismissed the subject, I set about drawing up my official report, and this charmingly common-place employment soon banished from my mind every more inviting subject!

It was nearly ten days after this my first ride into the wilds of Dinwiddie, before I again set out to look after the cavalry. The end of October was approaching. Grant had continued to hammer away along his immense line of earth-works; and day by day, step by step, he had gone on extending his left in the direction of the Southside railroad.

If the reader will keep this in view, he will understand every movement of the great adversaries. Grant had vainly attempted to carry Lee's works by assault, or surprise, — his only hope of success now was to gradually extend his lines toward the Southside road; seize upon that great war artery which supplied life-blood to Lee's army; and thus compel the Confederate commander to retreat or starve in his trenches. One thing was plain — that when Grant reached the Southside railroad, Lee was lost, unless he could mass his army and cut his way through the forces opposed to him. And this fact was so obvious, the situation was so apparent—that from the moment when the Weldon road was seized upon by General Grant, that officer and his great adversary never removed their eyes from the real point of importance, the true key of the lock—namely the Southside railroad, on Lee's right.

Elsewhere Grant attacked, but it was to cover some movement, still toward his left. He assaulted Lee's works, north of the James—but it was south of the Appomattox that he was looking. The operations of the fall and winter, on the lines around Petersburg were a great series of marches and counter-marches to and fro, suddenly bursting into battles. Grant massed his army heavily in front of the works in Charles City opposite the left of Lee; attempted to draw in that direction his adversary's main force; then suddenly the blue lines vanished; they were rushed by railroad toward Petersburg, and Grant hastened to thrust his columns still farther beyond Lee's right, in order to turn it and seize the Southside road.

That was not the conception of a great soldier, it may be, reader; but it was ingenious. General Grant was not a man of great military brain—but he was patient, watchful, and persevering. To defeat Lee, what was wanted was genius, or obstinacy—Napoleon or Grant. In the long run, perseverance was going to achieve the results of genius. The tortoise was going to reach the same goal with the hare. It was a question of time—that was all.

So, throughout October, as throughout September, and August, and July, General Grant thundered everywhere along his forty miles of earth-works, but his object was to raise a smoke dense enough to hide the blue columns moving westward. "Hurrah! we have got Fort Harrison!" exclaimed his enthusiastic subordinates. Grant would much rather have heard, "We have got the White Oak road!" Fort Harrison was a strong out-post simply; the White Oak road was the postern door into the citadel.

Gradually moving thus, from the Jerusalem plank road to the Weldon railroad, from the Weldon railroad to the Squirrel Level road, from the Squirrel Level road toward the Boydton road, beyond which was the White Oak road, Grant came, toward the end of October, to the banks of the Rowanty. As this long blue serpent unfolded its coils and stretched its threatening head into the Dinwiddie woods, Lee had extended his right to confront it. The great opponents moved *pari passu*, each marching in face of each other. Like two trained and skillful swordsmen, they changed ground without moving their eyes from each others' faces—the lunge was met by the parry; and this seemed destined to go on to infinity.

That was the unskilled opinion, however. The civilians thought that—Lee did not. It was plain that this must end somewhere. Lee's line would not bear much further extension. It reached now from a point on the Williamsburg road, east of Richmond, to Burgess's Mill, west of Petersburg. His forty thousand men were strung over forty miles. That made the line so thin that it would bear little more. Stretched a little farther still, and it would snap.

Lee called in vain for more men. The Government could not send them. He predicted the result of failure to receive them. They did not come.

And Grant continued to move on, and Lee continued to stretch his thin line, until it began to crack.

Such was the situation of affairs at the end of October—when Grant aimed a heavy blow to cut the line in pieces. The blue serpent raised its head, and sprung to strike.

XXVI
THE HOUSE NEAR MONK'S
NECK, AND ITS OWNER

Such was the critical condition of affairs when I again set out to make my regular tour of inspection of the cavalry.

Crossing Hatcher's Run at Burgess's Mill, I turned to the left, and soon found myself riding on between the lofty walls of pine, through which the roads of Dinwiddie wind like a serpent.

When near Monk's Neck, I determined to stop and feed my horse. I always carried, strapped behind my saddle, a small bag containing about a feed of corn for that purpose; and as I generally selected some wayside house where I could, myself, rest while my horse was feeding, I now looked about me to discover such.

My search was speedily rewarded. Three hundred yards from the road, in a clump of stunted trees, I saw a small house, which I soon reached. The surroundings of the establishment were poor and mean beyond expression. Through the open door I could see that the interior was even more poverty-stricken than the outside.

As I dismounted, a man came to this door. Are you fond of natural history, reader; and have you ever amused yourself by instituting comparisons between certain human beings and certain animals — beasts, birds, or fishes? I have seen men who resembled horses, owls, hawks, sheep, — and geese. This one resembled the bird called the penguin. Read the description of the penguins: "Their feet are placed more posteriorly than in any other birds, and only afford them support by resting on the tarsus, which is enlarged, like the sole of the foot of a quadruped. The wings are very small, and are furnished with rudiments of feathers only, resembling scales. Their bodies are covered with oblong feathers, harsh to the touch, and closely applied over each other. * * * * * Their motions are slow and awkward, and from the form of their wings, they can not fly."

The individual before me recalled the penguin—except that he was excessively lean instead of fat. The feet accorded with the above description; the arms were short, and hung like wings; the coat of the worthy was a ragged "cut-away," which ended in a point behind, like the tail of a bird; and the movements of the individual were "slow and awkward" to a degree which forbade the supposition that, under any circumstances, he could be induced to fly. Add a long, crane-like neck, two bleared eyes, a mouth stretching from ear to ear, and a nose like the bill of a duck. You will then have before you the gentleman who bore, as I soon discovered, the classic name of Mr. Alibi.

When the worthy, who had flapped his arms, by way of greeting, and shown me into his mansion, informed me that such was his name, I knew that the house at which I now found myself was the place of meeting agreed upon between Nighthawk and Swartz, at their interview in Richmond. Here, also, the man and woman, rescued by Swartz on the Nottoway, had been left, on his way to Petersburg, as the spy had informed us in the Wilderness.

"Well, general," croaked Mr. Alibi, with a smile, and in a nasal voice, "wha—a—t's the news?"

"I am only a lieutenant-colonel, Mr. Alibi."

"Well, colonel, any thing stirring?"

"Nothing, I think. Any news with you, Mr. Alibi? I have heard of you from a friend of yours."

"Eh! And who mout that be, colonel?"

"Mr. Nighthawk. Have you seen him lately?"

"Na—a—a—w," said Mr. Alibi, with a prolonged drawl through his nose, and flapping his arms in an uncouth fashion, "I ain't seen him for a long spell now."

"Nor Swartz, either?"

Mr. Alibi looked keenly at me.

"Na—a—a—w, nor him nuther, leftenant-colonel."

"Leave out the 'leftenant,' my dear Mr. Alibi; and call me 'colonel'—it is shorter," I said, laughing, as I looked at the queer figure. "And so you have not seen Swartz lately? He made an appointment to meet Nighthawk here."

"Made an app'intment, did he, leftenant—least ways, colonel?"

"Yes."

"With Mr. Nighthawk?"

"Yes."

"Well, I reckon they are both dead, or they'd 'a' kept their app'intment."

"Nighthawk dead!"

"He must be, sartain."

"You are mistaken, friend Alibi," said a voice behind him.

And Nighthawk, in person, entered the house.

XXVII
STARVATION

Nighthawk had appeared, as was his wont, as if he had risen from the earth.

But this circumstance disappeared from my mind at once. I was looking at his face. It had completely lost its benignant expression; was pale, and bore marks of great fatigue. Something of the old clerical benignity came to the eyes as he greeted me cordially; but sitting down in the nearest chair, as though completely wearied out, he became as dispirited as before.

"And what mout be the matter with you, Mr. Nighthawk?" said Mr. Alibi: "you look 's if the night hags had been a-riding of you with spurs on."

And Mr. Alibi flapped his wings, stretched out his neck, and seemed about to cackle.

"I am tired, Alibi," said Nighthawk, briefly, "go to the spring and get me some fresh water. You needn't come back in a hurry, as I wish to talk with Colonel Surry."

And Mr. Nighthawk rose, and carelessly sat down near the window, through which he could reconnoitre.

The object of this movement was soon evident. Mr. Alibi took a bucket, and went out as though to seek the spring. When he had gone a few paces, however, he turned to the right and disappeared behind the house, toward the opposite window, which was open.

Nighthawk rose, went to the door, and caught Mr. Alibi eavesdropping — the result of which was that the penguin hastily moved off, muttering. In a minute he had shambled along and disappeared.

No sooner had his figure vanished than Nighthawk turned hastily toward me.

"Will you go with me to-night, colonel, on an expedition I intend to make?" he said.

"An expedition, Nighthawk?"

"A work of mercy, colonel; let us talk quickly. That man, Alibi, is a spy—for both sides—and I wish to arrange every thing before he returns."

"Explain, Nighthawk."

"I will, colonel. Do you remember that night in Richmond, when Swartz made an appointment to meet me at a house near Monk's Neck?"

"Perfectly."

"Well, this is the house,—and I expected important results from that meeting. Unfortunately, I was prevented, by some pickets who arrested me, from reaching this spot on the appointed day. I was here two days afterward, however—asked for Swartz—he had not been here—and as that was the most unaccountable thing in the world to me, I set out to find him."

"In the enemy's lines?"

"Yes, colonel. I had no doubt I would come across him somewhere. So I went through the country behind the Federal lines; looked everywhere for my man, have been looking ever since I left you—and at last have found him."

"Where?"

"In the upper room of a deserted house, not three miles from this place, within the enemy's picket line."

"The upper room of a deserted house?"

"'Confined—put to starve there, colonel! The work of Darke, and that she-devil who goes about with him, I am willing to swear, colonel!"

"Good heavens! Is it possible?" I said, "Swartz is shut up and left to starve?"

"Exactly, colonel—and here is how I know it. I was coming back, worn out by my long search after Swartz, when in passing this house, I came suddenly upon a picket of about fifty men. To avoid being seen, I ran, being on foot, and got behind the house. I had no sooner done so, than I heard groans from the upper part of it—and as the house was entirely uninhabited, these sounds excited my curiosity—not to say astonishment. Well, I determined to, find the origin of them. I crawled through a broken window—reached the second floor by a dusty staircase, and went straight toward a door, behind which I heard the groaning. It was heavily locked, and I could not even shake it. Then I ran to the partition between the room and the passage—found it made of boards, between the cracks of which I could see—and looking in, I saw Swartz! He was sitting on an old broken chair, beside a table with three legs, and his hand was buried in his hair, as if he was trying to tear it out.

"When I called to him, he started, and his groans stopped. He turned his head. No sooner had he recognized me than he cried out with joy; and for some moments he could say nothing but 'Save me! save me! Nighthawk! They are starving me to death!'

"I will not lengthen out my story, colonel. I see Alibi coming back. I had scarcely exchanged ten words with Swartz, when I heard the gallop of a horse, and running to the window, saw *that woman* get off. A second's reflection told me that she was coming into the house; I knew that, if discovered, I would be shot or taken prisoner—and I decided on my course in a minute. I said to Swartz, 'wait a few hours—I will go and bring you help.' I glided through a back window, dropped to the ground, ran into the bushes—and here I am, colonel, waiting for night to come, to return and rescue Swartz."

"Can you do so?"

"With one companion—to look out while I pick the lock."

"Good—I'll go with you; and provide for contingencies, too."

I had seen a cavalryman passing along the road in front of the house, and as Mr. Alibi came in at the same moment, I sent him to hail the wayfarer, and bring him to the house. As soon as Mr. Alibi had left us on his errand, I tore a sheet from my note-book, obtained from Nighthawk an exact description of the locality where Swartz was confined, and writing a note to Mohun, informed him of our intention. If he could send a squadron of cavalry to drive in the picket near the house, it would insure the success of our design, I added.

As I finished this note, Mr. Alibi appeared with the cavalryman. He proved to belong to Mohun's command. I entrusted the note to him,

cautioning him that it was important, and must reach Mohun promptly —
then I looked at my watch.

It was four o'clock. Already the sun was declining toward the wooded
horizon; I looked toward it, and then at Nighthawk, who nodded.

"In an hour, colonel," he said, "and as I am broken down, I will sleep."

With these words, Nighthawk leaned back in his split-bottom chair,
covered his face with his handkerchief, and in ten seconds his long, quiet
breathing showed plainly that he was asleep.

"A cur'ous man, leftenant-colonel! a cur'ous man is Mr. Nighthawk!"
said Mr. Alibi.

And he flapped his arms, and wriggled about in a manner so
extraordinary that he looked more like a penguin than ever.

XXVIII
BIRDS OF PREY

Night came on. I left my horse at Mr. Alibi's; set off on foot with Nighthawk; crossed the Rowanty, separating the opposing pickets, by a moss-covered log, in a shadowy nook, and was approaching the house in which Swartz was shut up.

Nighthawk moved with the stealthy and gliding step of a wildcat. I could see the man was a born scout; intended by nature for the calling he had adopted—secret service. He scarcely uttered a word; when he did, it was in tones so low that they were lost in the whisper of the wind, amid the great trailing vines depending from the trees, and I was compelled to lean my ear close to catch the words.

Fifty paces from the bank, a shadowy object on horseback was visible by the dim light.

"The vedette," murmured Nighthawk, "but he need not see us."

And plunging, or rather gliding into the shadow of the trees, he led the way without noise, to a point directly in rear of the vedette.

A hundred yards farther a fire twinkled; and around this fire were the dusky figures of men and horses. This was evidently the picket.

Three hundred paces to the left, rose a dark object, sombre and lugubrious against the night, which it exceeded in blackness. Only in the upper portion of the house, a dim light, like a star, glittered.

"Some one is yonder," came from Nighthawk in a murmur as before, "let us go there, colonel."

And crouching down until his body nearly reached the earth, my companion glided, snake-like, toward the house. I imitated him; we passed unobserved, and almost immediately were behind the house.

Nighthawk then rose erect, and said in a whisper:—

"I am going to reconnoitre. Remain here, colonel. If I think you can come up without danger, I will make you a signal through that window."

With these words Nighthawk pointed to an open window about ten feet from the ground; glided past me through the broken sash of one beside which we were standing, and disappeared like a shadow.

I waited, holding my breath. From the upper portion of the house came the muffled sound of voices. I was endeavoring to distinguish the words uttered, when I saw Nighthawk appear at the upper window, and make me a sign.

That sign indicated that I might ascend with a reasonable amount of safety; and passing without noise through the window, I found myself in a bare and deserted apartment, with a single shutterless window opposite me. On the right was an open door. I passed through it, and found myself at the foot of a rough stairway, occupying half of a narrow passage.

Ascending, not without more than one creak, which, I must confess, sent a tingle through my nerves, I reached the upper landing, found myself in front of a closed door, and beside this door encountered the warning hand of Nighthawk.

"Look!" he said.

And drawing me toward him, he pointed through a crack in the board partition, which separated the passage from the apartment.

XXIX
DARKE'S PAST LIFE

Leaning on Nighthawk's shoulder, I placed my eye at the aperture.

On a broken chair beside the three-legged table sat Darke, booted, spurred, and armed with pistol and sabre. In an old rocking-chair, without arms, the singular woman, who seemed to accompany him everywhere, sat rocking to and fro, and carelessly tapping with a small whip, the handsome gray riding-habit which defined her slender and graceful figure.

Facing them, on an old bed frame, sat the unfortunate Swartz—but I would scarcely have recognized him, if I had not known that it was he. His frame had fallen away almost to nothing. His clothes hung upon him as upon a wooden pole. His cheeks were pale, sunken; his eyes hollow; his bearing, cowed, abject, and submissive beyond expression. Let me spare the reader one horror, however. Hunger was not torturing the unfortunate man at this moment. Beside him, on the floor, lay a piece of meat, and an unfinished loaf—thus it was evident that food had been brought to him; and as some of that food remained uneaten, he must have satisfied his hunger.

From Swartz, my glance passed to Darke. This second survey of the worthy proved to me that he was what is succinctly styled "half-drunk." But drink appeared not to have exhilarated him. It seemed even to have made him more morose. In the eyes and lips of the heavily bearded Hercules could be read a species of gloomy sarcasm—a something resembling bitter melancholy.

The woman in the gray dress, had never appeared cooler. She rocked to and fro in her chair with an air of perfect *insouciance*.

The interview had evidently lasted some time before our arrival at the house; but, as the reader will perceive, we came soon enough to overhear a somewhat singular revelation.

As I reached my position near the door, Darke was speaking to Swartz: —

"You ask why you are shut up here to starve," he said, "and as I have some time on my hands to-night, I am going to tell you. That might be called 'imprudent.' No! I am talking to a dead man! You see I hold out no false hopes — you will not leave this house alive probably — I will go back, and tell you something which will serve to explain the whole."

Darke paused a moment, and then gazed with a strange mixture of gloom and tenderness upon the gray woman.

"Perhaps you, too, madam," he said, speaking in a low tone, "may be ignorant of a part of my history. You know the worst — but not all. You shall know every thing. Listen; and I beg you will not interrupt me. About ten years ago, I chanced to be at Dinwiddie Court-House, a few miles only from this spot; and one day a certain Mr. George Conway visited the courthouse to receive a considerable sum of money which was to be paid to him."

At the words "a certain Mr. George Conway," uttered by the speaker, in a hoarse and hesitating voice, I very nearly uttered an exclamation. That name, which General Davenant's recent narrative had surrounded with so many gloomy associations, produced a profound effect on me, as it now escaped from this man's lips; and had it not been for Nighthawk's warning pressure on my arm, I should probably have betrayed our vicinity. Fortunately I suppressed the rising exclamation; it had attracted no attention; and Darke went on in the same low tone: —

"I was in the clerk's office of Dinwiddie when the money I refer to was paid to Mr. Conway. It amounted to about ten thousand dollars, and as I had at that time no business in the region more important than hanging around the tavern, and drinking and playing cards — as, besides this, I was at the end of my resources, having lost my last penny on the night before, at the card-table — the idea occurred to me that it would not be a bad plan to ride after Mr. Conway; accost him on the road; represent my necessities to him, and request a small loan out of his abundant means, to prevent myself from being deprived of my luxuries — liquor and cards. Is that a roundabout way of saying I intended to act the highwayman, perhaps the — murderer — on this occasion? By no means, madam! What is highway robbery? Is it not the brutal and wanton robbery of the poor as well as the rich? Well, I was not going to rob anybody. I was going to request a small loan—and so far from intending violence, or—murder—," he uttered that word always in a hesitating voice—"I swear, I had no such intention. I was entirely unarmed; upon my whole person there was not one deadly weapon—it was only by accident that I found, when riding out of the court-house, that I had a small pen-knife in my pocket. This I had picked up, by pure accident from the table of the clerk's office, where some one had laid it down. I had carelessly commenced paring my nails with it—my attention was attracted by something else. I finished paring my nails, and without being aware of what I was doing, put the knife in my pocket.

"Well, you may think, perhaps, all this is irrelevant. You are mistaken. Many things turned on that knife. The devil himself placed it in my grasp that day!"

XXX
STABBED "NOT MURDERED"

"Well," Darke continued, "I have told you my design, and now I will inform you how I carried it out.

"I saw Mr. George Conway receive the money — in notes, bank notes, and gold. That was enough; I knew the road he would take; and going to the stable of the tavern I saddled my horse, and rode out of the place in a western direction. When I was out of sight, however, I turned eastward toward Five Forks, pushed into the woods, and about sunset took my stand in a piece of timber, on the side of the road which — he — was coming by."

There was always a marked hesitation when he came to the name of his victim. He went on more rapidly now.

"Well, he came along about dusk. Some one followed him, but I could not make out who. Another man came on from the direction of Petersburg; passed me and *him*; and the other who had followed *him* out of the court-house turned into a by-road and disappeared. Then I saw that the game was in my own hands; I waited, looking at him as he approached me. I swear I did not intend to harm him. I was half-drunk, but I remember what I intended. He came on. I rode toward him, demanded the money, he refused. I threw myself on him, as he struck at me with the butt of his heavy riding-whip, then we both rolled to the ground, I under! His clutch was on my throat, I was choking. 'Help,' he cried, and I came near crying it, too! All at once my hand fell upon my pocket, I felt the knife, I drew it out, opened it, and stabbed him as he was strangling me!

"That was the whole! Do you call it a *murder*? I rose up, as *he* fell back. His breast was all bloody; his eyes turned round; he gasped something, and fell back dead."

The speaker paused and wiped his brow with his huge, muscular hand. His face was a strange spectacle. The most bitter and terrible emotions of the human heart were written there as with a pen of fire.

"Then I looked at him;" he went on, "I said to myself, 'this is a murder,' foolishly, for he was stabbed, not murdered; and my first thought was to conceal the body. I dragged it to the roadside, hid it in some bushes, and thinking I heard some one coming, leaped on my horse, who had stood by quietly—*his* had galloped away—and left the cursed spot as fast as I could go. The money was left on him. I swear I did not touch a penny of it, and would not have touched it, even if I had not been interrupted. I had not intended to kill him. It was the result of the struggle. I took nothing of *his* away from that place, but I left something of my own; the knife with which I had struck him!

"The devil had put the cursed thing into my hand; and now the devil made me drop it there, within ten feet of the dead body."

XXXI
THE TWO PAPERS

Darke had spoken in a low, dull, gloomy voice; and something like a shudder had passed through his frame as he painted, in brief words, the sombre scene. This emotion now seemed even to grow deeper. Was there good left in this wild animal?

"That knife," he continued, "was very nearly the means of hanging an innocent man. It belonged to a gentleman of the neighborhood who had accidentally laid it on the table of the clerk's office, a few moments before I, as accidentally, picked it up—and this gentleman had just had angry words with—*him*—about a trifle. What made things worse was that they had long been enemies—and when *he* was found there, dead in the bushes, next day, the owner of the knife found near the body was arrested as the murderer.

"Well, he went to jail, and the trial was coming on soon. The evidence against him was strong. He was the known enemy of—Mr. Conway. He had quarrelled with him on that day, and his knife was found by—the body—on which the money had not been touched. A robber, you see, would have taken the money; as it was untouched the crime must have been committed by a personal enemy. Who was that enemy? The prisoner—whose name was Davenant!

"Well, the trial was near. I had gone back to the court-house on *that day*, and was still hanging around the place. What was I to do? I had to determine whether I would let an innocent man be hanged for my crime, or go to the sheriff and say, 'release the prisoner—I am the murderer.' That was rather more than I was ready for, and I hit on a means which might serve. The knife was important evidence—the *most* important—and I was in the clerk's office one day, hanging round and listening, when I saw the sheriff put the knife in a drawer, to have it ready near court on the day of trial. Well, that night I broke into the court-house—stole the knife—and waited to see what would occur on the trial.

"As the day drew near I felt like a real murderer, and had the prisoner all the time before my eyes, hanging on a gallows. I drank harder than ever, but I could not get that picture out of my mind. I saw worse pictures than before. So I determined what to do. I sat down, wrote a full confession of the murder, which I signed; and a friend of mine carried this to the prisoner's wife. I had put on it 'In haste, this will save Mr. Davenant's life' — and his wife carried it, at full speed, with her own hands to the court-house, where she arrived just as the jury had retired.

"The prisoner opened and read it. When he had finished it, he folded it up and put it in his pocket. As he did so, the jury came in with a verdict of 'Not guilty' — and he went out of the court-room accompanied by a crowd of friends.

"So he was cleared, you see — without using the document which I had written. That was in his pocket; was of no further use; and as it might become dangerous I entered his house that night, broke open the desk in which he kept his private papers, and took this one out, reading and making sure that it was the genuine document, by the light of the moon which streamed in at the window.

"I was still looking at the paper, when a noise behind me attracted my attention, and turning round I saw — Mr. Davenant. He had heard the noise I made in breaking open the secretary; put on his dressing-gown; and coming down, pistol in hand, was on me before I knew it. The few minutes that followed were rather angry, and noisy. Unexpectedly, Mr. Davenant did not fire on me. After an interchange of compliments, I put the paper in my pocket, passed out through the window, and mounting my horse, rode away.

"After that I went far, and saw many persons. Among the rest you, madam; and our matrimonial life has been chequered!

"A word to you, now," he added, turning toward Swartz. "I shut you up here to starve you to death because you were trusted and have betrayed me. Listen, and I will tell you how. You are greedy for gold, and this greed has tempted you to an act which will be your destruction. In Pennsylvania, one night, just before the battle of Gettysburg, you were at my house, and stole a paper from madam, who was collecting every thing to hide it from the enemy. No matter how I know that; I have made the discovery, and you deny it — refusing to deliver up that paper, which you state you never had, and consequently have not in your possession. In saying that, you lied! You stole that paper, and promise yourself that you will sell it for a large sum of money—you have already been bargaining, and have tried to finish the business.

"Well, that paper is interesting—to madam at least; and she has kept it with care from the eyes of the very person you would sell it to! Folded with it was another paper which is no less valuable to me. Thus, you see, that we are interested; and we will probably be informed in a day from this time where to find both the documents—as you will then be starving, and will reveal every thing!

"You think me jesting, perhaps—you imagine I will spare you. Undeceive yourself—your life is a small matter compared with these two papers.

"One is the certificate of madam's marriage with your very humble servant; the other the letter which I took from Mr. Davenant's desk that night, in which I confess myself the—well! the murderer—of George Conway!"

XXXII
A PISTOL-SHOT

Darke's deep and gloomy voice ceased to resound, and for a moment the silence of the apartment was only disturbed by the slight creaking made by the chair of the woman, as she quietly rocked backward and forward.

Swartz had risen to his feet while Darke was uttering his final words. With clasped hands, and trembling lips, he was about to throw himself upon his knees; — when suddenly a shot resounded without, a cry was heard, and then this was succeeded by rapid firing, mingled with hoof-strokes, in the immediate vicinity of the house.

Darke rose to his feet, and in two strides was at the window.

"An attack!" he exclaimed. "Can the friends of this carrion be trying to catch me!"

And springing toward the door, he tore it open.

Suddenly, another thought seemed to come to him. Returning at a bound to the side of Swartz, he seized him by the throat, dragged him through the door, and rushed down the steps, still dragging the unfortunate man.

As he passed me, I drew my revolver and fired on him, but the ball did not strike him. Then I saw the woman dart past like a shadow. When Nighthawk and myself reached the foot of the stairs, she and Darke were already in the saddle.

The collar of Swartz was still in his clutch. He seemed determined to bear him off at the risk of being himself captured; for a second glance showed me that a party of Confederate cavalry was rushing headlong toward the house, led by an officer whom I made out to be Mohun.

Darke saw that the small force on picket could not contend with the attacking party.

By the starlight, I could see his face, as he glared over his shoulder at Mohun, whom he had evidently recognized. An expression of profound hate was in that glance; a hoarse growl issued from his lips; and I distinguished the low words addressed to Swartz, whom he was dragging on beside his horse.

"So, you are rescued, you think! You have laid this trap for me, jailbird!"

He drew his pistol as he spoke, and placed it close to the unhappy man's temple. I had mine in my hand, and, aiming at Darke, fired.

It was too late. The bullet did not strike him; and the report of his own weapon followed that of mine like an echo.

Swartz staggered back, threw up his hands, and uttering a wild cry, fell at full length upon the ground.

The scene which followed was as brief as this tragedy. Mohun charged, at the head of his men, and drove the picket force before him. In five minutes the whole party were dispersed, or captured.

Darke had escaped with the gray woman, in the darkness.

The pursuit did not continue far. The Federal lines were near; and Mohun soon recalled his men.

Grasping me cordially by the hand, he exclaimed: —

"Well, Surry! the prisoner! Where is Swartz?"

I pointed to the spot where his body lay, and went thither with Mohun.

Swartz lay perfectly dead, in a pool of blood. Darke had blown out his brains.

XXXIII
PRESTON HAMPTON

An hour afterward the body of the unfortunate man had been buried, and I had returned with Mohun and Nighthawk to the opposite bank of the Rowanty.

I had never seen Mohun so gloomy. He scarcely uttered a word during the whole march back; and when I announced my intention to spend the night at the house of Mr. Alibi, as the long tramp had wearied me out, he scarcely invited me to his head-quarters, and when I declined, did not urge me. Something evidently weighed heavily on the mind of Mohun, and a few moment's reflection explained the whole to me.

He had conversed rapidly and apart with Nighthawk near the lonely house; and his gloom had dated from that conversation. Nighthawk had evidently explained every thing: the cause of Swartz's imprisonment; his statement in reference to the paper—and now that Swartz was dead, the hiding-place of the document seemed forever undiscoverable.

If the reader does not understand the terrible significance of this fact, and Mohun's consequent gloom, I promise that he shall comprehend all before very long.

Mohun returned to his camp, and I remained at the house of Mr. Alibi until morning, stretched on a lounge, and wrapped in my cape.

I awoke about sunrise. As I opened my eyes, quick firing came from the direction of Burgess's Mill. The fire speedily became more rapid and continuous; I hastened to mount my horse; and as I did so, a courier passed at full gallop.

"What news?" I asked.

"The enemy are advancing in force! They have crossed!"

"Where?"

"Near Armstrong's!"

And the courier disappeared, at full speed, in the woods. In a moment I had abandoned my design of inspecting, and was riding back.

"Armstrong's" was a mill on the Rowanty, near the Boydton road. If the enemy had crossed there, in force, it was to make a heavy advance toward the Southside road.

I was not mistaken. Reaching the debouchment of the "Quaker road," I found the cavalry drawn up in order of battle—a dispatch had been sent to hurry up the rest—on the lower waters of the Rowanty, and General Hampton informed me of the situation of affairs.

The enemy had advanced in heavy force at sunrise, driven in the pickets, and, crossing the Rowanty, seized on the Boydton road and the bridge at Burgess's Mill. From prisoners taken, it was ascertained that the force consisted of the Second, Fifth, and part of the Ninth Corps; Grant, Meade, and Hancock, accompanying the troops in person.

That left nothing in doubt. If any remained, it was dispelled by the fact, stated to me by General Hampton, that the Federal troops "had eight days' rations, and were certainly bound for the Southside road."[1]

{Footnote 1: His words.}

I had scarcely received this intelligence from General Hampton, when a heavy attack was made upon General William H.F. Lee, holding the Quaker road.

From that moment the battle began to rage with determined fury, and the entire force of cavalry was engaged in an obstinate fight with the advancing enemy. It was a bitter and savage affair. The men charged; dismounted and fought behind impromptu breastworks of rails; fell back only when they were pushed by the weight of the great column rolling forward; and for hours the whole field was a hurly-burly of dust, smoke, blood, uproar, carbine shots, musket shots, and the long threatening roar of cannon.

The Stuart horse artillery fought like tigers. The men stuck to their guns amid a storm of bullets, and vindicated, as they had done before on many fields, the name of "my pets," given them by Stuart! Among the officers, Will Davenant was seen, sitting his horse amid the smoke, as calm as a May morning; and I shall never forget the smile on the face of this young bull-dog, when he said:—

"I think we can hold our ground, colonel."

And looking over his shoulder, in the direction of Five Forks, he murmured:—

"This is a good place to die, too."

A thundering cheer rose suddenly above the roar of the guns, and the line of dismounted sharp-shooters behind their rail breastworks opened a more steady and resolute fire as the enemy appeared to pause.

At the same moment young Preston Hampton, a son of the general, and one of my favorites, from his courage and courtesy, passed by at a gallop, cheering and encouraging the skirmishers.

I spurred after him. Just as I reached him, I saw the arm waving above his head suddenly drop; his sword escaped from his grasp, and he fell from the saddle to the ground.

In an instant I had dismounted, and with other officers who hastened up, had raised him from the earth.

As we did so, the group, consisting now of no less than seven, attracted the enemy's attention; a hot fire was opened on us, and before we could bear the dying youth in our arms beyond the reach of the fire, four out of the seven officers were shot.{1}

{Footnote 1: Fact}

The boy was placed in an ambulance, and borne to the rear; but the wound was fatal, and he soon afterward expired. A staff officer afterward informed me that General Hampton did not leave his tent for a fortnight — scarcely replying when he was spoken to, and prostrated by grief.

I could understand that. The death of the brave youth sent a pang to my own heart — and he was only my friend. The great heart of the father must have been nearly broken.

So fell Preston Hampton. Peace to his ashes! No kinder or braver spirit ever died for his country!

XXXIV
I AM CAPTURED

Hour after hour the battle continued to rage; the enemy making resolute attempts to brush off the cavalry.

It was now discovered that Hancock's corps had crossed the Rowanty, supported by Crawford's division, with two corps behind; and as General Hancock held the bridge at Burgess's, there seemed little probability that Lee could cross a force to attack him.

But this was done. While the cavalry fought the blue masses with obstinate courage on the Boydton road, Mahone, that daring soldier, crossed a column of three brigades over the Rowanty, below Burgess's; and suddenly the enemy found themselves attacked in flank and rear. Mahone did not pause. He advanced straight to the assault; swept every thing before him, and thrusting his small force in between Hancock and Crawford, tore from the former four hundred prisoners, three battle-flags, and six pieces of artillery.

The assault had been sudden and almost overwhelming. While hotly engaged with Hampton in front, the enemy had all at once staggered beneath the heavy blow dealt on their flank and rear. They turned to strike at this new foe; and the shock which followed was rude, the onset bloody.

Mahone met it with that dash and stubbornness now proverbial in the army; and, hurling his three brigades against the advancing column, broke through three lines of battle, and drove them back.{1}

{Footnote 1: "In the attack subsequently made by the enemy, General Mahone broke three lines of battle." — General Lee's Dispatch of October 28, 1864.}

Night was near, and the fighting still continued. The enemy seemed both to give up the ground; and were holding their position obstinately, when a determined charge from a brigade of Mahone's drove every thing in its front.

I had been to carry a message for General Hampton, upon whose staff I served during the battle, and now found myself swept forward by the brigade charging.

In front of them, I recognized General Davenant, on horseback, and sword in hand, leading the charge. His son Charley was beside him.

"We are driving them, colonel!" exclaimed the general, with a proud smile "and look! yonder are some of their general officers flying from that house!"

As he spoke, he pointed to three horsemen, riding at full speed from a house known as Burgess's; their splendid suit of staff officers indicated that they were of high rank.

In fact, the three horsemen who retired thus hastily, would have proved a rich prize to us. They were Generals Grant, Meade and Hancock.{1}

{Footnote 1: Fact.}

They made a narrow escape, and the question suggests itself, "What would have been the result of their capture?" I know not; I only know that Grant, Meade and Hancock, came near having an interview with General Lee that night—a peaceful and friendly talk at his head-quarters.

I did not think of all this then. The hot charge dragged me. I had come to participate in it by the mere chance of battle—but this apparent accident was destined to have very singular results.

I had ridden with General Davenant, as his brigade swept forward, and we were breasting a heavy fire on his front, when a sudden cry of "Cavalry! look out!" came from our left.

General Davenant wheeled his horse; went at full speed, accompanied by his son and myself, through the bullets, in the direction indicated; and carried onward by his animal, as I was by my own, rode right into a column of blue cavalry, advancing to attack our flank.

Such was the "chance of battle!" At one moment General Davenant was in command of a brigade which was driving the enemy, and sweeping every thing before it. At the next moment he had been carried by the powerful animal which he bestrode straight into the ranks of the Federal cavalry, hidden by the woods and approaching darkness—had been surrounded in an instant, fired upon, and half dragged from his saddle, and captured, together with his son Charley.

What was still more unfortunate to me, personally, was the fact that having followed the old soldier, I was surrounded, and made a prisoner in the same manner.

XXXV
FACE TO FACE

We had scarcely time to realize the truly disgusting fact, that we were captured at the very instant that the enemy were being driven, when the charge of the Federal cavalry was met by a hail-storm of bullets which drove them back in disorder.

For some moments the woods presented a singular spectacle. Horsemen flying in wild confusion; riderless animals darting madly toward the rear; the groans of wounded men tottering in the saddle as they rushed by—all this made up a wild scene of excitement, and confusion worse confounded.

General Davenant, his son, and myself had been ordered to the rear, under escort; and the old cavalier had turned his horse's head in that direction, boiling with rage at his capture, when the repulse ensued, and the Federal cavalry streamed by us toward the rear.

All at once a loud voice was heard shouting in the half darkness:—

"Halt! halt! you cursed cowards! Halt! and form column!"

The speaker rushed toward us as he spoke, mounted upon a huge black horse, and I heard the noise made by his sabre, as with the flat of it, he struck blows upon the brawny shoulders of the fugitives.

At his summons, and the blows of his sabre, the men halted, and again fell into column. Under the shadowy boughs of the woods, and in the gathering darkness, the long line of horsemen resembled phantoms rather than men. Near them glimmered some bivouac fires; and the flickering light illumined their persons, gleamed on their scabbards, and lit up the rough bearded faces.

"Cowardly scoundrels!" exclaimed their leader, in fierce accents, "where are the prisoners that ran into us?"

"Here, colonel. One is a general!" said a man.

"Let me see them!"

General Davenant struck the spur violently into his horse, and rode close to the Federal officer, in whom I had recognized Colonel Darke.

"Here I am, wretch!—look at me!" exclaimed General Davenant, foaming with rage. "Accursed be the day when I begat a murderer and a renegade!"

XXXVI
THE CURSE

Darke's hand unconsciously drew the rein, and man and horse both seemed to stagger back before the furious old soldier.

"General — Davenant!" muttered Darke, turning pale.

"Yes, General Davenant! — a gentleman, an honest man; not a traitor and a murderer!"

"Good God!" muttered Darke, "it is my father, truly — and my little brother! The proud face, the eyes, the mouth — and yet they told me you were killed."

"Ah! 'Killed!' Killing is a favorite topic with you!" exclaimed General Davenant, furiously; "well, kill *me*, now! — Strike your dastardly sword, or *your knife* if you have one, straight into my breast! Murder me, I say, as you murdered George Conway! — I have a purse in my pocket, and you can rob me when I am dead. Strike! strike! — but not with the sword! That is the weapon of a gentleman. Draw your knife, and stab me in the back — the knife is the weapon of the assassin!"

And crossing his arms upon his breast, the fiery old cavalier confronted his son, with eyes full of bitter wrath and disdain — eyes which I shall never forget; for their fire burnt them into my memory.

Darke did not dare to meet them. I had listened with amazement to those words, which indicated that the Federal officer was General Davenant's son; then this sentiment of astonishment, profound as it was, had yielded to one of expectation, if I may so express myself. What I expected was a furious outbreak from the man of fierce and violent passions, thus taunted and driven to bay by the repeated insults of the general. No outburst came, however. On the contrary, the Federal officer bowed his head, and listened in silence, while a mortal pallor diffused itself over his swarthy face. His gaze was bent upon the ground, and his brows so closely knit that they extended in an unbroken ridge of black and shaggy hair above his bloodshot eyes. He sat his horse, in the light of the camp-fire, — a huge cavalier upon an animal as powerful and forbidding in appearance as himself, — and for more than a minute after the scornful outburst from General Davenant, Darke remained silent and motionless, with his eyes still fixed upon the ground:

Then he raised his head, made a sign with his hand to an officer, and said, briefly: —

"Move back with the column — leave these prisoners here."

At the word, the column moved back slowly; the shadowy figures were lost sight of in the darkness; General Davenant, his son Charles, Darke, and myself, were left alone beside the camp-fire.

Then the Federal officer, with a face over which seemed to pass "the shadow of unutterable things," looked first with a long, wistful, absorbed glance toward the boy Charles, his brother — lastly, toward his father.

"Why do you taunt me?" he said, in a low tone. "Will that result in any good now? Yes, I committed murder. I intended, if I did not commit, robbery. I killed — yes, I killed! — with a knife — as a murderer kills. But I do not wish to kill you — or Charley — or this officer — or rob you. Keep your life and your money. There is the road before you, open. Go; you are free!"

General Davenant had sat his horse — the boy Charley beside him — listening in sullen wrath. As Darke ended, the general's hand went to the hilt of his sword, and he half drew it, by an instinctive movement, from the scabbard. "Well!" added the Federal officer, in the same low tone, with a deeper flush in his cheeks, "draw your sword, sir — strike me if you think proper. For myself, I am done with murder, and shrink from it, so that, if my father wishes to kill me, I will open my breast, to give him a fair opportunity. You see I am not altogether the murderous wretch you take me for. I am a murderer, it is true, and soiled with every vice — you see I am frank — but I will not resist, if you plunge your sword into my heart. Strike! strike! While I am dying I will have time to say the few words I have to say to you!"

General Davenant shuddered with wrath still, but a strange emotion was mingled with the sentiment now — an emotion which I could not fathom. Before he could open his lips, however, Darke resumed, in the same tone: —

"You hesitate — you are not ready to become my executioner. Well, listen, and I will utter that which may deprive you of all self-control. Yes, once more, I killed a man, and killed him for money; but *you* made me what I was! You petted, and spoiled, and made me selfish. In addition, you hated—that man. You had hated him for twenty years. When I grew up, I found out that. If you did not strike him, you had the desire to do so—and, like a good son, I shared my 'father's loves and hatreds.' I heard you speak of—him—harshly; I knew that an old grudge was between you; what matter if I met this enemy of the family on the high-road, and, with the dagger at his throat, said: 'Yield me a portion of your ill-gotten gains!' for that money was the proceeds of a forced sale for cash, by which the father of a family was turned out of house and home! Well, I did that—and did it under the effect of drink. I learned the habit at *your* table; wine was placed in my hands, in my very childhood, by you; you indulged all my vile selfishness; made me a miserable, arrogant wretch; I came to hang about the village tavern, and gamble, and fuddle myself, until I was made worthless! Then, when one day the devil tempted me, I committed a crime—and that crime was committed by *you*! for *you* cultivated in me the vile habits which led me on to murder!"

Darke's eyes were gloomy, and full of a strange fire. As he uttered the last words, he spurred close to his father, tore open his uniform until his bare breast was visible, and added in accents full of vehement and sullen passion:—

"Strike me! Bury your sword's point in my heart! I am your son. You are as noble a gentleman as Brutus was! Kill me, then! I am a murderer: but I am a Davenant, and no coward!"

From the fierce and swollen face, in which the dark eyes burned like firebrands, my glance passed to the countenance of General Davenant. A startling change had taken place in the expression of the old cavalier. He was no longer erect, fiery, defiant. His glance no longer darted scorn and anger. His chin had fallen upon his breast; his frame drooped; his cheeks, but now so flushed, were covered with a deep pallor.

For a moment he remained silent. The hand which had clutched at the sword hilt hung listless at his side. All at once his breast heaved, and with a sound which resembled a groan, he said, in low tones:—

"I am punished! Yes, my hatred has brought forth fruit, and the fruit is bitter! It was I who warped this life, and the tree has grown as I inclined it."

"Yes," said Darke, in his deep voice, "first warped—then, when cut down, cast off and forgotten!"

General Davenant looked at the speaker with bitter melancholy.

"Ah! you charge me with that, do you, sir?" he said, "You do not remember, then, that I have suffered for you—you do not know, perhaps, that for ten years I have labored under the imputation of that crime, and have preserved silence that I might shield your memory—for I thought you dead! You do not know that I never breathed a syllable of that letter which you sent to me on the day of my trial—that I have allowed the world to believe I was saved by a legal technicality! You have not heard, perhaps, that a daughter of Judge Conway is beloved by your brother, and that her father rejects with scorn the very idea of forming an alliance with *my* son—the son of one whom he regards as the murderer of his brother! Oh! yes, sir! truly I have cast off and forgotten you and your memory! I have not wept tears of blood over the crime you committed—over the dishonor that rested on the name of Davenant! I have not writhed beneath the cold and scornful eye of Judge Conway and his friends! I have not seen your brother's heart breaking for love of that girl; and suppressed all, concealed every thing, borne the brand on my proud forehead, and *his* young life, that *your* tombstone might at least not have 'murderer' cut on it! And now you taunt me with my faults!—with my injudicious course toward you when your character was forming. You sneer and say that I first hated George Conway, and that the son only inherited the family feud, and struck the enemy of the family! Yes, I acknowledge those sins; I pray daily to be forgiven for them. I have borne for ten years this bitter load of dishonor. But there is something more maddening even than my faults, and the stain on my name—it is to be taunted to my face, here, with the charge that I struck that blow! that I made you the criminal, and then threw you off, and drove you to become a renegade in the ranks of our enemies!"

The last words of the speaker were nearly drowned in a heavy fusillade which issued from the woods close by.

"Listen!" exclaimed General Davenant, "that is the fire of your hirelings, sir, directed at the hearts of your brethren! *You* are leading that scum against the gentlemen of Virginia! Well join them! Point *me*, and my son, and companion out to them! Tear us to pieces with your bullets! Trample us beneath your hireling heels! That will not prevent me from branding you again in your dishonored forehead!—from cursing you as renegade, debauchee, and murderer!"

The whistle of bullets mingled with these furious and resounding words; and then the crackle of footsteps was heard, the undergrowth suddenly swarmed with figures—a party of Confederates rushed shouting into the little glade.

Darke wheeled not from, but toward them, as though to charge them. The stern courage of the Davenant blood burned in his cheeks and eyes. Then, with a harsh and bitter laugh, he turned and pushed his horse close up beside that of his father.

"I would call this meeting and parting strange, if any thing were strange in this world!" he said, "but nothing astonishes me, or moves me, as of old! The devil has brought it about! he put a knife in my hands once! to-night he brings me face to face with you and my boy-brother—and makes you curse and renounce me! Well, so be it! have your will! Henceforth I am really lost—my father!"

And drawing his pistol, he coolly discharged barrel after barrel in the faces of the men rushing upon him; wheeled his horse, and dug the spurs into him; an instant afterward, with his sneering face turned over his shoulder, he had disappeared in the woods.

Two hours afterward I was on my way to Petersburg.

The enemy were already falling back from their adventurous attempt to seize the Southside road.

In the morning they had retired across the Rowanty, and disappeared.

So ended that heavy blow at Lee's great war-artery.

BOOK IV
THE PHANTOMS

I
RICHMOND BY THE THROAT

I was again back at the "Cedars," after the rapid and shifting scenes which I have endeavored to place before the reader.

The tragic incidents befalling the actors in this drama, had most absorbed my attention; but sitting now in my tent, with the newspapers before me, I looked at the fight in which I had participated, from the general and historic point of view.

That heavy advance on the Boydton road, beyond Lee's right, had been simultaneous with a determined assault on the Confederate left, north of James River, and on Lee's centre opposite Petersburg; and now the extracts from Northern journals clearly indicated that the movement was meant to be decisive.

"I have Richmond by the throat!" General Grant had telegraphed; but there was good ground to believe that the heavy attack, and the eloquent dispatch, were both meant to "make capital" for the approaching Presidential election.

These memoirs, my dear reader, are written chiefly to record some incidents which I witnessed during the war. I have neither time nor space for political comments. But I laid my hand yesterday, by accident, on an old number of the *Examiner* newspaper; and it chanced to contain an editorial on the fight just described, with some penetrating views on the "situation" at that time.

Shall I quote a paragraph from the yellow old paper? It will be bitter—we were all bitter in those days! though to-day we are so fraternal and harmonious. With his trenchant pen, Daniel pierced to the core of the matter; and the paper may give some idea of the spirit of the times.

I could fancy the great satirist sitting in his lonely study, and penning the lines I shall quote, not without grim smiles at his own mordant humor.

Here is the slip I cut out. The old familiar heading may recall those times to some readers, as clearly as the biting sentences, once read, perhaps, by the camp-fire.

* * * * * DAILY EXAMINER. * * * * * MONDAY MORNING OCT. 31, 1864. * * * * *

"Every day must now bring its brilliant bulletin to the Yankee nation. That nation does not regard the punctual rising of the sun as more lawfully due to it than a victory every morning. And those glorious achievements of SHERIDAN in the Valley were grown cold and

stale, and even plainly hollow and rotten — insomuch that, after totally annihilating the army of EARLY at least three times, and so

clearing the way to Lynchburg, instead of marching up to Lynchburg

the heroick victor goes whirling down to Winchester. Then the superb victory obtained on Sunday of last week over PRICE in Missouri, has taken a certain bogus tint, which causes many to believe that there was, in fact, no victory and no battle. This would not do. Something fresh must be had; something electrifying; above all, something that would set the people to cheering and firing off salutes about the very day of the election; — something, too, that could not be plainly contradicted by the events till after that critical day — then let the contradiction come and welcome: your true Yankee will only laugh.

"From this necessity came the great 'reconnoissance in force' of last Thursday on our lines before Richmond and Petersburg; a 'reconnoissance' in very heavy force indeed upon three points of our front at once both north and south of the James river; so that it may be very properly considered as three reconnoissances in force; made with a view of feeling, as it were, LEE'S position; and the object of the three reconnoissances having been fully attained — that is, LEE having been felt — they retired. That is the way in which the transactions of Thursday last are to appear in STANTON'S bulletin, we may be all quite sure; and this

*representation, together with the occupation of a part of the
Boydton plank-road (which road the newspapers can call for a few
days the Southside Road) will cause every city from Boston to
Milwaukee to fire off its inevitable hundred guns. Thus, the
Presidential election will be served, just in the nick of time; for
that emergency it is not the real victory which is wanted, so much
as the jubilation, glorification and cannon salutes.*

*"Even when the truth comes to be fully known that this was the
grand pre-election assault itself: the resistless advance on
Richmond which was to lift the Abolitionists into power again
upon
a swelling high-tide of glory unutterable — easily repulsed and
sent
rolling back with a loss of about six or seven thousand men in
killed, wounded and prisoners; even when this is known, does the
reader imagine that the Yankee nation will be discouraged? Very
far
from it. On the contrary it will be easily made to appear that from
these 'reconnoissances in force,' an advantage has been gained,
which is to make the next advance a sure and overwhelming
success.
For the fact is, that a day was chosen for this mighty movement,
when the wind was southerly, a soft and gentle breeze, which
wafted
the odour of the Yankee whiskey-rations to the nostrils of
Confederate soldiers. The Confederates ought to have been taken
by
surprise that morning; but the moment they snuffed the tainted
gale, they knew what was to be the morning's work. Not more
unerring is the instinct which calls the vulture to the
battle-field before a drop of blood is shed; or that which makes
the kites 'know well the long stern swell, that bids the Romans
close;' than the sure induction of our army that the Yankees are
coming on, when morn or noon or dewy eve breathes along the
whole*

line a perfumed savour of the ancient rye. The way in which this
discovery may be improved is plain. It will be felt and understood
throughout the intelligent North, that it gives them at last the
key to Richmond. They will say — Those rebels, to leeward of us,
smell the rising valour of our loyal soldiers: the filling and
emptying of a hundred thousand canteens perfumes the sweet
South as

if it had passed over a bed of violets, stealing and giving
odours: — when the wind is southerly it will be said, rebels know a
hawk from a handsaw. Therefore it is but making our next grand
assault on some morning when they are to windward of us —
creeping

up, in the lee of LEE, as if he were a stag — and Richmond is ours."

That is savage, and sounds unfraternal to-day, when peace and good feeling reign — when the walls of the Virginia capitol re-echo the stately voices of the conscript fathers of the great commonwealth and mother of States: conscript fathers bringing their wisdom, mature study, and experience to the work of still further improving the work of Jefferson, Mason, and Washington.

"I have Richmond by the throat!" General Grant wrote in October, 1864. In February, 1868, when these lines are written, black hands have got Virginia by the throat, and she is suffocating; Cuffee grins, Cuffee gabbles — the groans of the "Old Mother" make him laugh.

Messieurs of the great Northwest, she gave you being, and suckled you! Are you going to see her strangled before your very eyes?

II
NIGHTMARE

In truth, if not held by the throat, as General Grant announced, Richmond and all the South in that autumn of 1864, was staggering, suffocating, reeling to and fro under the immense incubus of all-destroying war.

At that time black was the "only wear," and widows and orphans were crying in every house throughout the land. Bread and meat had become no longer necessaries, but luxuries. Whole families of the old aristocracy lived on crusts, and even by charity. Respectable people in Richmond went to the "soup-houses." Men once rich, were penniless, and borrowed to live. Provisions were incredibly dear. Flour was hundreds of dollars a barrel; bacon ten dollars a pound; coffee and tea had become unknown almost. Boots were seven hundred dollars a pair. The poor skinned the dead horses on battle-fields to make shoes. Horses cost five thousand dollars. Cloth was two hundred dollars a yard. Sorghum had taken the place of sugar. Salt was sold by the ounce. Quinine was one dollar a grain. Paper to write upon was torn from old blank books. The ten or twenty dollars which the soldiers received for their monthly pay, was about sufficient to buy a sheet, a pen, and a little ink to write home to their starving families that they too were starving.

In town and country the atmosphere seemed charged with coming ruin. All things were in confusion. Everywhere something jarred. The executive was unpopular. The heads of departments were inefficient. The army was unfed. The finances were mismanaged. In Congress the opposition bitterly criticised President Davis. The press resounded with fierce diatribes, *pro* and *con*, on all subjects. The *Examiner* attacked the government, and denounced the whole administration of affairs. The *Sentinel* replied to the attacks, and defended the assailed officials. One could see nothing that was good. The other could see nothing that was bad. Their readers adopted their opinions; looking through glasses that were deep green, or else *couleur de rose*. But the green glasses outnumbered the rose-colored more and more every day.

Thus, in the streets of the city, and in the shades of the country, all was turmoil, confusion—a hopeless brooding on the hours that were coming. War was no longer an affair of the border and outpost. Federal cavalry scoured the woods, tearing the last mouthful from the poor people. Federal cannon were thundering in front of the ramparts of the cities. In the country, the faint-hearted gathered at the court-houses and cross-roads to comment on the times, and groan. In the cities, cowards croaked in the market-places. In the country, men were hiding their meat in garrets and cellars—concealing their corn in pens, lost in the depths of the woods. In the towns, the forestallers hoarded flour, and sugar, and salt in their warehouses, to await famine prices. The vultures of troubled times flapped their wings and croaked joyfully. Extortioners rolled in their chariots. Hucksters laughed as they counted their gains. Blockade-runners drank their champagne, jingled their coin, and dodged the conscript officers.

The rich were very rich and insolent. The poor were want-stricken and despairing. Fathers gazed at their children's pale faces, and knew not where to find food for them. Mothers hugged their frail infants to bosoms drained by famine. Want gnawed at the vitals. Despair had come, like a black and poisonous mist, to strangle the heart.

The soldiers were agonized by maddening letters from their families. Their fainting loved ones called for help. "Father! come home!" moaned the children, with gaunt faces, crying for bread. "Husband, come home!" murmured the pale wife, with her half-dead infant in her arms. And the mothers—the mothers—ah! the mothers! They did not say, "Come home!" to their brave boys in the army; they were too proud for that—too faithful to the end. They did not summon them to come home; they only knelt down and prayed: "God, end this cruel war! Only give me back my boy! Do not bereave me of my child! The cause is lost—his blood not needed! God, pity me and give me back my boy!"

So that strange autumn of that strange year, 1864, wore on. The country was oppressed as by some hideous nightmare; and Government was silent.

The army alone, kept heart of hope—Lee's old soldiers defied the enemy to the last.

III
LEE'S MISERABLES

They called themselves "Lee's Miserables."

That was a grim piece of humor, was it not, reader? And the name had had a somewhat curious origin. Victor Hugo's work, *Les Misérables*, had been translated and published by a house in Richmond; the soldiers, in the great dearth of reading matter, had seized upon it; and thus, by a strange chance the tragic story of the great French writer, had become known to the soldiers in the trenches. Everywhere, you might see the gaunt figures in their tattered jackets bending over the dingy pamphlets — "Fantine," "Cosette," or "Marius," or "St. Denis," — and the woes of "Jean Valjean," the old galley-slave, found an echo in the hearts of these brave soldiers, immured in the trenches and fettered by duty to their muskets or their cannon.

Singular fortune of a writer! Happy M. Hugo! Your fancies crossed the ocean, and, transmitted into a new tongue, whiled away the dreary hours of the old soldiers of Lee, at Petersburg! Thus, that history of "The Wretched," was the pabulum of the South in 1864; and as the French title had been retained on the backs of the pamphlets, the soldiers, little familiar with the Gallic pronunciation, called the book "Lees Miserables!" Then another step was taken. It was no longer the book, but themselves whom they referred to by that name. The old veterans of the army thenceforth laughed at their miseries, and dubbed themselves grimly "*Lee's* Miserables!"{1}

{Footnote 1: It is unnecessary to say that this is not a jest or fancy on the part of Colonel Surrey. It is a statement of fact. — ED.}

The sobriquet was gloomy, and there was something tragic in the employment of it; but it was applicable. Like most popular terms, it expressed the exact thought in the mind of every one — coined the situation into a phrase. Truly, they were "The Wretched," — the soldiers of the army of Northern Virginia, in the fall and winter of 1864. They had a quarter of a pound of rancid "Nassau bacon" — from New England — for daily rations of meat. The handful of flour, or corn-meal, which they received, was musty. Coffee and sugar were doled out as a luxury, now and then only; and the microscopic ration became a jest to those who looked at it. A little "grease" and cornbread—the grease rancid, and the bread musty—these were the food of the army.

Their clothes, blankets, and shoes were no better—even worse. Only at long intervals could the Government issue new ones to them. Thus the army was in tatters. The old clothes hung on the men like scarecrows. Their gray jackets were in rags, and did not keep out the chilly wind sweeping over the frozen fields. Their old blankets were in shreds, and gave them little warmth when they wrapped themselves up in them, shivering in the long cold nights. The old shoes, patched and yawning, had served in many a march and battle—and now allowed the naked sole to touch the hard and frosty ground.

Happy the man with a new blanket! Proud the possessor of a whole roundabout! What millionaire or favorite child of fortune passes yonder—the owner of an unpatched pair of shoes?

Such were the rations and clothing of the army at that epoch;—rancid grease, musty meal, tattered jackets, and worn-out shoes. And these were the fortunate ones! Whole divisions often went without bread even, for two whole days. Thousands had no jackets, no blankets, and no shoes. Gaunt forms, in ragged old shirts and torn pantaloons only, clutched the musket. At night they huddled together for warmth by the fire in the trenches. When they charged, their naked feet left blood-marks on the abatis through which they went at the enemy.

That is not an exaggeration, reader. These facts are of record.

And that was a part only. It was not only famine and hardship which they underwent, but the incessant combats—and mortal tedium—of the trenches. Ah! the trenches! Those words summed up a whole volume of suffering. No longer fighting in open field; no longer winter-quarters, with power to range; no longer freedom, fresh air, healthful movement—the trenches!

Here, cooped up and hampered at every turn, they fought through all those long months of the dark autumn and winter of 1864. They were no longer men, but machines loading and firing the musket and the cannon. Burrowing in their holes, and subterranean covered-ways, they crouched in the darkness, rose at the sound of coming battle, manned the breastworks, or trained the cannon—day after day, week after week, month after month, they were there in the trenches at their grim work; and some fiat of Destiny seemed to have chained them there to battle forever! At midnight, as at noon, they were at their posts. In the darkness, dusky figures could be seen swinging the sponge-staff, swabbing the cannon, driving home the charge. In the starlight, the moonlight, or the gloom lit by the red glare, those figures, resembling phantoms, were seen marshalled behind the breastworks to repel the coming assault. Silence had fled from the trenches—the crash of musketry and the bellow of artillery had replaced it. That seemed never to cease. The men were rocked to sleep by it. They slept on in the dark trenches, though the mortar-shells rose, described their flaming curves, and, bursting, rained jagged fragments of iron upon them. And to many that was their last sleep. The iron tore them in their tattered blankets. They rose gasping, and streaming with blood. Then they staggered and fell; when you passed by, you saw a something lying on the ground, covered with the old blanket. It was one of "Lee's Miserables," killed last night by the mortars—and gone to answer, "Here!" before the Master.

The trenches!—ah! the trenches! Were you in them, reader? Thousands will tell you more of them than I can. There, an historic army was guarding the capital of an historic nation—the great nation of Virginia—and how they guarded it! In hunger, and cold, and nakedness, they guarded it still. In the bright days and the dark, they stood at their posts unmoved. In the black night-watches as by day—toward morning, as at evening—they stood, clutching the musket, peering out into the pitchy darkness; or lay, dozing around the grim cannon, in the embrasures. Hunger, and cold, and wounds, and the whispering voice of Despair, had no effect on them. The mortal tedium left them patient. When you saw the gaunt faces contract, and tears flow, it was because they had received some letter, saying that their wives and children were starving. Many could not endure that. It made them forget all. Torn with anguish, and unable to obtain furloughs for a day even, they went home without leave—and civilians called them deserters. Could such men be shot—men who had fought like heroes, and only committed this breach of discipline that they might feed their starving children? And, after all, it was not desertion that chiefly reduced Lee's strength. It was battle which cut down the army—wounds and exposure which thinned its ranks. But thin as they were, and ever growing thinner, the old veterans who remained by the flag of such glorious memories, were as defiant in this dark winter of 1864, as they had been in the summer days of 1862 and 1863.

Army of *Northern Virginia!*—old soldiers of Lee, who fought beside your captain until your frames were wasted, and you were truly his "wretched" ones—you are greater to me in your wretchedness, more splendid in your rags, than the Old Guard of Napoleon, or the three hundred of Thermopylae! Neither famine, nor nakedness, nor suffering, could break your spirit. You were tattered and half-starved; your forms, were warworn; but you still had faith in Lee, and the great cause which you bore aloft on the points of your bayonets. You did not shrink in the last hour the hour of supreme trial. You meant to follow Lee to the last. If you ever doubted the result, you had resolved, at least, on one thing — to clutch the musket, to the end, and die in harness!

Is that extravagance — and is this picture of the great army of Northern Virginia overdrawn? Did they or did they not fight to the end? Answer! Wilderness, Spottsylvania, Cold Harbor, Charles City, every spot around Petersburg where they closed in death-grapple with the swarming enemy! Answer! winter of '64, — bleak spring of '65, — terrible days of the great retreat when hunted down and driven to bay like wild animals, they fought from Five Forks to Appomattox Court-House — fought staggering, and starving, and falling — but defiant to the last!

Bearded men were seen crying on the ninth of April, 1865. But it was *surrender* which wrung their hearts, and brought tears to the grim faces.

Grant's cannon had only made "Lee's Miserables" cheer and laugh.

IV
THE BLANDFORD RUINS

These memories are not cheerful. Let us pass to scenes more sunny—and there were many in that depressing epoch. The cloud was dark—but in spite of General Grant, the sun would shine sometimes!

After reading the *Examiner's* comments, I mounted my horse and rode into Petersburg, where I spent a pleasant hour in conversation with a friend, Captain Max. Do you laugh still, my dear Max? Health and happiness attend you and yours, my hearty!

As I got into the saddle again, the enemy began a brisk shelling. The shell skimmed the roofs of the houses, with an unearthly scream; and one struck a chimney which it hurled down with a tremendous crash. In spite of all, however, the streets were filled with young women, who continued to walk quietly, or to trip along laughing and careless, to buy a riband or some trifle at the stores.{1} That seemed singular then, and seems more singular to-day. But there is nothing like being accustomed to any thing—and the shelling had now "lost its interest," and troubled nobody.

{Footnote 1: Real.}

"Good!" I said, laughing, "our friends yonder are paying us their respects to-day. They have dined probably on the tons of turkey sent from New England, and are amusing themselves shelling us by way of dessert."

And wishing to have a better view of the lines, I rode toward Blandford.

Do you remember the ivy-draped ruins of the old "Blandford church," my dear reader? This is one of our Virginia antiquities, and is worth seeing. Around the ruins the large graveyard is full of elegant tombstones. Many are shattered to-day, however, by the Federal shell, as the spot was near the breastworks, and in full range of their artillery. In fact it was not a place to visit in the fall of 1864, unless you were fond of shell and a stray bullet. I was somewhat surprised, therefore, as I rode into the enclosure—with a hot skirmish going on a few hundred yards off—to see a young officer and a maiden sitting on a grass bank, beneath a larch tree, and conversing in the most careless manner imaginable.{1}

{Footnote 1: Real.}

Who were these calmly indifferent personages? Their backs were turned, and I could only see that the young lady had a profusion of auburn hair. Having dismounted, and approached, I made another discovery. The youth was holding the maiden's hand, and looking with flushed cheeks into her eyes—while she hung her head, the ringlets rippling over her cheeks, and played absently with some wild flowers, which she held between her fingers.

The "situation" was plain. "Lovers," I said to myself; "let me not disturb the young ones!"

And I turned to walk away without attracting their attention.

Unfortunately, however, a shell at that instant screamed over the ruin; the young girl raised her head with simple curiosity—not a particle of fear evidently—to watch the course of the missile; and, as the youth executed the like manoeuvre, they both became aware of my presence at the same moment.

The result was, that a hearty laugh echoed among the tombstones; and that the youth and maiden rose, hastening rapidly toward me.

An instant afterward I was pressing the hand of Katy Dare, whom I had left near Buckland, and that of Tom Herbert, whom I had not seen since the fatal day of Yellow Tavern.

V
LES FORTUNÉS

The auburn ringlets of Katy Dare were as glossy as ever; her blue eyes had still the charming archness which had made me love her from the first. Indeed her demeanor toward me had been full of such winning sweetness that it made me her captive; and I now pressed the little hand, and looked into the pretty blushing face with the sentiment which I should have experienced toward some favorite niece.

Katy made you feel thus by her artless and warm-hearted smile. How refrain from loving one whose blue eyes laughed like her lips, and whose glances said, "I am happier since you came!"

And Tom was equally friendly; his face radiant, his appearance distinguished. He was clad in a new uniform, half covered with gold braid. His hat was decorated with a magnificent black plume. His cavalry boots, reaching to the knee, were small, delicate, and of the finest leather. At a moderate estimation, Tom's costume must have cost him three thousand dollars!—Happy Tom!

He grasped my hand with a warmth which evidently came straight from the heart; for he had a heart—that dandy!

"Hurrah! old fellow; here you are!" Tom cried, laughing. "You came upon us as suddenly as if you had descended from heaven!"

"Whither you would like to send me back! Am I wrong, Tom?"

And I shot a glance of ancient and paternal affection at these two young things, whose *tete-à-tete* I had interrupted.

Katy blushed beautifully, and then ended by laughing. Tom caressed his slender mustache, and said:—-

"My dear fellow, I certainly should like to go to heaven—consequently to send my friends there—but if it is all the same to everybody, I think I would prefer—hem!—deferring the journey for a brief period, my boy."

"Until an angel is ready to go with you!"

And I glanced at the angel with the ringlets.

"Ah, my dear Surry!" said Tom, smoothing his chin with his hand, "you really have a genius for repartee which is intolerable, and not to be endured!"

"Let the angel sit in judgment!"

"Oh, you have most 'damnable iteration!'"

"I learned it all from you."

"From me, my boy?"

"Certainly — see the beauty of repetition in poetry."

And looking at the damsel, I began to repeat —

"Katy! Katy!

Don't marry any other!

You'll break my heart, and kill me dead,

And then be hanged for murder!"

The amount of blushing, laughter, pouting, good humor, and hilarity generally, which this poem occasioned, was charming. In a few minutes we were all seated again on the grassy bank, and Tom had given me a history of his adventures, which had not been either numerous or remarkable. He had been assigned to duty on the staff of General Fitzhugh Lee, and it was delightful to hear his enthusiasm on the subject of that gay and gallant officer.

"I tell you he's a trump, old fellow," quoth Tom, with ardor. "He's as brave as steel, a first-rate officer, a thorough gentleman, generous, kind, and as jolly as a lark! Give me Fitz Lee to fight with, or march with, or hear laugh! He was shot in the Valley, and I have been with him in Richmond. In spite of his wound, which is a severe one, he is as gay as the sunshine, and it would put you in good spirits only to go into his chamber!"

"I know General Fitz well, Tom," I replied, "and you are right about him; every word you say is true, and more to boot, old fellow. So you are cruising around now, waiting for your chief to recover?"

"Exactly, my dear Surry."

"And have captured the barque *Katy!*"

"Humph!" quoth Miss Katy, tossing her head, with a blush and a laugh.

"Beware of pirates," I said, "who make threats even in their verses, — and now tell me, Miss Katy, if you are on a visit to Petersburg? It will give me true pleasure to come and see you."

"Indeed you must!" she said, looking at me with the most fascinating smile, "for you know you are one of my old friends now, and must not neglect me. I am at my aunt's, Mrs. Hall, — uncle brought me a month ago from Buckland; but in the morning I shall go down to a cousin's in Dinwiddie."

"In Dinwiddie, Miss Katy?"

"Yes, near the Rowanty. My cousin, Mr. Dare, has come for me."

"Well, I will visit you there."

"Please do. The house is called 'Disaway's.'"

I bowed, smiling, and turned to Tom Herbert.

"When shall I see you again, Tom, and where? Next week—at Disaway's?"

Tom colored and then laughed. This dandy, you see, was a good boy still.

"Well, old fellow," he replied, "I think it possible I may visit Dinwiddie. My respected chieftain, General Fitz, is at present reposing on his couch in Richmond, and I am bearer of bouquets as well as of dispatches between him and his surgeon. But I am told he is ordered to Dinwiddie as soon as he is up. The country is a new one; the thought has occurred to me that any information I can acquire by—hem!—a topographical survey, would be valuable. You perceive, do you not, my dear friend? You appreciate my motive?"

"Perfectly, Tom. There will probably be a battle near 'Disaway's.'"

"And I'd better ride over the ground, eh?"

"Yes."

"Well, I'll do it!"

"Only beware of one thing!"

"What, my dear Surry?" asked Tom, anxiously.

"There is probably a conservatory at Disaway's."

"A conservatory?"

"Like that near Buckland, and the battle might take place *there*. If it does—two to one you are routed!"

Katy blushed exquisitely, smiled demurely, and burst into laughter. Then catching my eye she raised her finger, and shook her head with sedate reproach, looking at Tom. He was laughing.

"All right, I'll look out, Surry!"

"Resolve on one thing, Tom."

"What is that?"

"That you will never surrender, but be taken in arms!"

With which mild and inoffensive joke I shook hands with Tom, informing him where to find me; made Miss Katy a bow, which she returned with a charming smile and a little inclination which shook together her ringlets; and then leaving the young people to themselves, I mounted my horse, and returned to the Cedars.

All the way I was smiling. A charming influence had descended upon me. The day was brighter, the sunshine gayer, for the sight of the young fellow, and the pretty little maiden, with her blue eyes, like the skies, and her ringlets of silken gold!

VI
ON THE BANKS OF THE ROWANTY

When I again set out for the cavalry, a few days after the scene at Blandford church, the youth and sunshine of those two faces still dwelt in my memory, and I went along smiling and happy.

Not even the scenes on the late battle-field beyond the Rowanty, made my mood gloomy; and yet these were not gay. Graves were seen everywhere; the fences were broken down; the houses riddled by balls; and in the trampled roads and fields negroes were skinning the dead horses, to make shoes of their hides. On the animals already stripped sat huge turkey-buzzards feeding. My horse shied as the black vultures rose suddenly on flapping wings. They only circled around, however, sailing back as I disappeared.

Such is war, reader,—a charming panorama of dead bodies and vultures!

Turning into the Quaker road, I went on until I reached the head-quarters of General William H.F. Lee, opposite Monk's Neck. Here, under the crest of a protecting hill, where the pine thickets afforded him shelter from the wind, that gallant soldier had "set up his rest"—that is to say a canvass fly, one end of which was closed with a thick-woven screen of evergreens. My visit was delightful, and I shall always remember it with pleasure. Where are you to-day, general, and good comrades of the old staff? You used to laugh as hard as you fought—so your merriment was immense! Heaven grant that to-day, when the bugles are silent, the sabres rusting, you are laughing as in the days I remember!

Declining the friendly invitation to spend the night, I went on in the afternoon; and on my way was further enlivened by a gay scene which makes me smile even to-day. It was in passing General Butler's headquarters near the Rowanty. In the woods gleamed his white tents; before them stretched the level sandy road; a crowd of staff officers and others, with the general in their midst, were admiring two glossy ponies, led up by two small urchins, evidently about to run a race on them.

Butler—that brave soldier, whom all admired as much as I did—was limping about, in consequence of a wound received at Fleetwood. In the excitement of the approaching race he had forgotten his hurt. And soon the urchins were tossed up on the backs of their little glossy steeds—minus all but bridle. Then they took their positions about three hundred yards off; remained an instant abreast and motionless; then a clapping of hands was heard—it was the signal to start—and the ponies came on like lightning.

The sight was comic beyond expression. The boys clung with their knees, bending over the floating manes; the little animals darted by; they disappeared in the woods "amid thunders of applause;" and it was announced that the roan pony had won.

"Trifles," you say, perhaps, reader; "why don't our friend, the colonel, go on with his narrative?"

True,—the reproach is just. But these trifles cling so to the memory! I like to recall them—to review the old scenes—to paint the "trifles" even, which caught my attention during the great civil war. This is not a history, friend—only a poor little memoir. I show you our daily lives, more than the "great events" of history. That is the way the brave Butler and his South Carolinians amused themselves—and the figure of this soldier is worth placing amid my group of "paladins." He was brave—none was braver; thoroughbred—I never saw a man more so. His sword had flashed at Fleetwood, and in a hundred other fights; and it was going to flash to the end.

I pushed on after the pony race, and very soon had penetrated the belt of shadowy pines which clothe the banks of the Rowanty, making of this country a wilderness as singular almost as that of Spottsylvania. Only here and there appeared a small house, similar to that of Mr. Alibi's—all else was woods, woods, woods! Through the thicket wound the "military road" of General Hampton; and I soon found that his head-quarters were at a spot which I had promised myself to visit—"Disaway's."

Two hours' ride brought me to the place. Disaway's was an old mansion, standing on a hill above the Rowanty, near the "Halifax bridge," by which the great road from Petersburg to North Carolina crosses the stream. It was a building of considerable size, with wings, numerous gables, and a portico; and was overshadowed by great oaks, beneath which gleamed the tents of Hampton and his staff.

As I rode up the hill, the staff came out to welcome me. I had known these brave gentlemen well, when with Stuart, and they were good enough, now, to give me the right hand of fellowship,—to receive me for old times' sake, with "distinguished consideration." The general was as cordial as his military family—and in ten minutes I was seated and conversing with him, beneath the great oak.

A charming cordiality inspired the words and countenance of the great soldier. Nearly four years have passed, but I remember still his courteous smile and friendly accents.

All at once, the figure of a young woman appeared in the doorway. At a glance I recognized the golden ringlets of Katy Dare. She beckoned to me, smiling; I rose and hastened to greet her; in a moment we were seated upon the portico, conversing like old friends.

There was something fascinating in this child. The little maiden of eighteen resembled a blossom of the spring. Were I a poet, I should declare that her azure eyes shone out from her auburn hair like glimpses of blue sky behind sun-tinted clouds!

I do not know how it came about, or how I found myself there, but in a few moments I was walking with her in the autumn woods, and smiling as I gazed into the deep blue of her eyes. The pines were sighing above us; beneath our feet a thick carpet of brown tassels lay; and on the summit of the evergreens the golden crown of sunset slowly rose, as though the fingers of some unseen spirit were bearing it away into the night.

Katy tripped on, rather than walked—laughing and singing gayly. The mild air just lifted the golden ringlets of her hair, as she threw back her beautiful face; her cheeks were rosy with the joy of youth; and from her smiling lips, as fresh and red as carnations, escaped in sweet and tender notes, like the carol of an oriole, that gay and warbling song, the "Bird of Beauty."

Do you remember it, my dear reader? It is old—but so many good things are old!

> "Bird of beauty, whose bright plumage
> Sparkles with a thousand dyes:
> Bright thine eyes, and gay thy carol,
> Though stern winter rules the skies!"

Do you say that is not very grand poetry? I protest! friend, I think it superior to the *chef d'oeuvres* of the masters? You do not think so? Ah! that is because you did not hear it sung in the autumn forest that evening—see the ringlets of Katy Dare floating back from the rosy cheeks, as the notes escaped from her smiling lips, and rang clearly in the golden sunset. Do you laugh at my enthusiasm? Well, I am going to increase your mirth. To the "Bird of Beauty" succeeded a song which I never heard before, and have never heard since. Thus it is a lost pearl I rescue, in repeating some lines. What Katy sang was this:—

> *"Come under, some one, and give her a kiss!*
> *My honey, my love, my handsome dove!*
> *My heart's been a-weeping,*
> *This long time for you!*

> *"I'll hang you, I'll drown you,*
> *My honey, my love, my handsome dove!*
> *My heart's been a-weeping,*
> *This long time for you!"*

That was the odd, original, mysterious, incomprehensible poem, which Katy Dare carolled in the sunset that evening. It may seem stupid to some— to me the words and the air are charming, for I heard them from the sweetest lips in the world. Indeed there was something so pure and childlike about the young girl, that I bowed before her. Her presence made me better— banished all discordant emotions. All about her was delicate and tender, and pure. Like her "bird of bright plumage" she seemed to have flitted here to utter her carol, after which she would open her wings and disappear!

Katy ran on, in the pauses of her singing, with a hundred little jests, interspersed with her sweet childlike laughter, and I was more and more enchanted—when all at once I saw her turn her head over her shoulder. A bright flush came to her cheeks as she did so; her songs and laughter ceased; then—a step behind us!

I looked back, and found the cause of her sudden "dignity," her demure silence. The unfortunate Colonel Surry had quite disappeared from the maiden's mind.

Coming on rapidly, with springy tread, I saw—Tom Herbert! Tom Herbert, radiant; Tom Herbert, the picture of happiness; Tom Herbert, singing in his gay and ringing voice:—

> *"Katy! Katy!*
> *Don't marry any other!*
> *You'll break my heart and kill me dead,*
> *And you'll be hung for murder!"*

Wretch!—I could cheerfully have strangled him!

VII
THE STUART HORSE ARTILLERY

An hour afterward I was at the camp of the Stuart horse artillery.

Five minutes after greeting Tom, who had sought Katy, at "Disaway's"—been directed to the woods—and there speedily joined us—I left the young ones together, and made my way back to the mansion. There are few things, my dear reader, more disagreeable than—just when you are growing poetical—when blue eyes have excited your romantic feelings—when your heart has begun to glow—when you think "I am the cause of all this happiness, and gayety!"—there are few things I say—but why say it? In thirty seconds the rosy-faced youngster Tom, had driven the antique and battered Surry quite from the mind of the Bird of Beauty. That discomfited individual, therefore, took his way back sadly to Disaway's, leaving the children his blessing; declined the cordial invitations to spend the night, mounted his horse, and rode to find Will Davenant, at the horse artillery.

Their camp was in the edge of a wood, near the banks of the Rowanty; and having exchanged greetings with my old comrades of the various batteries, and the gallant Colonel Chew, their chieftain, I repaired to Will Davenant's head-quarters.

These consisted of a breadth of canvass, stretched beneath a tree in the field—in front of which burned a fire.

I had come to talk with Will, but our conversation was obliged to be deferred. The brave boys of the horse artillery, officers and men, gathered round to hear the news from Petersburg; and it was a rare pleasure to me to see again the old familiar faces. Around me, in light of the camp-fire, were grouped the tigers who had fought with Pelham, in the old battles of Stuart. Here were the heroes of a hundred combats; the men who had held their ground desperately in the most desperate encounters—the bulldogs who had showed their teeth and sprung to the death-grapple at Cold Harbor, Manassas, Sharpsburg, Fredericksburg, Chancellorsville, Fleetwood, Gettysburg, in the Wilderness, at Trevillian's, at Sappony, in a thousand bitter conflicts with the cavalry. Scarred faces, limping bodies, the one-armed, the one-legged,—these I saw around me; the frames slashed and mutilated, but the eyes flashing and full of fight, as in the days when Pelham thundered, loosing his war-hounds on the enemy. I had seen brave commands, in these long years of combat — had touched the hands of heroic men, whose souls fear never entered — but I never saw braver fighters than the horse artillery — soldiers more reckless than Pelham's bloodhounds. They went to battle laughing. There was something of the tiger in them. They were of every nation nearly — Frenchmen, Irishmen, Italians, — but one sentiment seemed to inspire them — hatred of our friends over the way. From the moment in 1862, when at Barbee's they raised the loud resounding *Marseillaise*, while fighting the enemy in front and rear, to this fall of 1864, when they had strewed a hundred battle-fields with dead men and horses, these "swarthy old hounds" of the horse artillery had vindicated their claims to the admiration of Stuart; — in the thunder of their guns, the dead chieftain had seemed still to hurl his defiance at the invaders of Virginia.

Looking around me, I missed many of the old faces, sleeping now beneath the sod. But Dominic, Antonio, and Rossini were still there — those members of the old "Napoleon Detachment" of Pelham's old battery; there still was Guillemot, the erect, military-looking Frenchman, — Guillemot, with his hand raised to his cap, saluting me with the profoundest respect; these were the faces I had seen a hundred times, and never any thing but gay and full of fight.

Doubtless they remembered me, and thought of Stuart, as others had done, at seeing me. They gave me a soldier's welcome; soon, from the group around the camp-fire rose a song. Another followed, then another, in the richest tenor; and the forests of Dinwiddie rang with the deep voices, rising clear and sonorous in the moonlight night.

They were old songs of Ashby and Stuart; unpublished ditties of the struggle, which the winds have borne away into the night of the past, and which now live only in memory. There was one of Ashby, commencing, —

"*See him enter on the valley,*"

which wound up with the words, —

"*And they cried, 'O God they've shot him!*
Ashby is no more!'
Strike, freemen, for your country,
Sheathe your swords no more!
While remains in arms a Yankee
On Virginia's shore!"

The air was sad and plaintive. The song rose, and wailed, and died away like the sigh of the wind in the trees, the murmuring airs of evening in the brambles and thickets of the Rowanty. The singers had fought under Ashby, and in their rude and plaintive song they uttered their regrets.

Then the music changed its character, and the stirring replaced the sad.

"If you want to have a good time,
J'ine the cavalry!"

came in grand, uproarious strains; and this was succeeded by the jubilant—

"Farewell, forever to the star-spangled banner,
No longer shall she wave o'er the land of the free;
But we'll unfurl to the broad breeze of heaven,
The thirteen bright stars round the Palmetto tree!"

At that song—and those words, "the thirteen bright stars round the Palmetto tree!"—you might have seen the eyes of the South Carolinians flash. Many other ditties followed, filling the moonlight night with song— "The Bonnie Blue Flag," "Katy Wells," and "The Louisiana Colors." This last was never printed. Here are a few of the gay verses of the "Irish Lad from Dixie:"—

"My sweetheart's name is Kathleen,
For her I'll do or die;
She has a striped straw mattress,
A shanty, pig, and sty.
Her cheeks are bright and beautiful,
Her hair is dark and curly,
She sent me with the secesh boys
To fight with General Early.

"She made our flag with her own hands,
My Kathleen fair and clever,
And twined its staff with shamrock green,
Old Ireland's pride forever!
She gave it into our trust,
Among our weeping mothers; —
'Remember, Irish men!' she said,
'You bear the Red Cross colors!'

"She told me I must never run;
The Rebel boys were brothers; —
To stand forever by our flag,
The Louisiana colors!
And then she said, 'If you desert,
You'll go to the Old Baily!'
Says I, 'My love, when I can't shoot,
I'll use my old shillalah!'

"And many a bloody charge we made,
Nor mind the battle's blaze;
God gave to us a hero bold,
Our bonny Harry Hays!
And on the heights of Gettysburg,
At twilight first was seen,
The stars of Louisiana bright,
And Katy's shamrock green.

"And oh! if I get home again,
I swear I'll never leave her;
I hope the straw mattress will keep,
The pig won't have the fever!
For then, you know, I'll marry Kate,
And never think of others.
Hurrah, then, for the shamrock green,
And the Louisiana colors!"

It was nearly midnight before the men separated, repairing to their tents. Their songs had charmed me, and made the long hours flit by like birds. Where are you, brave singers, in this year '68? I know not — you are all scattered. Your guns have ceased their thunder, your voices sound no more. But I think you sometimes remember, as you muse, in these dull years, those gay moonlight nights on the banks of the Rowanty.

VIII
"CHARGE! STUART! PAY OFF ASHBY's SCORE!"

These memories are beguiling, and while they possess me, my drama does not march.

But you have not been wearied, I hope, my dear reader, by this little pencil sketch of the brave horse artillerymen. I found myself among them; the moonlight shone; the voices sang; and I have paused to look and listen again in memory.

These scenes, however, can not possess for you, the attraction they do for me. To proceed with my narrative. I shall pass over my long conversation with Will Davenant, whose bed I shared. I had promised his father to reveal nothing of the events which I had so strangely discovered—and was then only able to give the young man vague assurances of a coming change for the better in his affair with Miss Conway. He thanked me, blushing, and trying to smile—and then we fell asleep beside each other.

Just at daylight I was suddenly aroused. The jarring notes of a bugle were ringing through the woods. I extended my arm in the darkness, and found that Will Davenant was not beside me.

What had happened? I rose quickly, and throwing my cape over my shoulders, went out of the tent.

The horse artillery was already hitched up, and in motion. The setting moon illumined the grim gun-barrels, caissons, and heavy horses, moving with rattling chains. Behind came the men on horseback, laughing and ready for combat.

As I was gazing at this warlike scene so suddenly evoked, Will Davenant rode up and pointed to my horse, which was ready saddled, and attached to a bough of the great tree.

"I thought I wouldn't wake you, colonel," he said, with a smile, "but let you sleep to the last moment. The enemy are advancing, and we are going to meet them."

He had scarcely spoken, when a rapid firing was heard two or three miles in front, and a loud cheer rose from the artillerymen. In a moment the guns were rushing on at a gallop, and, as I rode beside them, I saw a crimson glare shoot up above the woods, in the direction of the Weldon railroad. The firing had meanwhile grown heavier, and the guns were rushed onward. Will Davenant's whole appearance had completely changed. The youth, so retiring in camp, so cool in a hot fight, seemed burnt up with impatience, at the delay caused by the terrible roads. His voice had become hoarse and imperious; he was everywhere urging on the drivers; when the horses stalled in the fathomless mudholes, he would strike the animals, in a sort of rage, with the flat of his sabre, forcing them with a leap which made the traces crack, to drag the piece out of the hole, and onward. A glance told me, then, what was the secret of this mere boy's splendid efficiency. Under the shy, blushing face, was the passion and will of the born soldier—the beardless boy had become the master mind, and drove on every thing by his stern will.

In spite of every exertion to overcome the obstacles in the roads, it was nearly sunrise before we reached open ground. Then we emerged upon the upland, near "Disaway's," and saw a picturesque spectacle. From the hill, we could make out every thing. A hot cavalry fight was going on beneath us. The enemy had evidently crossed the Rowanty lower down; and driving in the pickets, had passed forward to the railroad.

The guns were rushed toward the spot, unlimbered on a rising ground, and their thunder rose suddenly above the forests. Shell after shell burst amid the enemy, breaking their ranks, and driving them back—and by the time I had galloped through a belt of woods to the scene of the fight, they lost heart, retreated rapidly, and disappeared, driven across the Rowanty again, with the Confederates pursuing them so hotly, that many of the gray cavalry punched them in the back with their empty carbines.{1}

{Footnote 1: Fact.}

Their object in crossing had been to burn a small mill; and in this they had succeeded, after which they retired as soon as possible to their "own side." Some queer scenes had accompanied this "tremendous military movement." In a house near the mill, resided some ladies; and we found them justly indignant at the course of the enemy. The Federal officers—general officers—had ordered the house-furniture to be piled up, the carriage to be drawn into the pile, and then shavings were heaped around, and the whole set on fire, amid shouts, cheers, and firing. The lady of the mansion remonstrated bitterly, but received little satisfaction.

"I have no time to listen to women!"{1} said the Federal general, rudely.

{Footnote 1: His words.}

"It is not *time* that you want, sir!" returned the lady, with great hauteur, "it is *politeness*!"{1}

{Footnote 1: Her words.}

This greatly enraged the person whom she addressed, and he became furious, when the lady added that all the horses had been sent away. At that moment an officer near him said: —

"General if you are going to burn the premises, you had better commence, as the rebs are pursuing us."

"Order it to be done at once!" was the gruff reply.

And the mill was fired, in the midst of a great uproar, with which mingled shouts of, "The Rebels are coming! The Rebels are coming!"

Soon they came, a hot fight followed, and during this fight a young woman watched it, holding her little brother by the hand near the burning mill. I had afterward the honor of making her acquaintance, and she told me that throughout the firing she found herself repeating over and over, unconsciously, the lines of the song, —

> "*Charge! Stuart! pay off Ashby's score,*
> *In Stonewall Jackson's way.*"{1}

{Footnote 1: Fact.}

The enemy had thus effected their object, and retreated hotly pursued. I followed toward the lower Rowanty, and had the pleasure of seeing them hurried over. So ended this immense military movement.

IX
MOHUN,
HIS THIRD PHASE

I was about to turn my horse and ride back from the stream, across which the enemy had disappeared, when all at once Mohun, who had led the pursuit, rode up to me, and we exchanged a cordial greeting.

"Well, this little affair is over, my dear Surry," he said; "have you any thing to occupy you for two or three hours?"

"Nothing; entirely at your service, Mohun."

"Well, I wish you to accompany me on a private expedition. Will you follow me blindfold?"

"Confidingly."

And I rode on beside Mohun, who had struck into a path along the banks of the Rowanty, leading back in the direction of Halifax bridge.

As we rode on, I looked attentively at him. I scarcely recognized, in the personage beside me, the Mohun of the past. His gloom so profound on that night when I parted with him, after the expedition to the lonely house beyond Monk's Neck, had entirely disappeared; and I saw in him as few traces of the days on the Rappahannock, in Pennsylvania, and the Wilderness. These progressive steps in the development of Mohun's character may be indicated by styling them the first, second, and third phases of the individual. He had entered now upon the third phase, and I compared him, curiously with his former self.

On the Rappahannock, when I saw him first, Mohun had been cynical, bitter, full of gloomy misanthropy. Something seemed to have hardened him, and made him hate his species. In the bloom of early manhood, when his life was yet in the flower, and should have prompted him to all kind and sweet emotions, he was a stranger to all—to charity, good-will, friendship, all that makes life endurable. The tree was young and lusty; the spring was not over; freshness and verdure should have clothed it; and yet it appeared to have been blasted. What had dried up its sap, I asked myself—withering and destroying it? What thunder-bolt had struck this sturdy young oak? I could not answer—but from the first moment of our acquaintance, Mohun became for me a problem.

Then the second phase presented itself. When I met him in the Wilderness, in May, 1864, a great change had come over him. He was no longer bitter and cynical. The cloud had plainly swept away, leaving the skies of his life brighter. Gayety had succeeded gloom. The rollicking enjoyment of the true cavalryman had replaced the recklessness of the man-hater. Again I looked at him with attention—for his courage had made me admire him, and his hidden grief had aroused my sympathy. A great weight had plainly been lifted from his shoulders; he breathed freer; the sap long dried up had begun to flow again; and the buds told that the leaves of youth and hope were about to reappear. What was the meaning of that?

Now the third phase of the man had come to excite in me more surprise and interest than the former ones. This time the change was complete. Mohun seemed no longer himself. Was the man riding beside me the old Mohun of 1863? Where was the gloomy misanthropy—where the rollicking humor? They had quite disappeared. Mohun's glance was gentle and his countenance filled with a charming modesty and sweetness. His voice, once so cold, and then so hilarious, had grown calm, low, measured, almost soft. His smile was exquisitely cordial; his glance full of earnestness and sweetness. The heaven-born spirit of kindness—that balm for all the wounds of human existence—shone in his eyes, on his lips, in every accent of his voice.

Colonel Mohun had been reckless, defiant, unhappy, or wildly gay. General Mohun was calm, quietly happy it seemed. You would have said of him, formerly, "This is a man who fights from hatred of his enemies, or the exuberant life in him." Now you would have said, "This is a patriot who fights from principle, and is worthy to die in a great cause."

What had worked this change? I asked myself once more. Was it love? Or was it the conviction which the Almighty sends to the most hardened, that life is not made to indulge hatred, but to love and perform our duty in?

I knew not; but there was the phenomenon before me. Mohun was certainly a new man, and looked on life and the world around him with a gentleness and kindness of which I had believed him incapable.

"I am going to take you to see a somewhat singular character," he said.

"Who is he?"

"It is a woman."

"Ah!"

"And a very strange one, I promise you, my dear Surry."

"Lead on, I'll follow thee!"

"Good! and I declare to you, I think Shakespeare would have examined this human being with attention."

"She is a phenomenon, then?"

"Yes."

"A witch?"

"No, an epileptic; at least I think so."

"Indeed! And where does she live?"

"On the Halifax road, some miles from the Rowanty."

"In the lines of the enemy, then?"

"Something like it."

"Humph!"

"Don't disturb yourself about that, Surry. I have sent out a scouting party who are clearing the country. Their pickets are back to Reams's by this time, and there is little danger."

"At all events, we'll share any, Mohun. Forward!"

And we pushed on to the Halifax bridge, where, as Mohun expected, there was no Federal picket.

The bridge—a long rough affair—had been half destroyed by General Hampton; but we forded near it, pushed our horses through the swamp, amid the heavy tree trunks, felled to form an abatis, and gaining the opposite bank of the Rowanty, rode on rapidly in the direction of Petersburg, that is to say, toward the rear of the Federal army.

X
AMANDA

Half an hour's ride through the swampy low grounds rising to gentle uplands, and beneath the festoons of the great vines trailing from tree to tree, brought us in front of a small house, half buried in a clump of bushes, like a hare's nest amid brambles.

"We have arrived!" said Mohun, leading the way to the cabin, which we soon reached.

Throwing his bridle over a bough near the low fence, Mohun approached the door on foot, I following, and when close to the door, he gave a low knock.

"Come in!" said a cheerful and smiling voice.

And Mohun opened the door, through which we passed into a small and very neat apartment containing a table, some chairs, a wide fireplace, in which some sticks were burning, a number of cheap engravings of religious scenes, framed and hanging on the wall, and a low bed, upon which lay a woman fully dressed.

She was apparently about thirty-five, and her appearance was exceedingly curious. Her figure was slender and of medium height; her complexion that of a Moorish or oriental woman, rather than that of the quadroon, which she appeared to be; her hair black, waving, and abundant; her eyes as dark and sparkling as burnished ebony; and her teeth of dazzling whiteness. Her dress was neat, and of bright colors. Around her neck she wore a very odd necklace, which seemed made of carved bone; and her slender fingers were decorated with a number of rings.[1]

{Footnote 1: "I have endeavored to give an exact description of this singular woman." Colonel Surry said to me when he read this passage to me: "She will probably be remembered by numbers of persons in both the Federal and Confederate armies. These will tell you that I describe her accurately, using her real name, and will recall the strange prediction which she made, and which I repeat. Was she an epileptic? I do not know. I have certainly never encountered a more curious character!" — EDITOR.}

Such was the personage who greeted us, in a voice of great calmness and sweetness, as we entered. She did not rise from the bed upon which she was lying; but her cordial smile clearly indicated that this did not arise from discourtesy.

"Take seats, gentlemen," she said, "and please excuse me from getting up. I am a little poorly to-day."

"Stay where you are, Amanda," said Mohun, "and do not disturb yourself."

She looked at him with her dark eyes, and said, in her gentle, friendly voice: —

"You know me, I see, General Mohun."

"And you me, I see, Amanda."

"I never saw you before, sir, but—am I mistaken?"

"Not in the least. How did you know me?"

The singular Amanda smiled.

"I have *seen you* often, sir."

"Ah—in your visions?"

"Yes, sir."

"Or, perhaps, Nighthawk described me. You know Mr. Nighthawk!"

"Oh, yes, sir. I hope he is well. He has often been here; he may have told me what you were like, sir, and then I *saw you* to know you afterward."

I looked at the speaker attentively. Was she an impostor? It was impossible to think so. There was absolutely no evidence whatever that she was acting a part—rather every thing to forbid the supposition, as she thus readily acquiesced in Mohun's simple explanation.

For some moments Mohun remained silent. Then he said: —

"Those visions which you have are very strange. Is it possible that you really *see* things before they come to pass—or are you only amusing yourself, and others, by saying so? I see no especial harm in the matter, if you are jesting; but tell me, for my own satisfaction and that of my friend, if you *really* see things."

Amanda smiled with untroubled sweetness.

"I am in earnest, sir," she said, "and I would not jest with you and Colonel Surry."

I listened in astonishment.

"Ah! you know me, too, Amanda!"

"Yes, sir—or I think I do. I think you are Colonel Surry, sir."

"How do you know that?"

"I have *seen you, too*, sir?" was the smiling reply.

I sat down, leaned my head upon my hand, and gazed at this incomprehensible being. Was she really a witch? I do not believe in witches, and at once rejected that theory. If not an impostor, then, only one other theory remained — that Nighthawk had described my person to her, in the same manner that he had Mohun's, and the woman might thus believe that she had seen me, as well as my companion, in her "visions."

To her last words, however, I made no reply, and Mohun renewed the colloquy, as before.

"Then you are really in earnest, Amanda, and actually see, in vision, what is coming to pass?" he said.

"I think I do, sir."

"Do you have the visions often?"

"I did once, sir, but they now seldomer come."

"What produces them?"

"I think it is any excitement, sir. They tell me that I lay on my bed moaning, and moving my arms about, — and when I wake, after these attacks, I remember seeing the visions."

"I hear that you predicted General Hunter's attack on Lexington last June."

"Yes, sir, I told a lady what *I saw*, some months before it came to pass."

"What did you see? Will you repeat it for us?"

"Oh, yes, sir. I remember all, and will tell you about it, as it seems to interest you. I saw a town, on the other side of the mountain, which they afterward told me was called Lexington — but I did not know its name then — and a great army of men in blue dresses came marching in, shouting and cheering. The next thing I saw was a large building on fire, and through the windows I saw books burning, with some curious-looking things, of which I do not know the names."

"The Military Institute, with the books and scientific apparatus," said Mohun, calmly.

"Was it, sir? I did not know."

"What did you see afterward, Amanda?"

"Another house burning, sir; the Federal people gave the ladies ten minutes to leave it, and then set it on fire."

Mohun glanced at me.

"That is strange," he said; "do you know the name of the family?"

"No, sir."

"It was Governor Letcher's. Well, what next?"

"Then they went in a great crowd, and broke open another building—a large house, sir—and took every thing. Among the things they took was a statue, which they did not break up, but carried away with them."

"Washington's statue!" murmured Mohun; and, turning to me, he added:—

"This is curious, is it not, Surry?"

I nodded.

"*Very* curious."

I confess I believed that the strange woman was trifling with us, and had simply made up this story after the event. Mohun saw my incredulity, and said, in a low tone:—

"You do not believe in this?"

"No," I returned, in the same tone.

"And yet one thing is remarkable."

"What?"

"That a lady of the highest character assured me, the other day, that all this was related to her before Hunter even entered the Valley."[1]

{Footnote 1: Fact.}

And turning to Amanda, he said:—

"When did you see these things?"

"I think it was in March, sir."

The words were uttered in the simplest manner possible. The strange woman smiled as sweetly as she spoke, and seemed as far from being guilty of a deliberate imposture as before.

"And you *saw* the fight at Reams's, too?"

"Yes, sir; I saw it two months before it took place. There was a man killed running through the yard of a house, and they told me, afterward, he was found dead there."

"Have you had any visions, since?"

"Only one, sir."

"Lately?"

"Yes, sir."

"What did you see?"

"It was not much, sir. I saw the Federal people on horses, watering their horses in a large river somewhere west of here, and the vision said the war would be over about next March."

Mohun smiled.

"Which side will be successful, Amanda?"

"The vision did not say, sir."{1}

{Footnote 1: Colonel Surry assured me that he had scrupulously searched his memory to recall the exact words of this singular woman: and that he had given the precise substance of her statements; often, the exact words. — ED.}

Mohun, who had taken his seat on a rude settee, leaned his elbow on his knee, and for some moments gazed into the fire.

"I have asked you some questions, Amanda," he said at length, "relating to public events. I *now come to some private matters* — those which brought me hither — in which your singular visions may probably assist me. Are you willing to help me?"

"Yes, indeed, sir, if I can," was the reply.

XI
DEEP UNDER DEEP

Mohun fixed his mild, and yet penetrating glance upon the singular woman, who sustained it, however, with no change in her calm and smiling expression.

"You know Nighthawk?"

"Oh, yes, sir. He has been here often."

"And Swartz?"

"Very well, sir—I have known him many years."

"Have you seen him, lately?"

"No, sir; not for some weeks."

"Ah! You saw him some weeks since?"

"Yes, sir."

"At this house?"

"Yes, sir."

"Do you know what has become of him?"

"No, sir; but I suppose he is off somewhere."

"He is dead!"

Her head rose slightly, but the smile was unchanged.

"You don't tell me, sir!"

"Yes, murdered; perhaps you know his murderer?"

"Who was it, sir?"

"Colonel Darke."

"Oh, I know *him*. He has been here, lately. Poor Mr. Swartz! And so they murdered him! I am sorry for him."

Mohun's glance became more penetrating.

"You say that Colonel Darke has been here lately?"

"Yes, sir."

"What was the occasion of his visit?"

"I don't know, sir; unless it was to hear me tell my visions."

"You never knew him before?"

Amanda hesitated.

"Yes, sir," she said at length.

"When, and how?"

"It was many years ago, sir; — I do not like to speak of these things. He is a terrible man, they say."

"You can speak to me, Amanda. I will repeat nothing; nor will Colonel Surry."

The singular woman looked from Mohun to me, evidently hesitating. Then she seemed suddenly to make up her mind, and said, with her eternal smile: —

"I will tell you, then, sir. I can read faces, and I know neither you nor Colonel Surry will get me into trouble."

"I will not — on my honor."

"Nor I," I said.

"That is enough, gentlemen; and now I will tell you what you wish to know, General Mohun."

As she spoke she closed her eyes, and seemed for some moments to be reflecting. Then opening them again, she gazed, with her calm smile, at Mohun, and said: —

"It was many years ago, sir, when I first saw Colonel Darke, who then went by another name. I was living in this same house, when late one evening a light carriage stopped before the door, and a gentleman got out of it, and came in. He said he was travelling with his wife, who had been taken sick, and would I give them shelter until morning, when she would be able to go on? I was a poor woman, sir, as I am now, and hoped to be paid. I would have given the poor sick lady shelter all the same, though — and I told him he could come in, and sleep in this room, and I would go into that closet-like place behind you, sir. Well, he thanked me, and went back to the carriage, where a lady sat. He took her in his arms and brought her along to the house, when I saw that she was a very beautiful young lady, but quite pale. Well, sir, she came in and sat down in that chair you are now sitting in, and after awhile, said she was better. The gentleman had gone out and put away his horse, and when he came back I had supper ready, and every thing comfortable."

"What was the appearance of the lady?" said Mohun, over whose brow a contraction passed.

"She was small and dark, sir; but had the finest eyes I ever saw."

"The same," said Mohun, in a low tone. "Well?"

"They stayed all night, sir. Next morning they paid me,—though it was little—and went on toward the south."

"They seemed poor?"

"Yes, sir. The lady's dress was cheap and faded—and the gentleman's threadbare."

"What names did they give?"

"Mr. and Mrs. Mortimer, sir."

Mohun's brow again contracted.

"Well, go on," he said, "or rather, go back, Amanda. You say that they remained with you until the morning. Did you not hear some of their conversation—gain some knowledge of whence they came, whither they were going, and what was the object of their journey?"

The woman hesitated, glancing at Mohun. Then she smiled, and shook her head.

"You will get me into trouble, sir," she said.

"I will not, upon my honor. You have told me enough to enable me to do so, however—why not tell me all? You say you slept in that closet there—so you must have heard them converse. I am entitled to know all— tell me what they said."

And taking from his purse a piece of gold, Mohun placed it in the hand extended upon the bed. The hand closed upon it—clutched it. The eye of the woman glittered, and I saw that she had determined to speak.

"It was not much, sir," she said. "I did listen, and heard many things, but they would not interest you."

"On the contrary, they will interest me much."

"It was a sort of quarrel I overheard, sir. Mr. Mortimer was blaming his wife for something, and said she had brought him to misery. She replied in the same way, and said that it was a strange thing in *him* to talk to *her* so, when she had broken every law of God and man, to marry the—"

"The—?" Mohun repeated, bending forward.

"The murderer of her father, she said, sir," returned Amanda.

Mohun started, and looked with a strange expression at me.

"You understand!" he said, in a low tone, "is the thing credible?"

"Let us hear more," I said, gloomy in spite of myself.

"Go on," Mohun said, turning more calmly toward the woman; "that was the reply of the lady, then—that she had broken all the laws of God and man by marrying the murderer of her father. Did she utter the name of her father?"

"Yes, sir."

"What was it?"

"A Mr. George Conway," replied Amanda, who seemed to feel that she had gone too far to conceal any thing.

"And the reason for this marriage?" said Mohun, in a low tone; "did she explain, or say any thing which explained to you, how such a union had ever taken place?"

"Yes, sir. They said so many things to each other, that I came to know all. The young lady was a daughter of a Mr. George Conway, and when she was a girl, had fallen in love with some worthless young man, who had persuaded her to elope with him and get married. He soon deserted her, when she fell in with this Mr. Mortimer and married him."

"Did she know that he was her father's murderer?"

"No, sir—not until after their marriage, I gathered."

"Then," said Mohun, who had suppressed all indications of emotion, and was listening coolly; "then it seems to me that she was wrong in taking shame to herself—or claiming credit—for the marriage."

"Yes, sir," returned Amanda, "and he told her as much."

"So they had something like a quarrel?"

"Not exactly a quarrel, sir. He seemed to love her with all his heart—more than she loved him. They went on talking, and laying plans to make money in some way. I remember he said to her, 'You are sick, and need every luxury—I would rather die than see you deprived of them—I would cheat or rob to supply you every thing—and we must think of some means, honest or dishonest, to get the money we want. I do not care for myself, but you are all that I have left in the world.' That is what he said, sir."

And Amanda was silent.

"Then they fell asleep?" asked Mohun.

"Yes, sir; and on the next morning he took her in his arms again, and carried her to the carriage, and they left me."

Mohun leaned his chin upon his hand, knit his brows, and reflected. The singular narrative plunged me too into a reverie. This man, Darke, was a veritable gulf of mystery—his life full of hidden and inexplicable things. The son of General Davenant, he had murdered his father's foe; permitted that father to be tried for the crime, and to remain under suspicion; disappeared, changed his, encountered the daughter of his victim, married her, had those mysterious dealings with Mohun, disappeared a second time, changed his name a second time, and now had once more made his appearance near the scene of his first crime, to murder Swartz, capture his father and brother, and complete his tragic record by fighting under the enemy's flag against his country and his family!

There was something diabolical in that career; in this man's life "deep under deep" met the eye. And yet he was not entirely bad. On that night in Pennsylvania, he had refused to strike Mohun at a disadvantage—and had borne off the gray woman at the peril of death or capture. He had released his captured father and brother, bowing his head before them. He had confessed the murder of George Conway, over his own signature, to save this father. The woman who was his accomplice, he seemed to love more than his own life. Such were the extraordinary contrasts in a character, which, at first sight, seemed entirely devilish; and I reflected with absorbing interest upon the singular phenomenon.

I was aroused by the voice of Mohun. He had never appeared more calm: in his deep tones I could discern no emotion whatever.

"That is a singular story," he said, "and your friend, Colonel Darke, is a curious personage. But let us come back to events more recent—to the visits of Swartz."

"Yes, sir," said Amanda, smiling.

"But, first, let me ask—did Colonel Darke recognize you?"

"You mean *know* me? Oh, yes, sir."

"And did he speak of his former visit—with his wife?"

"No, sir."

"And you—?"

Amanda smiled.

"I made out I didn't remember him, sir; I was afraid he would think I had overheard that talk with his wife."

"So he simply called as if to see you as a curiosity?"

"Yes, sir—and staid only a few minutes."

"But you know or rather knew poor Swartz better?"

"I knew him well, sir."

"He often stopped here?"

"Yes, sir."

Mohun looked at the woman keenly, and said:—

"I wish you, now, to answer plainly the question which I am about to ask. I come hither as a friend—I am sent by your friend Mr. Nighthawk. Listen and answer honestly—Do you know any thing of a paper which Swartz had in his possession—an important paper which he was guarding from Colonel Darke?"

"I do not, sir," said Amanda, with her eternal smile.

"For that paper I will pay a thousand dollars in gold. Where is it?"

The woman's eyes glittered, then she shook her head.

"On my salvation I do not know, sir."

"Can you discover?"

Again the shake of the head.

"How can I, sir?"

Mohun's head sank. A bitter sigh issued from his lips—almost a groan.

"Listen!" he said, almost fiercely, but with a singular smile, "you have visions—you see things! I do not believe in your visions—they seem folly—but only *see* where that paper is to be discovered, and I will believe! nay more, I will pay you the sum which I mentioned this moment."

I looked at the woman to witness the result of this decisive test of her sincerity. "If she believes in her own visions, she will be elated," I said, "if she is an impostor, she will be cast down."

She smiled radiantly!

"I will try, sir!" she said.

Mohun gazed at her strangely.

"When shall I come to hear the result?"

"In ten days from this time, sir."

"In ten days? So be it."

And rising, Mohun bade the singular personage farewell, and went toward his horse.

I followed, and we rode back, rapidly, in dead silence, toward the Rowanty.

XII
HOW THE MOMENT AT LAST CAME

Mohun rode on for more than a mile at full gallop, without uttering a word. Then he turned his head, and said, with a sigh:—

"Well, what do you think of your new acquaintance, Surry?"

"I think she is an impostor."

"As to her visions, you mean?"

"Yes. Her story of Darke I believe to be true."

"And I know it," returned Mohun. "A strange discovery, is it not? I went there to-day, without dreaming of this. Nighthawk informed me that Swartz had often been at the house of this woman—that the paper which I wish to secure might have been left with her for safe keeping—and thus I determined to go and ferret out the matter, in a personal interview. I have done so, pretty thoroughly, and it seems plain that she knows nothing of its present whereabouts. Will she discover through her visions—her spies—or her strange penetration, exhibited in the recognition of our persons? I know not; and so that matter ends. I have failed, and yet have learned some singular facts. Can you believe that strange story of Darke? Is he not a weird personage? This narrative we have just heard puts the finishing touch to his picture—the murderer marries the daughter of his victim!"

"It is truly an extraordinary history altogether," I said, "and the whole life of this man is now known to me, with a single exception."

"Ah! you mean—?"

"The period when you fought with him, and ran him through the body, and threw him into that grave, from which Swartz afterward rescued him on the morning of the 13th December, 1856."

Mohun looked at me with that clear and penetrating glance which characterized him.

"Ah! you know that!" he said.

"I could not fail to know it, Mohun."

"True—and to think that all this time you have, perhaps, regarded me as a criminal, Surry! But I am one—that is I was—in intent if not in reality. Yes, my dear friend," Mohun added, with a deep sigh, his head sinking upon his breast, "there was a day in my life when I was insane, a simple madman,—and on that day I attempted to commit murder, and suicide! You have strangely come to catch many glimpses of those past horrors. On the Rappahannock the words of that woman must have startled you. In the Wilderness my colloquy with the spy revealed more. Lastly, the words of Darke on the night of Swartz's murder must have terribly complicated me in this issue of horrors. I knew that you must know much, and I did not shrink before you, Surry! Do you know why? Because I have repented, friend! and thank God! my evil passions did not result, as I intended, in murder and self-destruction!"

Mohun passed his hand across his forehead, to wipe away the drops of cold perspiration.

"All this is gloomy and tragic," he said; "and yet I must inflict it on you, Surry. Even more, I earnestly long to tell you the whole story of which you have caught these glimpses. Will you listen? It will not be long. I wish to show you, my dear friend—you are that to me, Surry!—that I am not unworthy of your regard; that there are no degrading scenes, at least, in my past life; that I have not cheated, tricked, deceived—even if I have attempted to destroy myself and others! Will you listen?"

"I have been waiting long to do so, Mohun," I said. "Speak, but first hear me. There is a man in this army who is the soul of honor. Since my father's death I value his good opinion more than that of all others—it is Robert E. Lee. Well, come with me if you choose, and I will go to Lee with you, and place my hand upon your shoulder, and say: 'General, this is my friend! I vouch for him; I am proud of his regard. Think well of him, or badly of me too!' Are you satisfied?"

Mohun smiled sadly.

"I knew all that," he said. "Do you think I can not read men, Surry? Long since I gave you in my heart the name of *friend*, and I knew that you had done as much toward me. Come, then! Go to my camp with me; in the evening we will take a ride. I am going to conduct you to a spot where we can talk without interruption, the exact place where the crimes of which I shall speak were committed."

And resuming the gallop, Mohun led the way, amid the trailing festoons, through the fallen logs, across the Rowanty.

Half an hour afterward we had reached his camp.

As the sun began to decline we again mounted our horses.

Pushing on rapidly we reached a large house on a hill above the Nottoway, and entered the tall gateway at the moment when the great windows were all ablaze in the sunset.

XIII
FONTHILL

Mohun spurred up the hill; reined in his horse in front of the great portico, and, dismounting, fastened his bridle to the bough of a magnificent exotic, one of a hundred which were scattered over the extensive grounds.

I imitated him, and we entered the house together, through the door, which gave way at the first push. No one had come to take our horses. No one opposed our entrance. The house was evidently deserted.

I looked round in astonishment and admiration. In every thing appertaining to the mansion were the indications of almost unlimited wealth, directed by the severest and most elegant taste. The broken furniture was heavy and elaborately carved; the remnants of carpet of sumptuous velvet; the walls, ceiling, doorways, and deep windows were one mass of the richest chiselling and most elaborate fresco-painting.

On the walls still hung some faded portraits in the most costly frames. On the mantel-pieces of variegated marble, supported by fluted pillars, with exquisitely carved capitals, rested a full length picture of a gentleman, the heavy gilt frame tarnished and crumbling.

The house was desolate, deserted, inexpressibly saddening from the evident contrast between its present and its past. But about the grand mansion hung an august air of departed splendor which to me, was more striking than if I had visited it in the days of its glory.

"Let me introduce 'Fonthill' to you, or rather the remains of it, Surry," Mohun said, with a sad smile. "It is not pleasant to bring a friend to so deserted a place; but I have long been absent; the house is gone to decay like other things in old Virginia. Still we can probably find two chairs. I will kindle a blaze, and we can light a cigar and talk without interruption."

With these words, Mohun proceeded to the adjoining apartment, from which he returned a moment afterward, dragging two chairs with elaborately carved backs.

"See," he said, with a smile, "they were handsome once. That one with the ragged remnants of red velvet was my father's. Take a seat, my dear Surry. I will sit in the other—it was my mother's."

Returning to the adjoining room, Mohun again reappeared, this time bearing in his arms the broken remnants of a mahogany table, which he heaped up in the great fireplace.

"This is all that remains of our old family dining-table," he said. "Some Yankee or straggling soldier will probably use it for this purpose—so I anticipate them!"

And, placing combustibles beneath the pile, Mohun had recourse to the metallic match case which he always carried with him in order to read dispatches, lit the fuel, and a blaze sprung up.

Next, he produced his cigar case, offered me an excellent Havana, which I accepted, and a minute afterward we were leaning back in the great chairs, smoking.

"An odd welcome, this," said Mohun, with his sad smile; "broken chairs, old pictures, and a fire made of ruined furniture! But one thing we have—an uninterrupted opportunity to converse. Let us talk, therefore, or rather, I will at once tell you what I promised."

XIV
"LORD OF HIMSELF, THAT HERITAGE OF WOE"

Mohun leaned back in his chair, reflected for a moment with evident sadness, and then, with a deep sigh, said:—

"I am about to relate to you, my dear Surry, a history so singular, that it is probable you will think I am indulging my fancy, in certain portions of it. That would be an injustice. It is a true life I am about to lay before you—and I need not add that actual occurrences are often more surprising than any due to the imagination of the romance writer. I once knew a celebrated novelist, and one day related to him the curious history of a family in Virginia. 'Make a romance of that,' I said, 'it is an actual history.' But my friend shook his head. 'It will not answer my purpose,' he replied, smiling, 'it is too strange, and the critics would call me a "sensation writer"—that is, ruin me!' And he was right, Surry. It is only to a friend, on some occasion like the present, that I could tell my own story. It is too singular to be believed otherwise.

"But I am prosing. Let me proceed. My family is an old one, they tell me, in this part of Virginia; and my father, whose portrait you see before you, on the mantel-piece, was what is called an 'aristocrat.' That is to say, he was a gentleman of refined tastes and habits; fond of books; a great admirer of fine paintings; and a gentleman of social habits and feelings. 'Fonthill'—this old house—had been, for many generations, the scene of a profuse hospitality; my father kept up the ancient rites, entertaining all comers; and when I grew to boyhood I unconsciously imbibed the feelings, and clung to the traditions of the family. These traditions may be summed up in the maxims which my father taught me—'Use hospitality; be courteous to high and low alike; assist the poor; succor the unhappy; give bountifully without grudging; and enjoy the goods heaven provides you, with a clear conscience, whether you are called an aristocrat or a democrat!' Such were my father's teachings; and he practised them, for he had the kindest and sweetest heart in the world. He was aided in all by my mother, a perfect saint upon earth; and if I have since that time given way to rude passions, it was not for wanting a good example in the blameless lives of this true gentleman and pure gentlewoman.

"Unhappily, I did not have their example long. When I was seventeen my mother died; and my father, as though unable to live without her who had so long been his blessing, followed her a year afterward, leaving me the sole heir of the great possessions of the family. For a time grief crushed me. I was alone—for I had neither brother nor sister—a solitary youth in this great lonely house, standing isolated amid its twenty thousand acres—and even the guardian who had been appointed to look after my affairs, seldom came to see me and relieve my loneliness. The only associate I had was a sort of bailiff or steward, Nighthawk—you know him, and his attachment for me. It was hereditary—this attachment. My father had loved and trusted his; relieved the necessities of the humble family once when they were about to be turned adrift for debt. The elder Nighthawk then conceived a profound affection for his benefactor—and dying, left to his son the injunction to watch over and serve faithfully the son of his 'old master.'

"Do not laugh at that word, Surry. It is the old English term, and England is best of all, I think. So Nighthawk came to live with me, and take care of my interests. You know that he has continued to be faithful, and to serve me, and love me, to this moment.

"But in spite of the presence of this true friend, I was still lonely. I craved life, movement, company—and this I promised myself to secure at the university of Virginia, to which I accordingly went, spending there the greater portion of my time until I had reached the age of twenty. Then I returned to Fonthill—only to find, however, that the spot was more dreary than before. I was the master of a great estate, but alone; 'lord of myself,' I found, like the unhappy Childe Harold, and Randolph of Roanoke after him, that it was a 'heritage of woe.' There was little or no society in the neighborhood—at least suited to my age—I lived a solitary, secluded, dormant existence; and events soon proved that this life had prepared my character for some violent passion. A philosopher could have foretold that. Every thing in excess brings on reaction. The drunkard may abstain long, but the moment he touches spirit, an orgy commences. Men love, because the time and a woman have come—and that hour and person came all at once to arouse me from my lethargy.

"One day I was inert, apathetic, sluggish in my movements, careless of all things and all persons around me. On the next I was aroused, excited, with every nerve and faculty strung. I was becoming suddenly intoxicated, and soon the drunkenness of love had absorbed all the powers of my being.

"You know who aroused that infatuation, the daughter of George Conway."

XV
THE STORM

"At that time she was called Miss Mortimer. The commencement of our acquaintance was singular. Fate seemed to have decreed that all connected with our relations should be 'dramatic.'

"One night I was returning at full speed from the house of a gentleman in the neighborhood, whither I had been to make a visit. The night was as dark as a wolf's mouth, and a violent storm rushed down upon me, when I was still many miles from home. I have scarcely ever witnessed a more furious tempest; the thunder and lightning were fearful, and I pushed my horse to his utmost speed to reach Fonthill before the torrents of rain drenched me to the skin.

"Well, I had entered the Fonthill woods, a mile or two from the house, and was galloping at full speed through the black darkness which the lightning only occasionally illumined now, when all at once my horse struck his chest against something. I heard a cry, and then a dazzling flash showed me a light carriage which had evidently just been overturned. I was nearly unseated by the collision, but leaped to the ground, and at the same moment another flash showed me the form of a lady whom a man was extricating from the broken vehicle. I hastened to render my assistance. The lady was lifted in our arms, and then I aided in raising the fallen horse, who lay on his side, frightened and kicking violently.

"Ten minutes afterward I was placed in possession of what the lawyers call 'the facts of the case.' Mr. Mortimer, of Georgia, was travelling home from the North, with his sick sister in his carriage, for the benefit of her health. They had lost their way; the storm had caught them; their carriage had overturned in the darkness,—where could Mr. Mortimer obtain lodgings for the night? The condition of his sister rendered it imperative that they should not continue their journey until morning, even if the storm and broken vehicle permitted.

"I listened, and felt a warm sympathy for the poor sick girl—she was only a girl of eighteen, and very beautiful. I would gladly have offered my own house, but it was still some miles distant, and the young woman was so weak, and trembled so violently, that it would plainly be impossible to conduct her so far on foot. True, my carriage might have been sent for her, but the rain was now descending in torrents; before it arrived she would be drenched — something else must be thought of. All at once the idea occurred to me, 'Parson Hope's is only a quarter of a mile distant.' Mr. Hope was the parson of the parish, and a most excellent man. I at once suggested to Mr. Mortimer that his sister should be conducted thither, and as he assented at once, we half conducted, half carried the poor girl through the woods to the humble dwelling of the clergyman.

"The good parson received us in a manner which showed his conviction that to succor the stranger or the unfortunate is often to 'entertain angels unawares.' It is true that on this occasion it was something like a brace of devils whom he received into his mansion! The young lady threw herself into a seat; seemed to suffer much; and was soon conducted by the parson's old housekeeper — for he was a childless widower — to her chamber in which a fire had been quickly kindled. She disappeared, sighing faintly, but in those few minutes I had taken a good look at her. You have seen her; and I need not describe her. She is still of great beauty; but at that time she was a wonder of loveliness. Slender, graceful, with a figure exquisitely shaped; with rosy lips as artless as an infant's; grand dark eyes which seemed to burn with an inner light as she looked at you; such was *Miss Mortimer* at eighteen, when I first saw her on that night in the Fonthill woods."

XVI
ACT I

"An hour after the scene which I have tried to describe, I was at home; and, seated in this apartment, then very different in appearance, reflected deeply upon this romantic encounter with the beautiful girl.

"It was midnight before I retired. I fell asleep thinking of her, and the exquisite face still followed me in my dreams.

"These few words tell you much, do they not, Surry? You no doubt begin to understand, now, when I have scarcely begun the real narrative, what is going to be the character of the drama. Were I a romance writer, I should call your attention to the fact that I have introduced my characters, described their appearance, and given you an inkling of the series of events which are about to be unrolled before you. A young man of twenty is commended to your attention; a youth living in a great mansion; lord of himself, but tired of exercising that authority; of violent passions, but without an object; and at that very moment, presto! appeared a lovely girl, with dark eyes, rosy lips; whom the youth encounters and rescues under most romantic circumstances!

"Well, the 'lord of himself' acted in real life as he would have done in a novel. In other words, my dear Surry, I proceeded straightway to fall violently in love with *Miss Mortimer*; and it is needless to say that on the next day my horse might have been seen standing at the rack of the parsonage. I had gone, you see, as politeness required, to ask how the young lady felt after her accident.

"She was leaning back in an arm-chair, reading a 'good book,' and looked charming. The accident seemed to have greatly shocked the delicate frame of the young creature, but when I entered, she held out her hand, greeting me with a fascinating smile. Mademoiselle was imitated by

Monsieur. I mean Mr. Mortimer. I did not fancy the countenance of that gentleman much. It was dark and forbidden, but his manners were those of a person acquainted with good society; he thanked me 'with effusion,' as the French say, for my timely assistance on the night before; and then he strolled forth with the good parson to look at the garden, leaving me *tete-à-tete* with his sister.

"Why lengthen out my story by comment, reflections, a description of every scene, and the progressive steps through which the 'affair' passed? I was in love with Miss Mortimer. She saw it. Her eyes said, 'Love me as much as you choose, and don't be afraid I will not love you soon, in return.' At the end of this interview, which the worthy Mr. Mortimer did not interrupt for at least two hours, I rode home thinking with a throb of the heart 'If she will only love me?' Then the throb was succeeded by a sudden sinking of the same organ. 'But there will be no opportunity!' I groaned, 'doubtless in two or three days she will leave this part of the country!' A week afterward that apprehension had been completely removed. Miss Mortimer was still faint and weak, 'from her accident.' All her movements were slow and languid. She had not left the good parson's house, Surry — and what is more she was not going to leave it! She had learned what she desired to know about me; heard that I was a young man of great wealth; and had devised a scheme so singular that — but let me not anticipate! She proceeded rapidly. In our second interview she 'made eyes at me.' In the third, she blushed and murmured, avoiding my glances, when I looked at her. In the fourth, she blushed more deeply when I took her hand — but did not withdraw it. In the fifth, the fair head in some manner had come to rest on my shoulder — no doubt from weakness. And in a few days afterward the shy, embarrassed, loving, palpitating creature, blushing deeply, 'sunk upon my bosom,' as the poets say, and murmured, 'How can I resist you?'

"In other words, my dear friend, *Miss Mortimer* had promised to become *my wife*, and I need not say, I was the happiest of men. I thought with rapture of the bliss I was about to enjoy in having by my side, throughout life, this charming creature. I trembled at the very thought that the accident in the wood might not have happened, and I might never have known her! I was at the parsonage morning, noon, and night. When not beside *her* I was riding through the forest at full speed, with bared brow, laughing lips, and shouts of joy—in a word, my dear friend, I was as much intoxicated as ever youth was yet, and fed on froth and moonshine to an extent that was really astonishing!

"There was absolutely nothing to oppose our marriage. My old guardian, it is true, shook his head, and suggested inquiries into the family, position, character, etc., of the Mortimers; I was young, wealthy, heir of one of the oldest families, he said, and sharpers might deceive me. But all I heard was the word 'sharpers'—and I left my guardian, whose functions had ceased now, in high displeasure at his unworthy imputations. That angel a sharper! That pure, devoted creature, guilty of deception! I fell into a rage; swore never to visit my guardian again; and returning to the parsonage urged a speedy consummation of our marriage.

"The fair one was not loth. She indicated that fact by violently opposing me at first, but soon yielded. When I rode home that night I had made every arrangement for our union in one month from that time.

"So much for Act I., Surry!"

XVII
THE WILL

Mohun had commenced his narrative in a mild voice, and with an expression of great sadness upon his features. As he proceeded, however, this all disappeared; gradually the voice became harsh and metallic, so to describe it, and his face resumed that expression of cynical bitterness which I had observed in him on our first meeting. As he returned thus, to the past, all its bitterness seemed to revive; memory lashed him with its stinging whip; and Mohun had gone back to his "first phase,"—that of the man, stern, implacable, and misanthropic.

After uttering the words, "So much for Act I., Surry!" he paused. A moment afterward, however, he resumed his narrative.

"What I am now going to tell you is not agreeable to remember, my dear Surry, and I shall accordingly relate every thing as briefly as possible. I aim only to give you a clear conception of the tragedy. You will form your own opinion.

"I was impolite enough in introducing *Miss Mortimer* to you, at the parsonage, to describe that young lady as a 'devil.' No doubt the term shocked you, and yet it conveyed something very like the exact truth. I declare to you that this woman was, and is still, a marvel to me, a most curious study. How could she be such as she was? She had the lips of an infant, and the eyes of an angel. Was it not strange that, under all that, she should hide the heart of a born devil? But to continue my narrative.

"The month or two which elapsed between my engagement and my marriage was not an uninterrupted dream of bliss. The atmosphere was strangely disturbed on more than one occasion. Mademoiselle was frequently absent from the parsonage when I arrived, taking long walks with Monsieur, her brother; and when she returned from these excursions, I could see a very strange expression on her countenance as she looked at me. Occasionally her glance was like those lurid flashes of lightning which you may have seen issue from the depths of a black cloud. Her black eyes were the cloud—admire the simile!—and I assure you their expression at such moments was far from agreeable. What to make of it, I knew not. I am not constitutionally irritable, but on more than one occasion I felt a strange angry throb of the heart when I encountered those glances.

"Mademoiselle saw my displeasure, and hastened at once to soothe and dissipate it. The dark flash was always succeeded by the most brilliant sunshine; but, even in moments of her greatest apparent abandon, I would still meet suddenly, when she did not think I was looking at her, the sombre glance which appalled me.

"In spite of this strange phenomenon, however, the young girl possessed unbounded influence over me. I could not resist her fascinations, and was as wax in her hands. She took a charming interest in all that concerned me; painted the blissful future before us, in all the colors of the rainbow; and declared that the devotion of her whole life would not be sufficient to display 'her gratitude for my magnanimity in wedding a poor girl who had nothing but her warm love to offer me.'

"'That is more than enough,' I said, charmed by her caressing voice. 'I have few relations, and friends—you are all to me.'

"'And you to me!' she said. Then she added, with a sort of shudder, 'but suppose you were to die!'

"I laughed, and replied:—

"'You would be well provided for, and find yourself a gay young widow with hundreds of beaux?'

"She looked at me reproachfully.

"'Do you think I would ever marry again?' she said. 'No! I would take our marriage ring, and some little souvenir connected with you, leave your fine house, and go with my brother to some poor home in a foreign country, where the memory of our past happiness would be my solace!'

"I shook my head.

"'You will not do that,' I said, 'you will be the mistress of all my fortune, after my death!'

"'Oh, no!' she exclaimed.

"'Oh, yes!' I responded, laughing; 'and, to make every thing certain, I am going to draw up my will this very day, leaving you every thing which I possess in the world.'

"Her face suddenly flushed.

"'How can you think of such a thing!' she said. 'I did not know how much you loved me!'

"You will understand, my dear Surry, that those words did not change my resolution. When I left her I went home, and wrote the will in due form, and on my next visit she asked, laughing, if I had carried out my absurd resolution.

"'Yes,' I said, 'and now let us talk of a more interesting affair — our marriage!'

"She blushed, then turned pale, and again I saw the strange lurid glance. It disappeared, however, in an instant, and she was all smiles and fascinations throughout the remainder of the day. Never had I been so happy."

XVIII
THE MARRIAGE

"As the day of our marriage approached," continued Mohun, "I saw more than once the same singular expression in the lady's eyes, and I confess it chilled me.

"She seemed to be the prey to singular moods, and fits of silence. She took more frequent and longer walks with Mortimer than before. When they returned from these walks and found me awaiting them at the parsonage, both would look at me in the strangest way, only to quickly withdraw their eyes when they caught my own fixed upon them.

"I longed to speak of this curious phenomenon to some one, but had no friend. My best friend, Nighthawk, was alienated from me, and Mademoiselle had been the cause. From the first moment of our acquaintance, Nighthawk had seemed to suspect something. He did not attempt to conceal his dislike of Mortimer and the young lady. Why was that? I could not tell. Your dog growls when the secret foe approaches you, smiling, and, perhaps, Nighthawk, my faithful retainer, had something of the watch dog in him.

"Certain it is that he had witnessed my growing intimacy with Miss Mortimer, with ill-concealed distaste. As I became more and more attentive, he became almost sour toward me. When I asked him the meaning of his singular deportment, he shook his head—and then, with flushed cheeks and eyes, exclaimed: 'do not marry this young person, sir! something bad will come of it!' When he said that, I looked at him with haughty surprise—and this sentiment changed in a few moments to cold anger. 'Leave this house,' I said, 'and do not return until you have learned how to treat me with decent respect!' He looked at me for a moment, clasped his hands, opened his lips—seemed about to burst forth into passionate entreaty—but all at once, shaking his head, went out in silence. I looked after him with a strange shrinking of the heart. What could he mean? He was senseless!—and I mounted my horse, galloped to the parsonage, was received with radiant smiles, and forgot the whole scene. On the next day Nighthawk did not return—nor on the next. I did not see him again until the evening of the day on which I was married.

"To that 'auspicious moment' I have now conducted you, my dear Surry. The morning for my marriage came. I say 'the morning' — for my 'enchantress,' as the amatory poets say, had declared that she detested the idea of being married at night; she also objected to company; — would I not consent to have the ceremony performed quietly at the parsonage, with no one present but her brother and the excellent parson, Hope, and his old housekeeper? Then she would belong to me — I could do as I pleased with her — take her to Fonthill, or where I chose — she only begged that I would allow her to embark on the ocean of matrimony, with no one to witness her blushes but myself, her brother, the old housekeeper, and the good minister!

"I consented at once. The speech charmed me, I need not say — and I was not myself unwilling to dispense with inquisitive eyes and laughing witnesses. Infatuated as I was, I could not conceal from myself that my marriage was a hasty and extremely 'romantic' affair. I doubted whether the old friends of my father in the neighborhood would approve of it; and now, when Mademoiselle gave me a good excuse to dispense with their presence, I gladly assented, invited no one, and went to my wedding alone, in the great family chariot, unaccompanied by a single friend or relative.

"Mademoiselle met me with a radiant smile, and her wedding dress of white silk, made her look perfectly charming. Her lips were caressing, her eyes melting, but all at once, as she looked at me, I saw the color all fade out of the rosy lips of the lady; and from the great dark eyes darted the lurid flash. A chill, like that of death smote me, I know not why, but I suppressed my emotion. In ten minutes, I was standing before the excellent clergyman, the young lady's cold hand in mine — and we were duly declared man and wife.

"All my forebodings and strange shrinkings were completely dissipated at this instant. I was overwhelmed with happiness, and would not have envied a king upon his throne. With the hand of the lovely creature in my own, and her eyes fixed upon me with an expression of the deepest love, I experienced but one emotion — that of full, complete, unalloyed happiness.

"Let me hasten on. The storm is coming, my dear Surry. I linger on the threshold of the tragedy, and recoil even now, with a sort of shudder from the terrible scenes which succeeded my marriage. *Tragedy* is a mild word, as you will perceive, for the drama. It was going to surpass Aeschylus — and preserve the Greek 'unities' with frightful precision!

"Half an hour after the ceremony, I led madam to my chariot; followed her into the vehicle, and making a last sign of greeting to the good parson, directed the driver to proceed to Fonthill. Madam's excellent brother did not accompany us. He declared his intention to remain on that night at the parsonage. He would call at Fonthill on the next day—on the day after, he proposed to continue his way to Georgia. His eyes were not a pleasant spectacle as he uttered these words, and I observed a singular pallor came to madam's countenance. But I was in no mood to nourish suspicion. At the height of happiness, I looked serenely down upon all the world, and with the hand of *my wife* in my own, was driven rapidly to Fonthill.

"We arrived in the afternoon, and dined in state, all alone. Madam did the honors of *her table* with exquisite grace, but more than once I saw her hand shake in a very singular way, as she carried food or a glass to her lips.

"After dinner she bade me a smiling courtesy, leaving me to find company in my cigar, she said; and tripped off to her chamber.

"Well, I lit my cigar, retired to the library, and seating myself in an armchair before the fire, began to reflect. It was nearly the middle of December, and through the opening in the curtains I could see the moonlight on the chill expanse of the lawn.

"I had just taken my seat, when I heard a step in the passage, the door of the library opened, and Nighthawk, as pale as a ghost, and with a strange expression in his eyes, entered the apartment."

XIX
WEDDING ARRANGEMENTS

"I had recognized his step," continued Mohun, "but I did not move or turn my head, for I had not recovered from my feeling of ill humor toward the faithful retainer. I allowed him to approach me, and then said coldly, without looking at him—

"'Who is that?'

"'I, sir,' said Nighthawk, in a trembling voice.

"'What do you want?'

"'I wish to speak to you, sir.'

"'I am not at leisure.'

"'I *must* speak to you, sir.'

"I wheeled round in my chair, and looked at him. His pallor was frightful.

"'What does all this mean?' I said, coldly, 'this is a singular intrusion.'

"'I would not intrude upon you, if it was not necessary sir,' he said, in an agitated voice, 'but I must speak to you to-night!'

"There was something in his accent which frightened me, I knew not why.

"'Well speak!' I said, austerely, 'but be brief!'

"'As brief as I can, sir; but I must tell you all. If you strike me dead at your feet, I must tell you all, sir!'

"In spite of myself I shuddered.

"'Speak!' I said, 'what does this mean, Nighthawk?' Why do you look like a ghost at me?'

"He came up close to me.

"'What I have to tell you concerns your honor and your life, sir!' he said, in a low tone.

"I gazed at him in speechless astonishment. Was I the prey of some nightmare? I protest to you, Surry, I thought for a moment that I was dreaming all this. A tremor ran through my frame; I placed my hand upon my heart, which felt icy cold — then suddenly my self-possession and coolness seemed to return to me as by magic.

"'Explain your words,' I said, coldly, 'there is some mystery in them which I do not understand. Speak, and speak plainly.'

"'I will do so, sir,' he replied, in the same trembling voice.

"And going to the door of the apartment, he bent down and placed his ear at the key-hole. He remained in this attitude for a moment without moving. Then rising, he went to the window, and drawing aside the curtains, looked out on the chill moonlit expanse. This second examination seemed to satisfy him. At the same instant a light step — the step of madam — was heard crossing the floor of the apartment, above our heads; and this evidently banished Nighthawk's last fears.

"He returned quickly to the seat where I was sitting; looked at me for some minutes with eyes full of fear, affection, sympathy, fright, and said in a voice so low, that it scarce rose above a whisper: —

"'We are alone, sir, and I can speak without being overheard by these devils who have betrayed and are about to murder you! Do not interrupt me sir! — the time is short! — you must know every thing at once, in an hour it would be too late! The man calling himself Mortimer is probably within a hundred yards of us at this moment. The woman you have married is — — his wife. Stop, sir! — do not strike me! — listen! I know the truth of every thing now. She talked with him for an hour under the big cedar, near the parsonage last night. He will see her again to-night, and in this house — hear me to the end, sir! You will not harm him; you will care nothing for all this; you will not know it, for you will be dead, sir!'

"At these words I must have turned deadly pale, for Nighthawk hastened to my side, and placed his arm around me to support me. But I did not need his assistance. In an instant I was as calm as I am at this moment. I quietly removed the arm of Nighthawk, and said in a low tone: —

"'How do you know this?'

"'I overheard their talk,' he replied, in a husky voice, and looked at me with infinite tenderness as he spoke. 'I was coming to see you at the parsonage, where I thought you had gone, sir. I could not bear to keep away from my old master's son any longer; and let him get married without making up, and having him feel kindly again to me. Well, sir, I had just reached the big cedar, when I saw *the lady* come out of the house, hasten toward the cedar, and hide herself in the shadow, within a few feet of me. No sooner had she done so, than I saw a man come from the rear of the house, straight to the cedar, and as he drew nearer I recognized Mortimer.

Madam coughed slightly, as though to give him the signal; he soon reached her; and then they began to talk. I was hidden by the trunk of the tree, and the shadow of the heavy boughs, reaching nearly to the ground; so I heard every word they said, without being discovered.'

"'What was it they said?'

"'I can not repeat their words, sir, but I can tell you what I learned from their talk.'

"'Tell me,' I said.

"'First, I discovered that madam had been married to that man more than a year before you saw her.'

"'Yes.'

"'Before which she had been tried, convicted, and confined for six months in a prison in New York, as a thief. You turn pale, sir; shall I stop?'

"'No, go on,' I said.

"'These facts,' continued Nighthawk, 'came out in a sort of quarrel which madam had with the man. He reproached her with intending to desert him—with loving you—and said he had not rescued her from misery to be thus treated. She laughed, and replied that she was only following a suggestion of his own. They were poor, they must live; he had himself said that they must procure money either honestly or dishonestly; and he had fully approved of the plan she had now undertaken. *You*, sir—she added—were an "empty-headed fool,"—the idea of her "loving" you was absurd!—but you were wealthy; immensely wealthy; had made a will leaving her your entire property;—*if you died suddenly on your wedding night*, she and himself would possess Fonthill, and live in affluence.'

"'Go on,' I said.

"'At these words,' continued Nighthawk, 'I could see the man turn pale. He had not intended *that*, he said. His scheme had been, that madam should induce you to bestow upon her a splendid trousseau in the shape of jewels and money, with which they would elope. The marriage was only a farce, he added—he did not wish to turn it into a tragedy. But she interrupted him impatiently, and said she hated and would have no mercy on you. She would have all or nothing. Your will made her the mistress. What was a crime, more or less, to people like themselves! At these words he uttered a growl. In a word, she added, you were *an obstacle*, and she was going to *suppress you* — with or without his consent. She then proceeded to tell him her resolution; and it is a frightful, a horrible one, sir! All is arranged — you are about to be *murdered*!'

"'How, and when?' I said.

"'This very night, by poison!'

"'Ah!' I said, 'explain that.'

"'Madam has provided herself with strychnine, which she will place in the tea you drink to-night. Tea will be served in half an hour. *He* will be waiting — for she forced him to agree — and your cries will announce all to him. You will be poisoned between eight and nine o'clock in the evening, sir, — at ten you will already be dying, — and at midnight you will be dead. Then madam will banish every one from her chamber, in inconsolable grief — lock the door — tap on the window-pane — *he* will hear the signal, and come up the back staircase — when madam will open the private door for him to come in and take a look at your body! Do you understand now, sir?'

"'Yes,' I said. 'Remain here, Nighthawk. There is the step of the servant coming to tell me tea is ready!'"

XX
THE CUP OF TEA

"The door opened as I uttered the words, and my old major-domo—gray haired, and an heir-loom, so to say, of the family—bowed low, and announced that tea was served and madam waiting.

"I rose and looked into the mirror above the fireplace. I was pale, but not sufficiently so to excite suspicion; and with a smile which frightened Nighthawk, took my way toward the supper-room.

"Madam was awaiting me, as I suspected, and I had never seen her look more radiant. A single glance told me that she had made an elaborate toilet in honor of—my funeral! Her dark hair was in shining braids; her eyes sparkled with joy; her parted lips showed her white teeth;—the only evidence I saw of concealed emotion was in the bloodless cheeks. They were as white as the lace falling over her superb silk dress.

"'You see you keep me waiting!' she said, with playful *naiveté*, 'and your tea is growing cold, sir—which is worse for me than for you, as you do not care, but I care for you!'

"And as I passed her, she drew me playfully toward her, dragged me down, and held up her lips. I touched them with my own; they were as cold as ice, or the cheek my own face just touched in passing. I went to the table; took my seat; and madam poured out the tea, with a covert glance toward me. I was not looking at her, but I saw it.

"A moment afterward, the old waiter presented me the small gilt cup, smoking, fragrant, and inviting.

"I took it, looking, as before, out of the corner of my eye at madam. She was leaning forward, watching me with a face as pale as death. I could hear her teeth chatter.

"I placed the cup to my lips;—her hand, holding a spoon, trembled so that the spoon beat a tattoo on her saucer. She was watching me in breathless suspense; and all at once I turned full toward her.

"'The taste of this tea is singular,' I said, 'I should call it very bad.'

"'Oh, it is—excellent!' she muttered, between her chattering teeth.

"'The cup you send me is certainly wretched. Do me the *pleasure to taste it, madam.*'

"And depositing it upon the waiter of the old servant, I said:—

"'Take this to your mistress.'

"He did so; she just touched it with her lips, her hand trembling, then replaced it upon the waiter.

"'I perceive nothing disagreeable,' she murmured.

"'Swallow a mouthful,' I said, with a bitter smile.

"She looked at me with sudden intentness. Her eyes, full of wild inquiry, seemed attempting to read into my very soul.

"'Perhaps you object to drinking after me, as the children say,' I added—this time with a species of sneer, and a flash of the eye, I think.

"'Oh, no!' she exclaimed, with an attempt to laugh; 'and to show you—'

"With a quick movement she attempted—as though by accident—to strike the waiter with her elbow, in order to overturn the cup.

"But the old servant was too well trained. The lady's elbow struck the waiter, but the skilful attendant withdrew it quickly. Not a drop of the tea was spilled.

"A moment afterward I was beside madam.

"'I pray you to drink,' I said.

"'I can not—I feel unwell,' she murmured, cowering beneath the fire in my eye.

"'I beg you to drink from this cup.'

"'I have told you—I will not.'

"'I beseech you to humor me, madam. Else I shall regard you as a murderess!'

"She rose suddenly.

"'Your meaning, sir!' she exclaimed, as pale as death.

"I took the cup and poured the tea into a saucer. At the bottom was a modicum of white powder, undissolved. I poured the tea into the cup again—then a second time into the saucer. This time nothing remained—and I proceeded to pour cream into the saucer, until it was filled. Madam watched me with distended eyes, and trembling from head to foot. Then suddenly she uttered a cry—a movement of mine had caused the cry.

"I had gone to the fire where a cat was reposing upon the rug, and placed the saucer before her. In two minutes its contents had disappeared down the throat of the cat. Five minutes afterward the animal was seized with violent convulsions—uttered unearthly cries—tore the carpet with its claws—glared around in a sort of despair—rolled on its back, beat the air with its paws—and expired.

"I turned to madam, who was gazing at me with distended eyes, and pointing to the cat, said:—

"'See this unfortunate animal, madam! Her death is curious. She has died in convulsions, in consequence of drinking a cup of tea!'"

XXI
THE FOILS

"Up to this moment," continued Mohun, "madam had exhibited every indication of nervous excitement, and a sort of terror. Had that arisen from a feeling of suspense, and the unexpected discovery of her intent by the proposed victim? I know not; but now, when all was discovered, her manner suddenly changed.

"She glared at me like a wild animal driven to bay. Her pearly teeth closed upon her under lip until the blood started. Pallid, but defiant, she uttered a low hoarse sound which resembled the growl of a tigress from whom her prey has been snatched, and with a firm and haughty step left the apartment, glaring over her shoulder at me to the last.

"Then her step was heard upon the great staircase; she slowly ascended to her chamber; the door opened, then closed—and I sat down, overcome for an instant by the terrible scene, within three paces of the dead animal, destroyed by the poison intended for myself.

"This paralysis of mind lasted only for a moment, however. I rose coolly; directed the old servant, who alone had witnessed the scene, to retire, and carefully abstain from uttering a word of what had passed before him—then I leaned upon the mantel-piece, reflected for five minutes—and in that time I had formed my resolution.

"Mortimer was first to be thought of. I intended to put him to death first and foremost. It would have been easy to have imitated the old seigneurs of the feudal age, and ordered my retainers to assassinate him; but that was repugnant to my whole character. It should never be said that a Mohun had shrunk before his foe; that one of my family had delegated to another the punishment of his enemy. I would fight Mortimer—meet him in fair and open combat—if he killed me well and good. If not, I would kill him. And it should not be with the pistol. I thirsted to meet him breast to breast; to feel my weapon traverse his heart. To accomplish this was not difficult. I had often heard Mortimer, when at the parsonage, boast of his skill with the foils. I had a pair at hand. By breaking off the buttons, and sharpening the points, I would secure two rude but excellent rapiers, with which Mortimer and myself could settle our little differences, after the fashion of gentlemen in former ages! As to the place of combat,—anywhere—in the house, or a part of the grounds around the mansion—it was unimportant I said, so that one of us was killed. But a moment's reflection induced me to change my views. Under any circumstances *I* was going to die—that was true. My character, however, must be thought of. It would not do to have a stain rest on the last of the house of Mohun! Were I to kill Mortimer in the house, or grounds, it would be said that I had murdered him, with the aid of my servants—that I had drawn him thither to strike him—had acted the traitor and the coward. 'No,' I said, 'even in death I must guard the family honor. This man must fall elsewhere—in some spot far distant from this house—fall without witnesses—in silence—in fair fight with me, no one even seeing us.'

"I had formed this resolution in five minutes after the departure of madam from the supper-room. I went straight to the library; calmly stated my resolution to Nighthawk; and in spite of his most obstinate remonstrances, and repeated refusals, broke down his opposition by sheer force of will. It took me half an hour, but at the end of that time I had succeeded. Nighthawk listened, with bent head, and pale face covered with drops of cold perspiration, to my orders. These orders were to have the horses put to the carriage, which was to be ready at my call; then to proceed with a trusty servant, or more if necessary, to a private spot on the river, which I described to him; dig a grave of full length and depth; and when his work was finished, return and report the fact to me, cautioning the servant or servants to say nothing.

"This work, I calculated, would be completed about midnight—and at midnight I promised myself an interview with my friend Mortimer.

"Nighthawk groaned as he listened to my cold and resolute voice, giving minute instructions for the work of darkness—looked at my face, to discover if there were any signs of yielding there—doubtless saw none whatever—and disappeared, uttering a groan, to carry out the orders which he had received from me.

"Then I took the two foils from the top of the bookcase where they were kept; broke off the buttons by placing my heel upon them; procured a file, and sharpened the points until they would have penetrated through an ordinary plank. That was sufficient, I said to myself—they would pierce a man's breast—and placing them on the buffet, I went to a drawer and took out a loaded revolver, which I thrust into my breast.

"Two minutes afterward I had ascended to madam's chamber, opened the door, and entered."

XXII
WHILE WAITING FOR MIDNIGHT

"I did not arrive a moment too soon—in fact I came in the nick of time.

"Madam had hastily collected watches, chains, breastpins, necklaces, and all the money she could find; had thrust the whole into a jewel casket; thrown her rich furs around her shoulders; and was hurrying toward the door, in rear of the apartment which opened on the private staircase.

"She had not locked the main door of the apartment, doubtless fearing to excite suspicion, or knowing I could easily break the hasp with a single blow of my foot. She had plainly counted on my stupor of astonishment and horror at her crime, and was now trying to escape.

"That did not suit my view, however. In two steps, I reached the private door, turned the key, drew it from the lock, and placed it in my pocket.

"'Sit down, madam,' I said, 'and do not be in such a hurry to desert your dear husband. Let us talk for a few moments, at least, before you depart.'

"She glared at me and sat down. She looked regal in her costly furs, holding the casket, heaped with rich jewels.

"'What is your programme, madam, if I may ask?' I said, taking a chair which stood opposite to her.

"'To leave this house!' she said, hoarsely.

"'Ah! you are tired of me, then?'

"'I am sick of you!—have long been sick of you!'

"'Indeed!' I said. 'That is curious! I thought our marriage was a love affair, madam; at least you induced me to suppose so. What, then, has suddenly changed your sentiments in my direction? Am I a monster? Have I been cruel to you? Am I unworthy of you?'

"'I hate and despise you!'

"It was the hoarse growl of a wild animal rather than the voice of a woman. She was imperial at that moment—and I acknowledge, Surry, that she was 'game to the last!'

"'Ah! you hate me, you despise me!' I said. 'I have had the misfortune to incur madam's displeasure! No more connubial happiness—no more endearments and sweet confidences—no more loving words, and glances—no more bliss!'

"She continued to glare at me.

"'I am unworthy of madam; I see that clearly,' I went on. 'I am only a poor little, plain little, insignificant little country clodhopper! I am nothing—a mere nobody,—while madam is—shall I tell you, madam? While you are a convict—a bigamist,—and a poisoner! Are you not?'

"Her face became livid, but her defiant eyes never sank before my glance. I really admired her, Surry. No woman was ever braver than that one. I had supposed that these words would overwhelm her; that the discovery of my acquaintance with her past life, and full knowledge of her attempted crime, would crush her to the earth. Perhaps I had some remnant of pity for this woman. If she had been submissive, repentant! but, instead of submission and confusion, she exhibited greater defiance than before. In the pale face her eyes burned like coals of fire—and it was rage which inflamed them.

"'So you have set your spies on me!' she exclaimed, in accents of inexpressible fury. 'You are a chivalric gentleman, truly! You are worthy of your boasted family! You pretend to love and confide in me—you look at me with smiles and eyes of affection—and all the time you are laying a trap for me—endeavoring to catch me and betray me! Well, yes, sir! yes! What you have discovered through your spies is true. I *was* tried and sentenced as a thief—I *was* married when I first saw you—and it is this miserable creature, this offscouring of the kennels, this thief, that has become *the wife* of the proud Mr. Mohun—in the eyes of the world at least! I am so still—my character is untainted—dare to expose me and have me punished, and it is *your* proud name that will be tarnished! *your* grand escutcheon that will be blotted! Come! arrest me, expose me, drag me to justice! I will stand up in open court, and point my finger at you where you stand cowering, in the midst of jeers and laughter, and say: "There is Mr. Mohun, of the ancient family of the Mohuns,—he is the husband and the dupe of a thief!"'

"She was splendid as she uttered these words, Surry. They thrilled me, and made my blood flame. I half rose, nearly beside myself—then I resumed my seat and my coolness. A moment afterward I was as calm as I am at this moment, and said, laughing:—

"'So you have prepared that pretty little tableau, have you, madam? I compliment you on your skill;—and even more on your nerve. But have you not omitted one thing—a very trifling portion, it is true, of the indictment to be framed against you? I refer to the little scene of this evening, madam.'

"Her teeth closed with a snap. Otherwise she exhibited no emotion. Her flashing eyes continued to survey me with the former defiance.

"'Is there not an additional clause in the said indictment, madam?' I calmly continued, 'which the commonwealth's attorney will perhaps rely on more fully than upon all else in the document, to secure your conviction and punishment? You are not only a bigamist and an ex-convict,—you are also a poisoner, my dear madam, and may be hanged for that. Or, if not hanged— there is that handsome white house at Richmond, the state penitentiary. The least term which a jury can affix to your crime, will be eighteen years, if you are not sent there for life! For life!—think of that, madam. How very disagreeable it will be! Nothing around you but blank walls; no associates but thieves and murderers—hard labor with these pretty hands—a hard bed for this handsome body—coarse and wretched food for these dainty red lips—the dress, the food, the work, and the treatment of a convict! Disagreeable, is it not, madam? But that is the least that a felon, convicted of an attempt to poison, can expect! There is only one point which I have omitted, and which may count for you. This life in prison will not be so hard to you—since your ladyship has already served your apprenticeship among felons.'

"The point at last was reached. Madam had listened with changing color, and my words seemed to paint the frightful scene in all its horror. Suddenly fury mastered her. She rose and seemed clutching at some weapon to strike me.

"'You are *a gentleman*! you insult a woman.'

"'You are a poisoner, madam—you make tea for the gentleman!'

"'You are a coward! do you hear? a coward!'

"'I can not return, madam, the same reproach!' I replied, rising and bowing; 'it required some courage to attempt to poison me upon the very night of my wedding!'

"My words drove her to frenzy.

"'Beware!' she exclaimed, taking a step toward me, and putting her hand into her bosom.

"'Beware!' I said, with a laugh, 'beware of what, my dear Madam Laffarge?'

"'Of this!'

"And with a movement as rapid as lightning she drew from her breast a small silver-mounted pistol, which she aimed straight at my breast.

"I was not in a mood to care much for pistols, Surry. When a man is engaged in a little affair like that, bullets lose their influence on the nerves.

"'That is a pretty toy!' I said. 'Where did you procure it madam, the poisoner?'

"With a face resembling rather a hideous mask than a human countenance, she rushed upon me; placed the muzzle of the pistol on my very breast; and drew the trigger.

"The weapon snapped.

"A moment afterward I had taken it from her hand and thrown it into a corner.

"'Very well done!' I said. 'What a pity that you use such indifferent caps! Your pistol is as harmless as your tea!'

"She uttered a hoarse cry, but did not recoil in the least, Surry! This woman was a curiosity. Instead of retreating from me, she clenched her small white hand, raised it above her head, and exclaimed: —

"'If *he* only were here!'

"'*He*, madam?' I said. 'You refer to your respected *brother* — to Mr. Mortimer?'

"'Yes! *he* would make you repent your cowardly outrages and insults.'

"I looked at my watch, it was just eleven.

"'The hour is earlier than I thought, madam,' I said, 'but perhaps he has already arrived.'

"And advancing to the side of the lady, I took her arm, drew her toward the window, and said: —

"'Why not give your friend the signal you have agreed on, madam?'

"At a bound she reached the window, and struck a rapid series of blows with her fingers upon the pane.

"Five minutes afterward a heavy step was heard ascending the private staircase. I went to the door and unlocked it; the step approached — stopped at the door — the door opened, and Mortimer appeared.

"'Come in, my dear brother-in-law,' I said, 'we are waiting for you.'"

XXIII
THE RESULT OF THE SIGNAL

"Mortimer recoiled as if a blow had been suddenly struck at him. His astonishment was so comic that I began to laugh.

"'Good! you start!' I said. 'You thought I was dead by this time?'

"'Yes,' he coolly replied.

"As he spoke, his hand stole under the cloak in which he was wrapped, and I heard the click of a pistol as he cocked it. I drew my own weapon, cocked it in turn, and placing the muzzle upon Mortimer's breast, said:—

"'Draw your pistol and you are dead!'

"He looked at me with perfect coolness, mingled with a sort of curiosity. I saw that he was a man of unfaltering courage, and that the instincts of a gentleman had not entirely left him, soiled as he was with every crime. His eye was calm and unshrinking. He did not move an inch when I placed my pistol muzzle upon his breast. At the words which I uttered he withdrew his hand from his cloak—he had returned the weapon to its place—and with a penetrating glance, said:—

"'What do you wish, sir; as you declare you await me?'

"'Ask madam,' I said, 'or rather exert your own ingenuity.'

"'My ingenuity?'

"'In guessing.'

"'Why not tell me?'

"'So be it. The matter is perfectly simple, sir. I wish to kill you, or give you an opportunity to kill me—is that plain?'

"'Quite so,' replied Mortimer, without moving a muscle.

"'I can understand, without further words, that all explanations and discussions are wholly useless.'

"'Wholly.'

"'You wish to fight me,' he said.

"'Yes.'

"'To put an end to me, if possible?'

"'Yes.'

"'Well, I will give you that opportunity, sir, and, even return you my thanks for not killing me on the spot.'

"He paused a moment, and looked keenly at me.

"'This whole affair is infamous,' he said. 'I knew that when I undertook it. I was once a gentleman, and have not forgotten every thing I then learned, whatever my practice may be. You have been tricked and deceived. You have been made the victim of a disgraceful plot, and I was the author of the whole affair; though this lady would, herself, have been equal to that, or even more. You see I talk to you plainly, sir; I know a gentleman when I see him, and you are one. I was formerly something of the same sort, but having outlawed myself, went on in the career that brought me to this. I was poor—am poor now. I originated the idea of this pseudo-marriage, with a view to profit by it, but with no further—'

"He suddenly paused and looked at the woman. Their glances in that moment crossed like lightning.

"'Speak out!' she cried, 'say plainly—'

"'Hush! I did not mean to—I am no coward, madam!'

"'Say plainly that it was *I* who formed the design to get rid of this person!'

"And she pointed furiously at me.

"'Let no scruples restrain you—take nothing upon yourself—it was I, I!—I who planned his death!'

"Mortimer remained for an instant silent. Then he resumed, in the same measured voice as before:—

"'You hear,' he said. 'I tried to shield her, to take the blame—meant to give you no inkling of this—but she spoils all. To end this. I have offered you a mortal insult—soiled an ancient and honorable name—the last representative of the Mohuns has formed through me a degrading connection. I acknowledge all that. I am going to try to kill you, to bury every thing in the grave. I would have shrunk from assassinating you, though I wish your death. You offer me honorable combat, and you do me an honor, which I appreciate. Let us finish. The place, time, and weapons?'

"There was, then, something not altogether base in this man. I listened with joy. I had expected to encounter a wretch without a single attribute of the gentleman.

"'You accept this honorable combat, then?' I said.

"'With thanks,' he replied.

"'You wish to fight as gentlemen fight?'

"'Yes.'

"'You fence well?'

"'Yes—but you?'

"'Sufficiently well.'

"'Are you certain? I warn you I am excellent at the foils.'

"'They suit me—that is agreed on, then?'

"He bowed, and said:—

"'Yes. And now, as to the place, the time, and every detail. All that I leave to you.'

"I bowed in turn.

"'Then nothing will delay our affair. I have ordered a grave to be dug, in a private spot, on the river. The foils are ready, with the buttons broken, the points sharpened. The carriage has been ordered. A ride of fifteen minutes will bring us to the grave, which is done by this time, and we can settle our differences there, by moonlight, without witnesses or interruption.'

"Mortimer looked at me with a sinister smile.

"'You are provident!' he said, briefly. 'I understand. The one who falls will give no trouble. The grave will await him, and he can enter at once upon his property!'

"'Yes.'

"'And this lady?'

"'That will come afterward,' I said.

"'If I kill you—?'

"'She is your property.'

"'And if you kill me—?'

"'She is mine,' I said.

"The sinister smile again came to the dark features of Mortimer.

"'So be it,' he said, 'and I am ready to accompany you, sir.'

"I drew my pistol and threw it upon the bed, looking at Mortimer as I did so. He imitated me, and opening his coat, showed me that he was wholly unarmed. I did the same, and having locked the private door leading to the back staircase, led the way out, followed by Mortimer. He turned and looked at madam as he passed through the door. She was erect, furious, defiant, full of anticipated triumph. Was it a glance of gloomy compassion and deep tenderness which Mortimer threw toward her? I thought I heard him sigh.

"I locked the door, and we descended to the library."

XXIV
WHAT TOOK PLACE IN FIFTY MINUTES

"As we entered the apartment, the clock on the mantel-piece struck midnight.

"My body servant was within call, and I ordered my carriage, which Nighthawk had been directed to have ready at a moment's warning.

"In five minutes it was at the door, and I had just taken the two foils under my arm, when I heard a step in the passage. A moment afterward, Nighthawk entered.

"He was so pale that I scarcely recognized him. When his eyes encountered Mortimer, they flashed lightnings of menace.

"'Well?' I said, in brief tones.

"'It is ready, sir,' Nighthawk replied, in a voice scarcely audible. I looked at him imperiously.

"'And the servants are warned to keep silent?'

"'Yes, sir.'

"'Very well. Remain here until I return,' I said.

"And I pointed to a seat, with a glance at Nighthawk, which said plainly to him, 'Do not presume to attempt to turn me from my present purpose—it will be useless, and offensive to me.'

"He groaned, and sat down in the seat I indicated. His frame was bent and shrunken like that of an old man, in one evening. Since that moment, I have loved Nighthawk, my dear Surry; and he deserves it.

"Without delay I led the way to the carriage, which was driven by my father's old gray-haired coachman, and entered it with Mortimer, directing the driver to follow the high-road down the river. He did so; we rolled on in the moonlight, or the shadow, as it came forth or disappeared behind the drifting clouds. The air was intensely cold. From beyond the woods came the hollow roar of the Nottoway, which was swollen by a freshet.

"Mortimer drew his cloak around him, but said nothing. In ten minutes I called to the old coachman to stop. He checked his spirited horses—I had some good ones then—and I descended from the carriage, with the foils under my arm, followed by Mortimer.

"The old coachman looked on in astonishment. The spot at which I had stopped the carriage was wild and dreary beyond expression.

"'Shall I wait, sir?' he said, respectfully.

"'No; return home at once, and put away the carriage.'

"He looked at me with a sort of stupor.

"'Go home, sir?' he said.

"'Yes.'

"'And leave you?'

"'Obey me!'

"My voice must have shown that remonstrance would be useless. My old servitor uttered a sigh like the groan which had escaped from the lips of Nighthawk, and, mounting the box, turned the heads of his horses toward home.

"I watched the carriage until it turned a bend in the road, and then, making a sign to Mortimer to follow me, led the way into the woods. Pursuing a path which the moonlight just enabled me to perceive, I penetrated the forest; went on for about ten minutes; and finally emerged upon a plateau, in the swampy undergrowth near which stood the ruins of an old chimney.

"This chimney had served to indicate the spot to Nighthawk; and, before us, in the moonlight, was the evidence that he had found it. In the centre of the plateau was a newly dug grave—and in front of it I paused.

"'We have arrived,' I said.

"Mortimer gazed at the grave with a grim smile.

"'That is a dreary and desolate object,' he said.

"'It will soon be inhabited,' I returned; 'and the issue of this combat is indifferent to me, since in either event I shall be dead.'

"'Ah!' he exclaimed, 'explain that.'

"'Then you do not understand! You think this duel will end every thing? You deceive yourself! A family history like mine does not terminate with a duel. Have you read those tragedies where everybody is killed?— where not a single one of the *dramatis personae* escapes? Well, this is going to be a drama of that exact description. Do you wish to save that woman, yonder? To do so, you must kill *me*. I tell you that to warn you to do your best, sir!'

"Mortimer glared at me. It is hard to imagine a glance more sinister.

"'So you have arranged the whole affair?' he said; 'there is to be a wholesale killing.'

"'Yes.'

"'You are going to kill—*her*?'

"'Yes.'

"'Yourself, too?'

"'Yes.'

"Mortimer's smile became more sinister, as he raised his foil.

"'Take your position, sir,' he said; 'I am going to save you the latter trouble.'

"I grasped my weapon, and placed myself on guard.

"In an instant he had thrown himself upon me with a fury which indicated the profound passion under his assumed coolness. His eyes blazed; his lips writhed into something like a deadly grin; I felt that I had to contend rather with a wild animal than a man. The grave yawned in the moonlight at our very feet, and Mortimer closed in, with fury, endeavoring to force me to its brink, and hurl me into it.

"Ten minutes afterward the combat was over; and it was Mortimer who occupied the grave.

"He had given ground an instant, to breathe; had returned to the attack more furiously than before; a tremendous blow of his weapon snapped my own, eighteen inches from the hilt; but this had probably saved my life instead of destroying it, as Mortimer, from his fierce exclamation as the blade broke, evidently expected.

"Before he could take advantage of his success, I sprang at his throat, grasped his sword-arm with my left hand, and, shortening my stump of a weapon, drove the point through his breast.

"He uttered a cry, staggered, and threw up his hands; I released my clutch on his arm; and he fell heavily backward into the grave.

"'Now to end all,' I said, and I set out rapidly for Fonthill."

XXV
GOING TO REJOINMORTIMER

"I had not gone a hundred yards, when I heard the sound of wheels approaching.

"I had said to myself, 'I am going back to madam; she will hear my footsteps upon the staircase; will open the door; will rush forward to embrace me, under the impression that I am her dear Mortimer, returning triumphant from the field of battle; and then a grand tableau!' Things were destined to turn out differently, as you will see in an instant.

"The sound of wheels grew louder; a carriage appeared; and I recognized my own chariot.

"'Why have you disobeyed my orders?' I said to the old gray-haired driver, arresting the horses as I spoke, by violently grasping the bridles.

"The old coachman looked frightened. Then he said, in an agitated voice: —

"'Madam ordered me to obey her, sir.'

"'Madam?'

"'Yes, sir.'

"'Where is she?'

"'In the carriage, sir. As soon as I got back, she came down to the door — ordered me to drive her to *you* — and I was obliged to do so, sir.'

"'Good,' I said, 'you have done well.'

And opening the door of the carriage, through the glass of which I saw the pale face of the woman, I entered it, directing the coachman to drive to the 'Hicksford Crossing.'

A hoarse, but defiant voice at my side said: —

"'Where is Mr. Mortimer?'

"'Gone over the river,' I said, laughing, 'and we are going, too.'

"'To rejoin him?'

"'Yes, madam.'

"The carriage had rolled on, and as it passed the grave I heard a groan.

"'What is that?' said she.

"'The river is groaning over yonder, madam.'

"'You will not attempt to pass it to-night?'

"'Yes, madam. Are you afraid?'

"She looked at me with fiery eyes.

"'Afraid? No!' she said, 'I am afraid of nothing!'

"I really admired her at that moment. She was truly brave. I said nothing, however. The carriage rolled on, and ten minutes afterward the roar of the river, now near at hand, was heard. That sound mingled with the deep bellowing of the thunder, which succeeded the dazzling flashes at every instant dividing the darkness.

"All at once my companion said: —

"'I am tired of this — where is Mr. Mortimer?'

"'He awaits us,' I replied.

"'You are going to him?'

"'Yes.'

"We had reached the bank of the river, and, stopping the carriage, I sprung out. Madam followed me, without being invited. A small boat rose and fell on the swollen current. I detached the chain, seized a paddle, and pointed to the stern seat.

"'The river is dangerous to-night,' said madam, coldly.

"'Then you are afraid, after all?'

"'No!' she said.

"And with a firm step she entered the boat.

"'Go back with the carriage,' I said to the driver. He turned the heads of the horses, and obeyed in silence.

"Madam had taken her seat in the stern of the boat. I pushed from shore into the current, and paddling rapidly to the middle of the foaming torrent, filled with drift-wood, threw the paddle overboard, and took my seat in the stern.

"As I threw away the paddle, my resolution seemed to dawn for the first time upon my companion. She had become deadly pale, but said nothing. With folded arms, I looked and listened; we were nearing a narrow and rock-studded point in the river, where there was no hope.

"The frail boat was going to be overturned there, or dashed to pieces without mercy. I knew the spot—knew that there was no hope. The torrent was roaring and driving the boat like a leaf toward the jagged and fatal rocks.

"'Then you are going to kill me and yourself at the same time!' she said.

"The woman was fearless.

"'Yes,' I said, 'it is the only way. I could not live dishonored—you dishonored me—I die—and die with you!'

"And I rose erect, baring my forehead to the lightning.

"The point was reached. The boat swept on with the speed of a racehorse. A dazzling flash showed a dark object amid the foam, right ahead of us. The boat rushed toward it—the jagged teeth seemed grinning at us—the boat struck—and the next moment I felt the torrent sweep over me, roaring furious and sombre, like a wild beast that has caught its prey."

XXVI
AFTERWARD

"When I opened my eyes, the sun was shining in my face.

"I was lying on a mass of drift-wood, caught by a ledge of rock, jutting out into the river. I had apparently been hurled there, by the force of the current, stunned and bruised; the sunshine had aroused me, bringing me back to that life which was a burden and a mockery.

"And where was *she*? I shuddered as I asked myself that question. Had she been thrown from the boat? Had it been overturned? Was she drowned? I closed my eyes with a shudder which traversed my body, chilling my blood as with the cold hand of death.

"For a moment I thought of throwing myself into the river, and thus ending all my woes. But I was too cowardly.

"I turned toward the shore, groaning; dragged my bruised and aching limbs along the ledge of jagged rocks, through the masses of drift-wood; and finally reached the shore, where I sank down exhausted, and ready to die.

"I will not lengthen out the gloomy picture. At last I rose, looked around, and with bent head and cowering frame, stole away through the woods toward Fonthill. On my way, I passed within two hundred yards of *the grave*—but I dared not go thither. He was dead, doubtless—and he had been slain in fair combat! It was another form that haunted me—the form of a woman—one who had dishonored me—attempted to poison me—a terrible being—but still a woman; and I had—murdered her!

"I reached home an hour or two afterward. Nighthawk was sitting in the library, pale, and haggard, watching for me.

"As I entered, he rose with an exclamation, extending his arms toward me, with an indescribable expression of joy.

"I shrunk back, refusing his hand.

"'Do not touch that,' I groaned, 'there is blood on it!'

"He seized it, and kneeling down, kissed it.

"'Bloody or not, it is *your* hand—the hand of my dear young master!'

"And the honest fellow burst into tears, as he covered my hand with kisses.

"A month afterward, I was in Europe, amid the whirl and noise of Paris. I tried to forget that I was a murderer—but the shadow went with me!"

XXVII
MOHUN TERMINATES HIS NARRATIVE

Mohun had spoken throughout the earlier portions of his narrative in a tone of cynical bitterness. His last words were mingled, however, with weary sighs, and his face wore an expression of the profoundest melancholy.

The burnt-out cigar had fallen from his fingers to the floor; he leaned back languidly in his great arm-chair: with eyes fixed upon the dying fire, he seemed to go back in memory to the terrible scenes just described, living over again all those harsh and conflicting emotions.

"So it ended, Surry," he said, after a long pause. "Such was the frightful gulf into which the devil and my own passions pushed me, in that month of December, 1856. A hand as irresistible and inexorable as the Greek Necessity had led me step by step to murder—in intent if not in fact—and for years the shadow of the crime which I believed I had committed, made my life wretched. I wandered over Europe, plunged into a thousand scenes of turmoil and excitement—it was all useless—still the shadow went with me. Crime is a terrible companion to have ever at your elbow. The *Atra cura* of the poet is nothing to it, friend! It is a fiend which will not be driven away. It grins, and gibbers, and utters its gibes, day and night. Believe me, Surry,—I speak from experience—it is better for this world, as well as the next, to be a boor, a peasant, a clodhopper with a clear conscience, than to hold in your hand the means of all luxury, and so-called enjoyment, and, with it, the consciousness that you are blood guilty under almost any circumstances.

"Some men might have derived comfort from the circumstances of *that* crime. I could not. They might have said, 'I was goaded, stung, driven, outraged, tempted beyond my strength, caught in a net of fire, from which there was but one method of exit—to burst out, trampling down every thing.' Four words silenced all that sophistry—'She was a woman!' It was the face of that woman, as I saw it last on that stormy night by the lightning flashes, which drove me to despair. I, the son of the pure gentleman whose portrait is yonder—I, the representative of the Mohuns, a family which had acted in all generations according to the dictates of the loftiest honor—I, had put to death a woman, and that thought spurred me to madness!

"Of *his* death I did not think in the same manner. I had slain him in fair combat, body to body—and, however the law of God may stigmatize homicide, there was still that enormous difference. I had played my life against his, as it were—he had lost, and he paid the forfeit. But *the other* was *murdered*! That fact stared me in the face. She had dishonored me; tricked me; attempted to poison, and then shoot me. *She* had designed to murder *me*, and had set about her design deliberately, coolly, without provocation, impelled by the lust of gold only. She deserved punishment, but—she was a woman! I had not said 'Go!' either, in pointing to the gloomy path to death. I had said 'Come!'—had meant to die too. I had not shrunk from the torrent in which I had resolved she should be borne away. I had gone into the boat with her; accompanied her on her way; devoted myself, too, to death, at the same moment. But all was useless. I said to myself a thousand times—'at least they can not say that I was a coward, as well as a murderer. The last of the Mohuns may have blackened his escutcheon with the crime of murder—but at least he did not spare *himself*; he faced death with his victim.' Useless, Surry—all useless! The inexorable Voice with which I fenced, had only one reply—one lunge—'She was a woman!' and the words pierced me like a sword-blade!

"Let me end this, but not before I say that the dreadful Voice was *right*. As to the combat with Mortimer, I shall express no opinion. You know the facts, and will judge me. But the other act was a deadly crime. Gloss it over as you may, you can never justify murder. Use all the special pleading possible, and the frightful deed is still as black in the eyes of God and man as before. I saw that soon; saw it always; see it to-day; and pray God in his infinite mercy to blot out that crime from his book—to pardon the poor weak creature who was driven to madness, and attempted to commit that deadly sin.

"Well, to end my long history. I remained in Europe until the news from America indicated the approach of war—Nighthawk managing my estate, and remitting me the proceeds at Paris. When I saw that an armed collision was going to take place, I hastened back, reaching Virginia in the winter of 1860. But I did not come to Fonthill. I had a horror of the place. From New York, where I landed, I proceeded to Montgomery, without stopping upon the route; found there a prominent friend of my father who was raising a brigade in the Southwest; was invited by him to aid him; and soon afterward was elected to the command of a company of cavalry by his recommendation. I need only add, that I rose gradually from captain to colonel, which rank I held in 1863, when we first met on the Rappahannock — my regiment having been transferred to a brigade of General Lee's cavalry.

"You saw me then, and remember my bitterness and melancholy. But you had no opportunity to descry the depth and intensity of those sentiments in me. Suddenly the load was lifted. *That woman* made her appearance, as if from the grave, and you must have witnessed my wonder, as my eyes fell upon her. Then, she was not dead after all! I was not a murderer! And to complete the wonder, *he* was also alive. A man passing along the bank of the river, as I discovered afterward from Nighthawk, who ferreted out the whole affair — a man named Swartz, a sort of poor farmer and huckster, passing along the Nottoway, on the morning after the storm, had found the woman cast ashore, with the boat overturned near her; and a mile farther, had found Mortimer, not yet dead, in the grave. Succored by Swartz, they had both recovered — had then disappeared. I was to meet them again, and know of their existence only when the chance of war threw us face to face on the field.

"You know the scenes which followed. Mortimer, or Darke, as he now calls himself, confronted me everywhere, and *she* seemed to have no object in life but my destruction. You heard her boast in the house near Buckland that she had thrice attempted to assassinate me by means of her tool, the man Swartz. Again, at Warrenton, in the hospital, she came near poniarding me with her own hand. Nighthawk, who had followed me to the field, and become a secret agent of General Stuart, warned me of all this — and one day, gave me information more startling still. And this brings me, my dear Surry, to the last point in my narrative, I now enter upon matter with which you have been personally 'mixed up.'

"On that night when I attacked Darke in his house in Pennsylvania, Swartz stole a paper from madam — the certificate of her marriage with Mr. Mortimer-Darke, or Darke-Mortimer. The object of Swartz was, to sell the paper to me for a large sum, as he had gotten an inkling of the state of affairs, and my relation with madam. Well, Nighthawk reported this immediately, made an appointment to meet Swartz in the Wilderness, and many times afterward attempted to gain possession of the paper, which Swartz swore was a *bona fide* certificate of the marriage of these two persons *before the year* 1856, when I first met them.

"You, doubtless, understand now, my dear Surry, my great anxiety to gain possession of that paper. Or, if you do not, I have only to state one fact — that will explain all. I am engaged to be married to Miss Conway, and am naturally anxious to have the proof in my possession that I have not *one wife* yet living! I know *that woman* well. She will stop at nothing. The rumor that I am about to become the happy husband of a young lady whom I love, has driven madam nearly frantic, and she has already shown her willingness to stop at nothing, by imprisoning Swartz, and starving him until he produced the stolen paper. Swartz is dead, however; the paper is lost; I and madam are both in hot pursuit of the document. Which will find it, I know not. She, of course, wishes to suppress it—I wish to possess it. Where is it? If you will tell me, friend, I will make you a deed for half my estate! You have been with me to visit that strange woman, Amanda, as a forlorn hope. What will come I know not; but I trust that an all-merciful Providence will not withdraw its hand from me, and now dash all my hopes, at the very moment when the cup is raised to my lips! If so, I will accept all, submissively, as the just punishment of my great crime—a crime, I pray God to pardon me, as the result of mad desperation, and not as a wanton and wilful defiance of His Almighty authority! I have wept tears of blood for that act. I have turned and tossed on my bed, in the dark hours of night, groaning and pleading for pardon. I have bitterly expiated throughout long years, that brief tragedy. I have humbled myself in the dust before the Lord of all worlds, and, falling at the feet of the all-merciful Saviour, besought His divine compassion. I am proud—no man was ever prouder—but I have bowed my forehead to the dust, and if the Almighty now denies me the supreme consolation of this pure girl's affection,—if loving her as I do, and beloved by her, as I may venture to tell you, friend, I am to see myself thrust back from this future—then, Surry, I will give the last proof of my submission: I will bow down my head, and say 'Thy will, not mine, Lord, be done!'"

Mohun's head sank as he uttered the words. To the proud face came an expression of deep solemnity and touching sweetness. The firm lips were relaxed—the piercing eyes had become soft. Mohun was greater in his weakness than he had ever been in his strength.

When an hour afterward we had mounted our horses, and were riding back slowly through the night, I said, looking at him by the dim starlight:—

"This is no longer a gay young cavalryman—a mere thoughtless youth—but a patriot, fit to live or die with Lee!"

BOOK V
THE DEAD GO FAST

I
THE "DOOMED CITY" IN PROFILE
DECEMBER, 1864

The scenes just described took place in the month of November. In December I obtained the priceless boon of a few days' leave of absence, and paid a visit to Richmond.

There was little there of a cheerful character; all was sombre and lugubrious. In the "doomed city," as throughout the whole country, all things were going to wreck and ruin. During the summer and autumn, suffering had oppressed the whole community; but now misery clutched the very heartstrings. Society had been convulsed—now, all the landmarks of the past seemed about to disappear in the deluge. Richmond presented the appearance, and lived after the manner, of a besieged city, as General Grant called it. It no longer bore the least likeness to its former peaceful and orderly self. The military police had usurped the functions of the civil, and the change was for the worse. Garroters swarmed the streets of the city after dark. House-breakers everywhere carried on their busy occupation. Nothing was safe from these prowlers of the night; all was fish for their nets. The old clothes in rags and bales; the broken china and worn spoons; the very food, obtained through immense exertions by some father to feed his children—all became the spoil of these night-birds, who were ever on the watch. When you went to make a visit in the evening, you took your hat and cloak with you into the drawing-room, to have them under your eye. When you retired at night, you deposited your watch and purse under your pillow. At the hotels, you never thought of placing your boots outside the door; and the landlords, in the morning, carefully looked to see if the towels, or the blankets of the beds had been stolen. All things were thus unhinged. Misery had let loose upon the community all the outlaws of civilization; the scum and dregs of society had come to the top, and floated on the surface in the sunlight.

The old respectable population of the old respectable city had disappeared, it seemed. The old respectable habitudes had fallen into contempt. Gambling-houses swarmed everywhere; and the military police ignored them. "The very large number of houses," said a contemporary journal, "on Main and other streets, which have numbers painted in large gilt figures over the door, and illuminated at night, are faro banks. The fact is not known to the public. The very large numbers of flashily dressed young men, with villainous faces, who hang about the street corners in the daytime, are not gamblers, garroters, and plugs, but young men studying for the ministry, and therefore exempt from military duty. This fact is not known to General Winder." The quiet and orderly city had, in a word, become the haunt of burglars, gamblers, adventurers, blockade-runners. The city, once the resort of the most elegant society in Virginia, had been changed by war and misery into a strange chaotic caravanserai, where you looked with astonishment on the faces going and coming, without knowing in the least "who was who," or whether your acquaintance was an honest man or a scoundrel. The scoundrels dressed in excellent clothes, and smiled and bowed when you met them; it was nearly the sole means of identifying them, at an epoch, when virtue almost always went in rags.

The era of "social unrealities," to use the trenchant phrase of Daniel, had come. Even braid on sleeves and collars did not tell you much. Who was the fine-looking Colonel Blank, or the martial General Asterisks? Was he a gentleman or a barber's boy — an F.F. somewhere, or an exdrayman? The general and colonel dressed richly; lived at the "Spottswood;" scowled on the common people; and talked magnificently. It was only when some young lady linked her destiny to his, that she found herself united to quite a surprising helpmate — discovered that the general or the colonel had issued from the shambles or the gutter.

Better society was not wanting; but it remained largely in the background. Vice was strutting in cloth of gold; virtue was at home mending its rags. Every expedient was resorted to, not so much to keep up appearances as to keep the wolf from the door. Servants were sent around by high-born ladies to sell, anonymously, baskets of their clothes. The silk or velvet of old days was now parted with for bread. On the shelves of the bookstores were valuable private libraries, placed there for sale. In the shops of the silversmiths were seen breastpins, watches, bracelets, pearl and diamond necklaces, which their owners were obliged to part with for bread. "Could we have traced," says a late writer, "the history of a set of pearls, we should have been told of a fair bride, who had received them from a proud and happy bridegroom; but whose life had been blighted in her youthful happiness by the cruel blast of war—whose young husband was in the service of his country—to whom stark poverty had continued to come, until at last the wedding present from the dear one, went to purchase food and raiment... A richly bound volume of poems, with here and there a faint pencil-marked quotation, told perchance of a lover perished on some bloody field; and the precious token was disposed of, or pawned, when bread was at last needed for some suffering loved one."

You can see these poor women—can you not, reader? The bride looking at her pearl necklace, with flushed cheeks and eyes full of tears, murmuring:—"*He* gave me this—placed it around my neck on my wedding day—and I must *sell* it!" You can see too, the fair girl, bending down and dropping tears on the page marked by her dead lover; her bosom heaving, her heart breaking, her lips whispering:—"*His* hand touched this—we read this page together—I hear his voice—see his smile—this book brings back all to me—and now, I must go and sell it, to buy bread for my little sister and brother, who are starving!"

That is dolorous, is it not, reader?—and strikes you to the heart. It is not fancy. December, 1864, saw that, and more, in Virginia.

II
THE MEN WHO RUINED
THE CONFEDERACY

In the streets of Richmond, crowded with uniforms, in spite of the patrols, marching to and fro, and examining "papers," I met a number of old acquaintances, and saw numerous familiar faces.

The "Spottswood" was the resort of the *militaires*, and the moneyed people. Here, captains and colonels were elbowed by messieurs the blockade-runners, and mysterious government employees—employed, as I said on a former occasion, in heaven knows what. The officer stalked by in his braid. The "Trochilus" passed, smiling, in shiny broadcloth. Listen! yonder is the newsboy, shouting, "The *Examiner!*"—that is to say, the accurate photograph of this shifting chaos, where nothing seems stationary long enough to have its picture taken.

Among the first to squeeze my hand, with winning smiles and cordial welcome, was my friend Mr. Blocque. He was clad more richly than before; smiled more sweetly than ever; seemed more prosperous, better satisfied, firmer in his conviction than ever that the President and the administration had never committed a fault—that the world of December, 1864, was the best of all possible worlds.

"My dear colonel!" exclaimed Mr. Pangloss-Trochilus, *alias* Mr. Blocque, "delighted to see you, I assure you! You are well? You will dine with me, to-day? At five precisely? You will find the old company—jolly companions, every one! We meet and talk of the affairs of the country. All is going on well, colonel. Our city is quiet and orderly. The government sees farther than its assailants. It can not explain now, and set itself right in the eyes of the people—that would reveal military secrets to the enemy, you know. I tell my friends in the departments not to mind their assailants. Washington himself was maligned, but he preserved a dignified silence. All is well, colonel! I give you my word, we are all right! I know a thing or two—!" and Mr. Blocque looked mysterious. "I have friends in high quarters, and you can rely on my statement. Lee is going to whip Grant. The people are rallying to the flag. The finances are improving. The resources of the country are untouched. A little patience—only a *very* little patience! I tell my friends. Let us only endure trials and hardships with brave hearts. Let us not murmur at dry bread, colonel—let us cheerfully dress in rags—let us deny ourselves every thing, sacrifice every thing to the cause, cast away all superfluities, shoulder our muskets, and fight to the death! Then there *can* be no doubt of the result, colonel—good morning!"

And Mr. Blocque shook my hand cordially, gliding away in his shiny broadcloth, at the moment when Mr. Croker, catching my eye in passing, stopped to speak to me.

"You visit Richmond at an inauspicious moment, colonel," said Mr. Croker, jingling his watch-seals with dignity. "The country has at last reached a point from which ruin is apparent in no very distant perspective, and when the hearts of the most resolute, in view of the depressing influences of the situation, are well nigh tempted to surrender every anticipation of ultimate success in the great cause which absorbs the energies of the entire country—hem!—at large. The cause of every trouble is so plain, that it would be insulting your good judgment to dwell upon the explanation. The administration has persistently disregarded the wishes of the people, and the best interests of the entire community; and we have at last reached a point where to stand still is as ruinous as to go on—as we are going—to certain destruction and annihilation. Look at the finances, entirely destroyed by the bungling and injudicious course of the honorable Mr. Memminger, who has proceeded upon fallacies which the youngest tyro would disdain to refute. Look at the quartermaster's department,—the commissary department,—the State department, and the war department, and you will everywhere find the proofs of utter incompetence, leading straight, as I have before remarked, to that ruin which is pending at the present moment over the country. Our society is uprooted, and there is no hope for the country. Blockade-runners, forestallers, stragglers from the army—Good morning, Colonel Desperade; I was just speaking to our friend, Colonel Surry."

And leaving me in the hands of the tall, smiling, and imposing Colonel Desperade, who was clad in a magnificent uniform, Mr. Croker, forestaller and extortioner, continued his way with dignity toward his counting house.

"This is a very great pleasure, colonel!" exclaimed Colonel Desperade, squeezing my hand with ardor. "Just from the lines, colonel? Any news? We are still keeping Grant off! He will find himself checkmated by our boys in gray! The country was never in better trim for a good hard fight. The immortal Lee is in fine spirits—the government steadily at work—and do you know, my dear Colonel, I am in luck to-day? I am certain to receive my appointment at last, as brigadier-general—"

"Look out, or you'll be mistaken!" said a sarcastic voice behind us. And Mr. Torpedo, smoking a short and fiery cigar, stalked up and shook hands with me.

"Desperade depends on the war department, and is a ninny for doing so!" said Mr. Torpedo, member of Congress. "The man that depends on Jeff Davis, or his war secretary, is a double-distilled dolt. Jeff thinks he's a soldier, and apes Napoleon. But you can't depend on him, Desperade. Look at Johnston! He fooled *him*. Look at Beauregard—he envies and fears *him*, so he keeps him down. Don't depend on the President, Desperade, or you'll be a fool, my friend!"

And Mr. Torpedo walked on, puffing away at the fiery stump of his cigar, and muttering curses against President Davis.

An hour afterward, I was conversing in the rotunda of the capítol, with the high-bred and smiling old cavalier, Judge Conway, and he was saying to me:—

"The times are dark, colonel, I acknowledge that. But all would be well, if we could eradicate abuses and bring out our strength. A fatality, however, seems pursuing us. The blockade-runners drain the country of the little gold which is left in it; the forestallers run up prices, and debase the currency beyond hope; the able-bodied and healthy men who ought to be in the army, swarm in the streets; and the bitter foes of the President poison the public mind, and infuse into it despair. It is this, colonel, not our weakness, which is going to ruin us, if we are ruined!"

III

MY LAST VISIT TO JOHN M. DANIEL

On the night before my return to the army, I paid my last visit to John M. Daniel.

Shall I show you a great career, shipwrecked — paint a mighty ship run upon the breakers? The current of our narrative drags us toward passionate and tragic events, but toward few scenes more sombre than that which I witnessed on this night in December, 1864.

I found John M. Daniel in his house on Broad Street, as before; perched still in his high chair of black horse-hair, all alone. His face was thinner; his cheeks more sallow, and now haggard and sunken; his eyes sparkling with gloomy fire, as he half reclined beneath the cluster of globe lamps, depending from the ceiling, and filling the whole apartment with their brilliant light — one of his weaknesses.

He received me with grim cordiality, offered me a cigar, and said: —

"I am glad to see you, colonel, and to offer you one of the last of my stock of Havanas. Wilmington is going soon — then good-bye to blockade goods."

"You believe Wilmington is going to fall, then?"

"As surely as Savannah."

"Savannah! You think that? We are more hopeful at Petersburg."

"Hopeful or not, colonel, I am certain of what I say. Remember my prediction when it is fulfilled. The Yankees are a theatrical people. They take Vicksburg, and win Gettysburg, on their 'great national anniversary;' and now they are going to present themselves with a handsome 'Christmas gift' — that is the city of Savannah."

He spoke with evident difficulty, and his laboring voice, like his haggard cheeks, showed that he had been ill since I last saw him.

"Savannah captured, or surrendered!" I said, with knit brows. "What will be the result of that?"

"Ruin," was the curt response.

"Not the loss of a mere town?"

"No; the place itself is nothing. For Sherman to take it will not benefit him much; but it will prove to the country, and the President, that he is irresistible. Then they will *hack*; and you will see the beginning of the end."

"That is a gloomy view enough."

"Yes — every thing is gloomy now. The devil of high-headed obstinacy and incompetence rules affairs. I do not croak in the *Examiner* newspaper. But we are going straight to the devil."

As he uttered these words, he placed his hand upon his breast, and closed his eyes, as though he were going to faint.

"What is the matter?" I exclaimed, rising abruptly, and approaching him.

"Nothing!" he replied, in a weak voice; "don't disturb yourself about me. These fits of faintness come on, now and then, in consequence of an attack of pneumonia which I had lately. Sit down, colonel. You must really pardon me for saying it, but you make me nervous."

There was nothing in the tone of this singular address to take offence at, — the voice of the speaker was perfectly courteous, — and I resumed my seat.

"We were talking about Sherman," he said. "They call him Gog, Magog, anti-Christ, I know not what, in the clerical circles of this city!"

His lip curled as he spoke.

"One reverend divine publicly declared the other day, that 'God had put a hook in Sherman's nose, and was leading him to his destruction!' I don't think it looks much like it!"

The speaker was stopped by a fit of coughing, and when it had subsided, leaned back, faint and exhausted, in his chair.

"The fact is — Sherman — " he said, with difficulty, "seems to have — the hook in — *our* nose!"

There was something grim and lugubrious in the smile which accompanied the painfully uttered words. A long silence followed them, which was broken by neither of us. At last I raised my head, and said: —

"I find you less hopeful than last summer. At that time you were in good spirits, and the tone of the *Examiner* was buoyant."

"It is hopeful still," he replied, "but by an effort — from a sentiment of duty. I often write far more cheerfully than I feel, colonel."[1]

{Footnote 1: His words.}

"Your views have changed, I perceive—but you change with the whole country."

"Yes. A whole century has passed since last August, when you visited me here. One by one, we have lost all that the country could depend on—hope goes last. For myself, I began to doubt when Jackson fell at Chancellorsville, and I have been doubting, more or less, ever since. He was *a dominant man*, colonel, fit, *if any thing happened*, to rise to the head of affairs.{1} Oh! for an hour of Jackson! Oh! for a day of our dead Dundee!"{2}

{Footnote 1: His words.}

{Footnote 2: His words.}

The face of the speaker glowed, and I shall never forget the flash of his dark eye, as he uttered the words, "if any thing happened." There was a whole volume of menace to President Davis in those words.

"But this is useless!" he went on; "Jackson is dead, and there is none to take his place. So, without leaders, with every sort of incompetence, with obstinacy and stupidity directing the public councils, and shaping the acts of the administration, we are gliding straight into the gulf of destruction."

I could make no reply. The words of this singular man and profound thinker, affected me dolefully.

"Yes, colonel," he went on, "the three or four months which have passed since your last visit, have cleared away all mists from *my* eyes at least, and put an end to all my dreams—among others, to that project which I spoke of—the purchase and restoration of the family estate of Stafford. It will never be restored by me. Like Randolph, I am the last of my line."

And with eyes full of a profound melancholy, the speaker gazed into the fire.

"I am passing away with the country," he added. "The cause is going to fail. I give it three months to end in, and have sent for a prominent senator, who may be able to do something. I intend to say to him, 'The time has come to make the best terms possible with the enemy,' and I shall place the columns of the *Examiner* newspaper at his disposal to advocate that policy."{1}

{Footnote 1: This, I learned afterward, from the Hon. Mr. — —-, was duly done by Mr. Daniel. But it was too late.}

"Is it possible!" I said. "Frankly, I do not think things are so desperate."

"You are a soldier, and hopeful, colonel. The smoke blinds you."

"And yet General Lee is said to repudiate negotiations with scorn. He is said to have lately replied to a gentleman who advised them, 'For myself, I intend to die sword in hand!'"

"General Lee is a soldier—and you know what the song says: 'A soldier's business, boys, is to die!'"

I could find no reply to the grim words.

"I tell you the cause is lost, colonel!" with feverish energy, "lost irremediably, at this moment while we are speaking! It is lost from causes which are enough to make the devil laugh, but it is lost all the same! When the day of surrender, and Yankee domination comes—when the gentlemen of the South are placed under the heel of negroes and Yankees—I, for one, wish to die. Happy is the man who shall have gotten into the grave before that day!{1} Blessed will be the woman who has never given suck!{2} Yes, the best thing for me is to die—{3} and I am going to do so. I shall not see that *Dies Irae*! I shall be in my grave!"

{Footnote 1: His words.}

{Footnote 2: His words.}

{Footnote 3: His words.}

And breathing heavily, the journalist again leaned back in his chair, as though about to faint.

An hour afterward, I terminated my visit, and went out, oppressed and gloomy.

This singular man had made a reluctant convert of me to his own dark views. The cloud which wrapped him, now darkened me—from the black future I saw the lightnings dart already.

His predictions were destined to have a very remarkable fulfilment.

On the 21st of December, a few days after our interview, Sherman telegraphed to Lincoln:—

"I beg to present you, as a Christmas gift, the city of Savannah, with one hundred and fifty guns, and plenty of ammunition, and also about twenty-five thousand bales of cotton."

In January, Wilmington fell.

Toward the end of the same month, John M. Daniel was a second time seized with pneumonia, and took to his bed, from which he was never again to rise. He would see no one but his physician and a few chosen friends. All other persons were persistently denied admittance to his chamber. Lingering throughout the remainder of the winter, as spring approached, life seemed gradually leaving him. Day by day his pulse grew weaker. You would have said that this man was slowly dying with the cause for which he had fought; that as the life-blood oozed, drop by drop, from the bleeding bosom of the Southern Confederacy, the last pulses of John M. Daniel kept time to the pattering drops.

One morning, at the end of March, his physician came to see him, and found him lying on the outer edge of his bed. Not wishing to disturb him, the physician went to the window to mix a stimulant. All at once a noise attracted his attention, and he turned round. The dying man had, by a great effort, turned completely over, and lay on his back in the middle of the bed, with his eyes closed, and his arms folded on his breast, as though he were praying.

When the physician came to his bedside, he was dead.

It was four days before the fall of Petersburg and Richmond; and he was buried in Hollywood, just in time to escape the tramp of Federal feet around his coffin.

His prophecy and wish were thus fulfilled.{1}

{Footnote 1: These details are strictly accurate.}

IV
GARROTED

When I left Mr. John M. Daniel it was past ten at night, and designing to set out early in the morning for Petersburg, I bent my steps toward home.

The night was not however to pass without adventures of another character.

I was going along Governor Street, picking my way by the light of the few gas-lamps set far apart and burning dimly, when all at once I heard a cry in front, succeeded by the noise of a scuffle, and then by a heavy fall.

Hastening forward I reached the spot, which was not far from the City Hall; and a glance told me all.

A wayfarer had been garroted; that is to say, suddenly attacked while passing along, by one of the night-birds who then infested the streets after dark; seized from behind; throttled, and thrown violently to the ground — the object of the assailant being robbery.

When I reached the spot the robber was still struggling with his victim, who, stretched beneath him on the ground, uttered frightful cries. One hand of the garroter was on his throat, the other was busily rifling his pockets.

I came up just in time to prevent a murder, but not to disappoint the robber. As I appeared he hastily rose, releasing the throat of the unfortunate citizen. I saw a watch gleam in his hand; he bestowed a violent kick on his prostrate victim; — then he disappeared running, and was in an instant lost in the darkness.

I saw that pursuit would be useless; and nobody ever thought, at that period, of attempting to summon the police. I turned to assist the victim, who all at once rose from the ground, uttering groans and cries.

The lamp-light shone upon his face. It was the worthy Mr. Blocque — Mr. Blocque, emitting howls of anguish! Mr. Blocque, shaking his clenched hands, and maligning all created things! Mr. Blocque, devoting, with loud curses and imprecations, the assembled wisdom of the "city fathers," and the entire police force of the Confederate capital, to the infernal deities!

"I am robbed—murdered!" screamed the little Jewish-looking personage, in a shrill falsetto which resembled the shriek of a furious old woman, "robbed! rifled!—stripped of every thing!—garroted!—my money taken!—I had ten thousand dollars in gold and greenbacks on my person!—not a Confederate note in the whole pack—not one! gold and greenbacks!—two watches!—-I am ruined! I will expose the police! I was going to my house like a quiet citizen! I was harming nobody! and I am to be set on and robbed of my honest earnings by a highwayman—choked, strangled, knocked down, my pockets picked, my money taken—and this in the capital of the Confederacy, under the nose of the police!"

It was a shrill squeak which I heard—something unutterably ludicrous. I could scarce forbear laughing, as I looked at the little blockade-runner, with disordered hair, dirty face, torn clothes, and bleeding nose, uttering curses, and moaning in agony over the loss of his "honest earnings!"

I consoled him in the best manner I could, and asked him if he had lost every thing. That question seemed to arouse him. He felt hastily in his pockets,—and then at the result my eyes opened wide. Thrusting his hand into a secret pocket, he drew forth an enormous roll of greenbacks, and I could see the figures "100" on each of the notes as he ran over them. That bundle alone must have contained several thousands of dollars. But the worthy Mr. Blocque did not seem in the least consoled.

"He got *the other bundle!*" shrieked the victim, still in his wild falsetto; "it was ten thousand dollars—I had just received it this evening—I am robbed!—they are going to murder me!—Where is the police!—murder!"

I laid my hand upon his arm.

"You have lost a very considerable sum," I said, "but—you may lose more still."

And I pointed to the roll of bank notes in his hand, with a significant glance. At these words he started.

"You are right, colonel!" he said, hastily; "I may be attacked again! I may be robbed of all—they may finish me! I will get home as quickly as I can! Thank you, colonel! you have saved me from robbery and murder! Come and see me, colonel. Come and dine with me, my dear sir! At five, precisely!"

And Mr. Blocque commenced running wildly toward a place of safety.

In a moment he had disappeared, and I found myself alone—laughing heartily.

V
THE CLOAKED WOMAN

"Well," I said, as I walked on, "this is a charming adventure and conveys a tolerably good idea of the city of Richmond, after dark, in the year 1864. Our friend Blocque is garroted, and robbed of his 'honest earnings,' at one fell swoop by a footpad! The worthy citizen is waylaid; his pockets rifled; his life desolated. All the proceeds of a life of virtuous industry have disappeared. Terrible condition of things! — awful times when a good citizen can not go home to his modest supper of canvas-backs and champagne, without being robbed by — —his brother robber!"

Indulging in these reflections, not unaccompanied with smiles, I continued my way, with little fear, myself, of pickpockets or garroters. Those gentry were intelligent. They were never known to attack people with gray coats — they knew better! They attacked the black coats, in the pockets of which they suspected the presence of greenbacks and valuable papers; never the gray coats, where they would find only a frayed "leave of absence" for their pains!

I thus banished the whole affair from my mind; but it had aroused and excited me. I did not feel at all sleepy; and finding, by a glance at my watch beneath a lamp, that it was only half past ten, I resolved to go and ask after the health of my friend, Mr. X— —-, whose house was only a square or two off.

This resolution I proceeded at once to carry out. A short walk brought me to the house, half buried in its shrubbery; but as I approached I saw a carriage was standing before the house.

Should I make my visit then, or postpone it? Mr. X— —- evidently had company. Or had the carriage brought a visitor to some other member of the household? Mr. X——- was only a boarder, and I might be mistaken in supposing that *he* was engaged at the moment.

As these thoughts passed through my mind, I approached the gate in the iron railing. The carriage was half hidden by the shadow of the elms, which grew in a row along the sidewalk. On the box sat a motionless figure. The vehicle and driver were as still and silent as if carved out of ebony.

"Decidedly I will discover," I said, and opening the gate I turned into the winding path through the shrubbery, which led toward the rear of the house; that is to say, toward the private entrance to the room of Mr. X——-.

Suddenly, as I passed through the shadowy shrubs, I felt a hand on my shoulder. I started back, and unconsciously felt for some weapon.

"Don't shoot me, colonel!" said a voice in the darkness, "I am a friend."

I recognized the voice of Nighthawk.

"Good heavens! my dear Nighthawk," I said, drawing a long breath of relief, "you are enough to make Alonzo the Brave, himself, tremble? You turn up everywhere, and especially in the dark! What are you doing here?"

"I am watching, colonel," said Nighthawk, with benignant sweetness.

"Watching?"

"And waiting."

"Waiting for whom?"

"For a lady with whom you have the honor of being acquainted."

"A lady—?"

"That one you last saw in the lonely house near Monk's Neck. Hush! here she comes."

His voice had sunk to a whisper, and he drew me into the shrubbery, as a long bar of light, issuing from the door in the rear of the house, ran out into the night.

"I am going to follow her," whispered Nighthawk, placing his lips close to my ear, "she is at her devil's work here in Richmond, as Swartz was—."

Suddenly he was silent; a light step was heard. A form approached us, passed by. I could see that it was a woman, wrapped from head to foot in a gray cloak.

She passed so close to us that the skirt of her cloak nearly brushed our persons, and disappeared toward the gate. The iron latch was heard to click, the door of the carriage to open and close, and then the vehicle began to move.

Nighthawk took two quick steps in the direction of the gate.

"I am going to follow the carriage, colonel," he whispered. "I have been waiting here to do so. I will tell you more another time. Give my respects to General Mohun, and tell him I am on his business!"

With which words Nighthawk glided into the darkness—passed through the gate without sound from the latch—and running noiselessly, disappeared on the track of the carriage.

I gazed after him for a moment, said to myself, "well this night is to be full of incident!"—and going straight to the door in the rear of the house, passed through it, went to the door of Mr. X— —-'s room, and knocked.

"Come in," said the voice of that gentleman; and opening the door I entered.

VI
THE HEART OF A STATESMAN

Mr. X——- was seated in front of an excellent coal fire, in his great armchair, near a table covered with papers, and between his lips was the eternal cigar.

At sight of me he rose courteously—for he never omitted any form of politeness—and cordially shook my hand.

"I am glad to see you, colonel," he said. "Just from the army? Have a cigar."

And he extended toward me an elegant cigar-case full of Havanas, which he took from the table. I declined, informing him that I had been smoking all the evening in the sanctum of the editor of the *Examiner*.

"Ah! you have been to see Daniel," said Mr. X——-. "He is a very remarkable man. I do not approve of the course of his paper, and he has attacked me very bitterly on more than one occasion. But I bear no grudge against him. He is honest in his opinions. I admire the pluck of the man, and the splendid pith of his writings."

"My views accord with your own," I replied.

"Everybody thinks with us," said Mr. X——-, puffing at his cigar. "It is only ignoramuses who deny this man's courage and ability. I have never done injustice to Daniel—and I call that 'liberal' in myself, colonel! He has flayed me alive on three or four occasions, and it is not his fault that I am enjoying this excellent Havana."

"I read the attacks," I said.

"Were they not fearful?" said Mr. X——-, smiling tranquilly. "After reading them, I regarded myself as a moral and political monster!"

I could not forbear from laughing as the portly statesman uttered the words. He seemed to derive a species of careless enjoyment from the recollection of his "flayings."

"I expect to talk over these little affairs with Daniel hereafter," he said. "We shall have a great deal of time on our hands—in Canada."

And Mr. X— —- smiled, and went on smoking. It was the second time he had uttered that phrase—"in Canada."

I laughed now, and said:—

"You continue to regard Toronto, or Montreal, or Quebec, as your future residence?"

"Yes; I think I prefer Quebec. The view from Cape Diamond is superb; and there is something English and un-American in the whole place, which I like. The Plains of Abraham bring back the history of the past,—which is more agreeable to me at least than the history of the present."

"You adhere more than ever, I see, to your opinion that we are going to fail?"

"It is not an opinion, my dear colonel, but a certainty."

My head sank. In the army I had been hopeful. When I came to Richmond, those high intelligences, John M. Daniel and Mr. X— —-, did not even attempt to conceal their gloomy views.

"I see you think me a croaker," said Mr. X— —-, tranquilly smoking, "and doubtless say to yourself, colonel, that I am injudicious in thus discouraging a soldier, who is fighting for this cause. A year ago I would not have spoken to you thus, for a year ago there was still some hope. Now, to discourage you—if thinking men, fighting for a principle, like yourself, *could* be discouraged—would result in no injury: for the cause is lost. On the contrary, as the friend of that most excellent gentleman, your father, I regard it as a sort of duty to speak thus—to say to you 'Don't throw away your life for nothing. Do your duty, but do no more than your duty, for we are doomed.'"

I could find no reply to these gloomy words.

"The case is past praying for," said Mr. X— —- composedly, "the whole fabric of the Confederacy at this moment is a mere shell. It is going to crumble in the spring, and another flag will float over the Virginia capitol yonder—what you soldiers call 'The Gridiron.' The country is tired. The administration is unpopular, and the departments are mismanaged. I am candid, you see. The days of the Confederacy are numbered, and worse than all, nobody knows it. We ought to negotiate for the best terms, but the man who advises that, will be hissed at and called a 'coward.' It is an invidious thing to do. It is much grander to shout 'Death sooner than surrender!' I shouted that lustily as long as there was any hope—now, I think it my duty as a statesman, and public functionary, to say, 'There are worse things than death—let us try and avoid them by making terms.' I say that to you—I do not say so on the streets—the people would tear me to pieces, and with their sources of information they would be right in doing so."

"Is it possible that all is lost? That negotiations are our only hope?"

"Yes; and confidentially speaking—this is a State secret, my dear colonel—these will soon be made."

"Indeed!"

"You think that impossible, but it is the impossible which invariably takes place in this world. We are going to send commissioners to meet Mr. Lincoln in Hampton Roads—and it will be useless."

"Why?"

"We are going to demand such terms as he will not agree to. The commissioners will return. The war will continue to its legitimate military end, which I fix about the last days of March."

"Good heaven! so soon!"

"Yes."

"In three months?"

Mr. X— —- nodded.

"General Lee may lengthen the term a little by his skill and courage, but it is not in *his* power, even, to resist beyond the month of April."

"The army of Northern Virginia, driven by the enemy!"

"Forced to surrender, or annihilated; and in Virginia—it will never join Johnston. Its numbers are too small to cut a path through the enemy. Grant will be at the Southside road before the first of April; Lee will evacuate his lines, which he will be compelled to hold to the last moment; he will retreat; be intercepted; be hunted down toward Lynchburg, and either surrender, or be butchered. Cheerful, isn't it?"

"It is frightful!"

"Yes, Lee's men are starving now. The country is tired of the war, and disgusted with the manner in which we manage things. No recruits are arriving. The troops are not *deserting*, but they are leaving the army without permission, to succor their starving families. Lee's last hours are approaching, and we are playing the comedy here in Richmond with an immense appearance of reality; dancing, and fiddling, and laughing on the surface of the volcano. I play my part among the rest. I risk my head more even, perhaps, than the military leaders. I take a philosophic view, however, of the present and future. If I am not hung, I will go to Canada; meanwhile, I smoke my cigar, colonel."

And Mr. X— —- lazily threw away his stump, and lit a fresh Havana. It is impossible to imagine any thing more careless than his attitude. This man was either very brave or frightfully apathetic.

Five minutes afterward, I knew that any thing but apathy possessed him. All at once he rose in his chair, and his eyes were fixed upon me with a glance so piercing and melancholy, that they dwell still in my memory, and will always dwell there.

"I said we were playing a comedy here in Richmond, colonel," he said, in tones so deep and solemn that they made me start; "I am playing my part with the rest; I play it in public, and even in private, as before you to-night. I sit here, indolently smoking and uttering my jests and platitudes, and, at the moment that I am speaking, my heart is breaking! I am a Virginian—I love this soil more than all the rest of the world—not a foot but is dear and sacred, and a vulgar horde are about to trample it under foot, and enslave its people. Every pulse of my being throbs with agony at the thought! I can not sleep. I have lost all taste for food. One thought alone haunts me—that the land of Washington, Jefferson, Mason, Henry, and Randolph, is to become the helpless prey of the scum of Europe and the North! My family has lived here for more than two hundred years. I have been, and am to-day, proud beyond words, of my birthright! I am a Virginian! a Virginian of Virginians! I have for forty years had no thought but the honor of Virginia. I have fought for her, and her only, in the senate and cabinet of the old government at Washington. I have dedicated all my powers to her—shrunk from nothing in my path—given my days and nights for years, and was willing to pour out my blood for Virginia; and now she is about to be trampled upon, her great statues hurled down, her escutcheon blotted, her altars overturned! And I, who have had no thought but her honor and glory, am to be driven, at the end of a long career, to a foreign land! I am to crouch yonder in Canada, with my bursting brow in my two hands—and every newspaper is to tell me 'the negro and the bayonet rule Virginia!' Can you wonder, then, that I am gloomy—that despair lies under all this jesting? *You* are happy. You go yonder, where a bullet may end you. Would to God that I had entered the army, old as I am, and that at least I could hope for a death of honor, in arms for Virginia!"

VII
SECRET SERVICE

The statesman leaned back in his great chair, and was silent. At the same moment a tap was heard at the door; it opened noiselessly, and Nighthawk glided into the apartment.

Under his cloak I saw the gray uniform of a Confederate soldier; in his hand he carried a letter.

Nighthawk saluted Mr. X— —- and myself with benignant respect. His quick eye, however, had caught the gloomy and agitated expression of the statesman's countenance, and he was silent.

"Well," said Mr. X— —-, raising his head, with a deep sigh. Then passing his hand over his face, he seemed to brush away all emotion. When he again looked up, his face was as calm and unmoved as at the commencement of our interview.

"You see I begin a new scene in this comedy," he said to me in a low tone.

And turning to Nighthawk, he said:—

"Well, you followed that agreeable person?"

"Yes, sir," said Nighthawk, with great respect.

"She turned out to be the character you supposed? Speak before Colonel Surry."

Nighthawk bowed.

"I never had any doubt of her character, sir," he said. "You will remember that she called on you a week ago, announcing that she was a spy, who had lately visited the Federal lines and Washington. You described her to me, and informed me that you had given her another appointment for to-night; when I assured you that I knew her; she was an enemy, who had come as a spy upon *us*; and you directed me to be here to-night, and follow her, after your interview."

"Well," said Mr. X— —-, quietly, "you followed her!"

"Yes, sir. On leaving you, after making her pretended report of affairs in Washington, she got into her carriage, and the driver started rapidly, going up Capitol and Grace streets. I followed on foot, and had to run — but I am used to that, sir. The carriage stopped at a house in the upper part of the city — a Mr. Blocque's; the lady got out, telling the driver to wait, and went into the house, where she staid for about half an hour. She then came out — I was in the shadow of a tree, not ten yards from the spot, and as she got into the carriage, I could see that she held in her hand a letter. As the driver closed the door, she said, 'Take me to the flag-of-truce bureau, on Ninth Street, next door to the war office.' The driver mounted his box, and set off — and crossing the street, I commenced running to get a-head. In this I succeeded, and reached the bureau five minutes before the carriage.

"Well, sir, I hastened up stairs, and went into the bureau, where three or four clerks were examining the letters left to be sent by the flag-of-truce boat to-morrow. They were laughing and jesting as they read aloud the odd letters from the Libby and other prisons — some of which, I assure you, were very amusing, sir — when the lady's footsteps were heard upon the stairs, and she came in, smiling.

"I had turned my back, having given some excuse for my presence to one of the clerks, who is an acquaintance. Thus the lady, who knows me, could not see my face; but I could, by looking out of the corners of my eyes, see *her*. She came in, in her rich gray cloak, smiling on the clerks, and handing an open letter to one of them, said: — "'Will you oblige me by sending that to my sister in New York, by the flag-of-truce boat, to-morrow, sir?'

"'If there is nothing contraband in it, madam,' said the clerk.

"'Oh!' she replied, with a laugh, 'it is only on family matters. My sister is a Southerner, and so am I, sir. You can read the letter; it is not very dangerous!'

"And she smiled so sweetly that the clerk was almost ashamed to read the letter. He, however, glanced his eye over it, and evidently found nothing wrong in it. While he was doing so, the lady walked toward the mail-bags in which the clerks had been placing such letters as they found unobjectionable, the others being marked, 'Condemned,' and thrown into a basket. As she passed near one of the bags, I saw the lady, whom I was closely watching, flirt her cloak, as though by accident, across the mouth of one of the mail-bags, and at the same instant her hand stole down and dropped a letter into the bag. As she did so, the clerk, who had finished reading *the other letter*, bowed, and said: — -

"'There is nothing objectionable in this, madam, and it will be sent, of course.'

"'I was sure of that, sir,' replied the lady, with a smile. 'I am very much obliged. Good evening, sir!'

"And she sailed out, all the clerks politely rising as she did so.

"No sooner had the door closed than I darted upon the bag in which I had seen her drop the letter. The clerks wished to stop me, but I informed them of what I had seen. If they doubted, they could see for themselves that the letter, which I had easily found, was not sealed with the seal of the bureau. They looked at it, and at once acknowledged their error.

"'Arrest her!' exclaimed one of them, suddenly. The rapid rolling of a carriage came like an echo to his words.

"'It is useless, gentlemen,' I said. 'I know where to find the lady, and will look to the whole affair. You know I am in the secret service, and will be personally responsible for every thing. I will take this letter to the official who directed me to watch the lady who brought it.'

"To this, no objection was made, as I am known at the office. I came away; returned as quickly as possible; and here is the letter, sir."

With which words Nighthawk drew his hand from under his cloak, and presented the letter to Mr. X——-, who had listened in silence to his narrative.

VIII
BY FLAG-OF-TRUCE BOAT

MR. X— —- took the letter, broke the seal, and ran his eye over the contents.

"Decidedly, that woman is a skilful person," he said; "she fishes in troubled waters with the coolness of an experienced hand."

And presenting the letter to me, the statesman said: —

"Would you like to see a specimen of the sort of documents which go on file in the departments, colonel?"

I took the letter, and read the following words: —

"RICHMOND, 18 *Dec'r*, 1864.

"Tell, *you know who*, that I have just seen the honorable Mr. — —-" (here the writer gave the real name and official position of Mr. X— —-), "and have had a long conversation with him. He is fully convinced that I am a good Confederate, and spoke without reserve of matters the most private. He is in high spirits, and looks on the rebel cause as certain to succeed. I never saw one more blinded to the real state of things. Richmond is full of misery, and the people seem in despair, but this high official, who represents the whole government, is evidently certain of Lee's success. I found him in a garrulous mood, and he did not conceal his views. The government has just received heavy supplies from the south, by the Danville railroad — others are coming — the whole country in rear of Sherman is rising — and Lee, he stated, would soon be re-enforced by between fifty and seventy-five thousand men. What was more important still, was a dispatch, which he read me, from England. This startled me. There seems no doubt that England is about to recognize the Confederacy. When he had finished reading this dispatch, on the back of which I could see the English postmark, he said to me — these are his words: — 'You see, things were never brighter; it is only a question of time; and by holding out a little longer, we shall compel the enemy to retire and give up the contest. With the re-enforcements coming, Lee will have about one hundred thousand men. With that force, he will be able to repulse all General Grant's assaults. Things look dark at this moment, but the cause was never more hopeful.'

"He seemed insane, but I give you his words. It is certain that these are the views of the government, and that our authorities are much mistaken in supposing the Confederacy at its last gasp. It is impossible that the honorable Mr. — —- was attempting to deceive me; because I carried him a letter from — —-" (here the writer gave the name of a prominent official of the Confederate Government, which I suppress) "who vouched for me, and declared that I was passionately Southern in my sympathies.

"I shall see the honorable Mr. — —- in a day or two again. In the mean while, I am staying, *incognita*, at the house of our friend, Mr. Blocque, who has afforded me every facility in return for the *safeguard* I brought him, to protect his property when we occupy Richmond. The city is in a terrible state. Mr. Blocque has just come in, and informs me that he has been garroted near the capitol, and robbed of ten thousand dollars in good money. He is in despair.

"As soon as I have finished some important private business, which keeps me in the Confederate lines, I shall be with — —- again. Tell him to be in good spirits. This city has still a great deal of money hoarded in garrets — and we shall soon be here. Then we can retire on a competence — and when *Fonthill* is confiscated, we will purchase it, and live in affluence.

"LUCRETIA"

I looked at the back of the letter. It was directed to a lady in Suffolk. From the letter, my glance passed to the face of Mr. X— —-. He was smiling grimly.

"A valuable document," he said, "which madam will doubtless duplicate before very long, with additional particulars. I make you a present of it, colonel, as a memorial of the war."

I thanked him, and placed the letter in my pocket. To-day I copy it, word for word.

Mr. X— —- reflected a moment; then he said to Nighthawk: —

"Arrest this woman; I am tired of her. I have no time to waste upon such persons, however charming."

Nighthawk looked greatly delighted.

"I was going to beg that order of you, sir," he said, "as the 'private business' alluded to in the letter, concerns a friend of mine, greatly."

"Ah! well, here is the order."

And taking a pen, Mr. X— —- scrawled two lines, which he handed to Nighthawk. A glow of satisfaction came to that worthy's face, and taking the paper, he carefully placed it in his pocket.

As he did so, the bell in the capitol square struck midnight, and I rose to take my departure.

"Come and see me soon again, colonel," said Mr. X— —-, going to the door with me. He had made a sign to Nighthawk, who rose to go out with me, that he wished him to remain.

"What I have said to you, to-night," continued the statesman, gravely, "may have been injudicious, colonel. I am not certain of that—but I am quite sure that to have it repeated at this time would be inconvenient. Be discreet, therefore, my dear friend—after the war, tell or write what you fancy; and I should rather have my present views known then, than not known. They are those neither of a time-server, a faint heart, or a fool. I stand like the Roman sentinel at the gate of Herculaneum, awaiting the lava flood that will bury me. I see it coming—I hear the roar—I know destruction is rushing on me—but I am a sentinel on post; I stand where I have been posted; it is God and my conscience that have placed me on duty here. I will stay, whatever comes, until I am relieved by the same authority which posted me." And with the bow of a nobleman, the gray-haired statesman bade me farewell.

I returned to my lodgings, buried in thought, pondering deeply on the strange scenes of this night of December.

On the next morning I set out, and rejoined the army at Petersburg.

I, too, was a sentinel on post, like the statesman. And I determined to remain on duty to the last.

IX
TO AND FRO IN THE SPRING OF '65

The months of January and February, 1865, dragged on, sombre and dreary.

Two or three expeditions which I made during that woeful period, gave me a good idea of the condition of the country.

In September, 1864, I had traversed Virginia from Petersburg to Winchester, and had found the people — especially those of the lower Shenandoah Valley — still hopeful, brave, resolved to resist to the death.

In January and February, 1865, my official duties carried me to the region around Staunton; to the mountains west of Lynchburg; and to the North Carolina border, south of Petersburg. All had changed. Everywhere I found the people looking blank, hopeless, and utterly discouraged. The shadow of the approaching woe seemed to have already fallen upon them.

The army was as "game" as ever — even Early's little handful, soon to be struck and dispersed by General Sheridan's ten thousand cavalry. Everywhere, the soldiers laughed in the face of death. Each seemed to feel, as did the old statesman with whom I had conversed on that night at Richmond, that he was a sentinel on post, and must stand there to the last. The lava might engulf him, but he was "posted," and must stand until relieved, by his commanding officer or death. It was the "poor private," in his ragged jacket and old shoes, as well as the officer in his braided coat, who felt thus. For those private soldiers of the army of Northern Virginia were gentlemen. *Noblesse oblige* was their motto; and they meant to die, musket in hand!

Oh, soldiers of the army, who carried those muskets in a hundred battles! — who fought with them from Manassas, in 1861, to Appomattox, in 1865 — you are the real heroes of the mighty struggle, and one comrade salutes you now, as he looked at you with admiration in old days! What I saw in those journeys was dreary enough; but however black may be the war-cloud, there is always the gleam of sunlight somewhere! We laughed now and then, reader, even in the winter of 1864-'5!

I laugh still, as I think of the brave cannoneers of the horse artillery near Staunton—and of the fearless Breathed, their commander, jesting and playing with his young bull-dog, whom he had called "Stuart" for his courage. I hear the good old songs, all about "Ashby," and the "Palmetto Tree," and the "Bonnie Blue Flag"—songs sung with joyous voices in that dreary winter, as in other days, when the star of hope shone more brightly, and the future was more promising.

At Lynchburg, where I encountered a number of old friends, songs still sweeter saluted me—from the lips of my dear companions, Major Gray and Captain Woodie. How we laughed and sang, on that winter night, at Lynchburg! Do you chant your sweet "Nora McShane" still, Gray? And you, Woodie, do you sing in your beautiful and touching tenor to-day,—

"The heart bowed down by deep despair.

To weakest hopes will cling?"

Across the years comes once more that magical strain; again I hear your voice, filled with the very soul of sadness, tell how

"Memory is the only friend

That grief can call its own!"

That seemed strangely applicable to the situation at the time. The memory of our great victories was all that was left to us; and I thought that it was the spirit of grief itself that was singing. Again I hear the notes—but "Nora McShane" breaks in—"Nora McShane," the most exquisite of all Gray's songs. Then he winds up with uproarious praise of the "Bully Lager Beer!"—and the long hours of night flit away on the wings of laughter, as birds dart onward, and are buried in the night.

Are you there still, Gray? Do you sing still, Woodie? Health and happiness, comrades! All friendly stars smile on you! Across the years and the long leagues that divide us, I salute you!

Thus, at Staunton and Lynchburg, reader, gay scenes broke the monotony. In my journey toward North Carolina, I found food also, for laughter.

I had gone to Hicksford, fifty miles south of Petersburg, to inspect the cavalry; and in riding on, I looked with curiosity on the desolation which the enemy had wrought along the Weldon railroad, when they had destroyed it in the month of December. Stations, private houses, barns, stables, all were black and charred ruins. The railroad was a spectacle. The enemy had formed line of battle close along the track; then, at the signal, this line of battle had attacked the road. The iron rails were torn from the sleepers; the latter were then piled up and fired; the rails were placed upon the blazing mass, and left there until they became red-hot in the middle, and both ends bent down—then they had been seized, broken, twisted; in a wild spirit of sport the men had borne some of the heated rails to trees near the road; twisted them three or four times around the trunks; and there, as I passed, were the unfortunate trees with their iron boa-constrictors around them— monuments of the playful humor of the blue people, months before.

Hill and Hampton had attacked and driven them back; from the dead horses, as elsewhere, rose the black vultures on flapping wings: but it is no part of my purpose, reader, to weary you with these war-pictures, or describe disagreeable scenes. It is an odd interview which I had on my return toward Petersburg that my memory recalls. It has naught to do with my narrative—but then it will not fill more than a page!

I had encountered two wagons, and, riding, ahead of them, saw a courier of army head-quarters, whose name was Ashe.

I saluted the smiling youth, in return for his own salute, and said:—

"Where have you been, Ashe?"

"To Sussex, colonel, on a foraging expedition."

"For the general?"

"And some of the staff, colonel."

Ashe smiled; we rode on together.

"How did you come to be a forager, Ashe?" I said.

"Well this was the way of it, colonel," he said. "I belonged to the old Stonewall brigade, but General Lee detailed me at the start of the war to shoe the head-quarters horses. It was old General Robert that sent me with these wagons. I was shoeing the general's gray, and had just pared the hind-hoof, when he sent for me. A man had started with the wagons, and had mired in the field right by head-quarters. So old General Robert says, says he, 'Ashe, you can get them out.' I says, 'General, I think I can, if you'll give me a canteen full of your French brandy for the boys.' He laughed at that, and I says, 'General, I have been with you three years, and if in that time you have ever seen me out of the way, I hope you will tell me so.' 'No, Ashe,' says he, 'I have not, and you shall have the brandy.' And his black fellow went into the closet and drew me a canteen full; for you see, colonel, old General Robert always keeps a demijohn full, and carries it about in his old black spring wagon, to give to the wounded soldiers—he don't drink himself. Well, I got the brandy, and set the boys to work, building a road with pine saplings, and got the wagons out! From that time to this, I have been going with them, colonel, and sometimes some very curious things have happened."

I assumed that inquiring expression of countenance dear to story-tellers. Ashe saw it, and smiled.

"Last fall, colonel," he said, "I was down on the Blackwater, foraging with my wagons, for old General Robert, when a squadron of Yankees crossed in the ferryboat, and caught me. I did not try to get off, and the colonel says, says he, 'Who are *you?*' I told him I was only foraging with General Lee's head-quarters teams, to get something for the old general to eat, as nothing could be bought in Petersburg; and, says I, 'I have long been looking to be captured, and now the time has come.' As I was talking, I saw an uncle of mine among the Yankees, and says he, 'Ashe, what are you doing here?' 'The same you are doing there,' I says; and I asked the colonel just to let me off this time, and I would try and keep out of their way hereafter. He asked me, Would I come down there any more? And I told him I didn't know — I would have to go where I was ordered. 'Well,' says he, 'you can't beg off.' But I says, 'step here a minute, colonel,' and I took him to the wagon, and offered him my canteen of brandy. He took three or four good drinks, and then he says, says he, 'That's all I want! You can go on with your wagons.' And I tell you I put out quick, colonel, and never looked behind me till I got back to Petersburg?"[1]

{Footnote 1: In the words of the narrator.}

I have attempted to recall here, reader, the few gleams of sunshine, the rare moments of laughter, which I enjoyed in those months of the winter of 1864-'5.

I shrink from dwelling on the events of that dreary epoch. Every day I lost some friend. One day it was the brave John Pegram, whom I had known and loved from his childhood; the next day it was some other, whose disappearance left a gap in my life which nothing thenceforth could fill. I pass over all that. Why recall more of the desolate epoch than is necessary?

For the rest that is only a momentary laugh that I have indulged in. Events draw near, at the memory of which you sigh — or even groan perhaps — to-day, when three years have passed.

For this page is written on the morning of April 8, 1868.

This day, three years ago, Lee was staggering on in sight of Appomattox.

X
AEGRI SOMNIA.
MARCH, 1865

These letters and figures arouse terrible memories — do they not, reader? You shudder as you return in thought to that epoch, provided always that you then wore the gray, and not the blue. If you wore the blue, you perhaps laugh.

The South had reached, in this month of March, one of those periods when the most hopeful can see, through the black darkness, no single ray of light. Throughout the winter, the government had made unceasing efforts to bring out the resources of the country — efforts honest and untiring, if not always judicious — but as the days, and weeks, and months wore on, it became more and more evident that the hours of the Confederacy were numbered. The project of employing negro troops, which Congress long opposed, had been adopted at last, but only in time to be too late. The peace commissioners had held their interview with Lincoln, but effected nothing. The enemy continually advanced toward the achievement of their end. Sherman had safely made his famous "march to the sea" — Savannah and Charleston had fallen — the western army was about to unite with the army of Grant at Petersburg. There the great game went on, but the end was near. Lee had attempted, late in February, to evacuate his lines, but was overruled. His army was reduced to about forty thousand, while Grant's numbered about one hundred and fifty thousand. The Confederate troops were almost naked, and had scarce food enough to sustain life. They fought still, in the trenches, along the great line of works, but it was plain, as Lee said, that the line was stretched so far, that a very little more would snap it.

That line extended from the Williamsburg road, east of Richmond to Five Forks, west of Petersburg — a distance of nearly fifty miles. Gradually Grant had pushed westward, until his grasp was now very nearly upon the Southside road. Lee had extended his own thin line to still confront him. The White Oak road, beyond the Rowanty, had been defended by heavy works. The hill above Burgess's bristled with batteries. The extreme right of the Confederate line rested in the vicinity of Five Forks. Beyond that it could not be extended. Already it began to crack. Along the works stretching from east to west, there was scarce a soldier every ten yards. Grant was only prevented from bursting through by the masterly handling of Lee's troops — the rapid concentration of masses at the points which he threatened. The cavalry was almost paralyzed. The destruction of the Weldon road southward to Hicksford, in December, had been a death-blow nearly, to that arm of the service. The Confederate cavalry had depended upon it, hauling their forage from Stony Creek Station. Now they had been compelled to go south to Hicksford, the nearest point, fifty miles from Petersburg. The consequence was that Lee's right was almost undefended by cavalry. Grant's horsemen could penetrate, almost unchecked, to the Danville and Southside railroads. The marvel was, not that this was effected at the end of March, but that it was not effected a month sooner. But I anticipate.

To glance, for an instant before proceeding, at the condition of the country. It had reached the last point of depression, and was yielding to despair. The government was enormously unpopular — mismanagement had ceased to attract attention. The press roared in vain. The *Enquirer* menaced the members of Congress from the Gulf States. The *Examiner* urged that the members of the Virginia Legislature, to be elected in the spring, should be "clothed with the state sovereignty," to act for Virginia! Thus the executive and legislative were both attacked. The people said, "Make General Lee dictator." And General — —- wrote and printed that, in such an event, he "had the dagger of Brutus" for Lee. Thus all things were in confusion. The currency was nothing but paper — it was a melancholy farce to call it money. The Confederate note was popularly regarded as worth little more than the paper upon which it was printed. Fathers of families went to market and paid hundreds of dollars for the few pounds of meat which their households required each day. Officers were forced to pay one thousand dollars for their boots. Old saddle-bags were cut up, and the hides of dead horses carried off, to manufacture into shoes. Uniform coats were no longer procurable — the government had to supply them gratis, even to field officers. Lee subsisted, like his soldiers, on a little grease and corn bread. Officers travelling on duty, carried in their saddle-pockets bits of bacon and stale bread, for the country could not supply them. In the homes of the land once overflowing with plenty, it was a question each day where food could be procured. The government had impressed every particle, except just sufficient to keep the inmates alive. What the commissaries had left, the "Yankee cavalry" took. A lady of Goochland said to a Federal officer, "General, I can understand why you destroy railroads and bridges, but why do you burn mills, and the houses over women and children?" The officer bowed, and replied, "Madam, your soldiers are so brave that we can't beat you; and we are trying to *starve you!*"

The interior of these homes of the country was a touching spectacle. The women were making every sacrifice. Delicate hands performed duties which had always fallen to menials. The servants had gone to the enemy, and aristocratic young women cooked, washed, swept, and drudged — a charming spectacle perhaps to the enemy, who hated the "aristocracy," but woeful to fathers, and sons, and brothers, when they came home sick, or wounded. Clothes had long grown shabby, and were turned and mended. Exquisite beauty was decked in rags. A faded calico was a treasure. The gray-haired gentleman, who had always worn broadcloth, was content with patched homespun. It was not of these things that they were thinking, however. Dress had not made those seigneurs and dames — nor could the want of it hide their dignity. The father, and care-worn wife, and daughter, and sister, were thinking of other things. The only son was fighting beside Lee — dying yonder, in the trenches. He was only a "poor private," clad in rags and carrying a musket — but he was the last of a long line, perhaps, of men who had built up Virginia and the Federal government which he was fighting — he was "only a private," but his blood was illustrious; more than all, he was the treasure of the gray-haired father and mother; the head of the house in the future; if he fell, the house would fall with him — and it was nearly certain that he would fall!

So they mourned, and looked fearfully to the coming hours, in town and country. In the old homesteads — poverty and despair. In the cities — wasting cares and sinking hearts. More than ever before, all the vile classes of society rioted and held sway. The forestallers and engrossers drove a busy trade. They seemed to feel that their "time was short" — that the night was coming, in which not even rascals could work! Supplies were hoarded, and doled out at famine prices to the famine-stricken community; not supplies of luxuries, but of the commonest necessaries of life. The portly extortioner did not invite custom, either. Once he had bowed and smirked behind his counter when a purchaser entered. Now, he turned his back coldly, went on reading his newspaper, scarce replied to the words addressed to him, and threw his goods on the counter with the air of one reluctantly conferring a favor. Foreboding had entered even the hearts of the forestaller and extortioner. They had sold their souls for gain, and that gain was turning to dross. As at the wave of a magician's wand, their crisp new "Confederate notes" had become rags. The biter was bit. His gains were to count for nothing. Extortioner and victim were soon to be stripped equally naked — the cold blast of ruin was to freeze both alike. Thus, all things hastened toward the inevitable catastrophe. Brave hearts did not shrink, but they saw ruin striding on. Every thing crumbled—the Confederacy was staggering and gasping in the death agony. Day by day the cause was slowly, but certainly, being lost. Children cried aloud for bread—women moaned, and knelt, and prayed. Their last hope was leaving them. Lee's army was starving and dying. Hour by hour, nearer and nearer came the roar of the gulf of destruction. A sort of stupor descended. The country— prostrate and writhing—tried to rise, but could not. The government knew not where to turn, or what course to pursue. Grant was growing in strength hourly. Lee's little force was dwindling. Sherman was streaming through South Carolina. Grant was reaching out toward Five Forks. All-destroying war grinned hideously—on all sides stared gaunt Famine. The air jarred with the thunder of cannon. The days and nights blazed, and were full of wild cries—of shouts, groans, and reverberations. The ground shook—the grave yawned—the black cloud slowly drew on; that cloud from which the thunderbolt was about to fall.

How to describe in a volume like this, now near its end, that terrible state of coma—that approaching cataclysm, in which all things, social, civil, and military were about to disappear! The whole fabric of society was going to pieces; every hour flamed with battles; tragic events jostled each other; blood gushed; a people were wailing; a victorious enemy were rushing on; the whole continent trembled; Lee was being swept away, in spite of every effort which he made to steady his feet—and that torrent was going to engulf a whole nation!

All this I am to describe in the last few pages of this volume! The task is far beyond my strength. In the future, some writer may delineate that hideous dream—to do so to-day, in this year 1868, would tear the stoutest heart.

For myself, I do not attempt it. Were I able to paint the picture, there would be no space. My memoir is nearly ended. The threads of the woof are nearly spun out, and the loom is going to stop. Death stands ready with his shears to cut the ravelled thread, knit up the seam, and put his red label on the fabric!

XI
I VISIT GENERAL FITZHUGH LEE

The end of March, 1865, was approaching when I set out on what was to prove my last tour of duty amid the pine woods of Dinwiddie.

It was a relief to be back in the army; to see brave faces and smiles around me, instead of gloomy eyes and careworn cheeks, as in the city. I passed along the Boydton road almost gayly; crossed the Rowanty at Burgess's, and went on by General Lee's powerful works covering the White Oak road, beyond. Soon I was approaching Dinwiddie Court-House, in the vicinity of which was encamped our small force of starved and broken-down cavalry.

Hampton had gone to meet Sherman, and the cavalry was commanded now by General Fitzhugh Lee, who had recovered from his severe wound received at Winchester. I was greeted by this brave soldier and accomplished gentleman as warmly as I could have desired—for "General Fitz," as we always called him at Stuart's head-quarters, was the soul of good humor and good fellowship. You have seen him, have you not, reader—whether you wore gray or blue—fighting beside him, or meeting him in battle? You recall the open and manly features, the frank and soldierly glance of the eye, the long beard and heavy mustache, almost always curling with laughter? You remember the mirthful voice, the quick jest, the tone of badinage—that joyful and brave air which said, "as long as life lasts there is hope!" You have not forgotten this gay cavalier, the brother-in-arms of Stuart; this born cavalryman, with his love of adventure, his rollicking mirth, his familiar greeting of high and low, his charming abandon and ever-ready laughter. That was the character of the *individual*—of "Fitz Lee," the good companion. The commander-in-chief has defined for all, the traits of Major-General Fitzhugh Lee. It was General R.E. Lee who wrote him in 1863, "Your admirable conduct, devotion to the cause of your country, and devotion to duty, fill me with pleasure. I hope you will soon see her efforts for independence crowned with success, and long live to enjoy the affection and gratitude of your country."

These few lines were worth fighting hard for—were they not? All things change; many things fail. Chaos or monarchy may come, but the good opinion of Lee will survive all!

I talked with General Fitz Lee for an hour nearly, recalling the old days with Stuart, who had loved and confided in him more than in any other living man. It was a beautiful friendship, indeed, and each understood the value of the other as man and soldier. Stuart is dead, and can not give his testimony; but General Fitz Lee is alive, and can give his. Here and there a voice still denies Stuart's genius as a commander. Ask his friend who survives; and if tears do not choke the voice, you will learn the real rank of Stuart!

But I can not linger on these scenes. The narrative draws on.

I mounted my horse, after shaking hands with General Fitz Lee and his brave staff, and, for the first time, remembered to ask, "Where was Tom Herbert?"

At that question, a beaming smile came to every countenance.

"Done for!" said one.

"Captured!" laughed another.

"Demoralized, subjugated, and negotiating with the enemy!" said a third.

"Well, where is the place of meeting—where are the terms being arranged?" I said.

"At a place called Disaways, on the lower Rowanty!"

"Good! I know the road there," I said.

And with a laugh, which the general and his gay cavaliers echoed, I touched my gray with the spur, and set out toward the south.

XII
BY A FIRE IN THE WOODS

I pushed on, having resolved, after finishing my duties, to visit Disaways.

Soon Dinwiddie Court-House came in sight. I entered the small village, and looked attentively — as I had done on more than one occasion before — at the locality which General Davenant's narrative had surrounded with so strange an interest. There was the old tavern, with its long portico, where Darke had held his orgies, and from which he had set forth on his errand of robbery and murder. There was the county jail, in which General Davenant had insisted upon being confined, and where so many friends had visited him. There was the old court-house, in which he had been tried for the murder of George Conway; and I fancied I could distinguish upon one of the shutters, the broken bolt which Darke had forced, more than ten years before, in order to purloin the knife with which the crime had been committed.

For some miles, that tragic story absorbed me, banishing all other reflections. That was surely the strangest of histories! — and the drama had by no means reached its denouement. Between the first and last acts "an interval of ten years is supposed to pass." There was the stage direction! Darke was still alive, active, dangerous, bent on mischief. He had an able coadjutress in his female ally. That singular woman, with whom his life was so closely connected, was in prison, it was true, but the Confederate authorities might release her; she might, at any moment, recommence her *diablerie*. Had she found that paper — or had Mohun found it? In any event, she was dangerous — more so, even, than her male companion — that worthy whom I might meet at every turn in the road — that prince of surprises and tragic "appearances!"

"Decidedly, these are curiosities, this man and this woman!" I said; "they are two bottomless pits of daring and depravity. Mohun has escaped them heretofore, but now, when the enemy seem driving us, and sweeping every thing before them, will not Darke and madam attain their vengeance, and come out winners in the struggle?"

With that reflection, I dismissed the subject, and pushed on, over the narrow and winding roads, to make my inspections.

The day was cold and brilliant; the winds cut the face; and I rode on steadily, thinking of many things. Then the desire to smoke seized upon me. General Fitzhugh Lee had given me some excellent cigars, captured from the enemy, and I looked around to find some house where I could light my cigar. None appeared; but at two hundred yards from the road, in a hidden hollow, I thought I perceived the glimmer of a fire—probably made by some straggler. I rode toward it, descended into the hollow, approached the fire, beside which crouched a figure, wrapped in an overcoat. The figure raised its head—and I recognized Nighthawk.

He rose and smiled benignantly, as he shook hands with me.

"An unexpected meeting, Nighthawk," I said, laughing. "What on earth makes you come out and camp in the woods?"

"A little fancy, colonel; you know I am eccentric. I like this way of living, from having scouted so much—but I came here with an object!"

"What?"

"To be private. I thought my fire could not be seen from the road."

"Why should it not be?"

"Well, perhaps I exaggerate danger. But I am on an important scouting expedition—wanted to reflect, and not be seen—I am going, to-night, through the lines on a little affair of which you know something."

"Ah, what do you refer to?"

"That paper," said Nighthawk, succinctly. "It is in the hands of Alibi— there is a Yankee picket at his house—but I am going to see him, and force him to surrender it."

"Is it possible he has it! Do you know that?"

"Strangely enough, colonel. Do you remember that woman, Amanda?"

"Perfectly. I visited her with Mohun."

"He told me of your visit. Well, you no doubt remember also, colonel, that he offered her a large sum to discover the paper—that she offered to try and find it, or give him a clue to its whereabouts—he was to return in ten days, and hear her report."

"Yes," I said.

"Well, he returned, colonel, but Amanda could tell him nothing— which you no doubt have heard."

"Yes, from him."

"I have been more successful, at last, in dealing with this strange woman. I do not know if she is a witch or an epileptic, or what—but she has convinced me that Alibi has the paper we want."

And Nighthawk proceeded to explain. It was an exceedingly curious explanation. Amanda had first demanded of him a statement of all the facts. He had thereupon informed her of the appointment which he had made with Swartz in Richmond, to meet him three days afterward at the house of Alibi—of his detention by the pickets, so that he had been unable to keep the appointment—Alibi's statement when he saw him, that Swartz had not been to his house—and Swartz's confinement in the lonely house, ending in his murder by Darke. That was all he knew, he said—the paper was gone—where was it?

"At Mr. Alibi's," Amanda had replied; "I only asked you this, Mr. Nighthawk, to satisfy myself that my visions were true. I *saw* poor Mr. Swartz go to Mr. Alibi's, and ask for you, on the day you appointed. When he was told that you had not come, he seemed very low-spirited, and told Mr. Alibi that he *must* see you, to give you a paper. His life was threatened, he said, on account of that paper. An officer and a lady had discovered that he had that paper—it was as much as his life was worth to keep it on his person—if Mr. Alibi would take it, and for old times' sake, put it away until *he* came back, he would pay him as much gold as he could hold in both hands. Then he gave the paper to Mr. Alibi, and went away, telling him to say nothing of it."

"I then asked her," continued Nighthawk, "where the paper could be found. She replied that Alibi always carried it on his person. That was a few days ago. I am going to-night to see him, and recover the paper."

I had listened to this narrative with strange interest. This singular woman was a curious problem. Were her *visions* really such as she described them? Or did she only "put this and that together," as the phrase is, and by her marvellous acumen, sharpened possibly by disease, arrive at results which defied the most penetrating glance of the sane? I knew not—but reflecting often upon this subject since, have finally come to the latter conclusion, as the more philosophic of the two. Epilepsy is insanity of mind and body; and one of the most infallible characteristics of insanity is cunning—which is only another word for diseased and abnormal activity of brain. Amanda arrived at strange results, but I think she attained them by disease. Her acumen in this affair could be thus explained, almost wholly. As to the truth of the explanation, I felt a singular presentiment that it was correct.

"Well, that is curious enough," I said, "and I wish you success, Nighthawk. What of our other female friend—the fair lady you arrested in Richmond?"

"She is safe enough, colonel, and I don't think she will trouble us soon."

"I am glad of it. I think her the more dangerous of *the two*."

"And I agree with you."

"When did you see Darke, last?"

"I have not met him for three months."

"He can not be dead?"

"He may be wounded."

"And Mohun—is he at his head-quarters?"

Nighthawk smiled.

"He is at Five Forks, to-day, colonel."

"And Willie Davenant?"

"In Richmond, on business at the war department."

"Humph! So I shall see neither—but another time."

And mounting my horse, I added:—

"Good luck, Nighthawk."

"Thank you, colonel—the same to you."

And leaving Nighthawk crouching down beside his fire, I rode on.

XIII
DRINKING TEA UNDER DIFFICULTIES

Pushing on, I reached the cavalry and horse artillery, which I was soon done with—you see I dismiss "official" matters with commendable rapidity, reader—then I went on across Roney's bridge and along the "Flat Foot road" toward Disaways.

Following, amid a great wind and falling boughs, this winding road, stretching onward between its lofty walls of pines—a wild and deserted track, outside of the pickets, and completely untravelled. I recrossed Stony Creek, rode on over a bridle-path, and came just at sunset in sight of the hill upon which Disaways raised its ancient gables, near the Rowanty.

My horse neighed as he cantered up, and passed under the great oaks. He seemed to feel that this was something like home to him now, and that his day's march was over. In fact, all the months of winter I had regularly stopped at Disaways on my way to the cavalry at Hicksford. My friends had pathetically remonstrated—"there was not a single picket on the Rowanty in front of me, there, and I would certainly be captured some day,"—but I had persisted in stopping there still, on every tour which I made. How to resist the temptation! Disaways was just thirty miles from Petersburg. I always reached its vicinity as night fell, on the dark winter days. I was always cold, hungry, weary, depressed by the dull gray skies; and I knew what awaited me there—a blazing fire, a good supper, and Katy's smiles brighter than sunshine! She always ran to greet me, with both hands extended. Her blue eyes danced with joy, her rosy cheeks glowed, her lips laughed, and were like carnations, her golden ringlets fell in a shower over her white and delicate temples, or were blown back in ripples by the wintry wind.

Could you have resisted that, my dear reader? Would you have shrunk from Yankee scouting parties? For my part I thought I would risk it. I might be surprised and captured at any moment—the territory was open to the enemy — but I would have had a charming evening, would have been cheered by Katy's sunshine — while I was alive and free, I would have lived, and in a manner the most delightful!

Hitherto some angel had watched over me, and Disaways had been unvisited by the enemy's scouting parties, without so much as a vedette at the Halifax bridge, within half a mile. I had sat by the fire, eaten countless suppers, laughed and conversed with my good friends, slept soundly in a *real bed*, and gone on my way in the morning rejoicing.

I had thus always escaped surprise. No enemy ever annoyed me. It was the old adage, however, of the pitcher that went to the well so often! — but let me go on with my narrative.

As my horse uttered his shrill neigh now, ringing through the March evening, the door opened and Katy ran out to greet me. She had never looked more beautiful, and I recall still, as though I had seen it yesterday, the charming smile on her red lips. The wind blew back her ringlets till they resembled golden ripples — the rosy cheeks were flushed — there madam! (I say this to some one who is leaning over my shoulder, and laughing) don't begrudge me these smiling memories! Katy was only my little niece as it were — she is married and far away now. Nay, Surry ought to love and be grateful to the little lady who took such good care, in those grim days, of — your husband, madam!

Behind Katy appeared the faces of the excellent family, who cordially greeted me. Behind all appeared the blushing but dandified Tom Herbert.

"Ah! there is a straggler!" I said. "Why don't you send him back to his command, ladies? Every man should be at his post in this trying moment!"

"Oh, bother, my dear Surry! what a tongue you have!" exclaimed Tom.

"I see General Fitz was right, or his staff rather, in what they told me, Tom."

"What did they tell you, my dear boy?"

"That you were demoralized and captured!"

Sweet smile on the faces of the family at these words!

"That you had acknowledged your weakness, seen that further resistance was hopeless, and were already negotiating a surrender to the enemy. Well, Tom, what are the terms? Are they arranged?"

Suddenly I felt my hair pulled by an enemy from behind; and looking round I saw Miss Katy passing by, with an immense appearance of innocence. Her face was blushing; her lips emitted a low laugh; and seeing that no one was looking at her, she raised her finger in silent menace at me.

This caused a diversion, and Tom was enabled to rally his forces.

"My dear Surry," he said, smiling, with his delightfully foppish air, "it always charms me to meet you, for you are always sparkling, brilliant, full of wit; which reminds me of the good old days with Stuart! You have only one fault, my boy, you think yourself a philosopher. Don't do that, I beg, Surry! — But what's the news from Petersburg?"

I acquiesced in the change of topic, and gave Tom the news; but I was looking at Katy.

More than ever before I admired that little "bird of beauty," flitting about with charming grace, and an irresistible business air, to get me my supper, for the rest had just finished. This privilege she always claimed when I came to Disaways; fighting furiously, if the excellent lady of the manor attempted to supplant her. Looking at her, as she ran about now, engaged in her most admirable occupation, I thought her lovelier than ever before — certainly than when talking in the woods with Tom! You see she was getting my supper, reader! — and it seemed to be a labor of love. The little fairy ran on her tiptoes from sideboard to table; spread a snowy napkin, and placed a gilt china plate upon it; made tea; covered the table with edibles; and placed beside my plate a great goblet of yellow cream, of the consistency of syrup. Then she poured out my tea, set my chair to the table, and came with courtesy and laughing ceremony, to offer me her arm, and lead me to my seat.

Men are weak, worthy reader, and the most "romantic and poetical" of us all, have much of the animal in us. That is a mortifying confession. I was terribly hungry, and at that moment I think my attention was more closely riveted on the table, than even upon Miss Katy with her roses and ringlets.

I therefore unbuckled my sabre, placed the little hand on my arm, and was about to proceed toward the table, when a shot, accompanied by a shout, was heard from the direction of the Rowanty.

I went and buckled on my sword again. Then seeing Tom rise quickly — to get his horse ready, he said — I requested him to have my own resaddled, and returned to the table.

I had just raised the cup of tea to my lips, amid warnings from the family, to take care or I would be captured, when a cavalryman galloped up the hill, and stopped in front of the door.

"Look out, the Yankees are coming!" he cried.

I glanced through the window, and recognized a man of Mohun's command, who also recognized me.

"How near are they?" I said, attempting to swallow the burning tea.

"Not a quarter of a mile off, colonel!"

"That will give me time," I said.

And I applied myself again to the tea, which this time I poured out into the saucer, in order to cool it.

"Look out, colonel!" cried the man.

"Where are they?"

"At the gate."

I finished the tea, and the goblet of cream just as the man shouted: —

"Here they are, right on you, colonel!"

And I heard the sound of a galloping horse, accompanied by shots at the retreating cavalryman.

I went quickly to the window. A column of Federal cavalry was rapidly ascending the hill. By the last beams of day I recognized Darke at the head of the column; and by his side rode Mr. Alibi. I thought I could see that Darke was thin and very pale, but was not certain. The light was faint, and I had only one glance — discretion suggested a quick retreat.

I just grazed capture — passing through the door, in rear of the mansion, at the very moment when a number of the enemy, who had hastily dismounted, rushed in at the front door.

Tom was mounted, and holding my horse, which the good boy had saddled with his own hands. I leaped to saddle, and had scarcely done so, when a pistol bullet whizzed by my head. It had crashed through a pane of the window from within — and a loud shout followed. We had been perceived.

Under these circumstances, my dear reader, we always ran in the late war. Some persons considered it disgraceful to run or dodge, but they were civilians.

"Don't run until you are obliged to, but then run like the — —!" said a hard-fighting general.

And one day when a lady was telling General R.E. Lee, how a friend of hers had dodged once, the general turned to the laughing officer, and said in his deep voice, "That's right captain, dodge all you can!"

I have often dodged, and more than once have—withdrawn rapidly. On this occasion, Tom and I thought that retreat was the wisest course. In a moment we had disappeared in the woods, followed by pistol shots and some of the enemy.

They did not pursue us far. The Federal cavalry did not like the Virginia woods.

In ten minutes their shots were no longer heard; their shouts died away; and returning on our steps, we came once more in sight of Disaways and reconnoitred.

The enemy were not visible, and riding up, we dismounted and entered.{1}

{Footnote 1: "I have taken up too much space with this trifle," said Colonel Surry when I read this, "but that hot tea was a real cup of tea! I was really burned nearly to death, in attempting to swallow it! The dialogue with my friend, the cavalryman, was real; and it is just these trifles which cling to the memory, obscuring the 'greater events!'"}

XIV
MR. ALIBI

The enemy had eaten up my supper! A glance at the table told the whole tragic history;—but the unnerved family were scarce in a condition to think of my misfortune.

The enemy had staid for a few moments only, but in that time the family had gathered important information of their intentions. They were going to surprise and attack General Fitz Lee that night; and had not so much as halted, as they passed the house, to gain a by-road beyond. They were commanded, the men said, by a General Darke, and guided by a man living near Monk's Neck, whose name was Alibi.

This information of the enemy's design banished all other thoughts from my mind and Tom's. We ran to our horses—and I think I heard something like a kiss, in the shadow of the porch, as Tom and Katy parted.

We galloped into the woods, following a course parallel to that taken by the enemy's cavalry, and keeping as close to it as was safe.

"A sudden parting between yourself and Katy, Tom!" I said, as we galloped on. "A touching spectacle! When will you be married?"

"In a week or two—to answer seriously, old fellow," responded Tom.

"Is it possible!"

"Even so, my boy."

"Here, at Disaways?"

"No, in Richmond. Katy's family are refugees there, now; and I was going to escort her to Petersburg to-morrow, but for these rascals—and I will do it, yet."

"Good! I hope the way will be clear then! Let us go on. There is no time to lose in order to warn General Fitz!"

We pushed on, following bridle-paths, and making toward Dinwiddie Court-House. Half an hour thus passed, and we were near the Roney's Bridge road, when, suddenly, the whole forest on our right blazed with shots. Loud shouts accompanied the firing. The woods crackled as horsemen rushed through them. An obstinate fight was going on in the darkness, between the Federal and Confederate cavalry.

Plainly, the Confederates had not been surprised, and the dash and vim with which they met the Federal onset, seemed to dishearten their enemies. For fifteen minutes the combat continued with great fury, amid the pines; the air was filled with quick spirts of flame, with the clash of sabres, with loud cheers and cries; then the wave of Federal horsemen surged back toward the Rowanty; the Confederates pressed them, with cheer; and the affair terminated in a headlong pursuit.

Tom and myself had gotten into the *mêlée* early in the action, and my feather had been cut out of my hat by a sabre stroke which a big blue worthy aimed at me. This was my only accident, however. In fifteen minutes I had the pleasure of seeing our friends run.

I followed with the rest, for about a mile. Then I drew rein, and turned back—my horse was completely exhausted. I slowly returned toward Dinwiddie Court-House; hesitated for a moment whether I would lodge at the tavern; shook my head in a manner not complimentary to the hostelry; and set out to spend the night at "Five Forks."

I did not know, until some days afterward, that a serious accident had happened to the worthy Mr. Alibi, guide and friend of General Darke.

He had been struck by a bullet in the fight; had flapped his wings; cackled; tumbled from his horse; and expired.

Nighthawk's visit thus went for nothing.

Mr. Alibi was dead.

XV
FROM FIVE FORKS TO PETERSBURG

I shall not dwell upon the evening and night spent at "Five Forks"—upon whose threshold I was met and cordially greeted by the gray-haired Judge Conway.

In the great drawing-room I found the young ladies, who hastened to procure me supper; and I still remember that waiter of every species of edibles,—that smiling landscape above which rose the spire-like neck of a decanter! These incessant "bills of fare" will, I fear, revolt some readers! But these are my memoirs; and *memoirs* mean recollections. I have forgotten a dozen battles, but still remember that decanter-phenomenon in March, 1865. I spent the evening in cordial converse with the excellent Judge Conway and his daughters, and on the next morning set out on my return to Petersburg. Mohun had not been visible. At the first sound of the firing, he had mounted his horse and departed at a gallop.

So much for my visit to Five Forks. I pass thus rapidly over it, with real regret—lamenting the want of space which compels me to do so.

Do you love the queenly rose, and the modest lily of the valley, reader? I could have shown you those flowers, in Georgia and Virginia Conway. They were exquisitely cordial and high-bred—as was their gray-haired father. They spoke, and moved, and looked, as only the high-bred can. Pardon that obsolete word, "high-bred," so insulting in the present epoch! I am only jesting when I seem to intimate that I considered the stately old judge better than the black servant who waited upon me at supper!

Of Mohun and Will Davenant, I had said nothing, in conversing with the smiling young ladies. But I think Miss Georgia, stately and imposing as she was, looked at me with a peculiar smile, which said, "You are *his* friend, and cannot be a mere ordinary acquaintance to *me!*"

And here I ought to inform the reader, that since that first visit of mine to Five Forks, affairs had marched with the young lady and her friend. Mohun and Miss Georgia were about to be married, and I was to be the first groomsman. The woman-hating Benedict of the banks of the Rappahannock had completely succumbed, and the satirical Beatrice had also lost all her wit. It died away in sighs, and gave place to reveries — those reveries which come to maidens when they are about to embark on the untried seas of matrimony.

But I linger at Five Forks when great events are on the march. Bidding my hospitable host and his charming daughters good morning, I mounted my horse and set out over the White Oak road toward Petersburg. As I approached the Rowanty, I saw that the new defenses erected by Lee, were continuous and powerful. Long tiers of breastworks, and redoubts crowning every eminence, showed very plainly the great importance which Lee attached to holding the position.

In fact, this was the key to the Southside road. Here was to take place the last great struggle.

I rode on, in deep thought, but soon my reverie was banished. Just as I reached the hill above Burgess's, who should I see coming from the direction of the Court-House — but Tom Herbert and Katy Dare!

Katy Dare, on a little pony, with a riding skirt reaching nearly to the ground! — with her trim little figure clearly outlined by the fabric — with a jaunty little riding hat balanced lightly upon her ringlets — with her cheeks full of roses, her lips full of smiles, her eyes dancing like two blue waves, which the wind agitates!

Don't find fault with her, Mrs. Grundy, for having Tom only as an escort. Those were stern and troubled times; our poor girls were compelled often to banish ceremony. Katy had only this means to get back to her family, and went with Tom as with her brother.

She held out both hands to me, her eyes dancing. Three years have passed since then, but if I were a painter, I could make her portrait, reproducing every detail! Nothing has escaped my memory; I still hear her voice; the sun of 1868, not of 1865, seems to shine on the rosy cheeks framed by masses of golden ringlets!

I would like to record our talk as we rode on toward Petersburg — describe that ride — a charming episode, flashing like a gleam of sunlight, amid the dark days, when the black clouds had covered the whole landscape. In this volume there is so much gloom! Suffering and death have met us so often! Can you wonder, my dear reader, that the historian of such an epoch longs to escape, when he can, from the gloom of the tragedy, and paint those scenes of comedy which occasionally broke the monotonous drama? To write this book is not agreeable to me. I wear out a part of my life in composing it. To sum up, in cold historic generalities that great epoch would be little — but to enter again into the hot atmosphere; to live once more that life of the past; to feel the gloom, the suspense, the despair of 1865 again —

believe me, that is no trifle! It wears away the nerves, and tears the heart. The cheek becomes pale as the MS. grows! The sunshine is yonder, but you do not see it. The past banishes the present. Across the tranquil landscape of March, 1868, jars the cannon, and rushes the storm wind of March, 1865!

The cloud was black above, therefore, but Katy Dare made the world bright with her own sunshine, that day. All the way to Petersburg, she ran on in the most charming prattle. The winding Boydton road, like the banks of the lower Rowanty, was made vocal with her songs — the "Bird of Beauty" and the whole repertoire. Nor was Tom Herbert backward in encouraging his companion's mirth. Tom was the soul of joy. He sang "Katy! Katy! don't marry any other!" with an unction which spoke in his quick color, and "melting glances" as in the tones of his laughing voice. Riding along the famous highway, upon which only a solitary cavalryman or a wagon occasionally appeared, the little maiden and her lover made the pine-woods ring with their songs, their jests, and their laughter!

It is good to be young and to love. Is there any thing more charming? For my part I think that the curly head holds the most wisdom! Tell me which was the happier — the gray-haired general yonder, oppressed by care, or the laughing youth and maiden? It is true there is something nobler, however, than youth, and joy, and love. It is to know that you are doing your duty — to bear up, like Atlas, a whole world upon your shoulders — to feel that, if you fall, the whole world will shake — and that history will place your name beside that of Washington!

As the sun began to decline, we rode into Petersburg, and bidding Katy and Tom adieu, I returned to my Cedars.

I had taken my last ride in the "low grounds" of the county of Dinwiddie; I was never more to see Disaways, unless something carries me thither in the future. To those hours spent in the old mansion, and with my comrades, near it, I look back now with delight. Days and nights on the Rowanty! how you come back to me in dreams! Happy hours at Disaways, with the cavalry, with the horse artillery! you live still in my memory, and you will live there always! Katy Dare runs to greet me again as in the past — again her blue eyes dance, and the happy winds are blowing her bright curls into ripples! She smiles upon me still — as in that "winter of discontent." Her cheerful voice again sounds. Her small hands are held out to me. All things go — nothing lingers — but those days on the Rowanty, amid the sunset gilded pines, come back with all their tints, and are fadeless in my memory.

Going back thus in thought, to that winter of 1864, I recall the friendly faces of Katy, and all my old comrades — I hear their laughter again, touch their brave hands once more, and salute them, wishing them long life and happiness.

"Farewell!" I murmur, "Rowanty, and Sappony, and Disaways! *Bonne fortune!* old companions, little maiden, and kind friends all! It has not been time lost to gather together my recollections — to live again in the past, — to catch the aroma of those hours when kindness smoothed the front of war! We no longer wear the gray — my mustache only shows it *now*! but, thank heaven! many things in memory survive. I think of these — of the old comrades, the old times. Health and happiness attend you on your way through life, comrades! May the silver spare the gold of your clustering ringlets, Katy! Joy and gladness follow your steps! all friendly stars shine on you! Wherever you are, old friends, may a kind heaven send you its blessing!"

XVI
LEE'S LAST GREAT BLOW

I reached Petersburg on the evening of March 24, 1865.

The ride was a gay comedy—but a tragedy was about to follow it. On the very next morning, in the gray March dawn, Lee was going to strike his last great blow at Grant. A column under Gordon, that brave of braves, was going to be hurled headlong against Hare's Hill, the enemy's centre, just below Petersburg.

That design was evidently the result of supreme audacity, or of despair. In either case it indicated the terrible character of the crisis. There could be no two opinions upon that point. Lee aimed at nothing less than to cut General Grant's army in two—to root himself doggedly in the very centre of his enemies, and to force General Grant to draw back the entire left wing of his army, or run the risk, by holding his position, to have it destroyed.

Was Lee's motive to open the way for his retreat over the Boydton road toward Danville? I know not. Military critics say so, and it is certain that, a month before, he had endeavored to retreat. The government had checked him, then, but now, that step was plainly the only one left. He might effect his retreat by forcing Grant to draw in his left wing for the support of his centre. Lee could then retire from Hare's Hill; make a rapid march westward; push for North Carolina; and joining his forces with those of Johnston, continue the war in the Gulf States, falling back if necessary to Texas.

I have always thought that this was his design, but I was much too obscure a personage to gain any personal knowledge of his plans. It is certain that he designed one of two things—either to open the path for his retreat, or to relieve his right wing toward Five Forks, which was bending under the immense pressure upon it. Either motive was that of a good soldier—and what seemed wild audacity was sound common sense.

For the rest, there was little else to do. Some change in the aspect of things was vitally necessary. Grant had been re-enforced by a large portion of Sherman's army, and the Federal troops in front of Lee now numbered about one hundred and fifty thousand. As Lee's force, all told, on his entire line, was only about forty thousand, the rupture of the far-stretching defences, at some point, seemed only a question of time. And scarcely that. Rather, a question of the moment selected by Grant for his great blow.

At the end of March the hour of decisive struggle was plainly at hand. The wind had dried the roads; artillery could move; the Federal left was nearly in sight of the Southside road; one spring, and General Grant could lay hold on that great war-artery, and then nothing would be left to Lee but retreat or surrender.

Such was the condition of things at Petersburg, in these last days of March. Grant was ready with his one hundred and fifty thousand infantry to strike Lee's forty thousand. Sheridan was ready with his twelve thousand superbly mounted cavalry, to hurl himself against the two thousand half-armed horsemen, on starved and broken-down animals, under command of General Fitz Lee. A child could have told the result. The idea of resistance, with any hope, in the defences, any longer, was a chimera. Lee was a great soldier—history contains few greater. The army of Northern Virginia was brave—the annals of the world show none braver. But there was one thing which neither great generalship, or supreme courage could effect. Opposed by one hundred and fifty thousand well-fed troops, with every munition of war, forty thousand starving men, defending a line of forty miles, must in the end meet capture or destruction.

The country did not see it, but General Lee did. The civilians—the brave ones—had a superstitious confidence in the great commander and his old army. It had repulsed the enemy so uninterruptedly, that the unskilled people believed it invincible. Lee had foiled Grant so regularly that he was looked upon as the very God of Victory. Defeat could not come to him. Glory would ever follow his steps. On the banners of the old army of Northern Virginia, led by Lee, the eagles of victory would still, perch, screaming defiance, and untamed to the end.

While the civilians were saying this, Lee was preparing to retreat. Nothing blinded that clear vision—the eyes of the great chief pierced every mist. He saw the blow coming—the shadow of the Grant hammer as the weapon was lifted, ran before—on the 25th of March Lee's rapier made it last lunge. But when his adversary recoiled to avoid it, it was Lee who was going to retreat.

That lunge was sudden and terrible—if it did not accomplish its object. In the dark March morning, Gordon, "The Bayard of the army," advanced with three thousand men across the abatis in front of Hare's Hill.

What followed was a fierce tragedy, as brief and deadly as the fall of a thunder-bolt.

Gordon rushed at the head of his column over the space which separated the lines; stormed the Federal defences at the point of the bayonet; seized on Fort Steadman, a powerful work, and the batteries surrounding it, then as the light broadened in the East, he looked back for re-enforcements. None came — he was holding the centre of Grant's army with three thousand men. What he had won was by sheer audacity — the enemy had been surprised, and seemed laboring under a species of stupor; if not supported, and supported at once, he was gone!

An hour afterward, Gordon was returning, shattered and bleeding at every pore. The enemy had suddenly come to their senses after the stunning blow. From the forts and redoubts crowning every surrounding hill issued the thunder. Cannon glared, shell crashed, musketry rolled in long fusillade, on three sides of the devoted Confederates. Huddled in the trenches they were torn to pieces by a tempest of shell and bullets.

As the light broadened, the hills swarmed with blue masses hastening toward the scene of the combat, to punish the daring assailants. Grant's army was closing in around the little band of Gordon. No help came to them, they were being butchered; to stay longer there was mere suicide, and the few who could do so, retreated to the Confederate lines.

They were few indeed. Of the splendid assaulting column, led by Gordon, more than two thousand were killed or captured. He had split the stubborn trunk, but it was the trunk which now held the wedge in its obdurate jaws.

Gordon retreated with his bleeding handful — it was the second or third time that this king of battle had nearly accomplished impossibilities by the magic of his genius.

He could do only what was possible. To stay yonder was impossible. And the scarred veteran of thirty-three years, came back pale and in despair.

Lee had struck his last great blow, and it had failed.

XVII
THE WRESTLE FOR THE WHITE OAK ROAD

It is unsafe to wound the wild-boar, unless the wound be mortal. To change the figure, Grant had parried the almost mortal thrust of Lee; and now, with the famous hammer lifted and whirled aloft, aimed the final and decisive blow at the crest of his great adversary.

On Wednesday, March 29th, the Federal commander commenced the general movement, which had for its object the destruction of Lee's right wing, and the occupation of the Southside road.

Before dawn, the masses of blue infantry began to move westward across the Rowanty, laying down bridges over the watercourses, as the columns passed on; and on the night of the same day, the corps of Humphreys and Warren were near Dinwiddie Court-House with their extreme right guarded, by Sheridan's cavalry.

Such was the work of Wednesday. The great moment had evidently arrived. Lee penetrated at a single glance the whole design of his adversary; collected about fifteen thousand men, nearly half his army, and leaving Longstreet north of the James, and only a skirmish line around Petersburg, marched westward, beyond the Rowanty, to meet the enemy on the White Oak road.

On the morning of the 30th, all was ready for General Grant's great blow. But the elements were hostile to the Federal side. In the night, a heavy rain had fallen. All day on the 30th, it continued to rain, and military movements were impossible. The two great opponents looked at each other, — lines drawn up for the decisive struggle.

On the 31st, Grant was about to open the attack on Lee, when that commander saved him the trouble. The Virginian seemed resolved to die in harness, and advancing.

The corps of Humphreys and Warren had advanced from Dinwiddie Court-House toward the Southside road, and Warren was in sight of the White Oak road, when, suddenly, Lee hurled a column against him, and drove him back. The Confederates followed with wild cheers, endeavoring to turn the enemy's left, and finish them. But the attempt was in vain. Federal re-enforcements arrived. Lee found his own flank exposed, and fell back doggedly to the White Oak road again, having given the enemy a great scare, but effecting nothing.

As he retired, intelligence reached him that Sheridan's cavalry were advancing upon Five Forks. That position was the key of the whole surrounding country. If Sheridan seized and occupied this great *carrefour*, Lee's right was turned.

A column was sent without delay, and reached the spot to find Sheridan in possession of the place. Short work was made of him. Falling upon the Federal cavalry, Pickett and Fitzhugh Lee drove them back upon Dinwiddie—pushed rapidly after them—and, but for the terrible swamp, into which the late rains had converted the low grounds, would have followed them to the Court-House, and gotten in rear of the left wing of the Federal army.

That was the turning point. If Pickett and Fitz Lee had reached Dinwiddie court-house, and attacked in the enemy's rear, while Lee assailed them in front, it is difficult to believe that the battle would not have resulted in a Confederate victory.

Such was the alarm of General Grant at the new aspect of affairs, that late at night he withdrew Warren, and ordered him to hurry toward Dinwiddie Court-House, to succor Sheridan in his hour of need. Then if our flanking column could have pushed on—if Lee had then advanced—but all this is idle, reader. Providence had decreed otherwise. The flanking column could not advance—at ten at night it was withdrawn by Lee—midnight found the two armies resting on their arms, awaiting the morning of the first of April.

XVIII
THE BRIDEGROOM

I have endeavored to present a rapid, but accurate summary of the great events which took place on the lines around Petersburg, from the morning of the 29th of March, when General Grant began his general movement, to the night of the 31st, when he confronted Lee on the White Oak road, ready, after a day of incessant combat, which had decided little, to renew the struggle on the next morning for the possession of the Southside road.

This summary has been, of necessity, a brief and general one. For this volume has for its object, rather to narrate the fortunes of a set of individuals, than to record the history of an epoch, crowded with tragic scenes. I cannot here paint the great picture. The canvass and the time are both wanting. The rapid sketch which I have given will present a sufficient outline. I return, now, to those personages whose lives I have tried to narrate, and who were destined to reach the catastrophe in their private annals at the moment when the Confederacy reached its own.

I shall, therefore, beg the reader to leave the Confederate forces at bay on the White Oak road—the flanking column under Pickett and Johnson falling back on Five Forks—and accompany me to the house of the same name, within a mile of the famous *carrefour*, where, on the night of the 31st of March, some singular scenes are to be enacted.

It was the night fixed for Mohun's marriage. I had been requested to act as his first groomsman; and, chancing to encounter him during the day, he had informed me that he adhered to his design of being married in spite of every thing.

When night came at last, on this day of battles, I was wearied out with the incessant riding on staff duty; but I remembered my promise; again mounted my horse; and set out for "Five Forks," where, in any event, I was sure of a warm welcome.

Pushing on over the White Oak road, I turned southward at Five Forks, and riding on toward Judge Conway's, had just reached the road coming in from Dinwiddie Court-House, when I heard a cavalier approaching from that quarter, at a rapid gallop.

He was darting by, toward Five Forks, when by the starlight I recognized Mohun.

"Halt!" I shouted.

He knew my voice, and drew rein with an exclamation of pleasure.

"Thanks, my dear old friend," he said, grasping my hand. "I knew you would not fail me."

"Your wedding will take place, Mohun?"

"Yes, battle or no battle."

"You are right. Life is uncertain. You will hear cannon instead of marriage-bells probably, at your nuptials — but that will be inspiring. What is the news from the Court-House?"

"Our infantry is falling back."

"The condition of the roads stopped them?"

"Yes, it was impossible to get on; and they have been recalled by order of General Lee. Listen! There is the column coming — they are falling back to Five Forks, a mile north of Judge Conway's."

In fact, as we rode on now, I heard the muffled tramp of a column, and the rattle of artillery chains in the woods.

"The enemy will follow, I suppose?"

"Not before morning, I hope."

I smiled.

"Meanwhile you are making good use of the time to get married. What will you do with Miss Georgia?"

"You mean Mrs. Mohun, Surry!" he said, smiling.

"Yes."

"Well, she will be sent off — her father will take the whole family to Petersburg in the morning, to avoid the battle which will probably take place in this vicinity to-morrow."

"You are right. I predict a thundering fight here, in the morning."

"Which I hope I shall not balk in, my dear Surry," said Mohun, smiling.

"Is there any danger of that?"

"I really don't know. It is not good for a soldier to be too happy. It makes him shrink from bullets, and raises visions of a young widow, in mourning, bending over a tomb."

"Pshaw! stop that folly!" I said. "Is it possible that a stout-hearted cavalier like General Mohun can indulge in such apprehensions — and at a moment as happy as this?"

I saw him smile sadly, in the dim starlight. "I am much changed," he said, gently; "I no longer risk my life recklessly—trying to throw it away. Once, as you know, Surry, I was a poor outcast, and my conscience was burdened with a terrible crime. Life was little to me, then, and I would not have cared if a bullet cut it short. I was reckless, desperate, and had no hope. Now, I have hope—and a great deal more than all—I have happiness. My hands are not stained with the blood of that man and woman—I have the love of a pure girl who is going to give her life to me—and I have prayed to God for pardon, and been pardoned, I feel—else that All-merciful Being would not make my poor life bright again! But let me stop this talk! A strange conversation for a wedding night! Let me say again, however, my dear Surry, that I have no enmities now. I no longer hate *that man*, and would not harm *that woman* for aught on earth. Let them go—they are indifferent to me. I appeal to God to witness the purity of my sentiments, and the sincerity with which I have prayed, 'Forgive us our trespasses, as we forgive those who have trespassed against us!'"

I reached out my hand in the darkness, and pressed that of the speaker.

"You are right, Mohun—there is something greater, more noble, than vengeance—it is forgiveness. More than ever, I can say now of you, what I said after hearing your history that night."

"What was that, old friend?"

"That you were no longer the bitter misanthrope, hating your species, and snarling at all things—no longer the gay cavalier rushing to battle as a pastime—that you were altered, entirely changed, rather—that your character was elevated and purified—and that now, you were a patriotic soldier, fit to live or die with Lee!"

"Would that I were!" he murmured, letting his head fall upon his breast.

"That is much to say of any man; but I will add more. You are worthy of her—the blossom of Five Forks!"

As I uttered these words, we reached the gate.

A moment afterward we had entered the grounds, tethered our horses, and were hastening to the house.

XIX
THE CEREMONY

On the threshold we were met by Judge Conway, with a bow and a smile.

He pressed our hands cordially, but with a covert sadness, which I suppose comes to the heart of every father who is about to part with a beloved daughter—to give up his place as it were to another—and then we entered the great drawing-room where a gentleman in a white cravat and black coat awaited us. No other persons were visible.

The great apartment was a charming spectacle, with its brilliant lights and blazing fire. The frescoed walls danced in light shadows; the long curtains were drawn down, completely excluding the March air. Coming in out of the night, this smiling interior was inexpressibly home-like and delightful.

As we entered, the clerical-looking gentleman rose, modestly, and smiled.

"The Reverend Mr. Hope," said Judge Conway, presenting him. And Mr. Hope, with the same gentle smile upon his lips, advanced and shook hands.

At that name I had seen Mohun suddenly start, and turn pale. Then his head rose quickly, his pallor disappeared, and he said with entire calmness:

"Mr. Hope and myself are old acquaintances, I may even say, old friends."

To these words Mr. Hope made a gentle and smiling reply; and it was plain that he was very far from connecting the personage before him with the terrible tragedy which had taken place at Fonthill, in December, 1856. What was the origin of this ignorance? Had the worthy man, in his remote parsonage, simply heard of the sudden disappearance of Mohun, the lady, and *her brother*? Had his solitary life prevented him from hearing the vague rumors and surmises which must have followed that event? This was the simplest explanation, and I believe the correct one. Certain it is that the worthy Mr. Hope received us with smiling cordiality. Doubtless he recalled the past, but was too kind to spread a gloom over Mohun's feelings by *alluding to his loss*. In a few moments we were seated, and Judge Conway explained the presence of the parson.

The explanation was simple. Mohun, incessantly engaged on duty, had begged Judge Conway to send a message to the parson of his parish; the parson was absent, leaving his church temporarily in charge of his brother-clergyman, Mr. Hope; thus that gentleman by a strange chance, was about to officiate at Mohun's second marriage, as he had at his first.

I have explained thus, perhaps tediously, an incident which struck me at the time as most singular. Are there fatalities in this world? The presence of the Reverend Mr. Hope on that night at "Five Forks," resembled one of those strange coincidences which make us believe in the doctrine of destiny.

Having exchanged compliments with the clergyman, Mohun and I were shown to a dressing-room.

No sooner had the door closed, than I said to Mohun:—

"That is strange, is it not?"

"Singular, indeed," he replied, calmly, "but I am not averse to this worthy man's presence, Surry. I have no concealments. I have related my whole life to Judge Conway and Georgia. They both know the circumstances which lead to the conviction that *that woman* was already married, when she married *me*—that the proof of her marriage with Darke exists. Judge Conway is a lawyer, and knows that, in legal phraseology, the array of circumstances 'excludes every other hypothesis;' thus it is not as an adventurer that my father's son enters this house: all is known, and I do not shrink from the eye of this good man, who is about to officiate at my marriage."

"Does he know all?"

"I think not. I had half resolved to tell him. But there is no time now. Let us get ready; the hour is near."

And Mohun looked at his watch.

"Nine o'clock," he said. "The ceremony takes place at ten."

And he rapidly made his toilet. The light fell on a superb-looking cavalier. He was clad in full dress uniform, with the braid and stars of a brigadier-general. The erect figure was clearly defined by the coat, buttoned from chin to waist. Above, rose the proudly-poised head, with the lofty brow, the brilliant black eyes, the dark imperial and mustache, beneath which you saw the firm lips.

We descended to the drawing-room, where Judge Conway and Mr. Hope awaited us.

Fifteen minutes afterward light steps were heard upon the great staircase; the old statesman opened the door, and Miss Georgia Conway entered the apartment, leaning upon the arm of her father.

She was clad in simple white muslin, with a string of pearls in her dark hair; and I have never seen a more exquisite beauty. Her cheeks glowed with fresh roses; a charming smile just parted her lips; and her dark eyes, grand and calm, shone out from the snow-white forehead, from which her black hair was carried back in midnight ripples, ending in profuse curls. It was truly a *grande dame* whom I gazed at on this night, and, with eyes riveted upon the lovely face, I very nearly lost sight of Miss Virginia, who followed her sister.

I hastened to offer my arm to the modest little flower, and followed Judge Conway, who approached the parson, standing, prayer-book in hand, in the middle of the apartment.

In another instant Mohun was standing beside Miss Georgia, and the ceremony began.

It was not destined to proceed far.

The clergyman had nearly finished the exhortation with which the "form for the solemnization of matrimony," commences.

All at I once I was certain that I heard steps on the portico, and in the hall of the mansion.

The rest seemed not to hear them, however, and Mr. Hope continued the ceremony.

"Into this holy estate," he went on, "these two persons present come now to be joined. If any man can show just cause why they may not lawfully be joined together, let him now speak, or else hereafter forever hold his peace."

As he uttered the words the door was suddenly burst open, and Darke entered the apartment with *the gray woman.*

In the midst of the stupor of astonishment, she advanced straight toward Georgia Conway, twined her arm in that of the young lady, and said quietly:—

"How do you do, cousin? I am Lucretia Conway. Your father is my uncle. I have come to show just cause why you cannot marry General Mohun—my husband!"

XX
WHAT OCCURRED AT "FIVE FORKS," ON THE NIGHT OF MARCH 31, 1865

Mohun turned like a tiger, and was evidently about to throw himself upon Darke. I grasped his arm and restrained him.

"Listen!" I said.

The house was surrounded by trampling hoofs, and clattering sabres.

Darke had not drawn his pistol, and now glanced at me. His face was thin and pale—he was scarce the shadow of himself—but his eyes "burned" with a strange fire under his bushy brows.

"You are right, Colonel Surry!" he said, in his deep voice, to me, "restrain your friend. Let no one stir, or they are dead. The house is surrounded by a squadron of my cavalry. You are a mile from all succor. You can make no resistance. I am master of this house. But I design to injure no one. Sit down, madam," he added, to his companion, "I wish to speak first."

The sentences followed each other rapidly. The speaker's accent was cold, and had something metallic in it. The capture of the party before him seemed to be no part of his design.

All at once the voice of the strange woman was heard in the silence. She quietly released the arm of Georgia Conway, who had drawn back with an expression of supreme disdain; and calmly seating herself in a chair, gracefully cut some particles of dust from her gray riding habit with a small whip which she carried.

"Yes, let us converse," she said, with her eyes riveted upon Georgia Conway, "nothing can be more pleasant than these sweet family reunions!"

Judge Conway glanced at the speaker with eyes full of sudden rage.

"Who are you, madam," he exclaimed, "who makes this impudent claim of belonging to my family?"

"I have already told you," was the satirical reply of the woman.

"And you, sir!" exclaimed the old judge, suddenly turning and confronting Darke, "perhaps you, too, are a member of the Conway family?"

"Not exactly," was the cold reply.

"Your name, sir!"

"Mortimer Davenant."

Judge Conway gazed at the speaker with stupor.

"You that person?—you the son of General Arthur Davenant?"

"Yes, I am the son of General Arthur Davenant of the Confederate States army—General Davenant, whom you hate and despise as a felon and murderer—and I have come here to-night to relieve him of that imputation; to tell you that it was I and not he, who murdered your brother!

"A moment, if you please, sir," continued the speaker, in the same low, cold tone, "do not interrupt me, I beg. I have little time, and intend to be brief. You believe that your brother, George Conway, was put to death by General Davenant. Here is the fact of the matter: I saw him at Dinwiddie Court-House; knew he had a large sum of money on his person; followed him, attacked him, murdered him—and with General Davenant's pen-knife, which I had accidentally come into possession of. Then I stole the knife from the court-house, to prevent his conviction;—wrote and sent to him on the day of his trial a full confession of the murder, signed with my name—and that confession he would not use; he would not inculpate his son; for ten years he has chosen rather to labor under the imputation of murder, than blacken the name of a castaway son, whose character was wretched already, and whom he believed dead.

"That is what I came here, to-night, to say to you, sir. I am a wretch—I know that—it is a dishonor to touch my hand, stained with every vice, and much crime. But I am not entirely lost, though I told—my father—so, when I met him, not long since. Even a dog will not turn and bite the hand that has been kind to him. I was a gentleman once, and am a vulgar fellow now—but there is something worse than crime, in my estimation; it is cowardice and ingratitude. You shall not continue to despise my father; he is innocent of that murder. You have no right to continue your opposition to my brother's marriage with your daughter, for he is not the son of the murderer of your brother. *I* count for nothing in this. I am not my father's son, or my brother's brother. I am an outcast—a lost man—dead, as far as they are concerned. It was to tell you this that I have come here to-night—and for that only."

"And—this woman?" said Judge Conway, pale, and glaring at the speaker.

"Let her speak for herself," said Darke, coldly.

"I will do so, with pleasure," said the woman, coolly, but with an intensely satirical smile. That smile chilled me—it was worse than any excess of rage. The glance she threw upon Georgia Conway was one of such profound, if covert, hatred, that it drove my hand to my hilt as though to grasp some weapon.

"I will be brief," continued the woman, rising slowly, and looking at Georgia Conway, with that dagger-like smile. "General Darke-Davenant has related a pleasing little history. I will relate another, and address myself more particularly to Judge Conway—my dear uncle. He does not, or will not, recognize me; and I suppose I may have changed. But that is not important. I am none the less Lucretia Conway. You do not remember that young lady, perhaps, sir; your proud Conway blood has banished from your memory the very fact of her former existence. And yet she existed—she exists still— she is speaking to you—unbosoming herself in the midst of her dear family! But to tell my little story—it will not take many minutes. I was born here, you remember, uncle, and grew up what is called headstrong. At sixteen, I fell in love with a young Adonis with a mustache; and, as you and the rest opposed my marriage, obdurately refusing your consent, I yielded to the eloquence of Mr. Adonis, and eloped with him, going to the North. Here we had a quarrel. I grew angry, and slapped Adonis; and he took his revenge by departing without leaving me a wedding-ring to recall his dear image. Then I met that gentleman—General Darke-Mortimer-Davenant! We took a fancy to each other; we became friends; and soon afterward travelled to the South, stopping in Dinwiddie. Here I made the acquaintance of General Mohun—there he stands; he fell desperately in love with me—married me—Parson Hope will tell you that—and then attempted to murder me, without rhyme or reason. Luckily, I made my escape from the monster! rejoined my friend, General Darke-Davenant; the war came on; I came back here; have been lately arrested, but escaped by bribing the rebel jailers; only, however, to find that my naughty husband is going to marry my cousin

Georgia! Can you wonder, then, that I have exerted myself to be present at the interesting ceremony? That I have yielded to my fond affection, and come to say to my dear Georgia, 'Don't marry my husband, cousin!' And yet you frown at me—you evidently hate me—you think I am *lying*—that I was married before, perhaps. Well, if that be the case, where is the proof of that marriage?" "Here it is!" said a voice, which made the woman turn suddenly.

And opening the heavy window-curtains, which had, up to this moment, concealed him, Nighthawk advanced into the apartment, holding in his hand a paper.

A wild rage filled the eyes of the woman, but now so smiling. Her hand darted to her bosom, and I saw the gleam of a poniard.

"This paper," said Nighthawk, coolly, "was found on the dead body of a man named Alibi, who had stolen it. See, Judge Conway; it is in regular form. 'At Utica, New York, Mortimer Davenant to Lucretia Conway.' Attested by seal and signature. There can be no doubt of its genuineness."

Suddenly a hoarse exclamation was heard, and a poniard gleamed in the hand of the woman.

With a single bound, she reached Georgia Conway, and struck at her heart. The corsage of the young lady, however, turned the poniard, and at the same instant a thundering volley of musketry resounded without.

Furious cries were then heard; the wild trampling of horses; and a loud voice ordering: —

"Put them to the bayonet!"

Darke drew his sword, and reached the side of the woman at a bound. Throwing his arms around her, he raised her, and rushed, with his burden, through the hall, toward the lawn, where a fierce combat was in progress.

Suddenly the woman uttered a wild cry, and relaxed her grasp upon his neck. A bullet had buried itself in her bosom.

Darke's hoarse and menacing voice echoed the cry; but he did not release the body; with superhuman strength he raised it aloft, and bounded down the steps.

As he reached the bottom, a man rushed upon him, and drove his bayonet through his breast. It was withdrawn, streaming with blood.

"Put all to the bayonet!" shouted the voice of General Davenant, as he charged with his young son, Charles, beside him.

At that voice Darke stretched out both hands, and dropping his sword, uttered a cry, which attracted the general's attention.

For an instant they stood facing each other—unutterable horror in the eyes of General Davenant.

"I am—done for," exclaimed Darke, a bloody foam rushing to his lips, "but—I have told him—that *I* was the murderer—that *you* were innocent. Give me your hand, father!"

General Davenant leaped to the ground, and with a piteous groan received the dying man in his arms.

"I am a wretch—I know that—but I was a Davenant once"—came in low murmurs. "Tell Will, he can marry now, for I will be dead—kiss me once, Charley!"

The weeping boy threw himself upon his knees, and pressed his lips to those of his brother.

As he did so, the wounded man fell back in his father's arms, and expired.

XXI
FIVE FORKS

On the day after these events, Lee's extreme right at Five Forks, was furiously attacked, and in spite of heroic resistance, the little force under Pickett and Fitzhugh Lee was completely routed and dispersed.

Do you regard that term "heroic," as merely rhetorical, reader?

Hear a Northern writer, a wearer of blue, but too honest not to give brave men their due: —

"Having gained the White Oak road, Warren changed front again to the right, and advanced westward, so continually to take in flank and rear whatever hostile force still continued to hold the right of the Confederate line. This had originally been about three miles in extent, but above two-thirds of it were now carried. Yet, vital in all its parts, what of the two divisions remained, still continued the combat with unyielding mettle. Parrying the thrusts of the cavalry from the front, this poor scratch of a force threw back its left in a new and short crochet, so as to meet the advance of Warren, who continued to press in at right angles to the White Oak road. When the infantry, greatly elated with their success, but somewhat disorganized by marching and fighting so long in the woods, arrived before this new line, they halted and opened an untimely fusillade, though there had been orders not to halt. The officers, indeed, urged their men forward, but they continued to fire without advancing. Seeing this hesitation, Warren dashed forward, calling to those near him to follow. Inspired by his example, the color-bearers and officers all along the front, sprang out, and without more firing, the men charged at the *pas de course*, capturing all that remained of the enemy. The history of the war presents no equally splendid illustration of personal magnetism.... A charge of the cavalry completed the rout, and the remnants of the divisions of Pickett and Johnson fled westward from Five Forks, pursued for many miles, and until long after dark, by the mounted divisions of Merritt and McKenzie."

That is picturesque, is it not? It is amusing, too—though so tragic.

You can see that "poor scratch of a force" fighting to the death, can you not? You can see the poor little handful attacked by Sheridan's crack cavalry corps in front, and then suddenly by Warren's superb infantry corps in both their flank and rear. You can see them, game to the last, throwing back their left in the crochet to meet Warren; see that good soldier cheering on his men "greatly elated," but "somewhat disorganized," too—so much so that they suddenly halt, and require the "personal magnetism" of the general to inspire them, and bring them up to the work. Then the little scratch gives way—they are a handful, and two corps are pressing them. They have "continued the combat with unyielding mettle," as long as they could—now they are driven; and on rushes the thundering cavaliers to destroy them! Sound the bugles! Out with sabres! charge! ride over them! "Hurra!" So'the little scratch disappears.

General Warren, who won that fight, was a brave man, and did not boast of it. Tell me, general—you are honest—is any laurel in your hardwon wreath, labelled "Five Forks?" It would be insulting that other laurel labelled "Gettysburg," where you saved Meade!

In that bitter and desperate fight, Corse's infantry brigade and Lee's cavalry won a renown which can never be taken from them. The infantry remained unbroken to the last moment; and a charge of Lee's cavalry upon Sheridan's drove them back, well nigh routed.

But nothing could avail against such numbers. The Confederate infantry, cavalry, and artillery at last gave way. Overwhelmed by the great force, they were shattered and driven. Night descended upon a battlefield covered with heaps of dead and wounded, the blue mingled with the gray.

Among those wounded, mortally to all appearances, was Willie Davenant. He had fought with the courage of the bull-dog which lay *perdu* under the shy bearing of the boy. All the army had come to recognize it, by this time; and such was the high estimate which General R.E. Lee placed upon him, that it is said he was about to be offered the command of a brigade of infantry. Before this promotion reached him, however, the great crash came; and the brave youth was to fall upon the field of Five Forks, where he fought his guns obstinately to the very last.

It was just at nightfall that he fell, with a bullet through his breast.

The enemy were pressing on hotly, and there was no time to bring off the wounded officer. It seemed useless, too. He lay at full length, in a pool of blood, and was breathing heavily. To attempt to move him, even if it were possible, threatened him with instant death.

A touching incident followed. The enemy carried Five Forks as night descended. They had advanced so early, that Judge Conway and his daughters had had no time to leave their home. Compelled to remain thus, they did not forget their duty to the brave defenders of the Confederacy, and when the firing ceased, the old statesman and his daughters went to succor the wounded.

Among the first bodies which they saw was that of Will Davenant. One gleam of the lantern carried by the Federal surgeon told all; and Virginia Conway with a low moan knelt down and raised the head of the wounded boy, placing it upon her bosom.

As she did so, he sighed faintly, and opening his eyes, looked up into her face. The blood rushed to his cheeks; he attempted to stretch out his arms; then falling back upon her bosom the young officer fainted.

A cry from the girl attracted the attention of the Federal surgeon who was attending to the wounded Federalists. He was a kind-hearted man, and came to the spot whence he had heard the cry.

"He is dying!" moaned the poor girl, with bloodless cheeks. "Can you do nothing for him? Oh, save him, sir! — only save him! — have pity upon me!"

She could say no more.

The surgeon bent over and examined the wound. When he had done so, he shook his head.

"His wound is mortal, I am afraid," he said, "but I will do all I can for him."

And with a rapid hand he stanched the blood, and bandaged the wound.

The boy had not stirred. He remained still, with his head leaning upon the girl's breast.

"Can he live?" she murmured, in a tone almost inaudible.

"If he is not moved, he may possibly live; but if he is moved his death is certain. The least change in the position of his body, for some hours from this time, will be fatal."

"Then he shall not have to change his position!" exclaimed the girl.

And, with the pale face still lying upon her bosom, she remained immovable.

Throughout all the long night she did not move or disturb the youth. He had fallen into a deep sleep, and his head still lay upon her bosom.

Who can tell what thoughts came to that brave child as she thus watched over his sleep? The long hours on the lonely battle-field, full of the dead and dying, slowly dragged on. The great dipper wheeled in circle; the moon rose; the dawn came; still the girl, with the groans of the dying around her, held the wounded boy in her arms.{1}

{Footnote 1: Fact.}

Is there a painter in Virginia who desires a great subject? There it is; and it is historical.

When the sun rose, Willie Davenant opened his eyes, and gazed up into her face. Their glances met; their blushing cheeks were near each other; the presence of her, whom he loved so much, seemed to have brought back life to the shattered frame.

An hour afterward he was moved to "Five Forks," where he was tenderly cared for. The old statesman had forgotten his life-long prejudice, and was the first to do all in his power to save the boy.

A month afterward he was convalescent. A week more and he was well. In the summer of 1865 he was married to Virginia Conway.

As for Mohun, his marriage ceremony, so singularly interrupted, had been resumed and completed an hour after the death of the unfortunate Darke and his companion.

XXII
"THE LINE HAS BEEN STRETCHED UNTIL IT HAS BROKEN, COLONEL"

At nightfall, on the first of April, the immense struggle had really ended.

Lee's whole right was swept away; he was hemmed in, in Petersburg; what remained for General Grant was only to give the *coup de grace* to the great adversary, who still confronted him, torn and shattered, but with a will and courage wholly unbroken.

It is not an exaggeration, reader. Judge for yourself. I am to show you Lee as I saw him in this moment of terrible trial: still undaunted, raising his head proudly amid the crash of all around him; great in the hour of victory; in the hour of ruin, sublime.

Grant attacked again at dawn, on the morning of the second of April. It was Sunday, but no peaceful church-bells disturbed the spring air. The roar of cannon was heard, instead, hoarse and menacing, in the very suburbs of the devoted city.

There was no hope now—all was ended—but the Confederate arms were to snatch a last, and supreme laurel, which time can not wither. Attacked in Fort Gregg, by General Gibbon, Harris's Mississippi brigade, of two hundred and fifty men, made one of those struggles which throw their splendor along the paths of history.

"This handful of skilled marksmen," says a Northern writer, "conducted the defence with such intrepidity, that Gibbon's forces, surging repeatedly against it, were each time thrown back."

That is the generous but cold statement of an opponent; but it is sufficient. It was not until seven o'clock that Gibbon stormed the fort. Thirty men only out of the two hundred and fifty were left, but they were still fighting.

In the attack the Federal loss was "about five hundred men," says the writer above quoted.

So fell Lee's last stronghold on this vital part of his lines. Another misfortune soon followed. The gallant A.P. Hill, riding ahead of his men, was fired on and killed, by a small detachment of the enemy whom he had halted and ordered to surrender.

He fell from his horse, and was borne back, already dying. That night, amid the thunder of the exploding magazines, the commander, first, of the "light division," and then of a great corps—the hero of Cold Harbor, Sharpsburg, and a hundred other battles—was buried in the city cemetery, just in time to avoid seeing the flag he had fought under, lowered.

Peace to the ashes of that brave! Old Virginia had no son more faithful!

Fort Gregg was the last obstacle. At ten o'clock that had fallen, heavy masses of the enemy were pushing forward. Their bristling battalions, and long lines of artillery had advanced nearly to General Lee's head-quarters, a mile west of Petersburg.

As the great blue wave surged forward, General Lee, in full-dress uniform, and wearing his gold-hilted sword, looked at them through his field glasses from the lawn, in front of his head-quarters, on foot, and surrounded by his staff. I have never seen him more composed. Chancing to address him, he saluted me with the calmest and most scrupulous courtesy; and his voice was as measured and unmoved as though he were attending a parade. Do you laugh at us, friends of the North, for our devotion to Lee? You should have seen him that day, when ruin stared him in the face; you would have known then, the texture of that stout Virginia heart.

The enemy's column literally rushed on. Our artillery, on a hill near by, had opened a rapid fire on the head of the column; the enemy's object was to gain shelter under a crest, in their front.

They soon gained it; formed line of battle, and charged the guns.

Then all was over. The bullets rained, in a hurtling tempest on the cannoneer; the blue line came on with loud shouts; and the pieces were brought off at a gallop, followed by a hailstorm of musket-balls.

Suddenly the Federal artillery opened from a hill behind their line. General Lee had mounted his iron-gray, and was slowly retiring toward Petersburg, surrounded by his officers. His appearance was superb at this moment—and I still see the erect form of the proud old cavalier; his hand curbing his restive horse; his head turned over his shoulder; his face calm, collected, and full of that courage which nothing could break.

All at once a shell screamed from the Federal battery, and bursting close to the general, tore up the ground in a dozen places. The horse of an officer at his side was mortally wounded by a fragment, and fell beneath his rider other animals darted onward, with hanging bridle-reins, cut by the shell—but I was looking at General Lee, feeling certain that he must have been wounded.

He had escaped, however. Not a muscle of his calm face had moved. Only, as he turned his face over his shoulder in the direction of the battery, I could see a sudden color rush to his cheeks, and his eye flashed.

"I should now like to go into a charge!" he said to Stuart, once, after a disaster. And I thought I read the same thought in his face at this moment.

But it was impossible. He had no troops. The entire line on the right of Petersburg had been broken to pieces, and General Lee retired slowly to his inner works, near the city where a little skirmish line, full of fight yet, and shaking their fists at the huge enemy approaching, received him with cheers and cries which made the pulse throb.

There was no *hack* in that remnant—pardon the word, reader; it expresses the idea.

"Let 'em come on! We'll give 'em — —!" shouted the ragged handful. I dare not change that rough sentence. It belongs to history. And it was glorious, if rude. In front of that squad was a whole army-corps. The corps was advancing, supported by a tremendous artillery fire, to crush them— and the tatterdemalions defied and laughed at them.

This all took place before noon. Longstreet had come in from the north of the James with his skeleton regiments; and these opposed a bold front to the enemy on the right, while Gordon commanding the left, below the city, was thundering. A cordon hemmed in the little army now, in the suburbs of Petersburg. The right, on the Boydton road, was carried away; and the left beyond James River. One hope alone remained—to hold Petersburg until night, and then retreat.

I will not describe that day. This volume approaches its end; and it is fortunate. To describe at length those last days would be a terrible task to the writer.

Lee telegraphed to the President that he was going to retreat that night; and at the moment when the officers of the government hastily left Richmond by the Danville railroad, the army at Petersburg began to retire.

Did you witness what I describe, reader? What a spectacle!—the army of Northern Virginia, or what was left of it, rather, stealing away amid darkness. I sat my horse on the Hickory road, north of the Appomattox, near the city, and looked at the ragged column, which defiled by from the bridge over the river. In the starlight I could see their faces. There was not a particle of depression in them. You would have said, indeed, that they rejoiced at being out of the trenches—to be once more on the march, with Lee, riding his old iron-gray, in front of his old soldiers—with the battle-flags of a hundred battles still floating defiantly.

General Lee stood at the forks of the road, directing his column. He had said little during the day, and said little now, but his voice was as calm and measured, his eye as serene as before.

"This is a bad business, colonel!"[1] I had heard him say, at the moment when the shell burst near him in the morning.

{Footnote 1: His words.}

I heard but one other allusion which he made to the situation.

"Well, colonel," he said to an officer, in his deep and sonorous voice, "it has happened as I told them it would, at Richmond. The line has been stretched until it has broken."[1]

{Footnote 1: His words.}

So, over the Hickory road, leading up the northern bank of the Appomattox, in the direction of Lynchburg—amid the explosion of magazines, surging upward like volcanoes, the old army of Northern Virginia, reduced to fifteen thousand men, went forth, still defiant, into the night.

XXIII
WHAT I SAW FROM THE
GRAVE OF STUART

Three hours afterward I was in Richmond.

Sent with a message for General Ewell, I had taken the last train which left for the capital, and reached the city toward midnight.

The first person whom I saw was Tom Herbert, who ran to meet me. His face was pale, but his resolute smile still lit up the brave face.

"Come and wait on me, my dear old friend," he said; "I am to be married to-night!"

And in a few words he informed me that Katy had consented to have the ceremony performed before Tom followed General Lee southward.

Half an hour afterward I witnessed a singular spectacle: that of a wedding, past midnight, in the midst of hurry, confusion, uproar, universal despair—the scene, a city about to fall into the hands of the enemy—from which the government and all its defenders had fled.{1}

{Footnote 1: Real.}

Katy acted her part bravely. The rosy cheeks were unblanched still—the sweet smile was as endearing. When I took an old friend's privilege to kiss the smiling lips, there was no tremor in them, and her blue eyes were as brave as ever.

So Tom and Katy were married—and I bestowed upon them my paternal blessing! It was a singular incident—was it not, reader? But war is full of such.

I did not see Tom again until I met him on the retreat. And Katy—I have never seen her sweet face since—but heaven bless her!

An hour afterward I had delivered my message to General Ewell, who was already moving out with his small force to join Lee. They defiled across the bridges, and disappeared. For myself, tired out, I wrapped my cape around me, and stretching myself upon a sofa, at the house of a friend, snatched a little rest.

I was aroused toward daybreak by a tremendous explosion, and going to the window, saw that the city was in flames. The explosion had been caused, doubtless, by blowing up the magazines, or the rams in James River. The warehouses and bridges had been fired in anticipation of the approach of the enemy.

It behooved me to depart now, unless I wished to be captured. I had taken the precaution to provide myself with a horse from one of the government stables; the animal stood ready saddled behind the house; I bade my alarmed friends farewell, and mounting, rode through the streets of the devoted city toward the Capitol, amid bursting shell from the arsenal, exploding magazines, and roaring flames.

I can not describe the scenes which followed. They were terrible and would present a fit subject for the brush of Rembrandt. Fancy crowds of desperate characters breaking into the shops and magazines of stores — negroes, outcasts, malefactors, swarming in the streets, and shouting amid the carnival. The state prison had disgorged its convicts — the slums and subterranean recesses of the city its birds of the night — and now, felons and malefactors, robbers, cut-purses and murderers held their riotous and drunken carnival in the streets, flowing with whiskey. Over all surged the flames, roaring, crackling, tumultuous — the black clouds of smoke drifting far away, under the blue skies of spring.

Then from the Capitol hill, where I had taken my stand, I saw by the early light, a spectacle even more terrible — that of the enemy entering the city. They came on from Charles City in a long blue column resembling a serpent. Infantry and troopers, artillery and stragglers — all rushed toward the doomed city where they were met by a huge crowd of dirty and jabbering negroes and outcasts.

Suddenly a shout near at hand, thundered up to the hill. In front of the Exchange a column of negro cavalry, with drawn sabres rushed on. As they came, they yelled and jabbered — that was the darkest spectacle of all.

I remained looking at the frightful pageant with rage in my heart, until the advance force of the enemy had reached the railing of the Capitol. Then I turned my horse, and, pursued by carbine shots, rode out of the western gate, up Grace Street.

Fifty paces from St. Paul's I saw Colonel Desperade pass along — smiling, serene, in black coat, snow-white shirt, tall black hat, and with two ladies leaning upon his arms.

"Ah! gallant to the last, I see!" I growled to him as I rode by. "'None but the brave desert the fair!'"

The colonel smiled, but made no reply.

A hundred yards farther I met little Mr. Blocque joyously approaching.

In his hand he carried his safeguard, brought him by the gray woman. At his breast fluttered a miniature United States flag. The little gentleman was radiant, and exclaimed as he saw me: —

"What! my dear colonel! you are going to leave us? Come and dine with me — at five o'clock, precisely!"

My reply was not polite. I drew my pistol — at which movement Mr. Blocque disappeared, running, at the corner of St. Paul's.

On his heels followed a portly and despairing gentleman — Mr. Croaker.

"Save my warehouse! it is on fire! I shall be a beggar!" yelled Mr. Croaker.

I laughed aloud as the wretched creature rushed by, puffing and panting. Ten minutes afterward I was out of the city.

My last view of Richmond was from Hollywood Hill, near the grave of Stuart. The spectacle before me was at once terrible and splendid. The city was wrapped in a sea of flame. A vast black cloud swept away to the far horizon. A menacing roar came up from beneath those flames surging around the white Capitol; — the enemy's guns, troopers, musketeers and the rabble, were rushing with shouts, yells, and curses into the devoted city, which had at last fallen a prey to the Federal arms.

A last pang was to tear my heart. The sight before me was not enough, I had turned my horse to ride westward, throwing a parting glance upon the city, when suddenly the Virginia flag descended from the summit of the Capitol and the United States flag was run up.

I turned and shook my clenched hand at it.

"That is not my flag, and shall never be!" I exclaimed, aloud.

And taking off my hat as I passed the grave of Stuart, I rode on, thinking of the past and the present.

XXIV
THE RETREAT

Crossing James River, above the city, I pushed after the army, which I rejoined on the evening of the 4th, as it was crossing the Appomattox opposite Amelia Court-House.

It reached that village on Wednesday April 5th, and you could see at a glance that its spirit was unbroken. As to General Lee, his resolution up to that time had astonished all who saw him. Never had he seemed in more buoyant spirits.

"I have got my army safe out of its breastworks," he said, "and in order to follow me, my enemy must abandon his lines, and can derive no further benefit from his railroads, or James River."{1}

{Footnote 1: His words.}

It was only the faint-hearts who lost hope. Lee was not of those. Mounted upon his old iron-gray—at the head of his old army, if his little handful of about fifteen thousand men could be called such—Lee was still the great cavalier. The enemy had not yet checkmated him: his heart of hope was untouched. He would cut his way through, and the red flag should again float on victorious fields!

The army responded to the feeling of its chief. The confidence of the men in Lee was as great as on his days of victory. You would have said that the events of the last few days were, in the estimation of the troops, only momentary reverses. The veterans of Hill and Longstreet advanced steadily, tramping firm, shoulder to shoulder, with glittering gun barrels, and faces as resolute and hopeful as at Manassas and Chancellorsville.

"Those men are not whipped," said a keen observer to me, as he looked at the closed-up column moving. And he was right. The morale of this remnant of the great army of Northern Virginia was untouched. Those who saw them then will testify to the truth of my statement.

At Amelia Court-House a terrible blow, however, awaited them. General Lee had ordered rations to be sent thither from North Carolina. They had been sent, but the trains had gone on and disgorged them in

Richmond. When Lee arrived with his starved army, already staggering and faint, not a pound of bread or meat was found; there was nothing.

Those who saw General Lee at this moment, will remember his expression. For the first time the shadow of despair passed over that brave forehead. Some one had, indeed, struck a death-blow at him. His army was without food. All his plans were reversed. He had intended to reprovision his force at Amelia, and then push straight on. His plan, I think I can state, was to attack the detached forces of Grant in his front; cut his way through there; cross the Nottoway and other streams by means of pontoons, which had been provided; and, forming a junction with General Johnston, crush Sherman or retreat into the Gulf States. All this was, however, reversed by one wretched, microscopic incident. The great machine was to be arrested by an atom in its path. The rations were not found at Amelia Court-House; the army must have food, or die; half the force was dispersed in foraging parties throughout the surrounding country, and the delay gave Grant time to mass heavily in Lee's front, at Burksville.

Then all was decided. Lee had not doubted his ability to crush a corps, or even more, before the main force of the enemy came up. He saw as clearly now, that there was no hope of his cutting his way through Grant's army. It was there in his front—the failure of rations had caused all. With what must have been a terrible weight upon his heart, Lee directed his march toward Lynchburg, determined to fight to the end; and, as he had said during the winter, "die sword in hand."

Then commenced the woeful tragedy. What words can paint that retreat? There is only one other that equals it—Napoleon's retreat from Moscow. The army staggered on, fighting, and starving, and dying. Stalwart men fell by the roadside, or dropped their muskets as they tottered on. The wagons were drawn by skeleton mules, without food like the soldiers. If an ear of corn was found, the men seized and munched it fiercely, like animals. Covered with mud, blackened with powder, with gaunt frames, and glaring eyes, the old guard of the army of Northern Virginia still stood to their colors—fighting at every step, despairing, but not shrinking; and obeying the orders of Lee to the last.

You would not doubt that confidence in, and love for, their commander, reader, if you had witnessed the scene which I did, near Highbridge. The enemy had suddenly assailed Ewell and Custis Lee, and broken them to pieces. The blue horsemen and infantry pressing fiercely on all sides, and hunting their opponents to the death, seemed, at this moment, to have delivered a blow from which the Confederates could not rise. The attack had fallen like a thunderbolt. Ewell, Anderson, and Custis Lee were swept away by mere weight of numbers; the whole army seemed threatened with instant destruction.

Lee suddenly appeared, however, and the scene which followed was indescribable. He had rushed a brigade across, riding in front on his iron-gray; and at that instant he resembled some nobleman of the old age on the track of the wild-boar. With head erect, face unmoved, eyes clear and penetrating, he had reached the scene of danger; and as the disordered remnants of Ewell's force crowded the hill, hot and panting, they had suddenly seen, rising between them and the enemy, a wall of bayonets, flanked by cannon.

A great painter should have been present then. Night had fallen, and the horizon was lit up by the glare of burning wagons. Every instant rose, sudden and menacing, the enemy's signal rockets. On the summit of the hill, where the infantry waited, Lee rode among the disordered men of Ewell, and his presence raised a storm.

"It's General Lee!"

"Uncle Robert!"

"Where's the man who won't follow old Uncle Robert!"

Such were the shouts, cries, and fierce exclamations. The haggard faces flushed; the gaunt hands were clenched. On all sides explosions of rage and defiance were heard. The men called on the gray old cavalier, sitting his horse as calm as a statue, to take command of them, and lead them against the enemy.

No attack was made on them. An hour afterward the army moved again—the rear covered by General Fitzhugh Lee with his cavalry, which, at every step, met the blue huntsmen pressing on to hunt down their prey.

Such were some of the scenes of the retreat, up to the 7th. Who has the heart to narrate what followed in the next two days? A great army dying slowly—starving, fighting, falling—is a frightful spectacle. I think the memory of it must affect even the enemies who witnessed it.

It is only a small portion of the tragic picture that the present writer has the heart to paint.

XXV
HUNTED DOWN

On the morning of the 7th of April, and throughout the 8th, the horrors of the retreat culminated.

The army was fighting at every step. Hope had deserted them, but they were still fighting.

On every side pressed the enemy like bands of wolves hunting down the wounded steed.

Gordon and Longstreet, commanding the two skeleton corps of infantry, and Fitzhugh Lee the two or three thousand cavalry remaining, met the incessant attacks, with a nerve which had in it something of the heroic.

Fitz Lee had commanded the rear guard on the whole retreat. All along the route he had confronted the columns of Sheridan, and checked them with heavy loss.

At Paynesville he had driven Sheridan back, killing, wounding, and capturing two hundred of his men. At Highbridge he captured seven hundred and eighty more, killing many, among the rest the Federal General Read. On the morning of the 7th, beyond the river, he drove back a large column, capturing General Irwin Gregg.

That was a brave resistance made by the old army of Northern Virginia, reader, as it was slowly advancing into the gulf of perdition.

Beyond Farmville there was no longer any hope. All was plainly over. I shrink from the picture, but here is that of one of my friends. "It became necessary to burn hundreds of wagons. At intervals the enemy's cavalry dashed in and struck the interminable train, here or there, capturing and burning dozens on dozens of wagons. Hundreds of men dropped from exhaustion, and thousands let fall their muskets from inability to carry them any farther. The scenes were of a nature which can be apprehended in its vivid reality only by men who are thoroughly familiar with the harrowing details of war. Behind, and on either flank, a ubiquitous and increasingly adventurous enemy; every mud-hole and every rise in the road choked with blazing wagons; the air filled with the deafening reports of ammunition exploding, and shell bursting when touched by the flames; dense columns of smoke ascending to heaven from the burning and exploding vehicles; exhausted men, worn-out mules and horses, lying down side by side; gaunt famine glaring hopelessly from sunken lack-lustre eyes; dead mules, dead horses, dead men, everywhere; death many times welcomed as God's blessing in disguise—who can wonder if many hearts tried in the fiery furnace of four unparalleled years, and never hitherto found wanting, should have quailed in presence of starvation, fatigue, sleeplessness, misery, un-intermitted for five or six days, and culminating in hopelessness?"{1}

{Footnote 1: The Hon. Charles Francis Lawley, in the London *Times*.}

They did not "quail," they fell. It was not fear that made them drop the musket, their only hope of safety; it was weakness. It was an army of phantoms that staggered on toward Lynchburg—and what had made them phantoms was hunger.

Let others describe those last two days in full. For myself I can not. To sum up all in one sentence. The Army of Northern Virginia, which had for four years snatched victory upon some of the bloodiest battle-fields of history, fought, reeled, fired its last rounds, and fell dead from starvation, defying fiercely with its last breath, gurgling through blood in its throat, the enemy who was hunting it down to its death.

Call it what you will, reader—there was something in those men that made them fight to the last.

XXVI
THE LAST COUNCIL OF WAR OF THE ARMY OF NORTHERN VIRGINIA

On the night of the 8th of April, within a few miles of Appomattox Court-House, took place the last council of war of the army of Northern Virginia.

It was in the open air, beside a camp-fire, near which were spread General Lee's blankets; for throughout the retreat he had used no tent, sleeping, shelterless like his men, by the bivouac fire.

To this last council of war, none but the corps commanders were invited. Thus the only persons present were Gordon and Longstreet, commanding the skeleton corps of infantry, and Fitzhugh Lee, the cavalry of the army.

Gordon was stretched near Fitzhugh Lee, upon the blankets of the commander-in-chief; Gordon, with his clear complexion, his penetrating eyes, his firm lip, his dark hair, and uniform coat buttoned to his chin—the man to fight and die rather than surrender. Near him lay Fitz Lee, the ardent and laughing cavalier, with the flowing beard, the sparkling eyes, the top-boots, and cavalry sabre—the man to stand by Gordon. On a log, a few feet distant, sat the burly Longstreet, smoking with perfect nonchalance— his heavily bearded face exhibiting no emotion whatever. Erect, within a few paces of these three men, stood General Lee—grave, commanding, unmoved; the fire-light revealing every outline of his vigorous person, clad in its plain gray uniform, the gray beard and mustache, the serene eyes, and that stately poise of the head upon the shoulders, which seemed to mark this human being for command.

All these persons were composed. Their faces were haggard from want of rest, but there was nothing in their expressions indicating anxiety, though some gloom.

"It was a picture for an artist," said that one of them who described the scene to me afterward. The ruddy light brought out every detail of these martial figures. By that fire on the roadside had assembled for the last time General Robert E. Lee and his corps commanders.

The council was brief.

General Lee succinctly laid before his listeners the whole situation.

His army was on a strip of land between the James River and the enemy. He could not cross the river—if he could not break through the enemy in his front the army was lost. General Grant had understood his situation, and a correspondence had taken place. He would read General Grant's notes and copies of his own replies.

By the light of the fire, General Lee then proceeded to read the papers alluded too.

Grant had opened the correspondence. "The result of the last week must convince General Lee," he wrote, "of the hopelessness of further resistance on the part of the army of Northern Virginia." He therefore "asked the surrender" of that army to prevent bloodshed.

Lee had written in reply, requesting Grant to state the terms.

Grant had stated them on this 8th of April, and Lee had replied at once that he "did not intend to propose the surrender of the army of Northern Virginia, but to ask the terms of General Grant's proposition. To be frank," he had added, "I do not think the emergency has arisen to call for the surrender." But he would meet General Grant on the next morning to discuss the whole affair.

There the correspondence had terminated. What was the opinion of his corps commanders?

Their replies were brief and informal. The scene was august but simple. What was determined upon was this—-

That the army should continue its march on the next day toward Lynchburg, breaking through Sheridan's cavalry which was known to be in front; but in case the Federal infantry, a very different thing from the cavalry, was found to be "up," then Gordon, who was to lead the advance, should inform the commander-in-chief of that fact, when a flag of truce would be sent to General Grant acceding to the terms of capitulation proposed in his last note to General Lee.

Fitzhugh Lee only stipulated that if he saw that the Federal infantry in his front, rendered surrender inevitable, he should be allowed to go off with his cavalry to save the horses of his men.

This was agreed to, and it will be seen that Fitz Lee availed himself of the conmmander-in-chief's permission.

So ended that last council of war, by the camp fire.

With grave salutes and a cordial pressure of the brave hands, the famous soldiers took leave of Lee.

As they disappeared he drew his blanket around him and fell asleep by the blazing fire.

It was the night of April 8th, 1865 — three years, day for day, from the moment when these lines are written.

XXVII
THE NIGHT BEFORE THE SURRENDER

Throughout that strange night of the eighth of April, 1865, I was in the saddle, carrying orders.

Those who saw it will remember how singularly brilliant it was. The moon and stars shone. The light clouds sweeping across the sky scarcely obscured the mournful radiance. All was still. The two armies — one surrounded and at bay, the other ready to finish the work before it — rested silently on their arms, waiting for that day which would bring the thunder.

Every arrangement had been made by Lee to break through the force in his front, and gain Lynchburg, from which he could retreat to the southwest.

The column of infantry to open the way was about one thousand six hundred men, under Gordon. The cavalry, numbering two or three thousand, was commanded by Fitzhugh Lee. The artillery, consisting of three or four battalions, was placed under that brave spirit, Colonel Thomas H. Carter.

For the tough work, Lee had selected three braves.

I saw them all that night, and read in their eyes the fire of an unalterable resolution.

You know those men, reader. If *you* do not, history knows them. It was their immense good fortune to bear the red cross banner in the last charge on the enemy, and with their handful of followers to drive the Federal forces back nearly a mile, half an hour before Lee's surrender.

I had just left General Fitzhugh Lee, near Appomattox Court-House, and was riding through the pines, when a sonorous voice halted me.

"Who goes there?" said the voice.

"Surry, Mordaunt!"

For I had recognized the voice of the general of cavalry. We have seen little of him, reader, in this rapid narrative; but in all the long hard battles from the Rapidan to this night, I had everywhere found myself thrown in collision with the great soldier — that tried and trusty friend of my heart. The army had saluted him on a hundred fields. His name had become the synonym of unfaltering courage. He was here, on the verge of surrender now, looking as calm and resolute as on his days of victory.

"Well, old friend," said Mordaunt, grasping my hand and then leaning upon my shoulder; "as the scriptures say, what of the night?"

"Bad, Mordaunt."

"I understand. You think the enemy's infantry is up."

"Yes."

"Then we'll have hard work; but we are used to that, Surry."

"The work is nothing. It is death only. But something worse than death is coming Mordaunt."

"What?"

"Surrender."

Mordaunt shook his head.

"I am not going to surrender," he said. "I have sworn to one I love more than my life—you know whom I mean, Surry—that I would come back, or die, sword in hand; and I will keep my oath."

The proud face glowed. In the serene but fiery eyes I could read the expression of an unchangeable resolution.

"Another friend of ours has sworn that too," he said.

"Who?"

"Mohun."

"And just married! His poor, young wife, like yours, is far from him."

"You are mistaken; she is near him. She went ahead of the army, and is now at the village here."

"Is it possible? And where is Mohun?"

"He is holding the advance skirmish line, on the right of Gordon. Look! Do you see that fire, yonder, glimmering through the woods? I left him there half an hour since."

"I will go and see him. Do nothing rash, to-morrow, Mordaunt. Remember that poor Old Virginia, if no one else, needs you yet!"

"Be tranquil, Surry," he replied, with a cool smile. "Farewell; we shall meet at Philippi!"

And we parted with a pressure of the hand.

I rode toward the fire. Stretched on his cape, beside it, I saw the figure of Mohun. He was reading in a small volume, and did not raise his head until I was within three paces of him.

"What are you reading, Mohun?"

He rose and grasped my hand.

"The only book for a soldier," he said, with his frank glance and brave smile—"the book of books, my dear Surry—that which tells us to do our duty, and trust to Providence."

I glanced at the volume, and recognized it. I had seen it in the hands of Georgia Conway, at Five Forks. On the fly leaf, which was open, her name was written.

"That is *her* Bible," I said, "and doubtless you have just parted with her."

"Yes, I see you know that she is here, not far from me."

"Mordaunt told me. It must be a great delight to you, Mohun."

He smiled, and sighed.

"Yes," he replied, "but a sort of sorrow, too."

"Why a sorrow?"

Mohun was silent. Then he said:—-

"I think I shall fall to-morrow."

"Absurd!" I said, trying to laugh, "Why should you fancy such a thing?"

"I am not going to surrender, Surry. I swore to Chambliss, my old comrade, that I would never surrender, and he swore that to me. He was killed in Charles City—he kept his word; I will not break mine, friend."

My head sank. I had taken my seat on Mohun's cape, and gazed in silence at the fire.

"That is a terrible resolution, Mohun," I said at length.

"Yes," he replied, with entire calmness, "especially in me. It is hard to die, even when we are old and sorrowful—when life is a burden. Men cling to this miserable existence even when old age and grief have taken away, one by one, all the pleasures of life. Think, then, what it must be to die in the flush of youth, and health, and happiness! I am young, strong, happy beyond words. The person I love best in all the world, has just given me her hand. I have before me a long life of joy, if I only live! But I have sworn that oath, Surry! Chambliss kept his; shall I break mine? Let us not talk further of this, friend."

And Mohun changed the conversation, refusing to listen to my remonstrances.

Half an hour afterward I left him, with a strange sinking of the heart.

Taking my way back to the Court-House, I passed through the little village, rode on for a mile, and then, overwhelmed by fatigue, lay down by a camp fire in the woods, and fell asleep.

I was waked by a single gun, sending its dull roar through the gray dawn.

Rising, I buttoned my cape around me, mounted my horse, and rode toward the front.

As I ascended the hill, upon which stands Appomattox Court-House, a crimson blush suddenly spread itself over the fields and woods.

I looked over my shoulder. In the east, on the summit of the forest, the newly risen sun was poised, like a great shield bathed in blood.

Such was the spectacle which ushered in the ninth of April, 1865, at Appomattox Court-House.

XXVIII
THE LAST CHARGE OF THE OLD GUARD

I rode on rapidly to the front.

It was the morning of the ninth of April, 1865. Since that time three years, day for day, nearly hour for hour have passed; for these lines are written on the morning of the ninth of April, 1868.

Gordon had formed his line of battle across the road just beyond the court-house—and supported by Fitzhugh Lee's cavalry, and Carter's artillery on his right, was advancing with measured steps to break through the enemy.

It was a spectacle to make the pulse throb. The little handful was going to death unmoved. The red light of morning darted from the burnished gun-barrels of the infantry, the sabres of the cavalry, and the grim cannon following, in sombre lightnings.

Gordon, the "Bayard of the army," was riding in front of his line. The hour and the men had both come. Steadily the old guard of the army of Northern Virginia advanced to its last field of battle.

Suddenly, in front of them, the woods swarmed with the enemy's infantry, cavalry, and artillery. The great multitude had evidently employed the hours of night well. Grant's entire army seemed to have massed itself in Gordon's front.

But the force was not the question. Gordon's one thousand six hundred men were in motion. And when Gordon moved forward he always fought, if he found an enemy.

In five minutes the opponents had closed in, in stubborn fight, and the woods roared with musketry, cannon, and carbines.

Then a resounding cheer rose. The enemy had recoiled before Gordon, and he pressed forward, sweeping every thing in his path for nearly a mile beyond the court-house.

On his right Fitzhugh Lee's horsemen thundered forward on the retiring enemy; and Carter's guns advanced at a gallop, taking positions—

Starke to the left and Poague to the right of the road—from which they opened a rapid fire upon the Federal line of battle.

I had accompanied the advance and looked on with positive wonder. A miracle seemed about to be enacted before my very eyes. Gordon's poor little skirmish-line of less than two thousand men, with the half-equipped horsemen of Fitzhugh Lee, on their broken-down animals, seemed about to drive back the whole Federal army, and cut their way through in safety.

Alas! the hope was vain. In front of the handful were eighty thousand men! It was not Sheridan's cavalry only—that would have speedily been disposed of. During the night, General Grant's best infantry had pressed forward, and arrived in time to place itself across Lee's path. What Gordon and Fitzhugh Lee encountered was the Federal army.

Right and left, as in front, were seen dense blue columns of infantry, heavy masses of cavalry, crowding batteries, from which issued at every instant that quick glare which precedes the shell.

From this multitude a great shout arose; and was taken up by the Federal troops for miles. From the extreme rear, where Longstreet stood stubbornly confronting the pursuers, as from the front, where Gordon was trying to break through the immense obstacles in his path, came that thunder of cheers, indicating clearly that the enemy at last felt that their prey was in their clutch.

The recoil was brief. The great Federal wave which had rolled backward before Gordon, now rolled forward to engulf him. The moment seemed to have come for the old guard of the army of Northern Virginia to crown its victories with a glorious death.

The Federal line rushed on. From end to end of the great field, broken by woods, the blue infantry delivered their fire, as they advanced with wild cheers upon the line of Gordon and Lee.

The guns of Carter thundered in vain. Never were cannon fought more superbly; the enemy were now nearly at the muzzle of the pieces.

Gordon was everywhere encouraging his men, and attempting to hold them steady. With flaming eyes, his drawn sword waving amid the smoke, his strident voice rising above the din of battle, Gordon was superb.

But all was of no avail. The Federal line came on like a wave of steel and fire. A long deafening crash, mingled with the thunder of cannon, stunned the ear; above the combatants rose a huge smoke-cloud, from which issued cheers and groans.

Suddenly an officer of General Lee's staff passed by like lightning; was lost in the smoke; then I saw him speaking to Gordon. At the few words uttered by the officer, the latter turned pale.

A moment afterward a white flag fluttered—the order to surrender had come.

What I felt at that instant I can not describe. Something seemed to choke me. I groaned aloud, and turned toward the cavalry.

At fifty paces from me I saw Mordaunt, surrounded by his officers and men.

His swarthy face glowed—his eyes blazed. Near him, General Fitzhugh Lee—with Tom Herbert, and some other members of his staff—was sitting his horse, pale and silent.

"What will you do, general?" said Mordaunt, saluting with drawn sabre.

Fitzhugh Lee uttered a groan.

"I don't wish to be included in the surrender," he said. "Come, let's go. General Lee no longer requires my poor services!"{1}

{Footnote 1: His words.}

Mordaunt saluted again, as General Lee and his staff officers turned away.

"We'll go out sword in hand!" Mordaunt said. "Let who will, follow me!"

A wild cheer greeted the words. The men formed column and charged.

As they moved, a second cheer was heard at fifty paces from us. I turned my head, and saw Mohun, in front of about fifty cavalrymen, among whom I recognized Nighthawk.

In an instant I was at Mohun's side.

"You are going to charge!" I said.

"And die, Surry! A gentleman gives his word but once!"

And, following Mordaunt with long leaps, Mohun and his horsemen burst upon the enemy.

Then was presented a spectacle which made the two armies hold their breath.

The column of cavalry under Mordaunt and Mohun, had struck the Federal line of battle.

For an instant, you could see little, hear little, in the smoke and uproar. A furious volley unhorsed at least half of the charging column, and the rest were seen striking with their sabres at the blue infantry, who stabbed with their bayonets at the rearing horses.

Then a thundering shout rose. The smoke was swept away by the wind, and made all clear.

Mordaunt had cut his way through, and was seen to disappear with a dozen followers.

Mohun, shot through the breast, and streaming with blood, had fallen from the saddle, his foot had caught in the stirrup, and he was dragged by his frightened animal toward the Confederate lines.

The horse came on at a headlong gallop, but suddenly a cavalier came up with him, seized the bridle, and threw him violently on his haunches.

The new-comer was Nighthawk.

Leaping to the ground, he seized the body of Mohun in his arms, extricated his foot from the stirrup, and remounted his own horse, with the form of his master still clasped to his breast.

Then, plunging the spurs into his animal, he turned to fly. But his last hour had come.

A bullet, fired at fifty paces, penetrated his back, and the blood spouted. He fell from the flying animal to the earth, but his arms still clasped the body of Mohun, whose head lay upon his breast.

A loud cheer rose, and the blue line rushed straight upon him. Nighthawk's head rose, and he gazed at them with flashing eyes — then he looked at Mohun and groaned.

Summoning his last remains of strength, he drew from his breast a pencil and a piece of paper, wrote some words upon the paper, and affixed it to Mohun's breast.

This seemed to exhaust him. He had scarcely finished, when his head sank, his shoulders drooped, and falling forward on the breast of Mohun, he expired.

An hour afterward, all was still. On the summit of the Court-House hill a blue column was stationary, waving a large white flag.

General Lee had surrendered.

XXIX
THE SURRENDER

Lee had surrendered the army of Northern Virginia.

Ask old soldiers of that army to describe their feelings at the announcement, reader. They will tell you that they can not; and I will not attempt to record my own.

It was, truly, the bitterness of death that we tasted at ten o'clock on the morning of that ninth of April, 1865, at Appomattox Court-House. Gray-haired soldiers cried like children. It was hard to say whether they would have preferred, at that moment, to return to their families or to throw themselves upon the bayonets of the enemy, and die.

In that hour of their agony they were not insulted, however. The deportment of the enemy was chivalric and courteous. No bands played; no cheers were heard; and General Grant was the first to salute profoundly his gray-haired adversary, who came, with a single officer, to arrange, in a house near the field, the terms of surrender.

They are known. On the tenth they were carried out.

The men stacked the old muskets, which they had carried in a hundred fights, surrendered the bullet-torn colors, which had waved over victorious fields, and silently returned, like mourners, to their desolate homes.

Two days after the surrender, Mohun was still alive.

Three months afterward, the welcome intelligence reached me that he was rapidly recovering.

He had made a narrow escape. Ten minutes after the death of the faithful Nighthawk, the Federal line had swept over him; and such was the agony of his wound, that he exclaimed to one of the enemy: —

"Take your pistol, and shoot me!"

The man cocked his weapon, and aimed at his heart. Then he turned the muzzle aside, and uncocking the pistol, replaced it in its holster.

"No," he said, "Johnny Reb, you might get well!"

{Footnote: These details are all real.}

And glancing at the paper on Mohun's breast, he passed on, muttering —
"It's a general!"

The paper saved Mohun's life. An acquaintance in the Federal army saw it, and speedily had him cared for. An hour afterward his friends were informed of his whereabouts. I hastened to the house to which he had been borne. Bending over him, the beautiful Georgia was sobbing hopelessly, and dropping tears upon the paper, which contained the words —

"This is the body of General Mohun, C.S.A."

The army had surrendered; the flag was lowered: with a singular feeling of bewilderment, and a "lost" feeling that is indescribable, I set out, followed by my servant, for Eagle's Nest.

I was the possessor of a paper, which I still keep as a strange memorial.

"The bearer," ran this paper, "a paroled prisoner of the army of Northern Virginia, has permission to go to his home, and there remain undisturbed — with two horses!"

At the top of this document, was, "Appomattox Court-House, Va., April, 10, 1865." On the left-hand side was, "Paroled Prisoner's Pass."

So, with his pass, the paroled prisoner passed slowly across Virginia to his home.

Oh! that Virginia of 1865 — that desolate, dreary land! Oh! those poor, sad soldiers returning to their homes! Everywhere burned houses, unfenced fields, ruined homesteads! On all sides, the desolation of the torch and the sword! The "poor paroled prisoners," going home wearily in that dark April, felt a pang which only a very bitter foe will laugh at.

But all was not taken. Honor was left us — and the angels of home! As the sorrowful survivors of the great army came back, as they reached their old homes, dragging their weary feet after them, or urging on their jaded horses, suddenly the sunshine burst forth for them, and lit up their rags with a sort of glory. The wife, the mother, and the little child rushed to them. Hearts beat fast, as the gray uniforms were clasped in a long embrace. Those angels of home loved the poor prisoners better in their dark days than in their bright. The fond eyes melted to tears, the white arms held them close; and the old soldiers, who had only laughed at the roar of the enemy's guns, dropped tears on the faces of their wives and little children!

EPILOGUE

In the autumn of last year, 1867, I set out on horseback from "Eagle's Nest," and following the route west by Fredericksburg, Chancellorsville, Germanna Ford, Culpeper, and Orleans, reached "The Oaks" in Fauquier.

I needed the sunshine and bright faces of the old homestead, after that journey; for at every step had sprung up some gloomy or exciting recollection.

It was a veritable journey through the world of memory.

Fredericksburg! Chancellorsville! the Wilderness! the plains of Culpeper! — as I rode on amid these historic scenes, a thousand memories came to knock at the door of my heart. Some were gay, if many were sorrowful — laughter mingled with the sighs. But to return to the past is nearly always sad. As I rode through the waste land now, it was with drooping head. All the old days came back again, the cannon sent their long dull thunder through the forests; again the gray and blue lines closed in, and hurled together; again Jackson in his old dingy coat, Stuart with his floating plume, Pelham, Farley, all whom I had known, loved, and still mourned, rose before me — a line of august phantoms fading away into the night of the past.

Once more I looked upon Pelham, holding in his arms the bleeding form of Jean — passing "Camp-no-camp," only a desolate and dreary field now, all the laughing faces and brave forms of Stuart and his men returned — in the Wilderness I saw Jackson fight and fall; saw him borne through the moonlight; heard his sighs and his last greeting with Stuart. A step farther, I passed the lonely old house in the Wilderness, and all the strange and sombre scenes there surged up from the shadows of the past. Mordaunt, Achmed, Fenwick, Violet Grafton! — all reappeared, playing over again their fierce tragedy; and to this was added the fiercer drama of May, 1864, when General Grant invented the "Unseen Death."

Thus the journey which I made through the bare and deserted fields, or the mournful thickets, was not gay; and these were only a part of the panorama which passed before me. Looking toward the south, I saw as clearly with the eyes of the memory, the banks of the Po, the swamps of the

Chickahominy, the trenches at Petersburg, the woods of Dinwiddie, Five Forks, Highbridge — Appomattox Court-House! Nearer was Yellow Tavern, where Stuart had fallen. Not a foot of this soil of Old Virginia but seemed to have been the scene of some fierce battle, some sombre tragedy!

"Well, well," I sighed, as I rode on toward the Oaks, "all that is buried in the past, and it is useless to think of it. I am only a poor paroled prisoner, wearing arms no more — let me forget the red cross flag which used to float so proudly here, and bow my head to the will of the Supreme Ruler of all worlds."

So I went on, and in due time reached the Oaks, in Fauquier.

You recall the good old homestead, do you not, my dear reader? I should be sorry to have you forget the spot where I have been so happy. It was to this honest old mansion that I was conducted in April, 1861, when struck from my horse by a falling limb in the storm-lashed wood, I saw come to my succor the dearest person in the world. She awaited me now — having a month before left Eagle's Nest, to pay a visit to her family — and again, as in the spring of '63, she came to meet me as I ascended the hill — only we met now as bridegroom and bride!

This May of my life had brought back the sunshine, even after that black day of 1865. Two white arms had met the poor paroled prisoner, on his return to Eagle's Nest — a pair of violet eyes had filled with happy tears — and the red lips, smiling with exquisite emotion, murmured "All is well, since you have come back to me!"

It was this beautiful head which the sunshine of that autumn of 1867 revealed to me, on the lawn of the good old chateau of the mountains! And behind, came all my good friends of the Oaks — the kind lady of the manor, the old colonel, and Charley and Annie, who were there too! With his long gray hair, and eyes that still flashed, Colonel Beverly came to meet me — brave and smiling in 1867 as he had been in 1861. Then, with Annie's arm around me — that little sister had grown astonishingly! — I went in and was at home.

At home! You must be a soldier to know what that simple word means, reader! You must sleep under a tree, carry your effects behind your saddle, lie down in bivouac in strange countries, and feel the longing of the heart for the dear faces, the old scenes.

"Tell my mother that I die in a foreign land!" murmured my poor dear Tazewell Patton, at Gettysburg. I have often thought of those words; and they express much I think. Oh! for home! for a glimpse, if no more, of the fond faces, as life goes! You may be the bravest of the brave, as my dear

Tazewell was; but 'tis home where the heart is, and you sigh for the dear old land!

The Oaks was like home to me, for the somebody with violet eyes, and chestnut hair, was here to greet me.

The sun is setting, and we wander in the fields touched by the dreamy autumn.

"Look," says the somebody who holds my hand, and smiles, "there is the rock where we stopped in the autumn of 1862, and where you behaved with so little propriety, you remember, sir!"

"I remember the rock but not the absence of propriety. What were a man's arms made for but to clasp the woman he loves!"

"Stop, sir! People would think we were two foolish young lovers."

"Young lovers are not foolish, madam. They are extremely intelligent."

Madam laughs.

"Yonder is the primrose from which I plucked the bud," she says.

"That sent me through Stuart's head-quarters in April, 1863?" I say.

"Yes; you have not forgotten it I hope."

"Almost; Stay! I think it meant 'Come,'—did it not?—And you sent it to me!"

Madam pouts beautifully.

"You have 'almost forgotten' it! Have you, indeed, sir?"

"These trifles will escape us."

May loses all her smiles, and her head sinks.

I begin to laugh, taking an old porte-monnaie from my pocket. There is very little money in it, but a number of worn papers, my parole and others. I take one and open it. It contains a faded primrose.

"Look!" I say, with a smile, "it said 'Come,' once, and it brings me back again to the dearest girl in the world!"

A tear falls from the violet eyes upon the faded flower, but through the tears burst a smile!

They are curious, these earthly angels—are they not, my dear reader? They are romantic and sentimental to the last, and this old soldier admires them!

So, conversing of a thousand things, we return to the Oaks wandering like boy and girl through the "happy autumn fields." May Surry flits through the old doorway and disappears.

As she goes the sun sinks behind the forest. But it will rise, as she will, to-morrow!

The smiling Colonel Beverly meets me on the threshold, with a note in his hand.

"A servant has just brought this," he says, "it is from your friend, Mordaunt."

I opened the note and read the following words: —

"*My dear Surry*: —

"I send this note to await your appearance at the Oaks. Come and see me. Some old friends will give you a cordial greeting, in addition to

"Your comrade,

"Mordaunt."

I had intended visiting Mordaunt in a day or two after my arrival. On the very next morning I mounted my horse, and set out for the house in the mountain, anxious to ascertain who the "old friends" were, to whom he alluded.

In an hour I had come within sight of Mordaunt's mansion. Passing through the great gate, I rode on between the two rows of magnificent trees; approached the low mansion with its extensive wings, overshadowed by the huge black oaks; dismounted; raised the heavy bronze knocker, carved like the frowning mask of the old tragedians; and letting it fall sent a peal of low thunder through the mansion.

Mordaunt appeared in a few moments; and behind him came dear Violet Grafton, as I will still call her, smiling. Mordaunt's face glowed with pleasure, and the grasp of his strong hand was like a vice. He was unchanged, except that he wore a suit of plain gray cloth. His statuesque head, with the long black beard and mustache, the sparkling eyes, and cheeks tanned by exposure to the sun and wind, rose as proudly as on that morning in 1865, when he had charged and cut through the enemy at Appomattox.

Violet was Violet still! The beautiful tranquil face still smiled with its calm sweetness; the lips had still that expression of infantile innocence. The blue eyes still looked forth from the shower of golden ringlets which had struck me when I first met her in the lonely house in the Wilderness, in the gay month of April, 1861.

I had shaken hands with Mordaunt, but I advanced and "saluted" madam, and the cheek was suddenly filled with exquisite roses.

"For old times' sake, madam!"

"Which are the best of all possible times, Surry!" said Mordaunt, laughing.

And he led the way into the great apartment, hung round with portraits, where we had supped on the night of Pelham's hard fight at Barbee's, after Sharpsburg.

"You remember this room, do you not, my dear Surry?" said Mordaunt. "It escaped during the war; though you see that my poor little grandmother, the child of sixteen there, with the curls and laces, received a sabre thrust in the neck. But you are looking round for the friends I promised. They were here a moment since, and only retired to give you a surprise.

"See! here they are!"

The door opened, and I saw enter—Mohun and Landon!

In an instant I had grasped the hands of these dear friends; and they had explained their presence. Mohun had come to make a visit to Mordaunt, and had prolonged his stay in order to meet me. Then Mordaunt had written to Landon, at "Bizarre," just over the mountain, to come and complete the party—he had promptly arrived—and I found myself in presence of three old comrades, any one of whom it would have been a rare pleasure to have met.

Mohun and Landon were as unchanged as Mordaunt. I saw the same proud and loyal faces, listened to the same frank brave voices, touched the same firm hands. They no longer wore uniforms—that was the whole difference. Under the black coats beat the same hearts which had throbbed beneath the gray.

I spent the whole day with Mordaunt, After dinner he led the way into the room on the right of the entrance—that singular apartment into which I had been shown by accident on my first visit to him, and where afterward I witnessed the test of poor Achmed's love. The apartment was unchanged. The floor was still covered with the rich furs of lions, tigers, and leopards—the agate eyes still glared at me, and the grinning teeth seemed to utter growls or snarls. On the walls I saw still the large collection of books in every language—the hunting and battle pictures which I had before so greatly admired—the strange array of outlandish arms—and over the mantel-piece still hung the portrait of Violet Grafton.

Seated in front of a cheerful blaze, we smoked and talked—Mordaunt, Mohun, Landon, and myself—until the shades of evening drew on.

Landon told me of his life at "Bizarre," near the little village of Millwood, through which we had marched that night to bury his dead at the old chapel, and where he had surrendered in April, 1865. Arden and Annie lived near him, and were happy: and if I would come to "Bizarre," he would show me the young lady whom I had carried off, that night, from the chapel graveyard, on the croup of my saddle!

Landon laughed. His face was charming; it was easy to see that he was happy. To understand how that expression contrasted with his former appearance, the worthy reader must peruse my episodical memoir, *Hilt to Hilt*.

Mohun's face was no less smiling. He had lost every trace of gloom.

He gave me intelligence of all my old friends. General Davenant and Judge Conway had become close friends again. Will and Virginia were married. Charley was cultivating a mustache and speculating upon a new revolution. Tom Herbert and Katy were on a visit to "Disaways."

"Poor Nighthawk is the only one whom I miss, my dear Surry," said Mohun. "He died trying to save me, and I have had his body taken to Fonthill, where it is buried in the family graveyard."

"He was a faithful friend; and to be killed on that very last morning was hard. But many were. *You* had a narrow escape, Mohun."

"Yes, and was only preserved by a Bible."

"A Bible?"

"Do you remember that I was reading by the camp fire, when you came to visit me on the night preceding the surrender?"

"Yes—in your wife's Bible."

"Well, my dear Surry, when I had finished reading, I placed the volume in my breast, as usual. When I was shot, on the next morning, the bullet struck the book and glanced. Had the Bible not been there, that bullet would have pierced my heart. As it was, it only wounded me in the breast. Here is my old Bible—I carry it about me still."

As he spoke, Mohun drew from his breast the small leather-bound volume, in the cover of which was visible a deep gash.

He looked at it with a smile, and said:—-

"This book has been the salvation of my body and soul, Surry. I was haughty and a man-hater once—now I try to be humble. I had no hope once, now I am happy. I have one other souvenir of that memorable day at Appomattox—this scrap of paper between the leaves of my old Bible."

He drew out the scrap, which was dirty and discolored with blood.

Upon it was written in pencil, the words:—

"This is the body of General Mohun, C.S.A."

As Mohun pointed to it, a ray of sunset shot athwart the forest, and fell on his serene features, lighting them up with a sort of glory. The clear eyes gave back the ray, and there was something exquisitely soft in them. Mordaunt and Landon too, were bathed in that crimson light of evening, disappearing beyond the shaggy crest of the Blue Ridge—and I thought I saw on their proud faces the same expression.

"These three men are happy," I thought. "Their lot has been strange; they have been nearly lost; but heaven has sent to each an angel, to bring back hope to them. Ellen Adair, Georgia Conway, Violet Grafton—these fond hearts have changed your lives, Landon, Mohun, and Mordaunt!"

In an hour I was at the "Oaks."

A month afterward, I had returned to "Eagle's Nest."

And in this April, 1868, when the flowers are blooming, and the sun is shining—when a pair of violet eyes make the sunshine still brighter—I end the last volume of my memoirs.